T0130985

# DATA MINING
# AND UNCERTAIN
# REASONING

# DATA MINING AND UNCERTAIN REASONING

## An Integrated Approach

Zhengxin Chen

Department of Computer Science
University of Nebraska, Omaha

A WILEY-INTERSCIENCE PUBLICATION

**JOHN WILEY & SONS, INC.**

New York / Chichester / Weinheim / Brisbane / Singapore / Toronto

Copyright © 2001 by John Wiley & Sons. All rights reserved.

Published simultaneously in Canada.

For ordering and customer service, call 1-800-CALL-WILEY.

***Library of Congress Cataloging-in-Publication Data:***

Chen, Zhengxin.
  Data mining and uncertain reasoning : an integrated approach / Zhengxin Chen.
    p. cm.
  Includes index.
  ISBN 0-471-38878-5 (cloth)
  1. Data mining.  2. Expert systems (Computer science).  I. Title.
  QA76.9.D343 C47 2001
  006.3—dc21                                              2001024242

Printed in the United States of America.

10 9 8 7 6 5 4 3 2

To my late parents

# CONTENTS

# ACKNOWLEDGEMENTS

This work reflected in this book was supported, in part, by a DOD AFOSR grant. The author thanks colleagues and graduate students of Data Mining and Decision Support Systems (DMDSS) Lab at the College of Information Science and Technology, University of Nebraska at Omaha.

Z. CHEN

# 1

# WHAT THIS BOOK
# IS ABOUT

## 1.1   DATA MINING: CONVERGING THEMES AND DIVERGING TRENDS

Data mining, the objective of which is to make predictions or discoveries involving a large amount of data, is an exciting field for both researchers and practitioners. However, *data mining* means different things to different people. For example, the requirements and expectations for data mining in business and science-oriented applications may be quite different. Nevertheless, in parallel to diverging trends in various applications, important common themes have also emerged from various applications. This book examines a wide scope of issues—and provides a roadmap to various approaches—related to data mining. With the integrated treatment of data mining and uncertain reasoning, the book presents a unique approach to uncovering the nature of data mining. While concentrating on the prevalent and practical aspects of data mining such as infrastructure and the overall process of data mining, the book also focuses on selected algorithms and performance-related issues.

Articles or books on data mining are abundant. Data mining has been a favorite topic by academic researchers as well as business practitioners and is often discussed from very different perspectives. There are numerous books on data mining for practitioners, addressing practical concerns. However, these books usually provide a high-level overview of various approaches without technical detail. For example, Berry and Linoff (1997) presented a wide range of data mining methods, and Westphal and Blaxton (1998) described how to use existing commercial tools to conduct data mining. On the other hand, within academia, issues related to data mining have been studied from different perspectives such as statistics, pattern recognition, database management systems, and artificial intelligence (AI). Books on data mining from academia consist of edited conference proceedings or monographs. For example, the book by Fayyad et al. (1996) is a well-known volume on some research progress up to the year 1995. Monographs on data mining usually focus on some specific techniques for data mining. For example, Kennedy et al. (1997) discussed pattern recognition techniques for data mining, and Cios et al. (1998) promoted the use of computational intelligence techniques (such as rough set theory, fuzzy logic, artificial neural networks) for data mining. More recently, Han and Kamber (2000) presented an excellent discussion on data mining, mainly from a database perspective.

## 1.2   WHY THIS BOOK IS NEEDED

This book differs from other data mining books in that it provides a holistic view of the diversity of the exciting data mining world. As we have already indicated, there is a rich literature on data mining, but usually each book portraits the data mining world from a rather restrictive perspective, presenting materials from a specific discipline such as pattern recognition. Unlike these predecessors, this book presents a unique approach to advocate an integrated perspective on data mining. It serves as a bridge for practitioners from different applications, and fosters a dialog between researchers and practitioners. The book contains sketches of selected algorithms, but it is not designed as a collection of algorithms for data mining. By providing a concise description of various methods with certain important technical aspects, the book threads together up-to-date information on data mining. It provides an outline for a wide scope of issues related to data mining and uncertain reasoning, which thus far can be found only in separate resources.

The holistic perspective taken by this book incorporates uncertain reasoning into the main framework of data mining. The term *uncertainty* is a multifacet concept in literature. Various forms of uncertainty exist, include vagueness, incompleteness, missing value, and inconsistency. In general, scholastic books on reasoning under uncertainty predate research work in data mining, and fall in three categories: Collections of research papers, single book covering various methods, and books covering individual methods only. As a nice example of collections of papers, the volume by Shafer and Pearl (1990) contains 42 key papers from the literature, addressing the methods that have been used in artificial intelligence to build systems with the ability to manage uncertainty. As a concise book for comprehensive coverage of various methods in uncertain reasoning, Gryzmala-Busse (1991) starts with key issues such as knowledge acquisition in expert systems development, and covers several important methods of uncertain reasoning such as Bayesian approach, Dempster–Shafer theory, fuzzy logic, rough set theory, as well as others. There are also numerous books devoted to individual uncertain reasoning methods.

The treatise by Pawlak (1991) is the classical work on rough set theory. Yager (1987) presents the most important papers from Lotfi Zadeh, the "godfather" of fuzzy set theory and fuzzy logic. At the application side, Bojadziev and Bojadziev (1997) provide numerous examples on application of fuzzy logic in business world.

We have seen that there are many books on uncertain reasoning since the 1960s, as well as an increasing number of data mining books more recently. But *so far no single book covers both topics* (at least not in an explicit manner). A more recent book that is close to our objective is that by Cios et al. (1999), *Data Mining Methods for Knowledge Discovery*. However, although that book provides an excellent discussion on selected methods for uncertain reasoning using numerical approaches, it was written for advanced readers, and it was not intended to bridge the gap between research efforts made from numerical reasoning on data mining and those from database community.

Therefore, this current volume, *Data Mining and Uncertain Reasoning: An Integrated Approach*, represents one of the first serious efforts ever in the integration of uncertain reasoning and data mining. It examines the state of the art in both fields, and provides a roadmap for a coherent understanding for various related issues. In a sense, the book raises the *question* of the need for integration (because much research work is yet to be done in the future), although it also provides some *solutions* (or suggestions for solutions). This book is not intended to replace other data mining books, but it should accompany any of them, and serves as an important reference book for anybody who is interested in fundamental ideas of data mining.

Subjects covered in this book include the following: basics of data mining, including the infrastructure of data mining; data mining tasks (such association rule mining as well as other methods); uncertain reasoning approaches; relationship between data mining and uncertain reasoning; applications to decision support queries; and case studies, as well as future directions.

The relationship between data mining and uncertain reasoning is the central theme of this book, and it is impossible for us to provide a brief summary on this relationship at the beginning of the book. Nevertheless, some key observations can be outlined below. Both data mining and uncertain reasoning are concerned with analysis of data. Data mining is an in-depth explorative analysis of data—as deep as possible. As a new field dealing with decision support queries for organizations, data mining is aimed to discover knowledge patterns hidden in the data and predict future trends. In contrast to this, uncertain reasoning, as a traditional research area of artificial intelligence, is aimed at developing effective reasoning method involving uncertainty, namely, to derive what is behind data even the data is incomplete, inconsistent, or with other kinds of problems. For example, uncertainty reasoning may be used to recast a problem to a perturbation of a known problem (as in the case of fuzzy logic), thus converting a tough problem to a variation of a known problem.

Therefore, data mining and uncertain reasoning are two very different disciplines and have very different roots. Nevertheless, many uncertain reasoning methods, such as fuzzy set theory, rough set theory, neural net works, and genetic algorithms, are powerful computational tools for data analysis, and have good potential for data mining as well. However, we should keep in mind that these methods have been developed to provide *mechanisms* for the uncertain reasoning *process*, rather than discovery of what is hidden in the data. Consequently, if we want to make uncertain reasoning methods useful for data mining, a number of questions should be answered, such as: Why and how these methods can be used for uncertain reasoning? How can we extend their roles for data mining? For a certain technique, such as fuzzy logic or neural networks, what aspects can contribute to uncertain reasoning, and what aspects can contribute to data mining? Investigating these problems as well as others will provide significant hindsight to the nature of data mining and uncertain reasoning, and serve as a useful guide for using these techniques in various applications. The book deals with issues related to these considerations mentioned above. Since integration of data mining with uncertain reasoning is quite complex, and many aspects are still under investigation, it is impossible to provide a complete coverage of this topic in a single volume. However, we hope that the selected materials are representative enough to demonstrate various aspects related to this topic.

The need for integration of data mining and uncertain reasoning can be further strengthened from the following observation concerning the nature of these two tasks: In many cases, discovery of regularity in data mining closely parallels the process of removing uncertainty in uncertain reasoning. Uncertain reasoning can aid data mining in various ways, so they are two complementary tasks required by any sophisticated data analysis. Indeed, uncertainty handling can appear at different levels of real-world problem solving; a narrow, syntactic view is concerned with removing noise from data during data preparation or preprocessing, whereas a deeper, semantic perspective is to view it as the normal, intrinsic nature of data. Uncertainty is our lifetime friend in solving various problems involving real-world data. An integrated approach combining these two tasks will provide a good opportunity for a much-needed in-depth study of explorative data analysis, and benefit real-world applications.

As a note for methodology, we should mention that according to a modern definition, the field of *artificial intelligence* (AI) is the science of building intelligent agents. [The concept of intelligent agent will be presented in Chapter 5 and Chapter 6. For a further discussion on intelligent agents, see Chen (1999A).] In this sense, the problem of data mining is to developed intelligent agents that are able to interplay various techniques, including those developed for uncertain reasoning, for prediction or knowledge discovery involving large amount of data. The integrated perspective presented in this book thus provides an effective approach for building such types of agents.

## 1.3   WHO SHOULD READ THIS BOOK

The purpose of this book is to introduce useful techniques for data mining and uncertain reasoning, present a holistic perspective of uncertain reasoning for data mining, and aid college students and knowledge workers for their career in information technology. This book has been written for managerial personnel who are interested in data mining in general, for upper-level college students and first-year graduate students as a textbook in database management systems and artificial intelligence, and for researchers in data mining and AI as a reference book. This book will benefit this audience in that it provides readers a fresh look over various topics covered, presents basic ideas for a wide range of useful techniques, and broadens the visions of these readers by emphasizing the interrelationship of these methods. Various techniques useful for integrated data mining are presented in a concise manner, so that readers who lack data mining experience or the necessary background will not get lost in the forest of the data mining wonderland, nor become overwhelmed by the technical details if they were so presented.

Perspective readers should consider the most outstanding features of this book:

1. As indicated earlier, data mining and uncertain reasoning are both important topics in building intelligent agents. However, these two topics are usually discussed separately. In this book we take an integrated approach to combine both.
2. In addition, this book also address several related issues, such as the relationship between machine learning and data mining, and implementation issues related to scalability. We also cover other topics such as data warehousing as an enabling technique of data mining.
3. The organization of this book takes a modular design approach, and it should benefit readers with different needs. In fact, the book treats the contents of data mining in roughly three parts. The first part (Chapters 1–4) presents the basic, mainly nontechnical materials, followed (Chapters 5–7) by a more advanced, technical discussion (but without too much technical detail), and finally (Chapters 8 and 9) several case studies from a wide scope to illustrate the various concerns in data mining. In addition, chapters are designated to two categories: core chapters and more advanced chapters. Readers who are interested in general idea of data mining may focus on the basic part. Readers who want some technical exposure should read core chapters of all three parts. Each chapter of this book starts with a general overview to serve as a guideline for

coverage of the entire chapter, and is relatively standalone, so that readers can select specific chapters to explore.

Since data mining is pervasive in many applications, while writing the book, we have the general readership in mind. Readers with various backgrounds should be able to capture the most fundamental materials presented in this book. Efforts have been made to make this book self-contained. In order to understand the technical details of approaches presented in this book, however, knowledge of the basics of discrete and continuous mathematics, numerical methods, as well as knowledge of database management systems and artificial intelligence (AI), are desirable.

## 1.4   ORGANIZATION OF THE BOOK

As already stated in Section 1.3, this book can be roughly divided into three parts. The first part consists of the first four chapters, which present a nontechnical overview of the entire book. The second part consists of three chapters that provide a technical treatment of data mining with uncertainty. The third part consists of two chapters on case studies. A brief discussion of the future directions of data mining research is incorporated in these chapters.

*Chapter 1* presents an overview of the entire book. *Chapter 2* introduces basic concepts related to data mining and, in the context of these concepts, discusses the infrastructure of data mining, including integration of data mining into the decision support process of organization, the overall process of data mining, the role of database management in data mining, tasks of predictive and discovery types of data mining, and caling up and speeding up for data mining, as well as other issues. Both practical (emphasis on business-related applications) and theoretical aspects are discussed. Examination of the theoretical foundation of data mining reveals that integrating uncertain reasoning into data mining can be beneficial for a unified perspective of data mining. *Chapter 3* expands the discussion of Chapter 2. It examines enabling techniques and advanced features of data mining, such as the relationship between data warehousing and data mining, online analytical processing (OLAP) and data mining, semantic issues in data mining, the role of metadata, aspects related to sampling, and the general aspects of parallel data mining are discussed, and Web mining is briefly examined. *Chapter 4* presents an overview of the basic concepts related to data and knowledge uncertainty, existing approaches to dealing with uncertainty in database management systems and AI, and provides an outline on the relationship between data mining and uncertain reasoning.

*Chapter 5* is devoted to basic data mining tasks to knowledge discovery, which were briefly summarized in Chapter 2. Since many methods are rooted in symbolic reasoning in artificial intelligence (AI), this chapter starts with a discussion of the basics of AI, followed by discussions of symbol-based machine learning and induction and generalization. Attribute-oriented generalization is used to illustrate the basic idea of data mining algorithms. Several data mining tasks such as classification, clustering, and association rules are then examined. Emphasis of the discussion of different paradigms varies because of the different features of each paradigm. Some aspects discussed in previous chapters, such as parallel data mining, can now be discussed in more detail for specific algorithms. The chapter concludes with a discussion of the integration of data mining paradigms. *Chapter 6* resumes the discussion introduced in Chapter 4 by focusing on two uncertain reasoning approaches: Bayesian networks and artificial neural networks (ANNs). For both approaches, we first present the basic mechanisms for uncertain reasoning, and then discuss how the basic mechanism can be extended for data mining. *Chapter 7* continues the examination of uncertain reasoning and data mining, but the discussion focuses on a much wider scope. Important aspects of several well-known techniques, such as fuzzy logic, genetic algorithms, and rough set theory, are briefly summarized. Since a rich literature exists for these approaches, the discussion of these approaches focuses on how these approaches differ from each other, and how each of them can be used for data mining in some unique manner. Concludes with the chapter a discussion of the integration of these techniques.

*Chapter 8* summarizes the discussion of the whole book by presenting several case studies. Each case study has a different emphasis, such as to illustrate the overall process of data mining or how to deal with uncertainty during data mining. *Chapter 9* applies data mining techniques to intelligent conceptual query resolution with uncertainty, thus extending the main theme of the first eight chapters to a wider perspective. Three topics are selected to illustrate the rich areas where integrated data mining and uncertain reasoning techniques are applicable. Each topic is presented as a case study. The chapter concludes with a section summarizing these case studies as well as wrapping up the entire book.

## 1.5  HOW TO USE THE BOOK

The overall organization of the book is depicted in Figure 1.1. In this figure, the asterisk symbol * denotes a core chapter. Arrows with solid lines indicate the logical order of reading the chapters. Arrows with dashed lines indicate that materials presented in Chapters 3, 5, 6, and 7 are needed to understand the technical contents of Chapter 8 (although a casual reader or a reader at the first time reading may skip technical details).

The main reason of this organization is to emphasize the key concepts discussed in the book: data mining and uncertain reasoning. The main sequence of Chapter 1 → Chapter 2 → Chapter 4 → Chapter 8 indicates a quick path covering the basic materials (mainly for managerial personnel), making other materials somewhat optional. On the other hand, if a reader wants to know the

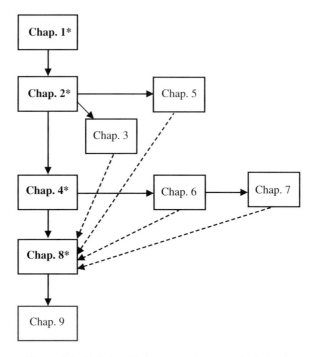

**Figure 1.1** Relationship between chapters of this book.

basics of data mining techniques, then Chapter 5 should be plugged into Chapter 2, and Chapters 6 and 7 should be plugged into Chapter 4.

This book is intended as a roadmap rather than a book of answers. Although we have tried to cover a wide range of topics, there are many issues, such as those are theoretical in nature, and those related to uncertainty but not have a close relationship with data mining, are not covered. For example, theoretical issues such as intractability versus uncertainty are beyond the scope of this book. There are also many interesting logical puzzles related to uncertainty, but since they are not closely related data mining, they are not discussed as well.

An ideal companion book would be *Computational Intelligence for Decision Support* (Chen 1999), which covers a wide area related to artificial intelligence, data and knowledge engineering, basics of data mining, and other related issues. In a sense, this current book is an expansion of several chapters of that book. However, that book (Chen 1999) also contains many other materials that are related to the theme of this current book, but are unable to be discussed in the present volume. As in that earlier book, this current book is concerned with integrated use of artificial intelligence, database management information systems, and other forms of information mechanism, but with a specific focus (namely, data mining with uncertainty).

Another important note about this current book is that it can accompany almost any existing data mining books (probably many future books as well), because it complements these books in that it is not solely about data mining; rather, it addresses problem solving in a more comprehensive context. This book is different from all the other data mining books, although it does present various data mining methods, more importantly, it shows the very idea of data mining, with a particular emphasis on integration with uncertain reasoning.

Since this book is intended to be a roadmap of integrated data mining and uncertain reasoning, we can afford to present only a brief sketch for various approaches. Interested readers can start from the presentation in the text, and use the references listed at the end of each chapter for further exploration.

Data mining is an exciting area that demonstrates the interesting relationship between the vertical (viz., historical) development of a single science or technology on one hand and the horizontal development of comparative sciences and technology on the other hand. The integrated examination on data mining and uncertain reasoning provides an excellent opportunity for exploring this methodological aspect. As pointed out in Chen (1999), there are many interesting "invariants" in science and technology development. They can also provide significant insight for business applications as well. Interested readers are encouraged to explore these issues on your own.

Enjoy the adventure of data mining with uncertainty!

# 2

# BASICS OF DATA MINING

## 2.1 OVERVIEW

To illustrate what data mining can achieve, let us consider the simple transaction database shown in Table 2.1. A *transaction database* is a relation consisting of transactions; each transaction [which is identified by a transaction identifier (TID) could be a customer receipt obtained from the supermarket cashier.

Since the database consists of many transactions, it would be interesting to ascertain whether any regularities exist in customer behavior. For example, what else is a customer who buys ice cream likely to buy? Discovery of such regularity or trends may provide important clues for store owners to promote their sales, yet benefit customers as well. For the database shown in Table 2.1, some rules mined are shown in Table 2.2. For example, the first row indicates the first rule; a customer who buys chocolate is likely to buy a biker's candy bar as well. Each rule will be referred to as an *association rule*. Mining association rule is only one kind of data mining task. An overview of data mining tasks is presented in this chapter, and a more detailed discussion is discussed in Chapter 5.

In this overview chapter we discuss the basic idea and basic features in data mining systems (which are also called *data miners*), as well as needed infrastructure for data mining, including architectures involved and the overall mining processes. We also characterize data mining in several aspects, including tasks, activities, technologies employed, and outcomes, from both technical and practical perspectives. In the next two sections we provide an overview of data mining: In Section 2.2 we discuss what data mining is, and point out the two major types of data mining: predictive data mining and knowledge discovery. In Section 2.3 we further consider several important issues for con-

**Table 2.1   A Small Transaction Database**

| TID | Customer | Item | Date | Price | Quantity |
|-----|----------|------|------|-------|----------|
| 100 | C1 | chocolate | 01/11/2001 | 1.59 | 2 |
| 100 | C1 | ice cream | 01/11/2001 | 1.89 | 1 |
| 200 | C2 | chocolate | 01/12/2001 | 1.59 | 3 |
| 200 | C2 | candy bar | 01/12/2001 | 1.19 | 2 |
| 200 | C2 | jackets | 01/12/2001 | 120.39 | 2 |
| 300 | C3 | jackets | 01/14/2001 | 168.88 | 1 |
| 300 | C3 | color shirts | 01/14/2001 | 27.95 | 2 |
| 400 | C4 | jackets | 01/15/2001 | 149.49 | 1 |

**Table 2.2   Some Discovered Rules**

| Rule | Bought this . . . | . . . also bought that |
|------|-------------------|------------------------|
| 1 | Chocolate | Ice cream |
| 2 | Candy bar | Chocolate |
| 3 | Ski pants | Colored shirt |
| 4 | Beer | Diaper |

ducting data mining in organizations. Then in two consecutive sections we pay attention to two types of data mining. In Section 2.4 we focus on data modeling for predictive data mining, and in Section 2.5 we provide a preview on tasks of knowledge discovery. The next three sections (2.6–2.8) are related to the data mining process. In Section 2.6 provide a high-level examination of data mining process, in Section 2.7 we provide some remarks on data mining performed in a database environment, and in Section 2.8 we take a closer look on the data mining process. The next two sections are devoted to two specific issues of data mining: Section 2.9 is on scalable and speedup data mining. Section 2.10 examines several philosophical and theoretical foundations for approaching data mining, and justifies the perspective taken by this book as stated in Chapter 1, namely, integrated data mining and uncertain reasoning. Section 2.11 sketches some trends and directions for data mining. This chapter is summarized in Section 2.12.

## 2.2   WHAT DATA MINING IS

### 2.2.1   Beyond Retrieval and Statistical Analysis of Data

Traditionally, the use of data sets largely falls in two categories: retrieve of individual elements of data (such as given the name of a particular product, find the price and producer information), or analysis (mainly using statistic methods) of the data as a whole, such as the average monthly sales amount and the deviation, etc. The advance of computer-related technology has brought the use of data to a new horizon. Not only can we handle a vast amount of data that was unthinkable in the past but new aspects and requirements of analyzing the data as well. The simple example shown in Section 2.1 illustrates a new direction of data analysis that should significantly benefit all walks of life.

Most organizations have been labeled "data-rich" and "knowledge-poor." Data mining enables complex business processes to be understood and re-engineered, thus rapidly changing this picture. This can be achieved through the discovery of patterns in data related to the previous behavior of a business process. Such patterns can be used to improve the performance of a process by exploiting favorable patterns and avoiding problematic patterns. In various business applications, data mining can reveal what factors affect the outcome of the business event or process and the patterns relating the outcome to these factors. Such patterns increase our understanding of these processes and therefore our ability to predict and affect the outcome. Data mining can answer various key business questions, such as

- Who will buy, what will they buy, and how much will they buy? This kind of analysis can be carried out as classification or prediction.
- What are the different types of visitors to your store or website? This example illustrates the need for segmentation of customers.
- What relationships exist between customers or Website visitors and the products? This kind of analysis illustrates the association type of data mining.
- What are the groupings hidden in the data? This illustrates the need for clustering analysis.

However, business applications represent only one domain of data mining. In basic science research, data mining has helped to "rediscover" scientific laws (Langley et al. 1987); and in applied research such as in bioinformatics, data mining techniques have been used to analyze human genes and discover hidden factors that cause cancerous diseases.

Therefore, *data mining* is the nontrivial extraction of implicit, previously unknown, interesting, and potentially useful information (usually in the form of knowledge patterns or models) from data. The extracted knowledge is used to describe the hidden regularity of data, to make prediction, or to aid human users in other ways. The ever-increasing popularity of data mining is due to demands from various real-world applications in decision making. Data mining applications fall into several groups according to their intent. The following are some typical cases:

- *Business Data Mining.* Ad hoc techniques are no longer adequate for sifting through vast collections of data. They are giving way to data mining for turning corporate data into competitive business advantage.

- *Scientific Data Mining.* Digesting millions of data points, each with tens or hundreds of measurements can be turned over to data mining techniques for data reduction, which functions as an interface between the scientist and large data sets. Knowledge discovery in database (KDD) applications in science may generally be easier than applications in business or finance, mainly because science users typically know their data in intimate detail.

- *Internet and Data Mining.* More recently, researchers and practitioners have advocated transforming the Web into a massive layered database to facilitate data mining, but the Web is too dynamic and chaotic to be tamed in this manner. As an alternative, proposals based on the structured Web hypothesis that information on the Web is sufficiently structured to facilitate effective Web mining have been advanced.

Note that different applications may have very different focuses. For example, scientific data mining seems to focus mostly on finding explanations for the most variable elements of the data set (i.e., to find and explain the outliers). For example, one may try to find an unexpected stellar object in a particular sky sweep or may attempt, mainly to understand the variations of the majority of the data set elements, with little interest in the outliers. For example, one may want to understand the purchasing habits of most of our customers (Skillicorn 1999). In this book we will study common data mining issues in these different applications.

Applications of data mining and knowledge discovery include

- Medicine, such as diagnosis and prognosis
- Control theory, such as predictive and adaptive control, model identification
- Engineering, such as diagnostics of mechanisms and processes
- Public administration
- Marketing and finance
- Data mining on the Web in text and heterogeneous data
- Scientific databases
- Fraud detection

### 2.2.2  Data Mining Primitives

It is important to understand fundamental elements needed to define a data mining task. These elements can be collectively called *data mining primitives*. At a very high level description, there are seven elements serving as data mining primitives: P (problem specification), D (task-relevant data), K (the kinds of knowledge to be mined), B (background knowledge), T (the specific data mining algorithms or techniques), M (models developed or knowledge patterns extracted, along with their presentation and visualization), I (interestingness or interesting measures), and U (user). Therefore, data mining can be described using a 8-tuple: (P, D, K, B, T, M, I, U).

The relationship between these eight elements could be quite complex, depending on the actual data mining process used and the actual data mining algorithms used. Nevertheless, in order to give readers a general idea of the interrelationship, we have tried to depict a rough picture, as shown in Figure 2.1. The user defines the data mining problem (P), while the data miner (the main data mining agent with K and T as its core components), utilizing D and B and incorporating user-specified interestingness (I), derives M to be returned to the user.

In the following paragraphs, we briefly describe each element in the data mining primitives.

- *Problem Specification*. An extremely important element in data mining is a well-defined problem specification.
- *Task-Relevant Data*. This portion of the database is related to a specific data mining problem.
- *The Kinds of Knowledge to Be Mined*. This specifies the data mining tasks to be performed. For example, in a data mining problem related to profit analysis, are you interested in finding classification rules or association rules?
- *Background Knowledge*. Background knowledge is the knowledge based on which data mining can be carried out. Usually background knowledge is closely related to the problem domain to be mined.

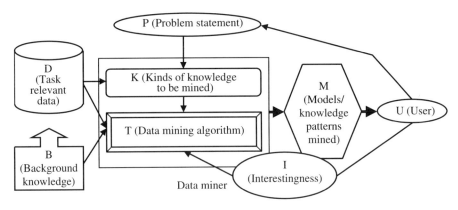

**Figure 2.1**  Data mining primitives.

- *Specific Data Mining Algorithms or Techniques*. Because of the complex nature of data mining, many algorithms and techniques have been developed. Appropriate algorithms or techniques should be used for the specific problem on hand.
- *Models Developed or Knowledge Patterns Extracted*. These are the major result of data mining. Equally important is their presentation and visualization
- *Interesting Measures*. The measures for interestingness serve as a guideline to measure the discovered knowledge so that the effort of data mining will not be wasted. Useful measures include simplicity, certainty, utility, novelty, and supporting active deployment (the concept of active deployment is briefly discussed in Section 2.8.7).
- *User*. After all, data mining should benefit human users. Although data mining could be an automated process, in most cases, it is a "person in the loop" process, and human users can play a very important role in guiding the mining process.

Interestingness of rules can be divided into *objective* and subjective (Silberschatz and Tuzhilin 1996). The objective measures appraise a pattern in terms of its structure and the underlying data used in the discovery process. In order to allow user's control, subjective measures have been introduced. They do not depend solely on the data on which they operate but also on the user who examines the patterns. The prior knowledge of the user is incorporated in the discovery process, and only the patterns that are interesting to the specific user are reported. This is a kind of personalization.

### 2.2.3   Major Categories of Data Mining Objectives

*2.2.3.1  Data Mining Objectives*   There are many different ways to categorizing data mining. One way is to examine data mining from the objectives. Two general categories in data mining are prediction and knowledge discovery. Fayyad et al. (1996) noted that the high-level primary goals of data mining in practice tend to be prediction and discovery (characterized by description):

- *Discovery* or *description* focuses on finding human-interpretable patterns describing the data. The relative importance of prediction and description for particular data mining applications can vary considerably. However, in the context of knowledge discovery, description tends to be more important than prediction. This is in contrast to pattern recognition and machine learning applications, where prediction is often the primary goal.
- *Prediction* involves using some variables or fields in the database to predict unknown or future values of other variables of interest. In order

to distinguish prediction from a kind of task (called *classification*) in discovery type, we may further require prediction works on continuous variables (Han and Kamber 2000).

For many applications, prediction is the strongest goal of data mining, has the greatest potential payoff, and has the most precise description. Knowledge discovery is an all-encompassing label for many topics related to decision support. Knowledge discovery (description) problems usually describe a stage prior to prediction, where information is insufficient for prediction. Knowledge discovery is complementary to predictive mining, but is closer to decision support than is decisionmaking. However, in some cases, the boundary between discovery and prediction is blurred. In fact, the task of classification in knowledge discovery can be considered as performing prediction on discrete data. For example, classification rules may help to identify potential home buyers of a high-price house. When a new resident comes to town, we may attempt to predict whether that person will buy such houses. In the following subsections, we discuss these types in a little more detail.

**2.2.3.2  *Predictive Modeling***  The aim of predictive modeling is to predict certain data values based on similar groups of data, such as predicting how much profit can be made in the first quarter for a retail chain. Patterns discovered from the data set are used to predict the future. However, we should note that the power of prediction is limited. They are carried out only on certain attributes. A well-known example to illustrate this is predicting identifier (ID): we are not able to predict the name of the next customer on the basis of information previously provided by other customers. It is important to determine the major factors that influence the prediction. Predictive modeling can utilize traditional modeling techniques developed in pattern recognition, to be summarized in Section 2.4. Predictive modeling can also utilize more contemporary data mining tasks, such as attribute-oriented generalization discussed in Chapter 5: we select relevant attributes and perform generalization through a conceptual hierarchy, perform high-level concept matching, and finally, perform predictions when sufficient evidence is available. Note that prediction will usually be a distribution, and may be utilize statistics analysis. While discovery finds patterns in data, predictive modeling applies the patterns to guess values for new data items. Predictive modeling also allows the user to submit records with some unknown field values, and the system will predict the unknown values on the basis of previous patterns discovered from the database. Kennedy et al. (1997) noted that pattern recognition is the association of an observation to past experience or knowledge. In the technical literature, the term *pattern recognition* often is used interchangeably with *classification*, which is the process of assigning one of a finite set of labels to an observation. However, a broader definition of pattern recognition could also encompasses estimation. Estimation is the process of assigning one of a (typically infinite) number of numerical labels to an observation (Kennedy et al. 1997). Estimation entails generating an approximation of some desired numerical value based on an observation. One example is estimating a person's age solely on the basis of physical appearance. The fundamental difference between estimation and classification is that classes in an estimation problem follow an explicit ordering (i.e., a sequence of values). Furthermore, in estimation problems, there is often an infinite continuum of classes, whereas in classification, the number of classes is finite. *Prediction* problems can be grouped into two main types: classification and regression. *Time series* is a specialized type of regression or occasionally a classification problem, where measurements are taken over time for the same features. Predictive data mining requires data modeling (which is different from data reduction). There is also a concern related to timelines in predictive data mining. From the perspective of database systems, the efficient storage and querying of timestamped information is a complex task. From a predictive data-mining perspective, the timestamped data greatly increase the dimensions of problem solving in a completely different direction. Instead of cases with one measured value for each feature, cases have the same featured measured at different times. Predictive data mining methods prefer the classical sample-and-case model of data but are characterized by difficulty in reasoning with time and its greatly increased dimensions.

Although the term *data mining* is relatively new, the concept of finding hidden regularity from data is not new. Research work in statistical analysis, pattern recognition, and machine learning (from artificial intelligence community) all contribute to data mining. In particular, we can examine the case of pattern recognition. Kennedy et al. (1997) used the terms *data mining* and *pattern recognition* interchangeably, as both concentrate on the extraction of information or relationships from data. They noted that the former term evolved primarily from the database marketing or database application realms, while the latter term was derived from engineering fields such as process control and quality inspection. It was argued that both terms deal with essentially the same ideas but represent the nomenclature developed from different industries. We believe this observation is largely true, but mainly at the infrastructure level. This observation is also useful, because as a matured field, pattern recognition can make important contributions to data mining, particularly in the mining process. However, pattern recognition emphasizes predictive mining, while data mining, as a more recent phenomenon, has a much richer meaning, with descriptive or discovery tasks as its focal point. In addition, we should also note that the term *pattern* is used in a sense narrower than the one used in the term *knowledge pattern*. Many techniques developed in pattern recognition are based on numerical approaches. However, data mining as discussed in business and many other fields has a strong emphasis on nonnumerical approaches, and is thus closely related to symbolic reasoning in artificial intelligence (AI). Some basic features of AI are briefly reviewed at the beginning of Chapter 5.

***2.2.3.3 Knowledge Discovery*** *Knowledge discovery in databases* (KDD) is the process of looking in a database to find hidden knowledge patterns (or regularities) without a predetermined idea or hypothesis about what the patterns may be. For example, the database only stores the information about who buys what, while hidden patterns may tell us whoever buys something (such as milk) would buy some other things as well (such as eggs). In other words, the program takes the initiative in finding what the interesting patterns are, and the user does not have to address the relevant questions first. In large databases, there are so many patterns that the user can never practically think of the right questions to ask. The key issue here is the richness of the patterns that can be expressed and discovered and the quality of the information delivered—determining the power and usefulness of the discovery technique.

Using the original definition given by Piatetsky-Shapiro and Frawley (1991), we can define knowledge discovery is the nontrivial extraction of implicit, previously unknown, interesting, and potentially useful information from data. Given a set of facts (data) $F$, a language $L$, and some measure of certainty $C$, a *pattern* is defined as a statement $S$ in $L$ that describes relationships among a subset $F_s$ of $F$ with a certainty $c$, such that in some sense $S$ is simpler than the enumeration of all facts in $F_s$. A pattern that is *interesting* and *certain* enough is referred to as *knowledge*; the output of a program that monitors the set of facts in a database and produces patterns in this sense is referred to as *discovered knowledge*. Note the term pattern actually refers to knowledge pattern and thus is used in a broad sense.

Sometimes the two terms KDD and data mining are used interchangeably. However, from a research-oriented perspective in computer science, knowledge discovery in databases, or KDD, is aimed to set up infrastructure for data mining, much at the organizational level. The acronym KDD is used to refer to the overall process of knowledge discovery, while the term *data mining* refers to the actual algorithms used in the discovery process. However, in business community the term *data mining* is used in a broader sense, because it refers to both the infrastructure and the algorithms. In addition, KDD implies that data reside in databases, while data mining could be conducted at data sets stored in any format (viz., it does not necessarily utilize database management system techniques). Since this book intends to address data mining aspects from a broad perspective and serves as a dialog for a wide readership, we will use the term *data mining* in this broad sense.

It is important to keep in mind that data mining is about why, about hidden regularities, and about important aspects related to perception, learning, and evolving. Data mining is the process of discovering actionable and meaningful patterns, profiles, and trends using appropriate technologies such as neural networks and machine learning and genetic algorithms. From a business perspective, Parsaye (1999) defined data mining as "a decision support process in which we search for patterns of information in data." This search may be done just by the user, (i.e., just by performing queries, in which case it is quite hard) or may be assisted by a smart program that automatically searches the database for the user and finds significant patterns. Once found, the information needs to be presented in a suitable form, with graphs, reports, and other documentation.

Knowledge discovery in databases has four main characteristics (Piatetsky-Shapiro and Frawley 1991):

1. The discovered knowledge is represented in a high-level language that can be understood by human users.
2. The discoveries accurately portray the contents of the database.
3. The discovered knowledge is interesting according to users.
4. The discovery process is efficient.

Important issues in data mining include the following:

- It should be human-centered; that is, it should be under the control of human users to satisfy human needs.
- It should incorporate subjective measures of *interestingness*, in particular unexpected and actionable suggestions for profit or other purposes.
- It should provide various types to satisfy different user needs.
- It should provide visualization to aid human thinking.

***2.2.3.4 Other Objectives of Data Mining*** Other kinds of data mining also exist. For example, *forensic analysis* is the process of applying the extracted patterns to find anomalous, or unusual data elements largely involved in business applications. To discover what is unusual, we first find the norm and then identify those items that deviate from the usual within a given threshold. For instance, once we notice that almost all users for accessing certain classified data are from project group A, we can wonder few individuals who are associated in different project group, such as B, also frequently accessed the data. These are unusual, and we do not know the reason. Note that while knowledge discovery helps us find "usual knowledge," forensic analysis looks for unusual and specific cases. In some applications, we may be interested in some specific items of data or single pieces of information (singular datum). Note that this is not simply to discover the outliers. The purpose of this type of analysis is to increase the efficiency of knowledge works. For example, this type of data mining may be useful in the fight against criminality, in particular in domains such as drug trafficking or the theft, transport, and sales of art objects or automobiles. Forensic analysis is interesting, but comparing with two other kinds of data mining, it is still in the explorations stage, and will not be the focus of our discussion in this book.

***2.2.3.5 Summary of Objectives of Data Mining*** As noted by Berry and Linoff (1997), an interesting phenomenon in data mining is that many publications (particularly those from academia) are concerned with descriptive tasks of data mining while most actual applications of data mining focus on prediction. This book takes a balanced approach: We respect the maturity of predictive approaches, and we also pay much attention to promote descriptive data mining, because it is relatively new and thus deserves more exploration.

### 2.2.4   What Data Mining Is Not

In order to better understand what data mining is, it is equally important to understand what data mining is not. One way to distinguish data mining from other tasks is to examine analysis versus monitoring. The majority of data mining applications are focused on analyzing information that has been previously collected. In contrast, monitoring often involves online pattern matching operations in which incoming data are compared against a set of conditions or boundaries. Monitoring systems often make quick responses in order to take advantage of information as it is being resented. These systems seldom perform data mining since they do not discover new patterns or classifications. They perform pattern matching rather than interactive discovery. As an example, a small gasoline purchase quickly followed by a series of other gasoline and product purchases is often flagged as a questionable pattern that is identified for further inquiry (i.e., monitoring), because criminals who steal credit cards often want to test the cards initially to determine whether they are valid before using them for a large purchase (Westphal and Blaxton 1998).

The process of discovering patterns from data is a process that combines various technologies since it requires hypothesis, exploration, and automatic discovery. Discovery as a data mining task should have at least some general goal in mind. Unexpected discovery such as discovery of Mendelev periodic tables of chemical elements, in general, is not in the current scope of data mining. Another example of unexpected discovery in human experience is one may discover something while not intended to do any discovery at all. Here is a traveler's story. A few years ago he tried to find a route for overnight train service across Germany. But after extensive search on the *Thomas Cook's Train Table*, he eventually gave up, because no such plan could be retrieved. Since overnight train service in Europe is so popular, he finally realized—and *discovered* unexpectedly—that after almost a decade of unification, Germany is still not united in full scope. Note that although we expect that knowledge discovery should give us some unexpected result at the content level, the activity of knowledge discovery itself should be planned. The current status of data mining has not reached such advanced format as yet.

### 2.2.5   Other Factors in Data Mining Categorization

Data mining has emerged from various applications in many different fields. This complex historical background has complicated the task of categorizing data mining. Data mining is categorized not only in terms of objectives but in many other ways as well.

Data mining methods can be distinguished by whether the original data should be retended or not.

- *Data Retention*. The top-level dichotomization of the data mining technologies can be based on the retention of data; that is, after we have mined the data, data could be maintained for future pattern matching. Obviously, these retention-based techniques apply only to the tasks of predictive modeling and forensic analysis, and not knowledge discovery since they do not distill any patterns. Approaches based on data retention quickly run into problems because of large data sets. The data are retained for pattern matching. When new data items are presented, they are matched against the previous data set.
- *Pattern Distillation*. In pattern distillation we analyze data, extract patterns, and then leave the data behind. This kind of technology can typically take a logical or mathematical approach. Each leaf of the tree shows a distinct method of implementing a system based on a technique (e.g., several types of decision tree algorithms). These technologies extract patterns from a data set, then use the patterns for various purposes. Naturally, the first two questions to ask here are what types of patterns can be extracted and how they are represented.

Note that not all approaches based on pattern distillation provide knowledge, since the patterns may be distilled into an "opaque" language or formalism not easily readable by humans such as very complex equations. Hence, some of these approaches produce "transparent" and understandable patterns of knowledge, while others produce patterns used only for opaque prediction.

Data mining methods can also be distinguished by the underlying data analysis methods. Data mining, as model construction or pattern search, may be performed by the user, for example, just by performing queries only (in which case it is quite difficult), or the user may be assisted by a more sophisticated program that searches the database by itself and finds significant patterns for knowledge discovery.

From a statistical standpoint, there are two types of analysis: confirmatory analysis and exploratory analysis. In *confirmatory analysis*, one has a hypothesis and either confirms or refutes it through a line of inferential statistical reasoning. However, the bottleneck for confirmatory analysis is the shortage of hypotheses on the part of the analyst. In *exploratory analysis*, one aims to find suitable hypotheses to confirm or refute. Automatic discovery automates the process of exploratory data analysis, allowing unskilled analysts to explore very large datasets much more effectively. Exploratory analysis is what we are interested in here. Of course, confirmatory data mining is related more to statistics. We will pay more attention to exploratory analysis later.

## 2.3 IMPORTANT ISSUES FOR CONDUCTING DATA MINING IN ORGANIZATIONS

### 2.3.1 Applicability of Data Mining

Data mining is emerging as a mature technology that is being incorporated into mainstream business applications. It has evolved beyond the point where the algorithms serve as the main criteria for assessing the technology. The following are some important considerations as to whether data mining should be conducted in an organization:

- The need for a data mining process supported effectively by the data mining environment. Such a need should be a result of careful analysis of an organization.
- The need for an interactive knowledge discovery environment in which the business knowledge of the user is combined with the power of the discovery algorithms in order to derive business knowledge from data. Without such a need, or the expected collaboration between user and the data mining system, data mining cannot become a reality.
- The effective and active deployment of the data mining models and patterns. Without such deployment, data mining is useless.
- Flexibility in addressing various computing architectures.
- Scalability and performance on large data volumes.

### 2.3.2 Integrating Data Mining into the Decisionmaking Process

Data mining is a business function and can provide a strategic advantage in developing, defining, and deploying competitive business strategies. There are two areas to consider in successfully ushering data mining into an information environment: skill sets and technology (Parsaye 1999).

Skill sets will vary by the data mining stakeholders in a business organization. The skill sets for each stakeholder are shown in Table 2.3.

Technology integration points include communication links between data mining software and both data and application domains. Data links include sourcing, transformation, and loading of input and output variables and result sets. Application links include the ability to invoke data mining tools from the data warehousing environment (see Chapter 3), access to mining results and visualizations, and ability to invoke analytic models for prediction and description from operational and decision support systems, both back-end and front-end.

Data mining has evolved from manual statistical methods to desktop mining to enterprise mining. With appropriate skill sets, the right team, a warehousing infrastructure, and data mining tools, companies can transition into agile competitors who maneuver quickly with the global demands of the marketplace. As

**Table 2.3  Data Mining Skill Sets in Business Organizations**

| Stakeholder | Skill Set |
|---|---|
| Data mining analyst | Analytics, model building, statistics, neural net development, research |
| Domain expert | Intensive business and data knowledge, experience, decisionmaker |
| Business user | Understand business and data, decisionmaker, user of mining results |
| Information technology technician | Support analytic environment, data model for new data mining components, integrate data mining (including tools, processes, results, models) into data warehousing |

a useful note, data mining can take advantage of *knowledge management*, which is the systematic process of finding, selecting, organizing, distilling, and presenting information in a way that improves an employee's comprehension in a specific area of interest. Knowledge management helps an organization gain insight and understanding from its own experience. Specific knowledge management activities help focus the organization on acquiring, storing, and utilizing knowledge for such things as problem solving, dynamic learning, strategic planning and decision making. It also protects intellectual assets from decay, adds to firm intelligence and provides increased flexibility. For more information, see http://www.equaljustice.org/techcenter/knowledge3.htm.

It is interesting to note that a culture clash is taking place between traditional marketers and database marketers that centers around the usage of data mining. Whereas traditional marketers rely on mass communication campaigns geared toward *acquiring new* customers, database marketers have embedded data mining techniques into their analysis processes, squeezing the most out of the *current* customer base. Database marketers clearly have more proof-of-performance numbers on their side. They are proficient at using data mining to make management comfortable by providing direct financial and economic return results from their promotional campaigns. The end result is that decisionmaking within the marketing discipline is split between informed and uninformed resource allocation decisions.

### 2.3.3  Major Categories of Data Mining Usage

It is necessary to distinguish the data mining processes discussed above in terms of the data mining activities in which the processes may be performed, and the users who perform them. First, are the users. Data mining activities are usually performed by three different classes of users: *executives*, *end users*, and *analysts*.

- *Executives* need top-level insights and spend far less time with computers than do the other groups; their attention span is usually a few minutes to less than half an hour. They may want information beyond what is available in their executive information system (EIS). Executives are usually assisted by end users and analysts.
- *End users* know how to use a spreadsheet, but they do not program—they can spend several hours a day with computers. Examples of end users are salespeople, market researchers, scientists, engineers, and physicians. At times, managers assume the role of both executive and end user.
- *Analysts* know how to interpret data and do occasional computing but are not programmers. They may be financial analysts, statisticians, consultants, or database designers. Analysts usually knows some statistics and Structured Query Language (SQL).

These users usually perform three types of data mining activity within a corporate environment of data mining duration. These three types are *episodic*, *strategic*, and *continuous* data mining.

- *Episodic Mining.* Data are mined from one specific episode such as a specific direct marketing campaign. We may try to understand this data set, or use it for prediction on new marketing campaigns. Episodic mining is usually performed by analysts.
- *Strategic Mining.* Larger sets of corporate data are mined with the intention of gaining an overall understanding of specific measures such as profitability. Typical questions to be answered by strategic mining include "Where do our profits come from?" and "How do our customer segments and product usage patterns relate to each other?"
- *Continuous Mining.* Data are mined in order understand how the world has changed within a given time period and to comprehend the factors that influence change. Questions to be answered in continuous mining include "How have sales patterns changed this month?" and "What were the changing sources of customer attrition last quarter?" Obviously, continuous mining is an ongoing activity and usually takes place once strategic mining has been performed to provide a first understanding of the issues.

There is natural connection between types of users and types of activities. Continuous and strategic mining are often directed toward executives and managers, although analysts may help them here. Different technologies are best suited to each of these types of data mining activity. A rough picture summarizing these relationships is shown in Figure 2.2, where different kinds of users, and different objectives, types, and tasks of data mining at the most abstract levels are depicted.

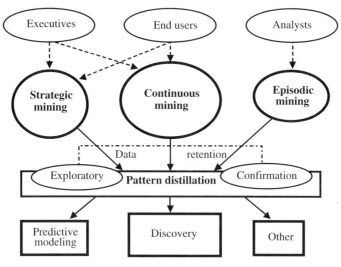

**Figure 2.2**   Data mining usage and types.

### 2.3.4   Data Mining and Privacy–Security Issues

As yet another caution to data mining in business organizations, we should note that although data mining is important, it may also bring some potential problems to database design, such as issues related to privacy and database security. Data mining should not be carried out with the price of violating privacy. A related but different problem is data security, because by using knowledge discovery techniques, an unauthorized user may derive highly sensitive knowledge from unclassified data.

Therefore, it is important to consider both the pros and cons of deriving implicit knowledge from databases. Two aspects need to be considered: (1) from the user's side, knowledge discovery techniques provide potential useful inference methods to better utilize the stored information (i.e., in addition to those explicitly stored information, implicit information can be derived and retrieved); and (2) from the system's side, inference methods can be used to derive knowledge about users to better serve users' information needs. Therefore, knowledge discovery techniques have great potential to enhance both system functionality and user-friendliness.

However, a potential negative side exists. One major concern is that knowledge discovery may become a threat to database security. The *inference problem* arises when a collection of data is more sensitive than the individual pieces (this is sometimes called the *aggregation problem* in database literature). The individual data items may be classified as low-sensitivity, but the relationship among the data items is highly sensitive.

From the system side, there are several aspects to deal with, including (1) eliminating derived sensitive data contents to detect and trace violating users by imposing active rules or, if necessary, (2) constructing new active rules. More discussion can be found in Chen (1994). On the other hand, data mining techniques can benefit computer systems to enhance security. The concept of *real-time data mining* has been developed for this purpose, and is an interesting research issue. Data mining can be used to analyze audit data, which is of a large quantity. Some of the most recent work on data mining and security includes that by Lee et al. (1999) and Warrender et al. (1999).

Here we sketch an interesting idea presented relatively recently. It illustrates that although security- and privacy-related issues have become our primary concern, they also serve as a catalyst stimulating new directions of research. Privacy-related concern has motivated the following investigation. Since the primary task in data mining is the development of models of aggregated data, can we develop accurate models without access to precise information in individual data records? Agrawal and Srikant (2000) investigated the specific case of building a decision-tree classifier (a classification system) from training data in which the values of individual records have been perturbed. While it is not possible to accurately estimate original values in individual data records, a novel reconstruction procedure has been proposed to accurately estimate the distribution of original data values. Therefore, by using the reconstructed distributions, we are able to build classifiers whose accuracy is comparable to the accuracy of classifiers built from the original data.

## 2.4  DATA MODELING FOR PREDICTIVE DATA MINING

### 2.4.1  General Aspects of Data Modeling

Data modeling is an important concept in data mining involving continuous variables. A model is usually represented by a math function to describe data classes or concepts. Consequently, classification is the process of finding a set of such models based on training sets. In fact, data modeling is at the heart of the classification or predictive data mining process; models are constructed and then used for prediction. In addition, although in discovery-type data mining we seldom use the term *modeling* explicitly, the knowledge patterns mined, collectively, could be viewed as a model of the underlying data (although not restricted to mathematic forms). Each pattern is a piece of knowledge identified as interesting by the user. The patterns reveal key characteristics behind the data. A model captures the general trends and correlations of data. Therefore, although the materials discussed in this section are directly related to predictive data mining, in many cases, they are also applicable to discovery type of data mining.

It is worth noting the difference between the terms between data *mining* and data *modeling*. While data modeling is about discovering a model that fits the data, regardless of whether the model is understandable (e.g., allowing a blackbox process such as a neural network), data mining sets more emphasis on discovering *understandable* patterns (trees, rules, or associations) in data. Therefore, data modeling is an effective way to achieve the objectives of data mining, even data modeling itself is not same as data mining.

### 2.4.2 Major Types of Models

There are various types of models or types of data mining in terms of solutions (Weiss and Indurkhya 1998). Roughly speaking, there are two categories: logical and mathematical. In a logical system the key operators are conditional (e.g., IF 2500 < sales < 3500 THEN profit is high). Logic can deal with both numeric and nonnumeric data. Mathematical models require all data to be numeric. In a mathematical model mathematical operators are used to relate variables together using regression, as in the case of $y = (a * X) + b$. Below we describe these two approaches.

***2.4.2.1 Logical Approaches*** Patterns expressed in logical languages are distinguished by two main features. On one hand they are readable and understandable; on the other hand, they are excellent for representing crisp boxes and groupings of data elements.

Decision trees express a simple form of conditional logic. Affinity logic is distinct from conditional logic in terms of both the language of expression and the data structures it uses. Affinity analysis (or association analysis) is the search for patterns and conditions that describe how various items "group together" or "happen together" within a series of events or transactions.

Knowledge patterns mined from discovery data mining can be considered as logical models. Related issues are summarized under the title of data mining tasks.

***2.4.2.2 Mathematical Model*** The relationship between inputs and desired outputs of a pattern recognition system is typically characterized by mathematical equations. Formulating these mathematical equations is referred to as "building a model," and the development process for building a model is called "modeling." Mathematical models are frequently used in predictive data mining.

*Fixed Models* The most straightforward approach to modeling involves formulating closed-form equations that define how the outputs are derived from the inputs. These equations can then be easily translated into a computer program to automate pattern recognition. A model produced in this manner is referred to as a *fixed model*, since all of its characteristics are fixed when the equations are derived. Expert systems studied in AI all into this category of models. The development of expert systems employs sophisticated techniques for producing explicit rules (equivalent to mathematical formulae) based on the knowledge of domain experts. Constructing such a fixed model is carried out as knowledge acquisition [see Chen (1999) for a little more discussion on knowledge acquisition].

*Parametric Models* When faced with an estimation problem, we might have a very good idea about how inputs and outputs interrelate, but not to the level of precision required by a fixed model. This can be handled by a parametric model. In general, the key feature of a parametric model is that explicit mathematical equations characterize the structure of the relationship between inputs and outputs, but a few parameters are unspecified. The unspecified parameters are chosen by examining data examples. Hence the stage of formulating mathematical equations allows for some flexibility in the model, which is fine-tuned by empirical analysis. Parametric modeling generally requires a fair amount of knowledge concerning the pattern recognition task at hand, although the degree of accuracy is less than required by a fixed model. However, this degree of understanding is frequently unavailable in real-world problems. The limitation of parametric modeling is obvious; they are not always applicable, and when they are used, the solution is inaccurate. Nevertheless, parametric models allow us to deal with real-world problems through a stereotyped and simplified approach, and provide acceptable solutions to these problems, which were unobtainable without such simplification. Parametric models can be considered as a specific form of data reduction (an issue to be discussed in Section 2.10), because only the model parameters instead of the actual data need to be stored.

*Nonparametric Models* Models relying heavily on the use of data, rather than domainspecific human expertise, are referred to as *nonparametric* or *data-driven models*. The popularity of nonparametric models has exploded since the late 1990s, as data have become increasingly available and computers have become fast enough to perform sophisticated analyses on huge amounts of data. Many nonparametric methods have been developed. Among these are methods associated with classical statistics, such as nearest cluster methods, as well as more modern machine learning algorithms, such as neural networks and decision trees. The primary difference between traditional and

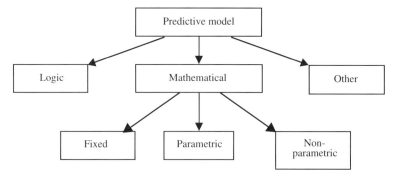

**Figure 2.3** Hierarchy of predictive models.

modern methods is that modern methods are generally geared toward the use of larger data sets and are able to work well with many input variables. In a more general sense, the term *nonparametric model* can be used to cover data mining methods such as clustering, sampling, and the use of histograms (Han and Kamber 2000).

Predictive modeling is summarized in Figure 2.3. For description-type data mining, knowledge patterns mainly take logic-based approaches (to be discussed in Section 2.5).

### 2.4.3 From Data to Model

Starting from the data, how can we construct a predictive model? The following are some important factors to be considered:

- *Model representation*, which is the language for describing discoverable patterns.
- *Model evaluation*, which estimates how well a particular pattern meets the criteria of the data mining process.
- *Model construction* (or model search), which refers to the process of constructing a model, including the search for parameters.
- *Formats of models*, which depend on the data to be analyzed and how they are to be displayed. For example, decision trees and rules make use of a simple representation form and are relatively easy to comprehend by the user. Nonlinear regression and classification methods consist of a family of techniques for predication that fit linear and nonlinear combinations of basics functions to combinations of input variables. In addition, various methods to be discussed in the next section can be used to construct models for discovery-type data mining.

## 2.5 AN OVERVIEW OF KNOWLEDGE DISCOVERY TASKS

### 2.5.1 Different Ways of Characterizing Data Mining Approaches

In this section we mainly focus on discovery type of data mining. As pointed out by Chen et al. (1996), data mining techniques can be classified by different criteria, such as according to which kinds of (1) databases to work on (relational databases, object-oriented databases, etc.), (2) knowledge to be mined (e.g., association rules or characteristic rules), or (3) techniques to be utilized (e.g., data-driven or query-driven).

In the next subsection, we briefly discuss primary data mining tasks (also called data mining functions or functionalities) according to the types of knowledge to be mined. In addition, as already discussed in Chapter 1, data mining tasks are closely related to pattern recognition, statistics, and other traditional data analysis methods, as well as uncertain reasoning tasks. These two issues are addressed in consecutive two subsections.

## 2.5.2   Primary Data Mining Tasks for Knowledge Discovery

The goals of discovery (and to a certain degree, prediction as well) are achieved by using various primary data mining tasks. A data mining task indicates what kind of knowledge should be mined, so it is also referred to as data mining functionality. The following is a brief discription of data mining tasks.

*Rule and Tree Induction*   *Rule* or *decision tree induction* is the most established and effective data mining technologies in use today. It is what can be termed *goal-driven* data mining in that a business goal is defined and rule induction is used to generate patterns that relate to that business goal. The business goal can be the occurrence of an event such as "response to mail shots" or "mortgage arrears" or the magnitude of an event such as *energy use* or *efficiency*. Rule induction will generate patterns relating the business goal to other data fields (attributes). The resulting patterns are typically generated as a tree with splits on data fields and terminal points (leaves) showing the propensity or magnitude of the business event of interest. *Tree induction* is goal driven discovery and is the most widely used technique involving the induction of patterns (trees) related to a business event (goal), such as mortgage arrears, customer attrition, energy consumption, and insurance claims. As an example of tree induction data mining, consider a data table that represents captured data in the process of loan authorization. The table should capture a number of data items concerning each loan applicant [sex, age, time lived at current address, residence status, occupation, employment tenure (length of time on current job), time with the bank (how long the customer has had an account), and monthly household expenses] as well as the decision made by the underwriters (to accept or reject). The objective of applying rule induction data mining to this table is to discover patterns related the decisions made by the loan underwriters to the details of the application.

*Characterization*   The objective of characterization is to generalize, summarize, and possibly contrast data characteristics. For example, we may want to know what kinds of people are typical home buyers in West Omaha for new homes priced $500,000 and above.

*Classification*   Frequently we want to classify data according to the values in a classifying attribute. This involves learning a function that maps (i.e., classifies) a data item into one of several predefined classes. For example, we may classify cars according to gas mileage on highways. In general, data classification is the process that finds the common properties among a set of objects in a database and classifies them into different classes, according to a classification model. The objective of the classification is to first analyze the training data and develop an accurate description or a model for each class using the features available in the data. Some machine learning techniques, such as ID3, are closely related to discovery of classification knowledge.

*Regression*  Regression involves learning a function that maps a data item to a real-valued prediction variable. This task is conceptually similar to classification. The major difference is that in regression the attribute to be predicted is continuous rather than discrete. The prediction of numeric values has been traditionally done by classical statistical methods, such as linear regression. However, regression can also be performed by the higher-level symbolic methods often used in the classification task.

*Association*  Also called *market basket analysis* (MBA) or *affinity analysis* in business applications, association is the discovery of associations between the various attributes or transactions. It may take several forms, such as

- *Discovery of Associations between Business Events or Transactions.* For example, we may want to know which items are purchased together in a supermarket, or which faults occur together, in a computer. As one example, we may have discovered that 30% of customers who buy product A will also buy product B. As another example, we may discover that in 60% of cases when fault 1 is encountered, then fault 7 is also encountered. (If the sequence of events is important, then another data mining technology for discovering sequences can be used.)
- *Discovery of Associations between the Attributes of Case Data.* This can be considered as a generalization of the basket data analysis. Case data are data that can be structured as a table of cases. Mortgage application records are an example of case data. In such data, associations can be found between data attributes (fields). For example, 70% of all applicants are over 40 and in managerial occupations and earning over $50,000 per year. Such associations can be used as a way of discovering clusters in the data. Note that this differs from rule induction on case data in that no outcome needs to be defined for the discovery process.

*Clustering*  Clustering involves grouping data into several new classes. It is a common descriptive task where one seeks to identify a finite set of categories or clusters to describe the data. For example, we may want to cluster houses to find distribution patterns. Data clustering is the process of grouping physical or abstract objects into classes of similar objects. Clustering analysis helps construct meaningful partitioning of a large set of objects based on a divide-and-conquer methodology that breaks a large-scale system down into smaller components to simplify design and implementation. The task of clustering is to maximize the intraclass similarity and minimize the interclass similarity. It is closely related to spatial data mining. An example of clustering would be segmenting a mortgage portfolio.

## 2.5.3 Other Data Mining Tasks

In addition, the following types of knowledge discovery have also been identified (Chen et al. 1996):

- *Dependency Modeling*. This method consists of finding a model that describes significant dependencies between variables. Dependency models exist at two levels: the structure level and the quantitative level.
- *Change Detection*. This method focuses on discovering the most significant changes in the data from previously measured or normative values.
- *Trend Analysis*. This method focuses on finding and characterizing evolution trend, sequential patterns, and deviation data, such as involved in stock analysis.
- *Deviation Detection*. This kind of task focuses on discovering significant deviations between the actual contents of data subset and its expected contents. Two major types of deviations are temporal deviations (which refer to significant changes in data along the dimension of time) and group deviations (which refer to unexpected differences between data in two subsets of data).
- *Link Analysis*. This method traces the connections between records to develop models based on patterns in the relationships by applying techniques based on graph theory. Link analysis uses a combination of binary relationships established between object representations to generate networks of interactions and associations from defferent data sets.
- *Pattern Analysis*. This method finds and characterizes specified patterns in large databases.
- *Spatiotemporal Data Mining*. This method is concerned with data mining involving spatial and/or temporal data. There is an interesting relationship between these spatial and temporal data mining (e.g., the problem of temporal data mining can be converted to spatial data mining).
- *Mining Path Traversal Patterns*. There is an interesting relationship between data mining and Internet. Mining path traversal patterns is a topic of *Web mining*, which has become increasingly popular. We will discuss issues related to Web mining in Chapter 3.
- *Mining Sequential Patterns*. This method involves the discovery of frequently occurring patterns in sequential data. The problem was first introduced as a problem of mining *sequential patterns* in a set of sequences, whose elements are sets of items. Another approach was presented in the context of sequences of events where various types of patterns, called *episodes*, are mined in one source data sequence.

## 2.5.4 Data Mining Tasks and Uncertain Reasoning Techniques

In addition to the data mining tasks summarized above, the objective of data mining can also be achieved through uncertain reasoning techniques, such as

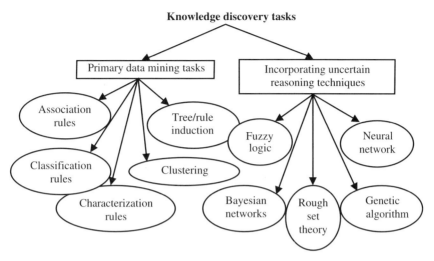

**Figure 2.4** Knowledge discovery tasks.

fuzzy logic, Bayesian networks, neural networks, rough set theory, and genetic algorithms. Of course, these two techniques have very different goals. However, both data mining and uncertain reasoning are aimed at data analysis. Uncertain reasoning is the process of reasoning with the existence of uncertainty; in can be used for many purposes, including data mining. In this sense, uncertain reasoning tasks can also serve as tasks for data mining. In fact, the integration of data mining and uncertain reasoning is the theme of this book. An overview of this issue is provided in Chapter 4, and several uncertain reasoning tasks are discussed in Chapters 6 and 7.

Data mining tasks for knowledge discovery, including useful techniques developed from uncertain reasoning, are summarized in Figure 2.4.

## 2.6 ENVIRONMENT FOR DATA MINING

Data mining may involve very different techniques for different purposes, and could be performed in various platforms. In its most straightforward form, data mining can be carried out from plain data sets, and data may reside in the main memory. Alternatively, in order to deal with huge amount of data in many real-world applications, we can perform data mining in a database management system (DBMS) environment, or in many cases, more preferably, even in a data warehouse environment. Figure 2.5 depicts different levels of data mining. We start with the original data sets. For relatively small size of data, they can be treated as plain files and to be processed in the main memory. In Figure 2.5, this kind of activity is denoted by a double-lined arrow. On the other hand,

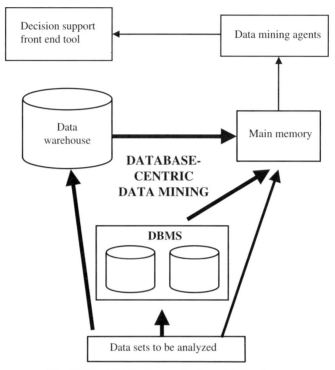

**Figure 2.5**   High-level examination of data mining.

in order to make huge amount of data manageable, they should take advantage of database management systems (DBMSs). Data are stored on disks, and are manipulated by DBMS for input/output (I/O) access. The integration of data mining and database management systems is referred to as *database-centric data mining*. The dark arrows in Figure 2.5 denote activities involved in this type of data mining, which we will pay attention to in the remaining part of the book.

Regardless of whether databases are involved, the data mining problem is taken care of by the data mining agents, which perform various kinds of duties such as data preparation and data mining proper, which may employ any data mining methods. Note also that some machine learning techniques originally developed in artificial intelligence community (see Chapter 5) and various software computing techniques (such as fuzzy set, genetic algorithms, as well as others) do not assume the use of DBMS. However, if DBMS is used, we can take advantage of functionalities of DBMS.

In addition, data used for data mining may come from different databases, and the DBMS need not necessarily be centralized. For example, data mining can be carried out in a mulitidatabase environment where multiple databases are involved. Furthermore, progress of data warehousing techniques has shown that data warehousing can significantly benefit data mining. Unlike multidatabase systems (where data are stored in multiple databases), in a data warehouse the consolidated data are stored in one database. The concept of data warehousing is explored further in Chapter 3.

There is a spectrum concerning varying degrees of coupling a data mining system with a database/data warehouse system. Several possible designs exist. In one extreme there is no coupling at all, while the other extreme requires tight coupling. Between these two extremes we may have loose coupling or semitight coupling. A popular opinion is that well-designed data mining systems should offer tight or semi-tight coupling with a database and/or data warehouse system (Han and Kamber 2000). However, there are also problems and challenges for such tight coupling. We will examine this issue in Chapter 3.

## 2.7  DATA MINING IN DATABASE MANAGEMENT SYSTEMS

We now take a closer look at data mining in the environment of database management systems (DBMSs). A data mining query goes a step beyond decision support query, inviting the system to decide where the focus should be. Naïve implementations of data mining queries will result in execution of large numbers of decision support queries, and may render this approach completely infeasible. Data mining stresses both the query optimization and DBMS components of a traditional database system, as well as extensions to database languages, such as language primitives that support efficient sampling of data (Garcia-Molina et al. 2000).

### 2.7.1  Data Mining and Database Management Systems

***2.7.1.1  A Pyramid for Data Mining***  In the case of tight integration between the DBMS and the data mining module, there may be a profound impact on DBMS functions. As indicated in Figure 2.6 in a pyramid for data mining, the operating system and communication network appears on the bottom. On the top of this are various layers including the database system, the data warehouse, data mining components, and other tools [such as online analytical processing (OLAP)] integrated together for decision support. Issues related to data warehousing and OLAP are discussed further in Chapter 3.

***2.7.1.2  Relevance of Database Management Systems to Data Mining***
In order to take advantage of database management systems for data mining, we should have a good understanding of the basic aspects of database management systems. Here we a briefly review some basic aspects of database management systems.

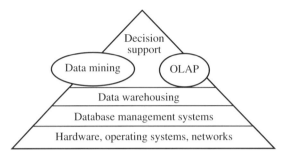

**Figure 2.6** A pyramid for data mining. [Revised from Thuraisingham (1999).]

- *Query Processing.* Various efforts have been made to examine query languages such as SQL (Structured Query Language) and determine what extensions are needed to support mining. Actually, various proposals exist. If there are additional constructs and queries that are complex, then the query optimizer has to be adapted to handle such cases. Closely related to query optimization is efficient storage structures, indexes, and access methods. In addition, special mechanisms may be introduced to support data mining in the query process.
- *Transaction Management.* In this case, mining may have relatively little impact, since mining is usually done on decision support data and not on transactional data [as used in traditional (OLTP) online transaction processing]. However, there are cases where transactional data are analyzed and mined for anomalies, such as credit card and telephone card anomalies. Analyzing the transactional data may help credit card or telephone companies detect abnormal usage patterns.
- *User Interface.* The system requirement includes an SQL query generator, the application generator, and a report generator. Users should select outcomes, approaches and techniques.

### 2.7.2 Data Mining from a Database Perspective

We can now address the issue of performing data mining in database management systems. Recall from the database literature, *integrity constraints* refer to the conditions with which data must comply (in order to guarantee the consistency of the database). There are several forms of integrity constraints, such as referential integrity, as well as functional or other forms of dependencies. The implicit relationship among data, as to be discovered by data mining, can be viewed as a relaxed (or generalized) form of integrity constraints. Therefore, data mining can be viewed as a study extended from the traditional context of integrity constraints (although they rarely are in a rigid manner as integrity constraints would require). For a discussion of integrity constraints, see Chen (1999).

Anther important aspect is that although database management systems have many nice features, they are developed for retrieval of data, rather than data mining. What major issues should be considered? For researchers from the DBMS community, the focus has been on the concern of database-centric data mining (as discussed in the previous section). In fact, data mining can be considered as an extension of the traditional DBMS querying process, as indicated in the two research programs proposed by Imielinski and Mannila (1996). The *short-term program* is concerned with developing efficient algorithms implementing data mining tools on the top of large databases and utilizing the existing DBMS support. The *long-term program* is concerned with building optimizing compilers for ad hoc queries and embedding queries in application programming interfaces. A discussion of SQL-aware data mining systems can be found in Chaudhuri (1998). For simplicity, we refer the database techniques needed for supporting data mining as *data mining mechanism.*

### 2.7.3 Data Mining for Database Management Systems

It would be interesting to examine what kind of data mining tasks can be done (or can only be done) in a DBMS environment, or how DBMS can take advantage of data mining. The following are some examples (Frietas and Lavington 1998):

- *Discovery of Semantic Query Optimization Rules.* Semantic query optimization rules transform an incoming database query into a new one by using semantic database knowledge (such as integrity constraints and functional dependencies) to produce a more efficient query. This is in contrast to conventional query optimization rules, which optimize an incoming query by performing a syntactical transformation in it, such as rearranging the order of execution of some relational operators. It is interesting to note that the task of discovering semantic query optimization rules has a requirement that is seldom specified for other data mining tasks. The selection of attributes to compose a semantic query optimization rule must necessarily take into account some aspect of the cost of the attributes (determined, e.g., by the access method and indexing scheme of the DBMS). This is necessary to determine the saving in query-processing time associated with the rule. Hence, cost-sensitive data mining algorithms are necessary for this task.
- *Discovery of Database Dependencies.* In the relational data model, the definitions of the relations in the database do not say anything about the relationship among their attributes. This relationship is specified through data dependencies, or integrity constraints. This kind of dependency, termed as database dependencies, is useful for the design and maintenance of a DBMS. Several methods have been devised to automatically discover database dependencies, such as algorithms for discovery of

foreign keys, and for discovery of unary inclusion dependencies and functional dependencies.

- *Mining Integration Knowledge.* This has been described by Srivastava and Chen (1999). Examples of such knowledge include rules that provide evidence for or against two objects from different databases representing the same real-world entity. Another example would be rules to determine the attribute values in the integrated database.

## 2.8 DATA MINING PROCESS

### 2.8.1 Overview

Having examined the overall infrastructure of data mining, we are now ready to take a closer look at data mining as a process. The following are the major stages in organizations for conducting data mining:

1. *Define the problem*, including accurately describing it, to determine the appropriateness of using data mining, to decide the form of input and output, to decide cost effectiveness, and so on.
2. *Collect and select data*, such as deciding which data to collect and how to collect them.
3. *Prepare data*, such as transform data to a certain format, data cleansing, or integrate data from different sources.
4. *Data preprocessing*; this task is concerned mainly with enhancement of data quality.
5. *Select an appropriate mining method*, which consists of two substeps:
   a. Selecting a model or an algorithm, such as deciding whether to use a parametric or nonparametric algorithm, or whether to use regression, use a particular algorithm in an artificial neural network, or use a particular clustering algorithm (such as the $k$-means algorithm)
   b. Selecting model/algorithm training parameters, such as the number of nodes at each level when an artificial neural network is used
6. *Training/testing* the data or applying the algorithm, where evaluation set of data is used in the trained architecture.
7. Final *integration* and *evaluation* of the generated model.

This discussion is expanded from the process of predictive data mining (Kennedy et al. 1997) so that it can also be applied to a broader context. The overview of this process is depicted in Figure 2.7. The overall process will be referred to as *data mining lifecycle*. Note that in an ideal agent-based data mining system, all of these steps can be conducted by multiple agents: While the main data mining agent takes care of the core data mining tasks, the other

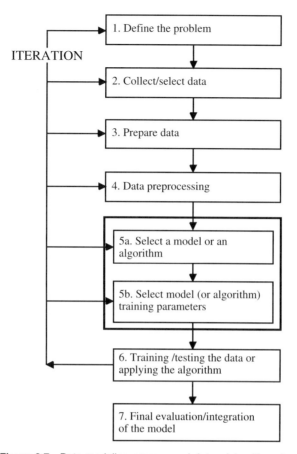

**Figure 2.7**   Data modeling process and data mining lifecycle.

agents perform one or more of other steps (such as data cleansing or data pre-processing). These agents corporate to carry out the data mining cycle. Note also that each step is associated with one or more DBMS and/or AI activities; for example, data cleaning and model development are related to query tools (Brachman and Anand 1996). Note also that the entire mining process is iter-ative, and the result obtained in step 6 (train and test) can be fed back to any of the previous five steps for improvement. For instance, the trained result may indicate there is a need redefine the problem, for collecting more data, or for a different way of preprocessing data, or for selecting a different algorithm or different parameters in the same algorithm. The loop will continue until is satisfactory result has been obtained.

A detailed discussion of these steps follows.

### 2.8.2   Defining the Problem

*Identifying the Objective.* The mining involves some advanced planning about what type and level of information the user intends to capture at the server and what additional data the user plans to match it with. This by itself will ensure data mining efforts will yield measurable business results. For example, in case of mining data from the Web for an organization headquarter, one needs to plan with the Web team what kind of log, cookie, and form of information is needed to capture at what juncture from the Web visitors. One may also need to decide with business, sales, and marketing teams what kind of demographic and household information is needed to purchase to merge with the server data. In addition, one should consider asking the information system team to help integrate the data mart or data warehouse and customer database with the Web data.

*Goal Definition.* This involves defining the goal or objective for the data mining project. This should be a business goal or objective which normally relates to a business event such as arrears in mortgage repayment, customer attrition (churn), energy consumption in a process.

*Problem Analysis.* This involves analyzing a business problem to assess if it is suitable for tackling using data mining. If it is, the availability of the data, the data mining technology to be used (induction, associations, etc.), and how the results of data mining will be deployed as part of the overall solution must be assessed.

### 2.8.3   Collecting and Selecting the Data

Once the business objective has been defined, one must then select the web server and company data for meeting this goal. Data selection is the process of identifying the data needed for the data mining project and the sources of this data. The following are some sample questions:

- Is there a need to connect your database to other databases? If yes, how?
- Will the data being mined remain unchanged and available after the analysis?
- What internal and external information is available for the analysis?
- How current and relevant are the data to the business objective?
- What joins are needed for the various database tables?
- Is there statistical information about the data available?

### 2.8.4   Data Preparation and Transformation

Data preparation plays an extremely important role in data mining. The task is to build "minable" data representations (Pyle 1999). In fact, most data mining practitioners agree that 50–80% of the total life cycle of a data mining project can be taken up by the data preparation stage. The objective of this stage is to cleanse the data and to transform it into a format suitable for the application of pattern discovery techniques.

Once the data have been acquired, one must decide which attributes to exclude and which attributes need to be converted into usable formats. The following are some sample questions:

- What condition are the data in, and what steps are needed to prepare them for analysis?
- What conversions and mapping of the data are required prior to the analysis?
- Are these processes acceptable to the users and the deliverable solution?
- How skewed are the data? Is log or square transformation needed to enhance the uniformity of data?
- Is there a need to normalize the data?
- Is there a need to convert data from one form to some other form, such as to convert yes/no field to 1/0?

Data preparation involves extracting the data and transforming it to the format required for specific data mining algorithms. This includes data cleansing, data aggregation, table joins, new attribute derivation, and normalization. In the context of data preparation, the term *normalization* usually refers to a kind of standard so that data from different input variables will have the same scale. This is because in many cases, particularly in nonparametric pattern recognition, algorithms implicitly assume distances in different directions (in the input space carry) the same weight. For example, the $k$ nearest-neighbor classifier using a Euclidean distance measure depends on all input dimensions being scaled equally. In this case, it is important to normalize the data along every input dimension. Also, in neural networks, the backpropagation (BP)/multilayer perceptron (MLP) model often performs better if all the inputs and outputs are normalized (Kennedy et al. 1997).

In many data mining tasks, particularly those related to predictive data mining, there is a need to divide the data into several sets:

- *Training set*—data used to build the initial model
- *Test set*—data used to adjust the initial model to make it more general
- *Evaluation set*—data used to gauge the likely effectiveness of the model when applied to unseen data

Note that when data mining is carried out in a relational database, and if a training set, a test set, and an evaluation set are used, they are all relations. Note also that some authors do not distinguish evaluation sets from the test sets.

As a specific issue, we make take a look at the issue of evaluating the data. One should evaluate the data to determine what type of data mining tools to use for analysis. The following are some sample questions:

- What is the ratio of categorical/binary attributes in the database?
- What is the nature and structure of the database?
- What is the distribution of the data set?
- How skewed is the data set?

In addition, derived ratios of input fields may be required in order to capture the impact or the true value of the inputs, or to capture the velocity of a client value, such as profit or propensity to buy. For example, a common derived ratio is debt-to-income, so that rather than using simply the debt and income attributes as inputs, more can be gained by the ratio rather than the individual values. If the data mining is carried out on the Web, the number of site visits or the number of purchases made over time may provide a better insight into the true value of a Website's customers. The following (where $N$ = number) is such a rule:

$$\frac{N \text{ purchases}}{N \text{ visits}} = 372/2500 = 0.15 \quad \text{propensity to purchase ratio}$$

$$\frac{\text{Amount of sales}}{N \text{ visits}} = \$13,162/2500 = \$5.26 \quad \text{profit ratio}$$

### 2.8.5 Data Preprocessing and Optional Steps

After data preparation, depending on the quality of data, various preprocessing activities can be carried out. Preprocessing aims at simplifying the relationships to be inferred by a model. (Note that the boundary between data preparation and preprocessing is clearcut. Some activities categorized in this book as preprocessing may be considered as preparation by other authors, and vice versa. Roughly speaking, while data preparation focuses on the data itself, data preprocessing consists of activities more directly related to the data mining proper.) Take a look at the case of nonparametric modeling. Although these models can infer arbitrary relationships from data, as the relationships become more complicated, more data and computational time are required. Therefore, preprocessing is crucial when the quantity of available data is a limiting factor. One commonly used type of preprocessing aims at reducing the number of input variables. Another type involves transforming a problem so that the relationships of the resulting problem are simpler, usually in the sense that the associated mapping becomes smoother. Other techniques are also used, and in general it is not easy to give general advice. There are also some optional steps before actual data mining is carried out, and many of them are highly recommended in various applications. We discuss several optional steps below.

*Conducting Analysis Session*   When using a data miner, an option is to bring a segment (and not a sample) of data from a warehouse (or other sources) to the data miner and perform discovery or prediction. The process of mining this data segment is referred to as an *analysis session*. For example, we may want to predict the response to a proposed direct mail campaign by analyzing previous campaigns for similar products, or we may want to know how customer retention has varied over various geographic regions.

An analysis session may be either structured or unstructured. A *structured* session is a more formal activity in which we set out with a specific task, such as analyzing profitability by customer segments and/or products. In fact, structured sessions are often performed in a routine manner; for example, we may analyze costs, revenues or expenses every quarter, and understand the reasons for the trends. As an alternative, we may routinely perform forecasting for various items such as product demand in various markets. We may also look for unusual transactions that have taken place in the past 4 weeks. An unstructured session is a wild ride through the database, where the user wanders around without a goal, hoping to uncover something of interest by serendipity. This type of abstract wild ride usually uncovers some very wild facts hidden in the data.

The data in the data miner often needs to be enriched with aggregations. How these aggregations are built is decided partly by a business analysis. For instance, we may need to look at the number of credit cards a customer has as an item. In some other cases, we may want to look at the volume of transactions the customer has had. These aggregations enrich the data and coexist with the atomic level data in the mine.

*Visualization*   The effectiveness of data mining as a business intelligence tool has been demonstrated with a large number of successful applications. However, in order to give data mining a wider appeal, it has become apparent that a methodology or process is required to allow non–data mining specialists to achieve the same degree of success as seasoned practitioners. Such a systematic and repeatable process will allow data mining to be successfully deployed by many people across organizations. Data visualization and exploration plays an important role throughout the data mining process, and has been incorporated into many software tools for data mining. In addition to giving the user a method of validating the accuracy and meaning of tree patterns, the pattern exploration process helps the user obtain a better understanding of the patterns being discovered and their implications.

*Data Reduction*   Various techniques have been developed for data reduction. Some basic issues on data reduction are discussed in Section 2.10. Below we present two cases to illustrate the idea. First, we can use data reduction such as discretization to reduce the possible values of a variable. As a preprocessing step for data mining, discretization consists of splitting the values of a continuous attribute into a small list of intervals. Each interval is then treated as a discrete value (a category) by the data mining algorithm. One effect of discetization is to significantly speed up the execution of several data mining algorithms. This is particularly true for algorithms in the rule induction task. The reason is that many rule induction algorithms have to sort the values of a continuous attribute when that attribute is a candidate attribute to extend a partially formed rule. Another example of data reduction is through *attribute selection*. When the data to be mined contain a large number of attributes, the processing time of a data mining algorithm can be reduced by applying this algorithm to a selected subset of the available attributes.

*Data Compression*    A particular form of data reduction is through data compression. Here *compression* is defined as the process of constructing a mapping from a source alphabet to a code and then reapplying that mapping to the file that contains the source alphabet. The most obvious advantage of data compression is to reduce storage requirements, which in turn reduces the overall program execution time. A wide range of data compression methods have been developed. In *reversible* data compression, all of the information is considered relevant and decompression will recover the original data representation. This is also known as lossless compression, as it involves no loss of information. If data has been losslessly compressed, the original data can be reconstructured exactly from the compressed data. To make data compression useful in many applications, *nonreversible* data compression methods are needed. These methods are referred to as *lossy compression* techniques, because they reduce the size of the physical representation of the data, but they do not necessarily preserve the whole set of information. When these techniques are used, only a subset of the original information considered relevant is preserved, and the original data can only be *approximately reconstructed* from the compressed data. The good thing about lossy compression techniques is that, if they are appropriately used, less important or noisy information is lost (filtered), and only the main features of the data will remain. Therefore, although data compression may not make direct contribution mining the knowledge patterns from data, it could be an effective step for data preparation in the overall data mining process. A particularly useful lossy data compression method is called *wavelet transforms*. As a linear signal processing technique, it transfers a data vector (consisting of values from all involved attributes) of length $L = 2^n$ to a numerically different vector of wavelet coefficients. Each transform involves applying two functions, which are applied to pairs of the input data, resulting in two sets of data of length $L/2$. The two functions are recursively applied to the sets of data obtained in the previous loop, until the resulting data sets are reduced to the size of length 2. Finally, only a small fraction of the wavelet coefficients that exceed a certain threshold will be retained, which is the compressed data. An interesting aspect of wavelet transform is that it can be used as a data cleaning method as well, because it removes noise without smoothing out the main features of the data.

*Other Issues*    Many other issues need to be considered. For example, a *sampling* technique can be used. This involves selecting representative data and is discussed further in Chapter 3. Another technique is *filtering*, which involves selecting and using "good" data only. Yet another issue is *data reduction*, which is discussed under the title of speeding data mining.

### 2.8.6    Model Construction and Pattern Discovery

Here the term *model* could be used in a generic sense; it may also refer to knowledge patterns.

#### 2.8.6.1    *Data Exploration*    Data exploration involves the exploration of the prepared data to get a better feel *prior to* pattern discovery and also to validate the results of the data preparation. Typically, this involves examining the statistics (minimum, maximum, average, etc.) and the frequency distribution of individual data fields. It also involves field–field graphs to understand the dependency between fields. It involves visualization-driven exploration, and its aim is to give the user a good feel for the data and to reveal any errors in the data preparation/extraction. It involves visualization driven exploration and its aim is to give the user a good feel for the data and to reveal any errors in the data preparation/extraction.

#### 2.8.6.2    *Formatting the Solution*    Several factors should be considered for selecting an appropriate format for data mining, such as

- What is the desired format of the solution: decision tree, rules, code (in C, C++, or some other programming language), graph, or something else?
- What is the solution used for: classification, regression, clustering, or segmentation?
- How will the knowledge gained be distributed?
- What are the available format options from the data mining process?
- What does management really need: insight or sales?

One may need to use multiple tools in order to come up with the ideal Web mining format for your Website. For example, one may need to extract rules from a clustering analysis. To do so one, will need to first perform the clustering analysis using an appropriate algorithm as discussed in Chapters 6 or 7. Next, one will need to run the identified clusters through a machine learning algorithm in order to generate the descriptive IF/THEN rules that characterize the extracted clusters. Conversely, one may need to first do an analysis using a machine learning algorithm on a data set with a large number of attributes in order to compress it, in order to identify a few significant attributes. Then run those significant attributes through a neural network for the final classification model.

***2.8.6.3  Selecting the Tools***  If a commercial software tool is used, a key criterion for a data mining tool is the data mining technologies it supports. To choose the right mining tool, you must not only select the right technology but also consider the characteristics and structure of your data. Here is a checklist of data-related issues you should considered when selecting a data mining tool:

- Number of continuous value fields
- Number of dependent variables
- Number of categorical fields
- Length and type of records
- Skewness of the data set

In order to select an appropriate tool for data mining, a basic understanding of machine learning is needed. Roughly speaking, machine learning refers to artificial intelligence (AI) tasks for better performance. (See chapter 5 for a brief discussion on machine learning.) In general, symbol-based machine learning algorithms perform better on skewed data sets with a high number of categorical attributes and a high number of fields per records, while neural networks do better with numeric data. Neural networks work best on data sets with a large number of numeric attributes. Machine learning algorithms incorporated in most decision tree and rule-generating data mining tools work best with data sets with a large number of records and a large number of attributes. Studies have shown that the structure of the data critically impacts on the accuracy of a data mining tool. For example, data sets with extreme distributions and with many binary or categorical attributes tend to favor machine-learning-based data mining tools (Parsaye 1999).

***2.8.6.4  Constructing the Model***  We now enter the model construction proper (again, we use the term *model* in a broad sense). It may take more specific form, such as pattern generation. This step involves using rule induction (automatic or interactive), associations discovery, as well as other algorithms to generate knowledge patterns. The process of pattern discovery is most effective when applied as an exploration process assisted by the discovery algorithm. This allows business users to interact with and to impart their business knowledge to the discovery process. During the mining process one searches for patterns in a data set and generate classification rules, decision trees, clustering, scores, and weights, and evaluate and compare error rates. The result of applying these algorithms will be referred to as a *model* (as discussed in Section 2.4.1). In order to construct a model in this sense, many issues should be considered, such as

- What are the model error rates, and are they acceptable, or can they be improved?

- Are additional data available that could help the performance of the models?
- Is a different methodology necessary to improve model performance?
- Should the output take the format of SQL syntax for distribution to end-users?
- Should we use supervised learning or unsupervised learning? (For these two types of learning, see Chapter 5.)
- Should we incorporate C code into a production system that manipulates IF/THEN-type rules?
- Should we integrate the obtained knowledge patterns into a decision support system?
- Should we use classification, prediction, or clustering?
- How can we monitor and evaluate the results?

In the case of inducing a tree, users can, at any point in the tree construction, examine and explore the data filtering to that path, examine the recommendation of the algorithm regarding the next data field to use for the next branch, and then use their business judgment to decide on the data field for branching. The pattern discovery stage also involves analyzing the ability of the discovered patterns to predict the propensity of the business event, and for verification against an independent data set.

### 2.8.7  Post–Model Processing and Pattern Deployment

***2.8.7.1  Main Forms of Post–Model Processing***  This stage involves the application of the discovered patterns to solve the business goal of the data mining project. This can take many forms:

- *Result (Patterns, Rules, etc.) Presentation.* The description of the patterns (or the graphical tree display) and their associated data statistics are included in a document or presentation. This requires the data mining tool to generate text reports representations of the result.
- *Validating and Interpreting the Discovered Patterns.* It is a very important step to validate the findings. A data mining analysis will most likely involve individuals from several departments, such as Information Systems, Marketing, Sales and Inventory. It most definitely will involve the administrators, designers, analysts, managers, and engineers responsible for designing and maintaining the database or Website. After data mining analysis is completed, it is important to share and discuss the findings within the group of people involved. Domain experts, people who are the specialists in their area, need to be briefed on the results of the analysis to ensure that the findings are correct and appropriate to your site's business objectives. This is the "sanity check" step. One need to be

objective and focused on your initial goal for mining. If data mining results are faulty, whether this is due to the data, tool, or methodology, one may need to do another analysis and reconstruct a new set of models with your domain experts' participation and input. Domain experts need to be briefed on the results of the analysis to ensure that the findings are correct and appropriate to the site's business objectives. This is the sanity check; one must be objective and focused on one's initial goal for mining the Website.

- *Delivering the Findings.* A report should be prepared documenting the entire mining process, including the steps taken in selecting and preparing data, the tools used and why, the tool settings, the findings, and an explanation of what the code that was generated is supposed to do.
- *Integrating the Solutions.* This final step is really a commitment to continue the process of learning from online transactions of the organization. This process involves incorporating the findings into the organization's business practices, marketing efforts, and strategic planning.

There are some other related tasks:

- *Data Scoring and Labeling.* The discovered patterns are used to score and/or label each data record in the database with the propensity and the label of the pattern it belongs to. This can be done directly by the data mining tool or through generation of SQL or C representation of the decision trees.
- *Incorporating Business Intelligence.* The discovered patterns are used as queries against a database to derive business intelligence reports.
- *Alarm Monitoring.* The discovered patterns are used as norms for a business process. Monitoring these patterns will enable deviations from normal conditions to be detected at the earliest possible time.
- *Pattern Deployment.* This step involves deploying the discovered patterns as designed in the problem analysis stage. Patterns are typically used in decision support systems, to produce reports/guidelines, or to filter data for further processing.
- *Maintenance of Discovered Knowledge, or Pattern Validity Monitoring.* As a business process changes over time, the validity of patterns discovered from historic data will deteriorate. It is therefore important to detect these changes at the earliest possible time by monitoring patterns with new data. Significant changes in the patterns will point to the need to discover new patterns from more recent data. For example, the issue of incremental maintenance of discovered association patterns will be briefly mentioned in Chapter 5.

***2.8.7.2 Pattern Deployment*** In many applications, the goal of data mining is to identify important patterns to guide organizations to take various actions, such as adjusting the product supply, or, in extreme cases, closing under-performing stores or opening new stores in certain locations. Therefore, pattern deployment, particularly active pattern deployment (Mena 1999) becomes a very important issue.

The format of a data mining analysis or data mining tools may vary. For example, it may be in the form of visualization, or in the form of IF/THEN rules, such as

IF      Website customer age is less than 30
THEN    response to offer is 25%

Still another possible solution available from the data mining process is a piece of code (such as in programming language C), which usually is representative of a set of weights, or formulas. These weights are usually extracted from a data mining tool incorporating a neural network as its core technology. Some data mining tools are also able to generate SQL syntax, which can be exported from the analysis and used in a production system to extract a set of records in the bases, which meet the parameters of the query.

Patterns discovered using data mining can be deployed in a number of ways to address the relevant business requirements. A number of deployment strategies can be used:

- *Reporting and Dissemination.* Graphical tree patterns can be generated in a way so that they can be easily embedded in Web applications.
- *Data Filtering.* The data miner can generate the discovered patterns as C code, SQL (structured query language) or SAS (Statistical Analysis System) procedures. This allows the user to select, for further processing, data records matching the discovered patterns.
- *Decision Support.* The decision tree, rules, or other forms of knowledge patterns discovered can be used as part of an online decision support system. This can be achieved by generating the tree patterns as C code.
- *Active Deployment.* Data and business specialists in an organization can create a specific data mining business scenario (usually referred to as a *vertical application*) to be deployed to a large number of data mining users inside or outside the organization.

We discuss active deployment in a little more detail [following Mena (1999) and Parsaye (1999)]. In active mining deployment, the users are empowered to discover and explore new patterns within the business scenario (solution) delivered to them. Activities include interactively developing new knowledge patterns in line with their business expertise and requirements; monitoring the impact of new data on existing patterns; and within the same business scenario, changing the outcome field and developing tree patterns for a new goal (or outcome). The active deployment of data mining turns data mining into vertical business applications for wide-scale use by business people who otherwise would not have the skills to develop a data mining process.

A number of software tools have been developed to support the active deployment of data mining. Some features of these tools are described in Chapter 8. These data mining software components allow the creation of vertical applications with embedded active data mining for use by business users (Parsaye 1999). For example, the *embedded data transformation engine* allows the data transformation process designed by the creators of the business scenario to be run against newly available data, without any technical intervention by the business user.

### 2.8.8  Summary of the Data Mining Process

In previous subsections, we examined each stage in the data mining process. Note that stage 7 in Figure 2.7 is not discussed in detail. In fact, the integration stage is optional, and is related largely to fusion of data mining tasks. For this reason, the discussion of integration is deferred to the last sections of Chapters 6 and 7.

As a final remark, we note that data mining is not a linear process. One very interesting aspect is that data mining can be embedded in one or more steps of the process. A well-known example is data mining embedded in data cleansing. As to data quality and integrity, one could apply mining techniques to detect bad data and improve the quality of the data.

## 2.9  SCALABLE AND ACCELERATED DATA MINING

### 2.9.1  Architecture for Data Mining

So far in this chapter we have discussed various aspects related to data mining infrastructure. We still need to take a look on the architecture for data mining from a technical perspective. This discussion is presented below. The data mining tools available today fall into one of two distinct architectures:

***2.9.1.1  Client-Based Mining***   These data mining tools run on client machines and mine data stored on the same client or data downloaded from a server, as data to the client for mining. These tools limit the size of data that can be mined, typically in the order of tens of thousands of records (table rows). These limits are imposed by client memory and processor speed restrictions, as well as network bandwidth restrictions. In this architecture the data to be mined are downloaded (extracted) and stored on the client machine (Windows 95 or NT). All the data preparation and mining is carried out on the client. Until relatively recently this approach was limited to mining tens of thousands of records (in acceptable times of under an hour). Technological advances have made it possible for millions of records to be mined on a client in tens of minutes (Al-Attar 1999).

#### 2.9.1.2 *Workstation (Server) Based Mining*

These tools run on workstations with very thin display clients. An advantage of this approach lies in high-performance workstations, and high bandwidth to the server overcomes the limitations of client-based mining tools. However, these tools have the disadvantages of high cost and the need to make copies of the data on the server. In this architecture the data are extracted and stored on a server but are mined from the client machine(s). There are two distinct flavors of this architecture:

- *Standard Platform Server.* In this scenario, the server is capable of running a data mining engine that is invoked by the data mining front end running on a client machine. This is the most common architecture for two-tier data mining.
- *High-Performance Dedicated Server.* In this scenario, the server is a dedicated machine that cannot run a data mining engine. Most data mining tools can address this situation only by extracting (copying) data from the dedicated server to another standard platform server. This approach is not preferred by users since in involve much data and hardware duplication. Advances has been made whereby the data in dedicated servers are mined in situ by the data mining client firing intelligent queries at the server.
- *Three-Tier Client/Server Data Mining.* This architecture typically involves a dedicated high-performance server, a standard platform middle tier, and a number of data mining clients. There are two subcategories:
  - *Thin Middle Tier.* This scenario is feasible only if the middle tier can have a data mining engine running on it that is invoked by the client, but that can mine the data in situ on the server. This involves the data mining engine on the middle-tier firing intelligent queries at the server.
  - *Fat Middle Tier.* This scenario involves the middle tier loading the data where they are mined on the middle tier and the results are passed on to the data mining client.

### 2.9.2 Scalable Data Mining

Extending the discussion of the architecture for data mining, we can further discuss what scalable data mining is, why it is needed, and the architectural and algorithmic requirements for achieving scalable data mining. *Scaleup* refers to handling larger tasks by increasing computing source.

With the decreasing costs of data processing and storage comes the data-rich organization. It is now a common place for small and medium-sized organizations to hold gigabytes of data relating to a business process. It is therefore essential that data mining tools can deliver acceptable performance on large volumes of data regardless of the computing platform or architecture being used. With the size of warehouses currently approaching many terabytes of information, data mining systems will need to access and process huge volumes of data in parallel. The task can be called *macromining*. Tight database integration that establishes parallel connections between the application and the parallel database is essential for feeding high volumes of transaction data to these data mining systems. A scalable data mining system can help to dramatically improve performance and increase company profits.

Scalable data mining systems must meet all the rigorous demands of corporate production environments, namely, mine on very large volumes of data without having to store extracts from the database to disk, integrate with the parallel database, mix and match traditional techniques with data mining techniques, port across platforms, use an open and flexible environment for running programs in parallel, and require no programming.

Sometimes the term *macromining* is used to refer to the ability to process large data volumes, while meeting performance and scalability requirements demanded by corporate departments. Macromining can process data sets on scalable servers where the data set size greatly exceeds that of memory. In contrast to macromining, *micromining* operates on small data volumes and typically in PC-based environments. Macromining greatly expands the set of business problems that can be solved by micromining applications.

It has been estimated that to build scalable applications, 80% of the effort involves moving the data, such as getting data off the mainframe and into the warehouse, feeding data to and through various phases of the application, and writing the result back into the warehouse. A data mining system is not just a collection of data mining algorithms but a system that is fully integrated with the parallel RDBMS (relational database management system), and one that can support in parallel such diverse data operations as cleaning, transformation, merging and sorting, analysis, extraction (from the database) without the need to store extracted data to disk, and insertion (into the database). To efficiently process the large volumes of data required by these applications, parallel connections must be established between the application and the database; anything less makes the task infeasible. One additional requirement is the ability to combine both relational and flat-file data.

Finally, we should remark on mix and match traditional techniques with data mining techniques. Data mining systems need to employ a variety of techniques for automating the information discovery process in very large databases. Many traditional techniques such as SQL queries and multidimensional analysis (see Chapter 3) are not sufficient for this task. Most users find that they need to build and run applications outside the database because application logic cannot be readily expressed using SQL. Consider a predictive modeling application that predicts which customers are good candidates for a targeted mailing. SQL-based applications are not expressive enough to address such questions. Similarly, multidimensional analysis techniques are limited to finding aggregations of measurements with respect to a predefined set of dimensions (such as finding the average of all sales by state for a given product). They cannot easily determine what factors influence the aggregated measurements (e.g., what factors influence sales). Thus a diversity of techniques are needed for information discovery, including traditional statistical techniques and more automatic data mining techniques.

### 2.9.3 From Machine Learning to Data Mining

Another very important aspect for scalable data mining is through efficient algorithms. The impact of the algorithmic aspect can be better examined from the evolutionary path from machine learning to data mining, as well as from statistical inference to data mining. An examination on the relationship between machine learning and data mining provides another perspective for scalable data mining.

As already mentioned, roughly speaking, *machine learning* refers to artificial intelligence tasks with improved performance. A brief overview of machine learning is provided in Chapter 5. An important form of machine learning is unsupervised learning from basic facts (axioms) or from data. Unlike supervised learning, when unsupervised learning is used, an algorithm is able to derive conclusions never taught by a teacher. This means that unsupervised learning acquires a strong data mining flavor. Despite the similarities between machine learning and data mining, however, one important factor we should bear in mind is that the size of data may make a big difference between them. Finding an appropriate structure to conduct machine learning could be a task which is NP-hard (Dean et al. 1995). In fact, computational learning theory has been developed for dealing with related computational problems. Although machine learning methods can be adopted for data mining purposes, it would also be desirable to explore new methods that directly address the need of decision support queries (see Section 3.2.1 for a brief discussion). Another difference is the objective. In fact, for machine learning, the emphasis of research has been on inference mechanisms involved in the learning process. Although much attention has been paid to developing efficient algorithms, and even though researchers are aware of the importance of scaling up, algorithms developed usually assume that the data are residing on the main memory. The driving force of machine learning research has been largely from academia, although many algorithms have found many applications (e.g., in the case of ID3 or C4.5). In contrast, the driving force of data mining is mainly from business and industry. Some machine learning techniques are not of interest to data mining practitioners, such as learning by analogy or by examples. The data mining community has also initiated some new types of rules, such as association rules (to be discussed in Chapter 5), which can be effectively studied by incorporating computational intelligence techniques. Therefore, data mining and machine learning differ from each other, but may also benefit each other.

As an important note, we point out that data mining differs from machine learning not only with respect to scalability. In fact, another difference is the different scope of tasks. Researchers have warned of several tricky issues in data mining. Inherited from machine learning methods, data mining may pursue a harmful equation of "knowledge = concepts." Research on automation of scientific discovery in natural sciences takes a broader perspective on knowledge. Since a narrow view of knowledge is accompanied by a narrow view of the discovery method, scientific discovery can shed some light on data mining with a broader vision of knowledge and discovery method (Zytkow 1997).

The relationship between machine learning and data mining can also be explained through a different perspective. The field of machine learning, mainly using inductive techniques, is aimed at guiding the system to learn (using training sets, as in supervised learning) or enabling the system to uncover previously unknown knowledge. If we are more interested in the result of machine learning (rather than the learning mechanism itself) on the huge amount of data in a certain domain as a basis for deciding on what actions to take in this domain (such as in the case of business or industry), or we make important breakthrough of this domain (such as in basic science), then we have shifted our interest to the field of data mining.

### 2.9.4 Approaches to Speeding up in Data Mining

***2.9.4.1 Overview*** *Speedup* refers to running a given task in less time by increasing the computing source. Broadly speaking, some approaches are directed at reducing or transforming the data to be mined without requiring modifications in the data mining algorithm. Hence, they can be termed as *data-*

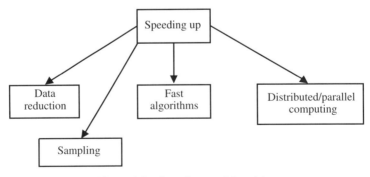

**Figure 2.8** Speeding up data mining.

*oriented approaches.* In contrast, there are algorithm-oriented approaches for speeding up data mining, which modify the algorithm without requiring modification to the data being mined. These approaches fall in three broad groups: fast algorithms, distributed data mining, and parallel data mining. (One can design fast data mining algorithms by restricting the rule space to be searched by the algorithm or by using algorithm optimization techniques, such as clever data structures.) A simple taxonomy is available in Figure 2.8. Since data reduction has been briefly discussed relative to data preprocessing (and will be discussed further in Chapter 7), and since a discussion of approaches related to sampling is available in Chapter 3, in the following we will briefly describe remaining categories.

### 2.9.4.2 Fast Algorithms

A rule induction–based data mining algorithm searches for rules in a very large rule space. In essence, the rule space associated with a data mining algorithm is the set of all rules that can be expressed in the representation language used by the algorithm. In practice, the rule space is too large to be exhaustively searched, and a data mining algorithm uses some heuristic to search only some parts of this space. However, heuristics based on greedy search are so commonplace in data mining that they can hardly be considered an approach to speed up data mining in large databases. A larger degree of restricted search is needed. This can be achieved either by designing a new algorithm or by choosing a suitable set of parameters for an existing algorithm. *Rule pruning*, such as the incremental rule pruning approach, has been used. In general, using heuristics to restrict the rule space can significantly reduce classification accuracy.

### 2.9.4.3 Distributed Data Mining and Parallel Data Mining

In essence, distributed data mining consists of three phases: (1) divide the data to be mined into data subsets and send each subset to a distinct processor, (2) ensure that each processor runs a (same or different) data mining algorithm on its local data subset, and then combine the local knowledge discovered by each data mining algorithm into a global, consistent discovered knowledge.

In Section 2.2.1, we discussed differences between business data mining and scientific data mining, and noted that scientific data mining seems to find and explain the outliers, while commercial applications seem to be aimed mainly at understanding the variations of the majority of the data set elements. Parallel data mining plays different roles in these two kinds of data mining. In application of finding explanation for outliers, parallel computing seems to be essential, while in applications for understanding the variations of the majority of the data set elements, the question is still open because it is not clear yet how effective sampling from a large data set might be at answering broader questions (Skillicorn 1999). Parallel and distributed processing for a particular kind of data mining, namely, association rule mining, will be discussed in Chapter 5.

## 2.10 THEORETICAL FOUNDATIONS OF DATA MINING

### 2.10.1 Examination of the Theoretical Foundations

Data mining has been carried out largely as a practical issue, but an examination of the theoretical (and in some degree, philosophical) foundations would be important for us to understand the nature of data mining. Here we provide a discussion on this issue. First, we summarize some existing perspectives (Mannila 2000).

***2.10.1.1 Reductionism*** *Reductionism* refers to reducing a problem to some other form, which is usually either simpler or better understood. There are several cases of reductionism, such as reducing the problem to a previously known, existing theory, or reducing the data representation.

1. *Reducing Data Mining to Existing Theory.* There are several ways to reduce data mining to an existing theory. For example, some people regard data mining as a subset of statistics, because the mined result can be viewed as a kind of data summarization. Some other people view data mining as an extended application of probability theory, because data mining can be viewed as the task of finding the underlying joint distribution of the variables in the data. Still others would relate data mining to machine learning, as we have already briefly discussed in Section 2.9. However, none of these reductions is adequate. For example, none of these theories is originated to deal with the size of data that data mining is intended to deal with, so the research disciplines of these theories are very different. In addition, both statistics and probability theory deal with only one particular form of uncertainty (viz., randomness), while data mining must deal with other forms of uncertainty (e.g., inconsistency or vagueness). Other differences between statistics and data mining include (1) although in many statistics problems it is sufficient to consider only samples of the data, in data mining, sampling is only a part of the entire problem solving; (2) in a statistical framework, modeling plays a central role, but algorithms play a much more central role in data mining; and (3) although in statisticians also talk about exploratory data analysis, much of statistics is about model fitting, or confirmatory analysis. In contrast, data mining is largely explorative in nature. See Hand (1999) for more detail.

2. *Reducing the Data Representation.* Data can be reduced to a simpler form; for example, continuous variables can be discretized to get range variables. If we push this viewpoint a little further, we can claim that *the task of data mining as a whole, can be viewed as a reduction process.* After all, the result of data mining is a more concise description of the original data themselves. The role of data mining is to discovery general patterns that describe the data. These patterns may have the form of rules, or some model. Each generated pattern represents a subset of the raw data. Knowledge extraction can

be achieved through data reduction. Some basic data mining techniques to be discussed in Chapter 5, such as clustering, sampling, along with some other methods such as visualization (such as the use of histograms), singular value decomposition, wavelets, regression, loglinear models, can be viewed as a kind of reduction method. A more recent technique, called the *rough set theory*, is a typical example of reductionist approach for data mining. (Rough set theory will be discussed in Chapter 7.)

As we will see in Chapter 3, *metadata*, which is data about data, can also be viewed as a kind of data reduction. Metadata can provide useful aid for data mining. Therefore, from the perspective of reductionism as just discussed above, we have the following interesting observation: data mining is the process of using raw data and metadata to derive another kind of data reduction (which is the extracted knowledge).

***2.10.1.2  Data Compression***  A particular variation of data reduction is data compression, which has specific emphasis on the use of encoding technique. According to this theory, the basis of data mining is to compress the given data by encoding in terms of bits, association rules, decision trees, clusters, and so on. Encoding based on the minimum description length principle states that the best theory to infer from a set of data is the one that minimizes the length of the theory and the length of the data when encoded using the theory as a predictor for the data. Encoding is typically carried out in bits.

According to the data compression approach, the goal of data mining is to compress the data set by finding some structure for it. That is, data mining looks for knowledge, where knowledge is interpreted as a representation that makes it possible to code the data using few bits. Several data mining tasks can be viewed as applications of this approach. For example, an accurate decision tree can be considered a compression method for the target (classification) attribute in terms of given properties; clustering of the data can be viewed as a way of compressing the data set so that data belonging to the same cluster are compressed to that cluster; and association rules can be viewed as ways of providing compression of portions of the data so that relevant items can be grouped together. Just like other reductionist approaches such as statistics or probability theory, however, the data compression approach is not adequate, because although it can explain some data mining tasks from a technical perspective, it does not take care of the semantics of data mining.

***2.10.1.3  Inductive Databases***  In contrast to reductionism, data mining can also be viewed by extending existing theories. One such perspective can be briefly discussed below. Relational database theory views queries as functions of mapping databases to databases. Data mining can be viewed as manipulating an *inductive database*, where database schema consists of data and patterns that are stored in the database. Data mining is therefore the problem of performing induction on databases, where the task is to query the data and the theory (i.e., patterns) of the database. The basic idea of inductive databases is that the query concept should be applied also to data mining and knowledge discovery tasks. One can benefit from viewing the typical data mining tasks not as dynamic operations constructing new nuggets of information, but as operations unveiling hitherto unseen but preexisting pieces of knowledge (Mannila 2000).

Intuitively, the term *inductive database* refers to a normal database plus the set of all patterns from a specified set of data that are true of the data. In contrast to a *deductive database* (which contains rules besides the conventional data), an inductive database does not contain all the rules that are true about the data stored in it; rather, the rules are constructed on demand. The schema of an inductive database consists of a normal relational database schema plus a schema for the generalizations. The perspective of inductive databases is gaining popularity in the database research community.

### 2.10.1.4 *From Pattern Recognition to Pattern Discovery*   The perspective discussed above extends relational database theory to a new kind of database that is able to perform induction. A similar consideration, although concerned with data sets in general (rather than relational databases as seen above), is to extend the theory of pattern recognition (for prediction) to pattern discovery. According to this theory, the basis of data mining is to discover patterns occurring in the database, such as associations, classification models, and sequential patterns. Tasks such as machine learning, neural networks, association mining, sequential pattern mining, and clustering contribute to this theory. This perspective apparently extends pattern recognition in at least two ways. First, the task of identifying a new pattern to some known pattern (as in the case of pattern recognition) is extended to discover patterns themselves. Consequently, a predictive task is combined with a discovery task. In addition the concept of pattern as used in knowledge discovery refers to conceptual patterns, and is far more general than the term pattern as used in pattern recognition literature.

### 2.10.1.5 *Microeconomic View*   The microeconomic view can be viewed as a restricted form of pattern discovery, because it considers data mining as the task of finding patterns that are interesting only to the extend that they can be used in the decisionmaking process of some enterprise. The starting point of the microeconomic aspect of data mining is about finding actionable patterns; the only interest is in patterns that can somehow be used to increase utility. This view is one of utility, in which patterns are considered interesting if they can be acted on. Enterprises are regarded as facing optimization problems where the object is to maximize the utility or value of a decision. In this theory, data mining becomes a nonlinear optimization problem.

### 2.10.1.6  *Reconstructability Analysis*

A rarely mentioned approach for data analysis is called reconstructability analysis. System reconstruction (Klir 1985) refers to the following problem: given a behavior system, viewed as an overall system, determine which sets of its subsystems are adequate for reconstructing the given system with an acceptable degree of approximation, solely from the information contained in the subsystems.

The problem of data mining can be reexamined from a system-theoretic perspective. In fact, the collection of data stored in a database describes a system. The task of system reconstruction and the task of knowledge discovery from databases (which can be viewed as systems) are of course quite different. The relationship between these two seems to be recovery of existing system versus discovery of previously unknown knowledge. However, discovery of something that was unknown does not necessarily mean that that thing did not exist before it was discovered. Take a look at the case of archeology. Because it is the science of reconstructing an ancient society, archeology does not create any thing that is physically new, but breakthroughs made in archeology do bring new knowledge to modern society. Similarly, system reconstruction may reveal important, interesting, and previously hidden features of the system. It is thus reasonable for us to hope that reconstruction of the system could be an effective process for the discovery of new knowledge.

System reconstruction and data mining share some common concerns, as well as some techniques utilized, such as statistics and information theory. Significant differences also exist between them. For example, reconstructability analysis requires that subsystems should adequately reconstruct the given system with an acceptable degree of approximation; this requirement is much more rigorous than the criteria used for determining an acceptable result in data mining, where heuristic rules are often deemed as sufficient. The theory developed for system reconstruction may not always be useful to data mining, and some data mining problems may not (or need not) be treated as reconstruction problems. Nevertheless, reconstructability analysis can benefit data mining due to some common interests and common techniques. Since reconstructability analysis is usually more rigorous than data mining, it may help to alleviate some problems faced by the data mining community. A discussion of data mining from this perspective can be found in Chen (1994).

Reconstructability analysis can be viewed as a study related to a more general topic, namely, inverse problems. Although reconstructability analysis has not been a popular approach for data mining, there have been some discussions on data mining and inverse problems. For example, the task of reconstructing original distribution from a given distribution, as exemplified in the case related to privacy-preserving data mining [Agrawal and Srikant (2000), as summarized in Section 2.3.4] can be viewed as a specific form of inverse problems. As another example (as reported in Gunopulos and Rastogi (2000), researchers have exploited results obtained from computational geometry for answering reverse nearest-neighbor (RNN) queries, namely, to find the set of data points that have the query point as the nearest neighbor. (A discussion of the nearest neighbor algorithm can be found in Chapter 5.)

### 2.10.2   Uncertain Reasoning Perspective on Data Mining

Summarizing our discussion in Section 2.10.1, we have seen that there are competing perspectives on the nature of data mining. Note, however, each perspective has its limitations, and can accommodate only some of the techniques in data mining. Therefore, it is reasonable to suggest that data mining may need multiple foundations; in other words, data mining is a multifacet process. Note also that these theories are not mutually exclusive. For example, although pattern discovery has been considered as extending the theory of pattern recognition, it can also be seen as a form of data reduction or data compression, with the patterns as the result of reduction or compression.

Ideally, a theoretical framework could be developed to incorporate all concerns addressed in different perspectives; it should be able to model typical data mining tasks (such as association, classification, and clustering), have a probabilistic nature, be able to handle different forms of data, and consider the iterative and interactive essence of data mining.

Before such a framework is developed, however, we do have a simple way to unify different perspectives. Although this perspective (not discussed in Section 2.10.1) cannot fulfill the wish list mentioned above, it turns out very useful. This is the integrated approach of dealing with data mining *and* uncertain reasoning. In fact, there is a *hidden factor* underlying all the above-mentioned perspectives, namely, *uncertainty* involved in the mining process. Uncertainty could be involved in data values, in the various algorithms used for data mining, or from other aspects. Approaches sketched in previous subsections all have something to do with uncertainty. Let us examine them one by one.

- First, data reduction or data compression makes sense, because uncertainty involved in the data provides us an opportunity to represent the original data in a more concise way. Reducing data mining theory to probability theory or statistics makes sense (even it is not adequate), because each theory has been developed to deal with a particular form of uncertainty.

- The perspective of extending pattern recognition to pattern discovery makes sense, because without considering uncertainty, which is usually intrinsic in the data or without allowing uncertainty in the discovered patterns, discovery of patterns, would be either straightforward (and thus would not deserve further research), not needed (because the regularity in the data could be apparent), or not possible at all (because the requirement for 100% percent accuracy of the result may prohibit any effort in dealing with nonperfect data).

- The perspective of viewing data mining as manipulating an inductive database differs the other approaches in that it takes a logic approach. However, this approach relies on induction, which is not a sound technique. Therefore, this approach represents a logic-based approach to dealing with uncertainty.

- The microeconomic view is intended to maximize the utility or value of a decision. The uncertainty in an optimization problem comes from the conditions with which the optimization problem is subjected to comply, so this perspective represents a mathematical treatment of uncertainty handling subjecting to certain constraints.

- Finally, the approach of using reconstrutability analysis shares the common concern of other forms of inverse problems, namely, how to construct the original system in an acceptable accuracy. Since accuracy and uncertainty are two sides of the same coin, the role of uncertainty is obvious in this perspective.

In summary, we have seen uncertainty handling is a hidden factor of all kinds of data mining perspectives. So why don't we take a close look at the role of uncertainty handling in data mining? In fact, advantages of integrating uncertain reasoning into data mining have been clearly stated in Chapter 1, where we emphasized the differences of these two sets of techniques, as well as common interests shared by them. In the rest of this book, we will exploit all the related aspects in some detail.

## 2.11 RESEARCH ISSUES, TRENDS, AND DIRECTIONS OF DATA MINING

As a relatively young field, there are many challenging and interesting issues to be further explored in data mining. The following are some remarks.

At the practical side, methodologies are needed that promises a degree of generality within one or more stages of the discovery process, such as preprocessing, mining, visualization, use of prior knowledge, knowledge refinement, and evaluation. We will revisit this issue at the end of Chapter 8, where some research directions are identified in a brief summary of existing software tools.

At the theoretical side, research is needed to demonstrate how the proposed theoretical contribution advances the discovery process. In addition to aspects related to integrated data mining as discussed in Section 2.10, Other issues are also of theoretical interest. In the following we briefly examine some topics of data mining from a theoretical perspective. This examination is restricted largely to data mining proper. Topics related to data mining from a broader perspective will be discussed in the next chapter.

A wide scope of issues exist that are of theoretical interest. Many of them are related to data preprocessing:

- Identify necessary and useful preprocessing operations and tools, specifically, to get the application know-how from the algorithm developer.
- Examine how these preprocessing operations can be represented (e.g., for documentation and reuse) as well as executed efficiently on large datasets.
- Compare the different data mining approaches with respect to their input requirements.
- Compare different (logical) representations of the problem and discuss their advantages and disadvantages.
- Assess the impact of unsatisfiable data mining results on further preprocessing.
- Establish usability criteria for different machine learning-approaches with respect to data mining, such as
  - *Scalability*: number of records, number of attributes, multiple relations versus learning time and space requirements
  - *Robustness*: handling of missing values, missing related tuples, noise tolerance, nominal attributes with many different values, and similar
  - *Learning goal*: classification, clustering, rule learning, and so on
  - *Understandability*: size und presentation of mining results
  - *Parameter settings* of the data mining algorithm and their impact on the mining result

As for the trends in data mining, several directions have been identified (Han and Kamber 2000, Chanduri et al. 2000). For example

- *Application-Specific Data Mining Systems.* Since generic data mining systems may have limitations in dealing with application-specific problems, we may see a trend toward the development of more application-specific data mining systems. In a sense, this trend is parallel to the phenomenon of knowledge-based systems where domain knowledge is incorporated to effective problem solving.
- *Scalable Data Mining Methods.* One important direction toward improving the overall efficiency of the mining process while increasing user interaction is constraint-based mining, which provides users with added control by allowing the specification and use of constraints to guide data mining systems in their search for interesting patterns.
- *Integration of Data Mining with Database Systems, Data Warehouse Systems, and Web Database Systems.* A desired architecture for a data mining system is the tight coupling with database and data warehouse systems. Transaction management, query processing, online analytical

processing, and online analytical mining should be integrated into one unified framework. This will ensure data availability, data mining portability, scalability, high performance, and an integrated information processing environment for multidimensional data analysis and exploration.

Other issues include

- Standardization of data mining language
- Visual data mining, which is an effective way to discover knowledge
- New methods for mining complex types of data
- Research to provide theoretical ground for mining techniques for complex types of data mining, and such as mining on multimedia data, text mining, and Web mining
- Privacy protection and information security in data mining
- A systematic analysis on artificial intelligence contributions to data mining
- Statistics and probability in data mining
- Logic-based perspective on data mining
- Human–machine interaction in data mining, including visualization of data, visualization of knowledge, user-friendly discovery interfaces, and interactive data mining: human and computer contributions
- High-performance computing for data mining, including hardware support for data mining, parallel discovery algorithms and complexity, distributed data mining, scalability in high-dimensional datasets, and decomposition of large data tables
- Machine learning and automated scientific discovery, including the process from concept learning to concept discovery, expanding the autonomy of data miners, embedding learning methods in data mining systems, conceptual clustering in knowledge discovery, applications of scientific discovery systems to databases, scientific hypothesis evaluation that transfers to data mining, and hypothesis spaces of scientific discovery useful in data mining
- Quality assessment of data mining results, including multicriteria knowledge evaluation, benchmarks and metrics for system evaluation, statistical tests in data mining applications, and usefulness and risk assessment in decisionmaking

## 2.12 SUMMARY

In summary, we have discussed the infrastructure of data mining: the basics, types, and processes, as well as some key practical and theoretical issues. These aspects depict the most fundamental part of data mining. Additional issues with this infrastructure are examined in Chapter 3, where we further examine data mining in a larger scope. After we provide an overview on uncertainty handling in Chapter 4, we will reexamine many aspects of this chapter (including the data mining process) by incorporating uncertainty issues in this overall process. At the end of Chapter 4, Figure 4.4 summarizes important techniques useful in data mining. These techniques will be examined in the rest of the book.

We wrap up this overview chapter on data mining with a remark on the lifecycle of technology adoption, which includes several stages: innovators, early adopters, chasm, early majority, late majority, and laggards. Data mining is now in a stage called *chasm*, which represents the hurdles or challenges that must be met before the method can become widely accepted as a mainstream technology (Han and Kamber 2000).

# 3

# ENABLING TECHNIQUES AND ADVANCED FEATURES OF DATA MINING

## 3.1 OVERVIEW

In Chapter 2 we discussed the general infrastructure related to data mining. In order to make data mining a reality in various applications, we have to consider supporting environment and enabling techniques for data mining. For example, the headquarters of a discount retail chain may want to analyze sales trend from its stores scattered throughout the world. In this case, the sales data and related information (such as locations of stores, economic information of these locations, etc.) should be first collected before data mining or any other form of analysis can be carried out.

In general, since data mining is hardly an isolated phenomenon, we should explore environments where data mining is usually carried out. Although data warehouses are not a necessary requirement for data mining, they do significantly benefit data mining by serving as an enabling technique. Not intended to provide a full coverage of data warehousing, in this chapter, we focus on some important aspects of data warehouses related to data mining. These aspects are addressed in Section 3.2, based on the popular definition of data warehousing given by W. H. Inmon. We also discuss the relationship between data warehousing and OLAP (online analytical processing). Later subsections of Section 3.3 reexamine the concept of data warehouse from a more theoretical perspective, where a data warehouse is characterized by materialized views. This perspective naturally extends the basics of relational database theory, bridging data mining and relational query processing. In particular, focus on a particular form of materialized view: data cube. Data cubes were originally proposed for OLAP, but more recently they have also found many applications in data mining.

A very important component in a data warehouse is metadata. In a sense, the metadata repository is a highly condensed version, or a miniature of the data warehouse itself, even though there are no actual, object-level data stored in the repository. Data mining techniques can take advantage of the high-level description of data from repository. For this purpose, a general discussion on the role of metadata in data mining is provided in Section 3.3.

Since OLAP and data mining are two basic activities in data warehouses, one may wonder how they can benefit each other. In particular, we are interested in how OLAP techniques can be incorporated into data mining. In Section 3.4, we discuss this issue, and propose an architecture for integrated OLAP and data mining.

Data warehousing provides excellent opportunity for integrated use of data, but it also raises challenging questions. We present two advanced issues related to this topic; both extend our discussion in Chapter 2. One issue is sampling and segmentation (Section 3.5). This discussion also reminds us the importance of dealing with uncertainty, a theme that will be further examined in Chapter 4. Another issue is distributed and parallel data mining integrated with data warehousing (Section 3.6), a theme continued from Chapter 2. In addition, since the basic concepts of data warehousing have naturally made their way onto the web, and some of the most popular Websites on the Internet are basically databases, our discussion of data warehousing is further extended to Web mining (Section 3.7).

## 3.2   DATA WAREHOUSES AND ONLINE ANALYTICAL PROCESSING (OLAP)

### 3.2.1   Basic Concepts of Data Warehousing

Data mining may involve data from multiple data sources, which may reside in a distributed database system, or in a tighter form, multidatabase. The complexity involved in distributed database systems has stimulated organizations to find alternative ways to achieve decision support. Data warehousing is an emerging approach for effective decision support. According to a popular definition, a *data warehouse* is a "subject-oriented, integrated, time-varying, non-volatile collection of data that is used primarily in organizational decision making" (Inmon 1996). Data warehousing provides an effective approach to deal with complex decision support queries over data from multiple sites. The key to this approach is to create a copy (or derivation) of all the data at some one location, and to use the copy rather than going to the individual sources. Note that the original data may be on different software platforms or belong to different organizations.

Data warehouses contain consolidated data from many sources (different business units), spanning long time periods, and augmented with summary information. Warehouses are much larger than other kinds of databases, sizes are much larger, typical workloads involve ad hoc, fairly complex queries, and fast response times are important. Data warehousing encompasses frameworks, architectures, algorithms, tools, and techniques for bringing together selected data from multiple databases or other information sources into a single repository suitable for direct querying or analysis. Data warehousing is especially important in industry today because of a need for enterprises to gather all of their information into a single place for in-depth analysis and the desire to decouple such analysis from their traditional online transaction processing (OLTP) systems. Since decision support often is the goal of data warehousing, clearly warehouses may be tuned for decision support, and perhaps vice versa.

In its simplest form, data warehousing can be considered as an example of asynchronous replication, in which copies are updated relatively infrequently. However, a more advanced implementation of data warehousing would store summary data or other kind of information derived from the source data. In other words, a data warehouse stores materialized views (plus some local relations if needed).

It is common in a data warehousing environment for source changes to be deferred and applied to the warehouse views in large batches for efficiency. Source changes received during the day are applied to the views in a nightly batch window (the warehouse is not available to the users during this period). Most current commercial warehousing systems (e.g., Prism, Redbrick) focus on storing the data for efficient access, and on providing extensive querying facilities at the warehouse. Maintenance of warehousing data (in a large degree, maintenance of materialized views) is thus an important problem.

The widespread adoption of Internet technology will profoundly affect *online analytical processing* (OLAP), which refers to applications dominated by stylized queries that typically involve group-by and aggregation operators for analysis purpose. Such queries are extremely important to organizations for analysis of important trends so that better decisions can be made in the future. In addition, most vendors of OLAP engines have focused on Internet-enabling their offerings. The true promise of the Internet is in making OLAP a mainstream technology, that is, moving OLAP from the domain of analysts to consumers. Electronic commerce (e-commerce) has emerged as one of the largest applications of the Internet in decision support. The basic concepts of data warehousing and aggregation have naturally made their way onto the web. In fact, some of the most popular Websites on the Internet are basically databases. For example, search engines such as AltaVista and Lycos attempt to warehouse the entire Web. Aggregation as a means to navigate and comprehend the vast amounts of data on the Internet also must be recognized. Directory services such as Yahoo and Excite attempt to aggregate the entire web into a category hierarchy and give users the ability to navigate this hierarchy. The infrastructure for decision support is also undergoing improvement.

The need for data warehouses is justified by the concerns behind decision support queries, such as OLAP and data mining. An agent-based data mining process prefers tightly coupled environments so that data mining becomes part of the database management process. Data warehouses provide such support.

*Decision support queries* are ad hoc user queries in various business applications. In these applications, current and historical data are comprehensively analyzed and explored, identifying useful trends and creating summaries of the data, in order to support high-level decision making in data warehousing environment. A class of stylized queries typically involve group-by and aggregation operators. Applications dominated by such queries are referred to as *online analysis processing* (OLAP) (Chaudhuri and Dayal 1997).

More recently the importance of integrating OLAP and data mining has been widely addressed by database practitioners from the industry perspectives (Parsaye 1999). As a reply from academia for this practical need, studies on multiple-level data mining (Han et al. 1994) can be viewed as a step closer to the goal of this integration. The various ways of mining knowledge at multiple concept levels, such as progressive deepening, progressive generalization, and interactive up and down, bear significant similarities with OLAP operations (such as rollup and drilldown).

Decision support queries are intended to comprehensively analyze or explore current and historical data, identify useful trends, and create summaries of data to support high-level decisionmaking for knowledge workers (executives, managers, analysts) (Chaudhuri and Dayal 1997). Both OLAP and data mining are two important tasks of decision support queries.

### 3.2.2   Architecture and Design of Data Warehouses

**3.2.2.1   *Components in Data Warehouses***   The data warehouse is an integrated environment, containing integrated data, detailed and summarized data, historical data, and metadata. An important advantage of performing data mining in such an environment is that the data miner can concentrate on mining data, rather than cleansing and integrating data.

Data warehousing provides an effective approach to deal with complex decision support queries over data from multiple sites. According to a popular definition, a *data warehouse* is a subject-oriented, integrated, time-varying, nonvolatile collection of data that is used primarily in organizational decisionmaking (Inmon 1996). The key to the data warehousing approach is to create a copy of all the data at some one location, and to use the copy rather than going to the individual sources. Data warehouses contain consolidated data from many sources (different business units), spanning long time periods, and augmented with summary information. Warehouses are much larger than other kinds of databases, sizes are much larger, typical workloads involve ad

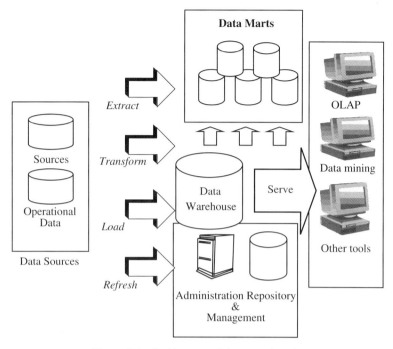

**Figure 3.1**    Architecture of data warehousing.

hoc, fairly complex queries, and fast response times are important. Since decision support often is the goal of data warehousing, clearly warehouses may be tuned for decision support, and perhaps vice versa.

A typical data warehousing architecture consists of the following components (as depicted in Figure 3.1):

- A *warehouse server*; as the data warehouse proper, it stores the corporate data (usually using the relational database technology). Here data volumes are very high as multiterabyte data warehouses are beginning to appear more frequently.

- *Data marts*, which are departmental subsets focused on selected subjects. The data mart is where departmental data is stored, and often various external data items are added. The data volumes are usually 15–30% of warehouse sizes, and the envelope is being pushed toward the terabyte limit. These databases are also usually either based on star schemas or are in a normalized form. They deal mostly with the data space, but at times some multidimensional analysis is performed.

- *Back-end* (system components providing functionality such as extract, transform, load and refresh data) and *front-end* (e.g., OLAP and data mining) tools and utilities.

- *Metadata*—the system catalogs associated with a warehouse are very large, and are often stored and managed in a separate database called a *metadata repository*.
- Other components (depending on the design methods and the specific needs of the organizations).

The architecture depicted in Figure 3.1 is basically two-tier, namely, warehouse and its front ends. A variation of data warehouse architecture consists of three tiers. The bottom tier is a warehouse database server, which is typically a relational database system. The middle tier is an OLAP server, and the top tier is a client, containing query and reporting tools.

***3.2.2.2  Star Schema***   Most data warehouses use *star schemas* to represent the multidimensional data model. In a star schema, there is a single fact table (which is at the center of a star schema and contains most of the data stored in the data warehouse) and a set of dimension tables that can be used to in combination with the fact table (a single table for each dimension). An example of star schema is shown in Figure 3.2, which is slightly revised from the example appearing in many recent publications [e.g., Chaudhuri and Dayal (1997)]. In this example, the fact table has the name `sales`, while the dimension tables are `order`, `costumer`, `store`, `product`, `date`, and `city`. Each dimension table has a primary key; for example, the dimension table product

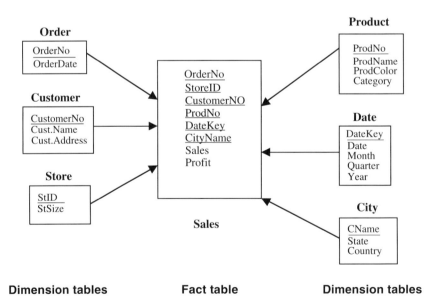

**Figure 3.2**   A star schema.

has `prodno` as its primary key, and dimension table has `datekey` as its primary key. Note also that the schema of the fact table has corresponding foreign keys, so that fact table can be joined with various dimension tables. Dimension tables may supply hierarchical information that can be used to perform OLAP operations (such as rollup or drilldown, as to be discussed further in Sections 3.2.4 and 3.2.5).

Join operations in a star schema may be performed only between the fact table and any of its dimensions. Data mining has frequently been carried assuming that is joined by the fact table with one or more dimension tables, followed by possible project and select operations. In addition, to facilitate data mining, such a kind of view is usually materialized (a concept to be discussed in the next subsection).

A variation of the star schema model is call *snowflake* schema. In such a schema, some dimension tables are normalized to reduce redundancies.

### 3.2.2.3 *Data Warehouse Design*
There are several approaches for data warehouse design. In general, data warehouse design process consists of the following steps (Inmon 1996, Kimball et al. 1998):

1. Choose a business process to model, such as sales, or shipments.
2. Choose the grain of the business process. The grain is the granularity (viz., fundamental, atomic) level of the data used in the fact table. The data stored there are the primary data based on which OLAP operations can be performed.
3. Choose the dimensions that will apply to records in the fact table(s). For example, time is a typical dimension. Dimensions are important because based on which various OLAP operations can be performed.
4. Choose the measures that will populate each fact table record. Measures are numeric additive quantities such as sales amount or profit.

### 3.2.3 Data Warehousing, Materialized Views, and Indexing

### 3.2.3.1 *Data Warehouses as Materialized Views*
A data warehouse could be an enterprise warehouse consisting of all the subject-relevant information, or a collection of data marts, or a set of materialized views over operational databases. In this last scenario, we have the so-called virtual warehouse (Han and Kamber 2000). According to fundamentals of database management systems, relational views are the most important asset of the relational model. Recall that we have the following basic concepts in relational databases:

*Relation* (base table)—this is a stored table.

*External view* (virtual view, or simply view)—this is a virtual table (derived relation defined in terms of base relations).

*Materialized view*—a view is materialized when it is stored in the database, rather than computed from the base relations in response to queries.

The general idea of the approach is to materialize certain expensive computations that are frequently inquired, especially those involving aggregate
functions, such as count, sum, average, and max, and to store such materialized views in a multidimensional database (called a *data cube*) for decision
support, knowledge discovery, and many other applications.

Traditionaly, commercial relational database products are used to discard
views immediately after they are delivered to the user or to a subsequent execution phase. The cost for generating the views is for one-time use only instead
of being amortized over multiple and/or shared results. Caching query results
or intermediate results for speeding up intra- and interquery processing has
been studied widely. All these techniques share one basic idea: the reuse of
views to save cost.

In a data warehouse where query execution and I/O are magnified, the
mandate for reuse cannot be ignored. In addition, in an OLAP environment,
updates come in bulk rather than in small numbers, making incremental
update techniques more effectively amortized. Therefore, query optimizers
based on materialized view fragments are a necessity. Note that amortization
and reuse of views can be possible only if they can be discovered by the query
optimizer that decides to invoke those views that reduce the cost of the query.
The most common techniques for discovering views (in any of its forms) in its
most general form is an undecidable problem, but for the most common
queries can be reduced to an NP-complete problem. Furthermore, for simple
conjunctive query views, the time complexity is reduced to polynomial-time
and very efficient algorithms.

The benefit of using materialized views is significant. Index structures can be
built on the materialized view. Consequently, database access to the materialized view can be much faster than recomputing the view. A materialized view
is just like a cache, which is a copy of the data that can be accessed quickly.

Materialized views are useful in new applications such as data warehousing, replication servers, chronicle or data recording systems, data visualization,
and mobile systems. Integrity constraint checking and query optimization can
also benefit from materialized views, but will not be emphasized in our current
context.

### 3.2.3.2 *Indexing Techniques for Implementation*   Due to the close rela-
tionship between materialized views and indexing, here we provide a brief
examination on the issue of indexing. Traditional indexing techniques (as
briefly mentioned in Chapter 4) can be used, but there are also additional
issues that are unique in a data warehousing environment.

The mostly read environment of OLAP systems makes the CPU overhead
of maintaining indices negligible, and the requirement of interactive response
times for queries over very large datasets makes the availability of suitable
indices very important.

*Bitmap Index*. The idea here is to record values for sparse columns as a
sequence of bits, one for each possible value. For example, the biologi-

cal gender of a customer (male or female) can be represented using bitmap index. This method supports efficient index operations such as union and intersection; this is more efficient than hash index and tree index.

*Join Index*. This method is used to speed up specific join queries. A join index maintains the relationships between a foreign key with its matching primary keys. The specialized nature of star schemas makes join indices especially attractive for decision support.

We use the following example to illustrate the join index. Let us consider the two relations "Sale" and "Product" shown in Tables 3.1 and 3.2.

If we perform join on sale.prod-id = prod-id, and precompute the result, we can obtain the *join index* as shown in Table 3.3. Note that the result shown in Table 3.3 has the same effect of Table 3.4, which represents a materialized view.

In bitmap indexing, each attribute has its own bitmap index table. Bitmap indexing reduces join, aggregation, and comparison operations to bit arithmetic. Join indexing records the joinable tuples of two or more relations from a relational database, reducing the overall cost of OLAP join operations. Bitmapped join indexing, which combines the bitmap and join methods, can be used to further speed up OLAP query processing.

Suppose we have very few products to consider, then the bitmap can be used for products. (This is a very important condition to check. It is not appropriate if there are many products.) The join index table after bitmap technique is incorporated is shown in Table 3.5.

Indexing is important to materialized views for two reasons. Indexes for a materialized view reduce the cost of computation to execute an operation (analogous to the use of an index on the key of a relation to decrease the time

**Table 3.1  The Sale Table**

| Rid | Prod-id | Store-id | Date | Amount |
|-----|---------|----------|------|--------|
| R1  | P1      | C1       | 1    | 12     |
| R2  | P2      | C1       | 1    | 11     |
| R3  | P1      | C3       | 1    | 50     |
| R4  | P2      | C2       | 1    | 8      |
| R5  | P1      | C1       | 2    | 44     |
| R6  | P1      | C2       | 2    | 4      |

**Table 3.2  The Product Table**

| ID | Name | Price |
|----|------|-------|
| P1 | Bolt | 10    |
| P2 | nut  | 5     |

Table 3.3    Example of a Join Index

| Product-id | Rid |
|------------|-----|
| P1 | R1, R3, R5, R6 |
| P2 | R2, R4 |

Table 3.4    A Materialized View

| Rid | Prod-id | Name | Price | Store-id | Date | Amount |
|-----|---------|------|-------|----------|------|--------|
| R1 | P1 | Bolt | 10 | C1 | 1 | 12 |
| R2 | P2 | Nut | 5 | C1 | 1 | 11 |
| R3 | P1 | Bolt | 10 | C3 | 1 | 50 |
| R4 | P2 | Nut | 5 | C2 | 1 | 8 |
| R5 | P1 | Bolt | 10 | C1 | 2 | 44 |
| R6 | P1 | Bolt | 10 | C2 | 2 | 4 |

Table 3.5    Combined Join/Bitmap Indexing

| P1 | P2 | Sale.prod-id |
|----|----|--------------|
| 1 | 0 | R1, R3, R5, R6 |
| 0 | 1 | R2, R4 |

needed to locate a specified tuple); indexing also reduces the cost of maintenance of the materialized views. One important problem in data warehousing is the maintenance of materialized views due to changes made in the source data. Maintenance of materialized views can be a very time consuming process. There need to be some methods developed to reduce this time (one method is use of supporting views and/or the meterializing of indexes).

The star schema model of data warehouses makes join indexing attractive for cross-table search, because the connection between a fact table and its corresponding dimension tables are the foreign key of the fact table and the primary key of the dimension table. Join indexing maintains relationships between attribute values of a dimension and the corresponding rows in the fact table. Join indices may span multiple dimensions to form composite join indices. Data mining algorithms can take advantage of this kind of facility. In fact, usually data mining algorithms are presented on a single table. Join indexing makes such kind of assumption reasonable.

### 3.2.4    Basic Concepts of OLAP

Decision support functions in a data warehouse involve hundreds of complex aggregate queries over large volumes of data. To meet the performance demands so that fast answers can be provided, virtually all OLAP products resort to some degree of these aggregates. According to a popular opinion from the OLAP Council, a data warehouse is usually based on relational technology, while OLAP uses a multidimensional view of aggregate data to provide quick access to strategic information for further analysis. A data warehouse stores tactical information that answers "Who?" and "What?" questions about past events. OLAP systems go beyond those questions; they are able to answer "What if?" and "Why?" questions. A typical OLAP calculation is more complex than simply summarizing data.

As indicated in Figure 3.2, OLAP or multidimensional analysis is a method of viewing aggregate data called *measurements* (e.g., sales, expenses) along a set of dimensions such as product, brand, stored, month, and city and state. An OLAP typically consists of the following conceptual elements:

- *Dimension*. Each dimension is described by a set of attributes. A related concept is *domain hierarchy*, for example, "country," "state" and "city" form a domain hierarchy.
- *Measure*. Each numeric measure depends on a set of dimensions, which provide the context for the measure. The dimensions together are assumed to uniquely determine the measure. Therefore, the multidimensional data view a measure as a *value* in the multidimensional space of dimensions.

### 3.2.5  Data Cubes

A special form of materialized views is called a *data cube*. Data cubes present materialized views involving multidimensional data. A data cube consists of a lattice of cuboids, each corresponding to a different degree of summarization of the given multidimensional data. (Recall that a *lattice* is a partially ordered set in which every subset consisting of two elements has a least upper bound and a greatest lower bound.) *Partial materialization* refers to the selective computation of a subset of the cuboids in the lattice. *Full materialization* refers to the computation of all the cuboids in the lattice. If the cubes are implemented using MOLAP, then multiway array aggregation can be used. A four-dimensional data cube is depicted in Figure 3.3, where A, B, C, D could represent different dimensions such as time, location, customer and store information. Each cuboid represents a different degree of summarization such as customer and time.

Discovery-driven exploration of data cubes uses precomputed measures and visual cues to indicate data exceptions at all levels of aggregation, guiding the user in the data analysis process. Multifeature cubes compute complex queries involving multiple dependent aggregates at multiple granularities. The computation of cubes for discovery-driven exploration and of multifeature cubes can be achieved efficiently by taking advantage of efficient algorithms for standard data cube computation.

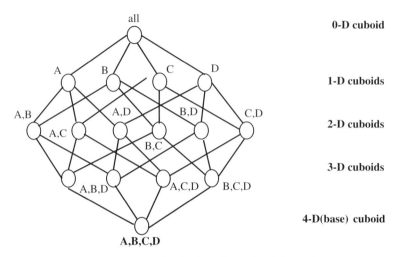

**Figure 3.3** Example of a four-dimensional data cube.

### 3.2.6 OLAP Operations in Data Cubes

We now take a closer look on OLAP operations, particularly with data cube in mind. The two best-known operations for OLAP queries are

- *Rollup*. This operation takes the current data object and does a further group-by on one of the dimensions. For example, given total sale by day, we can ask for total sales by month.
- *Drilldown*. As the converse of rollup, this operation tries to get more detailed presentation. For example, given total sale by model, we can ask for total sale by model by year.

Other operations include

- *Pivot*—its result is called a cross-*tabulation*.
- *Slice*—this is an equality selection, reducing the dimensionality of data.
- *Dice*—this is the range selection.

In the following we illustrate the motivation behind the operation of pivot. This example also illustrates the basic idea of the rollup operator. Consider a relational database on auto sales. The database is assumed to be in 3NF. Being more specific, let us consider a relation in this database with schema ("Model," "Year," "Color," "Dealer," "Sales date"). Now we want to have data aggregated by "Model," then by "Year," and finally by "Color." Suppose that the result is as shown in Table 3.6.

**Table 3.6    Sales Rollup**

| | | | Sales | | |
|---|---|---|---|---|---|
| Model | Year | Color | by model by year by color | by model by year | by model |
| Toyota | 1998 | Black | 130 | | |
| | | Light | 120 | | |
| | | | | 250 | |
| Toyota | 1999 | Black | 130 | | |
| | | Light | 110 | | |
| | | | | 240 | |
| | | | | | 490 |

**Table 3.7    Toyota Sales Cross-Tabulation**

| Toyota | 1998 | 1999 | Total (*all*) |
|---|---|---|---|
| Black | 130 | 130 | 260 |
| Light | 120 | 110 | 230 |
| Total (*all*) | 250 | 240 | 490 |

For a better summary, we can use the *cross tabulation* (namely, pivot) as shown in Table 3.7. The operation involved here is called the *pivot*. Note how the cross tabulation table can be obtained in a systematic way; when pivot is performed, *the values that appear in columns of the original presentation* (such as "black," "light" for "Color," and "1998," "1999" for "Year") now *become labels of axes in the result presentation.*

The cross-tabulation in this example is a 2D (two-dimensional) aggregation. But this is just a special case. For example, if other automobile models (Dodge, Ford, etc.) are added, it becomes a 3D aggregation. Generally speaking, the traditional GROUP BY clause in SQL can be used to generate the core of the $N$-dimensional *data cube*. The $N - 1$ lower-dimensional aggregates appear as points, lines, plains, cubes or hyper-cubes in the original data cube.

More examples of OLAP operations are depicted in Figure 3.4.

## 3.3    THE ROLE OF METADATA

### 3.3.1    Basics of Metadata

The development of data warehouses and data mining has significantly extended the role of metadata in the tradition DBMS environment. Metadata describe the data in the database, including information on access methods,

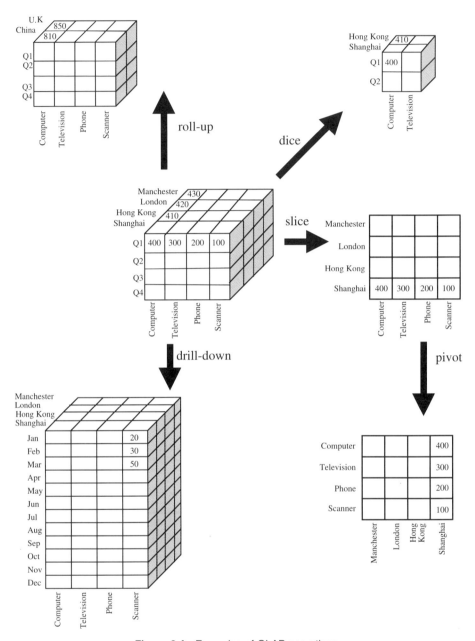

**Figure 3.4**   Examples of OLAP operations.

index strategies, security, and integrity constraints, as well as policies and procedures (optional).

Metadata become a major issue with some of the recent developments in data management such as digital libraries. Metadata in distributed and heterogeneous databases guide the schema transformation and integration process in handling heterogeneity, are used to transform legacy database systems to new systems. Metadata can be used for multimedia data management (metadata themselves could be multimedia data such as video and audio). Metadata for the Web includes information about various data sources, locations and resources on the Web, usage patterns, policies, and procedures.

Metadata for warehousing include metadata for integrating the heterogeneous data sources. Metadata can guide the transformation process from layer to layer in building the warehouse and also can be used to administer and maintain the warehouse. Metadata are used in extracting answers to the various queries posed.

### 3.3.2  Metadata for Data Mining

Regardless of the actual form of metadata, metadata can be viewed as a kind of data reduction. This is an interesting point, because in most cases when the relationship between metadata and data mining is considered, metadata are used to aid data mining, where the mined result can be viewed as a kind of data reduction as well (see Section 2.10 for a discussion of reductionism for data mining).

Metadata benefits data mining in many forms. First, metadata helps in managing the data warehouse where the data reside. More directly, metadata could benefit data mining because metadata can guide the mining process. The mining tool could consult the meta database and determine the type of queries to pose to the DBMS. Note that metadata could be updated during the mining process. Typically, a *repository* is used to store possibly all the metadata. The repository consists of information about the structure, as well as content and interdependencies of data warehouse components. It is important to structure the metadata to facilitate data mining.

Figure 3.5 illustrates metadata management in a data warehouse. The metadata repository stores and maintains information about the structure and the content of the data warehouse components. In addition, all dependencies between the different layers of the data warehouse environment, including operational layer, data warehouse layer, and business layer, are represented in this repository.

Figure 3.5 also depicts the roles of three different types of metadata (Stohr et al. 1999, Singh 1999):

- *Semantic (or Business) Metadata.* These data intend to provide a business-oriented description of the data warehouse content. A repository addressing semantic metadata should cover the types of metadata of the conceptual enterprise model, multidimensional data model, and similar, as well as their interdependencies.

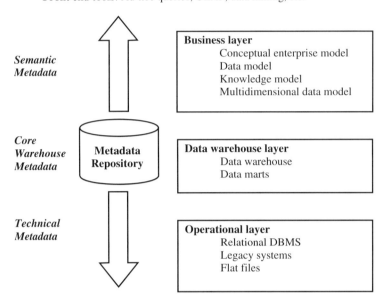

**Figure 3.5**    Metadata management in a data warehouse.

- *Technical Metadata.* These data cover information about the architecture and schema with respect to the operational systems, the data warehouse, and the OLAP databases, as well as the dependencies and mappings between the operational sources, the data warehouse, and the OLAP databases on the physical and implementation level.
- *Core Warehouse Metadata.* These data are subject-oriented and are based on abstractions of the real world. They defines how the transformed data are to be interpreted, as well as any additional views that may have been created.

Metadata for specific types of data mining require specific techniques. For example, for multimedia data, metadata may be extracted from the multimedia databases and then used to mine the data. In particular, metadata related to security and privacy can be regarded as part of the metadata, and can thus be used guide the process of data mining so that privacy issues are not compromised through mining. Another type is metadata for Web mining. Since Web information is semistructured, direct mining may be challenging. We may need to extract metadata from the data, then either mine these metadata or use them to guide in the mining process. XML (Extensible Markup Language) could play a role in describing metadata for Web documents. Web mining is discussed further in Chapter 8.

Note that types of metadata form a hierarchy. Topmost are the metadata for the data warehouse; underneath are metadata for mappings and transformations, followed by metadata for various data sources.

### 3.3.3  Mining the Metadata

Although most of time we talk about using metadata for data mining, the metadata themselves can be mined. This is an interesting issue. It involves conducting data mining on the metadata, because the data in the database may be incomplete, inaccurate, or unstructured, and the metadata could provide more meaningful information. Issues need to be considered are when to mine metadata and what kinds of technique are appropriate. Metadata (such as metadata in repository) can be mined to extract useful information in cases where the data themselves are not analyzable. For example, we can find characterizing rules that characterize an unstructured Web document, and store the mined features as a description of the document and store it in the metadata repository.

## 3.4  INTEGRATED ONLINE ANALYTICAL PROCESSING (OLAP) AND DATA MINING

### 3.4.1  Relationship between Data Warehousing and OLAP

Having described the basic architecture of data warehouses, we may further examine the relationship between data warehousing and OLAP, which can be elaborated as follows. Decision support functions in a data warehouse involve hundreds of complex aggregate queries over large volumes of data. To meet the performance demands so that fast answers can be provided, virtually all OLAP products resort to some degree of these aggregates. According to a popular opinion from the OLAP Council, a data warehouse is usually based on relational technology, while OLAP uses a multidimensional view of aggregate data to provide quick access to strategic information for further analysis. A data warehouse stores tactical information that answers "Who?" and "What?" questions about past events. OLAP systems go beyond those questions; they are able to answer "What if?" and "Why?" questions. A typical OLAP calculation is more complex than simply summarizing data.

### 3.4.2  Integration of OLAP and Data Mining

There are significant semantic differences between data mining and OLAP. Although both OLAP and data mining deal with analysis of data, the focus and methodology are quite different. However, since they are complementary to each other, it would be ideal to integrate these two directions of data analysis. For this purpose, on-line analytical mining (OLAM) has been proposed

(Han and Kamber 2000). In this section, we provide a much-needed discussion on this issue and use several examples to illustrate these differences. We point out the difference of data mining carried out at different levels, including how different types of queries can be handled, how different semantics of knowledge can be discovered at different levels, as well as how different heuristics may be used.

We note that different kinds of analysis can be carried out at different levels:

- What are the features of products purchased along with promotional items? The answer for this query could be association rule(s) at the granularity level, because we need to analyze actual purchase data for each transaction that is involved in promotional items (we assume information about promotional items can be found in product price).
- What kinds of products are most profitable? This query involves aggregation, and can be answered by OLAP alone.
- What kinds of customers bought the most profitable products? This query can be answered by different ways. One way is to analyze individual transactions and obtain association rules between products and customers at the granularity level. An alternative way is to select all most profitable products, project the whole set of customers who purchased these products, and then identify the characteristics of these customers. In this case we are trying to answer the query by discovering characteristic rules at an aggregation level. (For example, customers can be characterized by their addresses.)

This discussion further suggests that data mining at different levels may involve different semantics. Since most people are familiar with semantics of knowledge discovered at the granularity level, here we will provide a discussion emphasizing what kind of difference is made by the semantics of knowledge discovered at aggregation levels (which will be referred to as aggregation semantics). Aggregation semantics for classification and association rules with respect to data mining paradigms are discussed in Chapter 5.

Nevertheless, OLAP and data mining should—and can—be integrated for decision support. This results in the integrated architecture shown in Figure 3.6. Note here that data mining can be conducted both online and offline. The dedicated OLAP engine will deal with queries with OLAP aspects, in parallel to online data mining.

### 3.4.3   Issues in Integrated OLAP and Data Mining

Using the integrated architecture as a guideline, we now discuss three specific issues related to combined OLAP/data mining: (1) how to use and reuse of intensional historical data, (2) the benefits of using OLAP for data mining, and (3) how to enrich data mining using concepts related to OLAP.

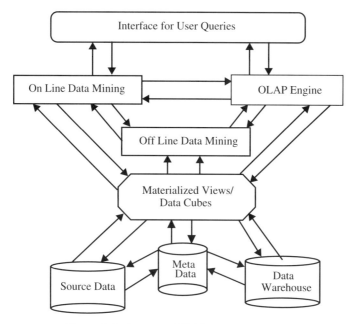

**Figure 3.6**   Integrated OLAP and data mining.

### 3.4.3.1 *On the Use and Reuse of Intensional Historical Data*   First, we provide some remarks on the use of reuse of discovered rules. In many cases, the rules (or other forms of knowledge) discovered from previous data are stored; they become intensional historical data and can be used or reused. Here the term "intensional" is used in the same sense as in intensional data-bases. Also note that the word "historical" refers to the knowledge discovered from previous data. The discovered knowledge (i.e., the intensional historical data) itself may or may not be time-sensitive. This feature (or the absence of the feature) may impact how the intensional historical data may be used or reused.

To use a previously discovered rule is to apply that rule directly. The following are some examples to indicate how a previously discovered rule can be used in the case of non-time-sensitive data:

- *Provide prediction.* Suppose we have the following intensional historical data available: "*Rule 6.* In September 1998, the number of orders for blue products whose price marked $x\%$ down increased $1.5x\%$ ($10 < x < 20$)." If a user wants to know in September 1999, when the price of a blue jacket is to be marked down 20%, how the number of orders will be affected, using rule 6, a predicted increase of 30% will be provided to the user with a quick response.

- *Offer suggestions.* Rule 6 can also be used to guide users' decisionmaking. For example, it can be used to advise users to mark down the price for blue products if they want to have a significant increase in orders.
- *Perform inference.* The preceding examples indicated the use of inference (e.g., modus ponens was used in prediction). Furthermore, the inference process can be carried out so that inference chains can be constructed. Suppose, from the combined historical and current data, that the following rule is discovered: "*Rule 7.* For whatever product, the number of orders increased 15% or above will always bring significant profit." Rules 6 and 7 can be used together to infer that "If we mark down the price for blue jacket in September 1999 by 12%, then significant profit may be made." In addition, time-sensitive intensional historical data can also be used for future data analysis and data mining, as exemplified in the following case.
- *Perform second-order data mining.* Generalization or other forms of induction can be used to perform further data mining on intensional historical data. For example, consider the summary table in Table 3.8, which was constructed from intensional historical data (i.e., each tuple is a rule discovered from previous sales):

In this summary table, we may perform further data mining on various directions, such as the impact of the color or store size without considering years, or the general trend of color or store size over years. Since the purpose of this kind of analysis is to perform data mining on the intensional historical data, it will be referred to as the *second-order data mining.* Second-order data mining provides an approach to derive rules at aggregation levels.

*Reuse* of a previously discovered rule differs from direct use of a rule in that some adaptation or revision is needed before the discovered knowledge can be used. Just like reuse of a piece of a previously developed software component, reuse of a rule requires necessary changes of some parameters. A kind of mapping may occur, which may take the form of analogical reasoning. The result of reusing a rule may be a derived *candidate* rule whose validity should be carefully checked.

**Table 3.8   A Summary Table**

| Year | Product Color | Store Size | Profitable |
|------|---------------|------------|------------|
| 1996 | Blue          | Large      | Low        |
| 1997 | Yellow        | Small      | High       |
| . . . | . . .        | . . .      | . . .      |
| 1998 | Yellow        | Large      | Very high  |

### *3.4.3.2 How Data Mining Can Benefit OLAP* In the following we outline several sample cases in which data mining may benefit OLAP. A more detailed discussion can be found in Chen (1999).

*Construction and Maintenance of Materialized Views* Many data mining techniques have already implicitly assumed the use of some basic functions of OLAP techniques; for example, the materialized view constructed from the star schema to be used for data mining. However, OLAP alone cannot decide which attributes should be used to form the schema of the view to be used for data mining. The feedback of data mining can be used to identify most important attributes (i.e., to determine schema for constructing materialized views), as well as the most important conditions for selecting the data to be included in the materialized views. Data mining may also provide help to handle indexing issues in evolving databases in data warehouse environment.

*Data Mining–Guided Aggregation for OLAP* In order to determine which view should be materialized (precomputed), the common interests of *ad hoc* queries from existing and potential users should be studied. Data mining on historical data may also provide a kind of guide for aggregation (namely, what to aggregate, and how to aggregate).

*Instructed Construction of Materialized Views for Data Mining* Furthermore, the need for data mining can instruct OLAP aggregation so that various materialized views can be constructed which can be used to discover rules at aggregation levels. By placing the group-by operator at different attributes, various materialized views can be constructed for data mining at aggregation levels or at mixed granularity–aggregation levels. In general, knowledge discovered earlier can always provide refined instructions for the construction of materialized views.

### *3.4.3.3 OLAP-Enriched Data Mining* There is another direction of connection between OLAP and data mining; namely, OLAP can benefit data mining. We use drilldown data mining as an example to illustrate how OLAP may provide a useful guide for data mining. First we note that summary data shows the general picture but lack of detail. For example, during a certain period, the sale of milk in Nebraska increased 10% while during the same period, the sale of milk dropped 5% in neighboring Iowa. This could be due to several reasons. If we know during the same period, the sales of all kinds of goods had dropped in Iowa but increased in Nebraska, then we may not need to pursue further analysis. On the other hand, if no convincing explanation exists, then we may have to perform some kind of data mining. In this case, the data mining process is drilldown in nature, because we should examine several dimensions in more detail.

We illustrate how the OLAP-related concerns can enrich the study of data mining by studying a variation of association patterns. (A more detailed discussion of association rules is given in Chapter 5.) This study addresses some concerns related to aggregation semantics as discussed earlier. Given a transaction database, where each transaction is a set of items, an association rule is an expression of the form $X \rightarrow Y$, where $X$ and $Y$ are sets of items. However, association patterns may be limited to market basket data. For instance, in a sales database, the query "How does product color affect profits?" promotes "color" and "profit" to be the objects of analysis. The data domain of color or profit is not the same as of basket items, such as hat or glove. Moreover, the association between color and profit (which is a numeric measure) suggests a new type of pattern—an influence pattern, which has not been covered by conventional association rules. The major purpose of influence patterns is to describe the influences of one set of objects, called *influencing factors*, on another set of objects, called *influence objects*. Algorithms have been proposed for discovery of influential association rules. Moreover, when conflicts exist for rules discovered at granularity and aggregation levels, a rule refinement process is invoked to resolve the conflicts. This refinement process resembles the drilldown operation of OLAP.

A set of algorithms for discovery and maintenance of influential association rules have been developed and a prototype system has been implemented. A very brief outline of the main algorithm for rule discovery is shown below (Chen et al. 1999). A case study of using this algorithm is presented in Chapter 8.

### Algorithm Influence Analysis

*Input*:    A relational view that contains a set of records and the questions for influence analysis.

*Output*:    An influential association rule.

*Method*:

*Step 1.* Specify the dimension attribute and the measure attribute.

*Step 2.* Identify the dimension itemsets and calculate support counts.

*Step 3.* Identify the measure itemsets and calculate support counts.

*Step 4.* Construct sets of candidate rules, and compute the confidence and aggregate value.

*Step 5.* Form a rule at the granularity level with greatest confidence, and form a rule at the aggregation level with largest abstract value of the measure attribute.

*Step 6.* Compare the assertions at different levels, exit if comparable (i.e., there is no inconsistency found in semantics at different levels).

*Step 7.* For the case where the discovered rules are not comparable, and derive the refined measure itemset and the framework of the rule.

*Step 8.* If the value of the measure consists of both negative and positive values, form a rule indicating the summary value; otherwise, form a rule concerning average value.

*Step 9.* Construct the final rule.

### 3.4.3.4 *Detecting Deviants in Data Cubes*

Data cubes are frequently used as the basic building blocks of data warehouses, and are the place where data mining in data warehouse is performed (Palpanas 2000). As an example, let us take a look at the issue of detecting deviants in data cubes. Consider the problem of identifying outliers in data cubes. The current practice in OLAP systems is to facilitate hypothesis-driven exploration of data cubes. In contrast, Sarawagi et al. (1998) proposes the discovery-driven exploration paradigm, in when the system recommends user potentially interesting paths of exploration in the data cube. The algorithm mines the data for exceptions, and summarizes the results at different levels of the hierarchy.

### 3.4.4 Pros and Cons of Integrated Data Warehousing and Data Mining

So far we have emphasized the integration of data mining and OLAP. Parsaye (1999A) suggested to sandwich the warehousing effort between two layers of mining—thus understanding the data before warehousing it. According to Parsaye, the data miner module, where the data are reorganized for analysis and information is extracted from the data. In practice, the data volumes here are the same as the "data mart" (thus smaller than the data warehouse), but the data is much more richly structured and is no longer just departmental. The data here refer to a specific business objective and is analyzed for the purpose of information extraction. The content of the data in the miner is often different from the data in the warehouse, because it is often enriched by additional external data not found within the warehouse. The data structures in the datamine need to be both denormalized and superdimensional. Parsaye further suggested that data miner can exist in three basic forms:

1. *Data miner is above the warehouse, as a set of conceptual views.* Data mining above the warehouse provides a minimal architecture for discovery and analysis. It is suitable only in cases where data mining is not a key objective for the warehouse.
2. *The data mining is beside the warehouse, as a separate repository.* The major advantage of this separation is that data mining can be effectively performed beside the warehouse, with data structures that lend themselves to detailed analyses.
3. *Data mining within the warehouse, as a distinct set of resources.* In some cases, where the warehouse is a very large, massively parallel processing (MPP) computer, the data mine may actually reside as a separate repository within the large warehouse. This is very similar to a data miner beside the warehouse, where the miner uses a portion of the physical warehouse, but is independent of the warehouse structures.

Therefore, although the design of the data space may be subject to compromises to please the various user groups, there should be no compromises in design of the data miner where serious and detailed analyses take place. The data mine should be optimized to deliver effective results by focusing on specific business needs, because influence analysis is so much harder than data access.

## 3.5  SAMPLING AND RELATED TECHNIQUES FOR DATA MINING

So far in this chapter we have emphasized how to perform data mining in the data warehousing environment. We should note, however, data warehousing also imposes significant challenges for data mining. To illustrate this, in this section, we examine sampling and related issues for data mining.

### 3.5.1  Sampling

Due to the huge amount of data stored in a data warehouse, sampling techniques may be needed to select a representative subset of the data for analysis. Sampling techniques have been extensively studied in statistics for many years, and various sampling techniques have been developed. In a sense, use or not use sampling distinguishes statistic analysis from data mining: While statistical analysis is typically applied on a set of sample data for analysis, it is preferable that the entire set of data is used for data mining. However, this is not to say sampling is not important in data mining. In fact, sampling could be a crucial step in both predictive and discovery types of data mining, because it allows a mining algorithm to run in complexity that is potentially sublinear to the size of the data.

One thing we should keep in mind is that when sampling is used, it may not necessarily reduce database I/Os: If data are stored on disks and we take one sample from each page where the data reside, since we can only access one page at a time, there is no reduction of I/O access. Also note that simple random sampling may have very poor performance in the presence of skew. To remedy this, we can develop adaptive sampling methods such as stratified sampling. It approximates the percentage of each class (or subpopulation of interest) in the overall database and is used in conjunction with skewed data.

Note that in reality the issue of sampling also strongly depends on the data representation. Consider the example provided by Parsaye (1999). Suppose that a supermarket wants to predict, for each day of the month, whether the amount of sales will be significantly higher than the one in a typical, average day. Suppose that (1) the supermarket is located just beside a large company that pays its employees on a weekly basis, always on Thursdays; and (2) many of the company's employees spend part of their weekly salary in the supermarket, right after they leave their jobs on Thursdays. Now consider a data representation in which one of the predicting attributes contains the amount of sales for each day of the month. In this case, there will be 4 or 5 days of the month with an amount of sales significantly higher than the average. These days, corresponding to Thursdays, will be separated from each other by a period of 7 days. Hence, tuples corresponding to significantly higher than average sales will be spread across the dimension day of the month in the database, leading to the occurrence of several small disjuncts. Clearly, this problem can be tackled by changing the data representation of the corresponding attribute from day of the month to day of the week. This would have the effect of merging several small disjuncts (separated from each other by a 7-day period) into a single large disjunct, corresponding to Thursdays. In practice this kind of data representation transformation is a very difficult issue when the underlying database contains many attributes that interact in a complex way. Even in the above very simple example, the data representation transformation required background knowledge involving information external to the supermarket, namely, the frequency of payment of the company. Since large real-world databases are multipurpose systems, where data were collected for purposes other than data mining, it is likely that these databases contain many small disjuncts. This suggests that, unless large amounts of background knowledge are given to the data mining algorithm, sampling tends to be an ineffective approach to mine large real-world database, since sampling is very sensitive to the existence of small disjuncts.

As we will see from later chapters, scalability and sampling in data mining are closely related to the actual tasks (or functionalities) of data mining (such as clustering or association). We will revisit this issue in Chapter 5 after we have discussed various kinds of data mining tasks.

Approaches that are more elaborate than pure random sampling, involving several sampling iterations, have been proposed, and they can sometimes speed up data mining.

- *Window Technique.* This technique is used in some early implementations of induction tree construction (see Chapter 5 for a brief discussion). At first a tree is built from a small subset of randomly-selected tuples (a window). The remaining tuples are then classified by this tree. The misclassified tuples are added to the window, and the process is repeated until all tuples are correctly classified. Windowing tends to considerably increase the running time, particularly in noisy domains.
- *Peepholing.* This heuristic method iteratively computes estimates of the rule evaluation measure from small random subsets of the database and uses these estimates to avoid examining all attributes and their entire range of values.
- *Dynamic Sampling.* Each iteration consists of picking a small sample from the data being mined, applying a data mining algorithm to this sample and evaluating the resulting classification accuracy. In each iteration the sample size is increased by a constant number of tuples, until the difference between classification accuracy on the sample and the evaluated resulting classification accuracy is smaller than a user-specified

value. In each iteration the sample size is increased by a constant number of tuples, until the difference between classification accuracy on the sample and the estimated classification accuracy on the entire data being mined is smaller than a user-specified value. When this condition is satisfied, the method halts and the knowledge discovered from the current sample is the knowledge returned to the user. An interesting feature of the method is that the classification accuracy on the entire data being mined can be estimated (without actually mining the data) by taking into account the history of classification accuracy achieve for the variable sample sizes used in previous iterations of the method. In addition, this method takes into account the performance of the data mining algorithm when deciding whether to stop the process of increasing sample size. However, this method has not been evaluated on very large real-world databases.

A discussion on samples from Finnish scholars and a discussion from Weiss and Indurkhya (1998). A principal approach to case reduction is to train on increasingly larger random subsets of cases, observe the trends and stop when no progress is made. The issue of sampling techniques in finding association rules is briefly discussed in Chapter 5.

### 3.5.2   Segmentation

In order to make the size of the data under control, another technique is segmentation. By *segmentation* we mean the data is divided into segments, and each segment is analyzed separately. When segmentation is used, we analyze one subset of the data at a time (e.g., one model year for auto sales), sharpening the focus of the analysis. Therefore, segmentation is an inherently different task from sampling. But segmentation can also be used along with sampling. For example, we can divide the data into segmentations, and take samples from each segment for analysis.

The need for segmentation can be justified by an interesting paradox between large warehouses and useful knowledge patterns (Parsaye 1999). On one hand, the larger a warehouse, the richer its pattern content, that is, as the warehouse grows the more patterns it includes. On the other hand, after a point, if we analyze too large a portion of a warehouse, patterns from different data segments begin to dilute each other and the number of useful patterns begins to decrease. Therefore we have the following paradox—the more data in the warehouse, the more patterns there are; however, the more data we analyze, the fewer patterns we will be able to find. Therefore, an interesting and challenging issue is how to combine the knowledge patterns mined from different segmentations. Consider, for example, the various stores of a discount retail chain. Supposes we segment the data by regions. From one region, we found that stores are profitable if they are located in the downtown

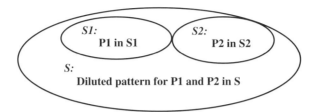

**Figure 3.7**   Illustration of diluted pattern.

area, while in another region, we found that stores located in suburbs are more profitable. If we combine these two sets together, the rules found in different regions would dilute each other.

A more general case is shown in Figure 3.7, where P1, the pattern discovered in subset S1; and P2, the pattern discovered in subset S2, are not consistent. Therefore, in the overall data set S, there is a diluted pattern for P1 and P2. Note that the inconsistency (or dilution of knowledge patterns) demonstrated here denotes a kind of nonmonotonic reasoning: This term was originally developed in logic to indicate that the reasoning process is not necessarily "the more you know, the more conclusion you can draw" (which is monotonic).

In summary, in many cases in real-world applications, it does not make sense to analyze all of a large warehouse because patterns are lost through dilution. To find useful patterns in a large warehouse, we usually have to select a segment (rather than a sample) of data that fits a business objective, prepare it for analysis and then perform data mining. Looking at all of the data at once often hides the patterns, because the factors that apply to distinct business objectives often dilute each other.

### 3.5.3   Summarization

While sampling may seem to offer a short-cut to faster data analysis, the end results are often less than desirable. Sampling was used within statistics because it was so difficult to have access to an entire population, that is, one could not interview a million people, or have access to a million manufactured components. Hence, sampling methods were developed to allow us to make some rough calculations about some of the characteristics of the population without access to the entire population. Sampling will almost always result in a loss of information, in particular with respect to data attributes with a large number of nonnumeric values.

Apart from sampling, summarization may be used to reduce data sizes. In summarization, individual data elements are replaced by the summary data; for example, individual sales from each store are now replaced by the total sales from all stores. But summarization can also cause problems. In fact, the summarization of the same data set with two sampling or summarization methods may produce the same result, and the summarization of the same data set with two methods may produce two different results.

As another intuitive example of how information loss and information distortion can take place through summarization, consider a retail chain, whose sales from Monday to Friday are exceptionally low for some stores, while weekend sales are exceptionally high for others. The summarization of daily sales data to weekly amounts will totally hide the fact that weekdays are money losers, while weekends are money makers for some stores. In other words, key pieces of information are often lost through summarization, and there is no way to recover them by further analysis (Parsaye 1999). Therefore, summarization should be used with caution.

### 3.5.4 Other Issues Related to Sampling

Additional issues have been discussed related to sampling. For example, an additive approach has been proposed to predict data mining costs. The additive approach takes small sample sizes at early stages of data mining when the costs are still low compared to the costs at the later stages when more data are required, and based on small sample sizes tries to make a prediction on how much would the total costs be for a given large database (Brumen et al. 2000).

Another issue deals with the problem of imbalanced data sets [see Japkowicz (2000); see also http://www.cs.dal.ca/~nat/Workshop2000/description.html]. Some data mining systems are evolved from machine learning systems. However, majority of learning systems previously designed and tested on toy problems or carefully crafted benchmark data sets usually assumes that the training sets are well balanced. In the case of concept learning, for example, classifiers typically expect that their training set contains as many examples of the positive as of the negative class.

This balanced assumption is often violated in real-world settings. Indeed, there exist many domains for which one class is better represented than the other. This is the case, for example, in fault monitoring tasks where nonfaulty examples are plentiful since they typically involve recording from the machine during normal operation whereas faulty examples involve recording from a malfunctioning machine, which is not always possible, easy, or financially worthwhile. More generally, the problem of imbalanced data sets occurs wherever one class represents a circumscribed concept, while the other represents the counterpart of that concept. The imbalanced data set problem can thus take two distinct forms: (1) either the counterpart class is undersampled relative to the concept class (as in the example above) or (2) it is over-sampled but particularly sparse (e.g., it includes the profile of a large number of patients who do not have lung cancer).

Although the imbalanced data set problem is starting to attract researchers' attention, attempts at tackling it have remained isolated. It is our belief that much progress could be achieved with a concerted effort and a greater amount of interactions between researchers interested in this issue. The purpose of our workshop is to provide a forum to foster such interactions and identify future research directions.

The following categories of methods capable of tackling the imbalanced set problem in concept learning tasks have been identified:

- Methods in which the class represented by a small data set is oversampled in order to match the size of the other class.
- Methods in which the class represented by the large data set can be downsized to match the size of the other class.
- Methods that ignore (or makes little use of) one of the two classes, altogether, by using a recognition-based instead of a discrimination-based inductive scheme.
- Methods that internally bias the discrimination-based process so as to compensate for the class imbalance.

### 3.5.5   Summary: A Remark on Uncertainty

In this section we examined two related issues for data mining using multiple data sources: sampling and segmentation. In fact, as long as data are integrated from different sources, these issues also arise even without using data warehousing. But the advent of data warehouses makes these issues more significant. The issues discussed in this section also exemplify the need for dealing with uncertainty, because the difficulties described in this section demonstrate that the knowledge minded from the result may be inconsistent, an indication of uncertainty. In fact, there are many other indications of uncertainty in the overall data mining process. A more detailed discussion on uncertainty will be continued in Chapter 4.


### 3.6   PARALLEL DATA MINING INTEGRATED WITH DATA WAREHOUSING

Two basic integrated frameworks are discussed. One is server-based, where the data mining algorithm is run on the parallel database server. The other is hybrid client/server-based, where some procedures of the data mining algorithm are performed on the client while other procedures (the data-intensive, time-consuming ones) are performed on the parallel database server. We also present generic, set-oriented primitives for the hybrid client/server-based framework. In addition, parallel data mining can use specialized hardware parallel database servers (Freitas and Lavington 1998).

According to the basic architecture of most large data warehouses, the data warehouse is stored on a parallel database server, while users access the data warehouse through client machines, typically PCs and/or workstations. Two

Client

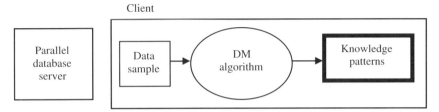

**Figure 3.8**   Conventional client-based data mining network.

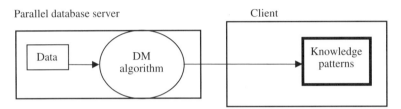

**Figure 3.9**   Server-based data mining network.

integrated data mining and data warehouse frameworks are referred to as server-based and hybrid client/server-based. They differ from a conventional, client-based framework where no integration takes place. Options are as follows:

1. *Conventional, Client-Based Data Mining Framework* (*No Integration*). As depicted in Figure 3.8, a small data sample is downloaded from the server to the client, and all the procedures of the data mining algorithm are executed on the client. Therefore, the parallel database server has no participation at all in the execution of the data mining algorithm.

2. *Server-Based Data Mining Framework.* As depicted in Figure 3.9, under this framework, the data mining algorithm is fully embedded on the parallel database server underlying the data warehouse. The client sends a single command to the server, requesting the execution of a given data mining algorithm. All the procedures of this algorithm are run on the parallel database server, and the discovered knowledge is then returned for the client. Note that the data being mined are kept on the parallel database server underlying the data warehouse during all data mining activity. This framework maximizes performance.

3. *Hybrid Client/Server-Based Data Mining Framework.* Combining the different approaches discussed above, in a hybrid framework, the data mining algorithm is partially embedded on the parallel database server. As in the pure server-based data mining framework, the data being mined are kept on the

parallel database server underlying the data warehouse during all data mining activity. Unlike the server-based data mining framework, however, the circle representing the data mining now consists of tow parts, with the majority representing data handling procedures (which are the most time-consuming operations when mining very large databases) and the minority representing search control procedures, executed on the client. The data mining algorithm does not have direct access to the data; it simply sends database queries to the parallel database server. This server uses automatic parallel query optimization methods to efficiently access the data and returns the query results to the client. The query results returned to the client are in the form of summarized information (rather than raw tuples), so that in this framework part of the functionality of the data mining algorithm is pushed down into the parallel database server. From a data mining users perspective, the hybrid framework has much more flexibility than the pure server-based data mining framework, but with less desirable performance.

There are some advantages of the integrated architecture:

- *Minimization of Data Exporting*. Data mining is an inherently iterative process, and multiple runs of data mining algorithms are necessary to discovery high-quality knowledge. The data exporting has a significant cost. By keeping the data being minded on the parallel database server during all data mining activity, we can avoid data exporting altogether.

- *Improved Scalability*. In general, data warehouses are designed to efficiently support the execution of ad hoc queries accessing large amounts of data in a complex and unpredictable way. A tight integration between data mining algorithms and the data warehouse allows the former to capitalize on efficiency-oriented database facilities (such as specialized forms of indexing) offered by the latter. Hence, this integration allows data mining algorithms to scale up to large databases.

- *Data Reuse and Minimization of Data Redundancy*. The conventional, client-based data mining framework consists of extracting the data to be mined from the data warehouse and performing the data mining process separately from other database applications. This approach goes against the philosophy of DBMS of data independence and allowing reuse of data for many applications. The integrated frameworks corrected this. In addition, a tight integration between data mining and data warehouse avoids data redundancy between the data stored in the data warehouse and the data used by the data mining algorithm.

## 3.7   FROM DATA MINING TO WEB MINING

Web mining demonstrates many basic features of data mining as discussed so far, but with a special concern of the Internet. In this section we present some additional concerns related to Web mining.

### 3.7.1   Basic Concepts and Business-Oriented Considerations

*3.7.1.1  Data to be Mined and the Web*   We start with a brief remark on the relationship between data warehousing and Internet. Through the merger of a company's data warehouse and website, several deliverables are possible, including the identification of profitable customers and potential future clients. With this profile, one can target and develop new potential clients while they visit the Website. The true promise of the Internet is in making OLAP a mainstream technology, that is, moving OLAP from the domain of analysts to consumers. E-commerce has emerged as one of the largest applications of the Internet in decision support. The basic concepts of data warehousing and aggregation have naturally made their way onto the Web. In fact, some of the most popular Websites on the Internet are basically databases. For example, search engines such as AltaVista and Lycos attempt to warehouse the entire web. Aggregation as a means to navigate and comprehend the vast amounts of data on the Internet has to also be recognized. Directory services such as Yahoo and Excite attempt to aggregate the entire Web into a category hierarchy and give users the ability to navigate this hierarchy. The infrastructure for decision support is also in the process of improvement (Mena 1999).

The Web provides companies an unprecedented opportunity to collect and analyze patterns of consumer behavior. Most companies fail to see that in e-commerce long-term success is dependent on how their Web data are leveraged to convert visitors into customers and customers into loyal clients. The Web data that is generated with a single sale is of more value than the sale itself since it can lead to a long and profitable relationship with that customer.

Each action of a Web user is a digital gesture exhibiting habits, preferences, and tendencies. These interactions reveal important trends and patterns that can help a company design a Website that effectively communicates and markets its products and services. Companies can aggregate, enhance, and mine Web data in order to learn what sells, what works and what doesn't, who is buying, and who is not.

Before an organization starts to mine the data, one must define the objective and what information is needed to achieve the objective. For example, the Web master in an organization may need to issue visitor identification cookies when they complete registration forms at its Website. This will enable the organization to match the information captured from various forms, such as the visitor's zipcode, with the transaction information generated from the cookies. It will also allow the organization to merge its cookie information, which will provide the detail the locations where visitors visited, with the specific attributes like age and gender from the forms owned by the organization. In addition, a zipcode or visitor address will allow the Web master to match the company's cookie and form data with demographics and household information matched from third-party data resellers.

One will likely need to scrub and prepare the data from the Website before beginning any sort of data mining analysis. Log files, for example, can be fairly redundant since a single "hit" generates a record of not only that HTML (Hyper Text Markup Language) but also of every graphic on that page. However, once a template, script, or procedure has been developed for generating the proper recording of a single visit, the data can be input into a database format from which additional manipulations and refinements can take place. If a site traffic analyzer tool is used, these data may already be format-ready for additional mining analysis (Mena 1999).

### 3.7.1.2  *Creating and Enhancing Web Data*

Web data are diverse and voluminous. In order to analyze e-commerce data one must assemble the divergent data components captured via server log files, form databases, and emails generated by visitors into a cohesive, integrated and comprehensive view. This requires careful planning.

Server log files provide domain types, time of access, keywords, and search engine used by visitors and can provide some insight into how a visitor arrived at a Website and what keywords they used to locate it. Cookies dispensed from the server can track browser visits and pages viewed and can provide some insight into how often this visitor has been to the site and what sections they wander into.

All this internal and external information can be implemented using a database management product such as Oracle, or using a flat file, which then can be linked or imported into a data mining tool. These include automated tools, which have principally been used in data warehouses to extract patterns, trends and relationships and new easy-to-use data mining data mining tools with graphical user interface (GUI) interfaces that are designed for business and marketing personnel. These data mining analyses can provide actionable solutions in many formats, which can be shared with those individuals responsible for the design, maintenance and marketing of an e-commerce site.

### 3.7.1.3  *Using Metadata for Web Mining*

Metadata, as discussed in Section 3.3, can also be used for data mining. This is depicted in Figure 3.10. It shows that in order to carry out data mining tasks, the data miner (the main data mining agent) can incorporate metadata for various data sources, as well as metadata from other resources, policies or history over the Internet. The same configuration will allow us to perform mining on the metadata itself, as already briefly discussed in Section 3.3.3.

### 3.7.1.4  *Mining Web Data*

Various data mining techniques can be used for Web mining. For example, using a data mining tool incorporating a machine learning algorithm, one can segment a Website database can into unique groups of visitors, each with individual behavior. These same tools perform statistical tests on the data and partition them into multiple market segments

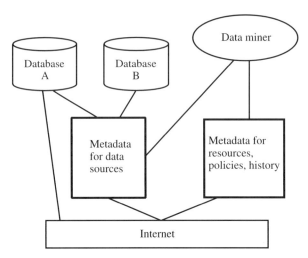

**Figure 3.10**   Using metadata for Web mining.

independent of the analyst or marketer. These types of data mining tools can autonomously identify key intervals and ranges in the data, which distinguish the good from the bad prospect. These types of data mining tools generally output their results in the form of graphical decision trees or IF/THEN rules. This type of Web mining allows a merchant to make some projections about the profitability potential of its visitors in the form of business rules, which can be extracted, directly from the web data:

> IF search keywords are "e-commerce" and "B2B"
> AND search engine YAHOO
> AND subdomain .AOL
> AND gender male
> AND age 25–34
> THEN average projected sale amount is $1000 → High

On the other hand, predicting customer propensity to purchase can also be done using a data mining tool incorporating a backpropagation neural network. Neural networks can be used to construct customer behavior models that can predict who will buy, or how much they are likely to buy. The ability to learn is one of the features of neural networks.

**3.7.1.5   *Other Issues of Web Mining***   There are some additional issues after Web mining proper is carried out. The following are some sample issues.

*Acting on Mining Solutions*   Most likely one will need to do Web mining on a separate server dedicated to analysis. After the analysis one will need to validate the results through some sort of mechanism such as a marketing test email campaign. Web mining is not an isolated process carried in a vacuum; it must be integrated into the entire electronic retailing and marketing processes. Electronic retailing changes not only the distribution and marketing of products, but more importantly, it also alters the process of consumption and the related transactions of buying and selling.

*Web Marketing, Mining and Messaging*    An organization should use segmentation analysis to stratify its email offers to prospects it has identified via the mining analysis, use targeted email to provide incentives only to those individuals likely to be interested in one's products or services, and use the Web mining analysis to discover customers demographics, consumer preferences, values, and lifestyles. Incorporate such knowledge about customers in the tone, manner and method by which the company would communicate with them. The company can also track marketing ad efforts to know what works and why. It is of paramount importance that retailers in a networked economy be adaptive and receptive to the needs of their customers. In this expansive, competitive, and volatile environment web mining will be a critical process impacting every retailer's long-term success, where failure to quickly react, adapt, and evolve can translate into customer "churn" with the click of a mouse.

*Web Trackers Fine-tunning Mining Consumer Interests*    Various techniques can be used, many of them emphasize personalization. The personalization industry can be divided into three camps. One is the platforms, the software applications that Web publishers and marketers use to create their sites and campaigns. Another is the companies that make analysis and reporting tools; and the third is composed of those who enable marketers to take actions such as sending email or serving up dynamic content. Of course, some vendors might dispute that breakdown or argue over which group they fit.

## 3.7.2   Technical Issues in Web Mining

### 3.7.2.1   *Approaches to Web Mining*    We now take a look at some technical issues related to Web mining. In general, it is a good example of an integrated use of various methods discussed in this chapter. More recent work has shown that the analysis needs of Web usage data have much in common with those of a data warehouse, and hence OLAP techniques are quite applicable. In the following we briefly examine this topic by following the presentation of Cooley et al. (1997) and Srivastava et al. (2000).

Web mining can be broadly defined as the discovery and analysis of useful information from the World Wide Web. According to Kosala and Blockeel (2000), we can categorize Web mining into three areas of interest based on which part of the Web to mine: Web content mining, Web structure mining, and Web usage mining.

- *Web content mining* describes the discovery of useful information from the Web contents, Web data, or Web documents.
- *Web structure mining* discovers the model underlying the link structures of the Web.
- *Web usage mining* discovers regularity of the data generated by the Web user's sessions or behaviors.

In addition, for Web content mining, there are two ways of viewing it: We can view it from an *information retrieval* (IR) perspective, where the Web documents are treated as *unstructured* documents, or we can take a database view where the Web documents are treated as *semistructured* documents stored at various Websites (which are viewed as databases). [For a brief discussion on information retrieval and its relevance to Web search, see Chen (1999).] Web mining categories are summarized in Figure 3.11.

These factors have prompted researchers to develop more intelligent tools for information retrieval. These tools include intelligent Web agents, as well as to extend database and data mining techniques to provide a higher level of organization for semi-structured data available on the Web. In Chapter 5 we describe the basic architecture of Web search. In the following we further summarize some efforts for Web mining conducted in this basic architecture:

- *Agent-Based Approach.* The agent-based approach to Web mining involves the development of sophisticated computational intelligence systems that can act autonomously or semiautonomously on behalf of a particular user, to discover and organize Web-based information. Generally, the agent-based Web mining systems can be placed into the following three categories: (1) intelligent search agents, (2) information filtering/categorization, and (3) personalized Web agents.

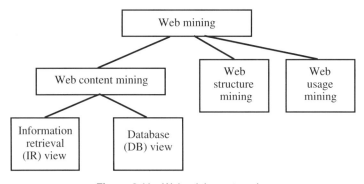

**Figure 3.11**   Web mining categories.

- *Database Approach.* The database approaches to Web mining have generally focused on techniques for integrating and organizing the heterogeneous and semistructured data on the Web into more structured and high-level collections of resources, such as in relational databases, and using standard database querying mechanisms and data mining techniques to access and analyze this information.

- *Multilevel Database Approach.* Several researchers have proposed a multilevel database approach to organizing Web-based information. The main idea behind these proposals is that the lowest level of the database contains primitive semi-structured information stored in various Web repositories, such as hypertext documents. At the higher level(s) metadata or generalizations are extracted from lower levels and organized in structured collections such as relational or object-oriented databases.

- *Web Query Systems.* There have been many Web-base query systems and languages developed recently that attempt to utilize standard database query languages such as SQL, structural information about Web documents, and even natural language processing for accommodating the types of queries that are used in Web searches. Some Web-based query systems are summarized in Florescu et al. (1998).

### 3.7.2.2  *Discovery Techniques in Web Transactions*

As already introduced earlier, *Web usage mining* is the type of Web mining activity that involves the automatic discovery of user access patterns from one or more Web servers. Organizations often generate and collect large volumes of data in their daily operations. Most of this information is generated automatically by Web servers and collected in server access logs. Analyzing such data can help these organizations determine the lifetime value of customers, cross-marketing strategies across products, and effectiveness of promotional campaigns, among other things. Analysis of server access logs and user registration data can also provide valuable information on how to better structure a Website in order to create a more effective presence for the organization.

Web usage mining employs many important ideas of basic data mining techniques as summarized in Chen et al. (1996). There are several types of access pattern mining that can be performed depending on the needs of the analyst. Below we briefly discuss these types and illustrate them using simple examples.

- *Path Analysis.* Using path analysis may be able to discover that "50% of new investors who accessed /fund-family/products/purchase.html did so by starting at /fund-family, and proceeding through /fund-family/top-performance, and /fund-family/products/minimum-investment.html."

- *Association Rule Discovery.* For example, using association rule discovery techniques, we can find correlations such as "25% of clients who accessed /SuperStar.com/announcements/promotion-item.html, placed an online order in /SuperStar.com/products/fancy-computer."

- *Sequential Patterns.* The problem of discovering sequential patterns is to find intertransaction patterns such that the presence of a set of items is followed by another item in the timestamp ordered transaction set. By analyzing this information, the Web mining system can determine temporal relationships among data items such as "37% of clients who placed an online order in /SuperStar/products/fancy-computer.html, also placed an online order in /SuperStar/products/digitalTV within 30 days."

- *Clustering and Classification.* Discovering classification rules allows one to develop a profile of items belonging to a particular group according to their common attributes. For example, "40% of clients who placed an online order in /SuperStar/products/fancy-computer, were in the 25–28 age group with income in high 5-digits." Clustering analysis allows one to group together clients or data items that have similar characteristics.

After the patterns are discovered, the next task is the analysis of discovered patterns. Website administrators are extremely interested in questions such as "How are people using the site?", "Which pages are being accessed most frequently?" Techniques and tools for enabling the analysis of discovered patterns are expected to draw upon a number of fields, including visualization techniques, data warehousing and OLAP techniques, and usability analysis, as well as data and knowledge querying. Given the large number of patterns that may be mined, there is a need for a mechanism to specify the focus of the analysis. A query mechanism will allow the user (usually, an analyst) to provide more control over the discovery process by specifying various constraints. The user may provide control by placing constraints on the database to restrict the portion of the database to be mined for, or by querying the knowledge that has been extracted by the mining process.

More recent studies in Web usage analysis have brought a number of interesting issues, including modeling users, discovering association rules and navigation patterns, and interestingness measures (Masand and Spiliopoulou 2000).

## 3.8 SUMMARY

In this chapter we have examined data warehousing as an enabling technique for data mining. We started with the concepts of data warehouse and online analytical processing (OLAP). We discussed architecture and design of data warehouses, basic operations of OLAP and data cubes, as well as more a more theoretical examination of data warehousing using materialized views and indexing. We discussed the concept of metadata, as well as its role in data mining. In addition, we discussed issues related to integrated OLAP and data mining. Several related issues, such as sampling and segmentation, and distributed and parallel data mining, have also been discussed. Finally, we addressed the issue of how to extend data mining for Web mining.

In addition to issues that are already covered, there are many other issues related to data warehousing and knowledge discovery, such as:

- *Data Mining Support for the Design of a Data Warehouse.* So far we have examined the how data warehouses can be used for data mining. Now there is the inverse problem—how can we take advantage of data mining techniques to aid the design of data warehouses?
- *Discovery Techniques for Data Cleaning.* This can be considered as a special case of the issue discussed above, and has already been used in business applications, although a more theoretical analysis is still needed.
- *From Data Warehousing to Knowledge Warehousing.* Since the 1960s or 1970s, we have witnessed the evolution from database management systems to knowledge-based systems. Will this phenomenon be repeated in warehousing environment? In other words, is there any reason to warehouse the knowledge, in the same way that we warehouse the data? If knowledge warehousing is even needed, what are the similarities with data warehousing? What are the differences?

These issues, along with many other issues, should be further investigated.

So far, we have not put particular emphasis on dealing with uncertainty in data mining. However, some problems encountered in sampling and segmentation as presented in this chapter reminded us that uncertainty handling should not be overlooked when we discuss data mining. In the next chapter, we will examine various aspects and approaches related to uncertainty handling.

# 4

# DEALING WITH UNCERTAINTY IN MANIPULATION OF DATA

## 4.1  OVERVIEW

In Chapters 2 and 3 we presented some most important concepts about data mining. Although we have noted the importance of dealing with uncertainty (such as inconsistency in sampling and segmentation), most of time we skipped this issue to make the main line of discussion straight. In this chapter, uncertainty comes to center stage. The organization of this chapter closely follows the presentation of the two previous chapters. The contents of this chapter fall into two lines of discussion. In one line of discussion, we review different kinds of uncertainty, different sources of uncertainty, and different existing approaches in databases and artificial intelligence (AI) to dealing with uncertainty. The other line of discussion is more directly related to data mining, where we discuss how to deal with uncertainty in various stages of data mining, including data preparation, model construction, and post–order processing.

In order to explain how this chapter is organized, we offer the following remarks on the terminology "data mining." First, we focus on the word "data." In real-world applications, data are usually far from perfect. First of all, data should be distinguished from noise. In addition, data used in mining usually need to be cleansed, because of unsatisfactory data quality, such as missing or incomplete. The second term, "mining," which originated as an analogy, in the context of (intelligent) information processing, refers to discovery of implicit knowledge patterns by employing reasoning techniques due largely to the practice of artificial intelligence (AI). Recall that when we discussed data mining primitives in Chapter 2, the main result of data mining is the data model which may contain a set of knowledge patterns. Here we give a more detailed description about the concept of knowledge pattern.

Given a set of facts (data) $F$, a language $L$ used for description, and some measure of certainty $C$, a knowledge *pattern* is defined as a statement $S$ in $L$ that describes relationships among a subset $F_s$ of $F$ with a certainty $c$, such that in some sense $S$ is simpler than the enumeration of all facts in $F_s$ (Piatetski-Shapiro and Frawley 1991). This definition clearly indicates where the uncertainty comes from. The knowledge patterns to be discovered are uncertain (that is why $c$ is needed to control the degree of certainty); what is more, the reasoning process itself is uncertain (because we may not know what is the most appropriate technique to be used, and what factors we should focus on). In fact, uncertainty may take various forms in the entire lifetime of any form of information processing.

Following this perspective, in this chapter, we present an overview of dealing with reasoning process on uncertain data. To underscore the importance of studying uncertainty related to data analysis, we start with a discussion on the importance of studying uncertainty (including a brief discussion on philosophy) in general (Section 4.2). As to the uncertainty in data analysis itself, we note that this topic actually consists of multiple aspects: (1) the inherit uncertainty residing in the *data*, (2) various forms of uncertainty in the reasoning *process* caused from the data uncertainty, and (3) the impact of uncertainty to the *result* of this reasoning process due to both data uncertainty and the uncertain reasoning process. The discussion of this chapter, in turn, consists of three parts. We first examine the uncertainty associated with data (Section 4.3). A discussion on sources and types of uncertainty (including various types of errors) in information processing systems is in order (Section 4.4). We then discuss the process of dealing with uncertainty data in database management systems and in artificial intelligence systems (Sections 4.5 and 4.6). Only common aspects underlying various approaches are identified; details on these specific techniques are left to a later chapter (Chapter 6). As to the impact of uncertainty to data mining, we examine the case of predictive modeling to show how to deal with the uncertainty in the modeling process and the result of data analysis (Section 4.7). In addition, the discussion of uncertainty allows us to again examine discovery-type data mining when uncertainty is involved (Section 4.8). To illustrate the diversity of handling uncertainty, we included several relatively recent developments (Section 4.9). We summarize this chapter in Section 4.10, which includes a discussion of what should be learned from uncertainty handling.

## 4.2    IMPORTANCE OF STUDYING UNCERTAINTY

We start with a somewhat philosophical discussion on the importance of studying uncertainty: the nature underneath surface. For this purpose, let us take a short detour before we get back to the main theme.

One of the most important results related to uncertainty is from theoretical physics. The theory of quantum mechanics implies that if $\Delta x$ is the uncertainty in the position of a particle and $\Delta p$ is the uncertainty in the momentum, then $\Delta x \, \Delta p \geq h/4\pi$, where $h$ is Planck's constant. This statement is the mathematical version of the well-known *Heisenberg uncertainty principle*. It is concerned with the role of the Observer: the act of observation changes the system irrevocably. The system is not the same after observation as before. This is fundamental to modern physics. It tells us that any attempt to measure some of the properties of a subatomic particle therefore introduces an unavoidable uncertainty into the result. Thus, in the world of very small particles, one can never measure all properties exactly. Therefore, quantum-mechanical theory implies that it is not possible to determine the present state (both the position and momentum) of every particle in the universe, and therefore we cannot predict all future events. Some possible interpretations to these results are

- The theory of quantum mechanics implies that there is an observer-independent absence of precise future values of observables.
- The theory of quantum mechanics implies that it is not possible to determine whether there is an observer-independent absence of precise future values for observables.
- The quantum-mechanical description of physical reality is incomplete. The principal efforts to extend the existing theory were the development of hidden variable theories. Consequently hidden variable theories do not appear very plausible.

So, what is the important indication of this seemingly irrelevant discussion? Uncertainty is prevalent in the physical world; it is a way of life, and it is not avoidable. In addition, uncertainty serves as a driving force for exploration in many subject areas. In many cases, uncertainty is the tip of the iceberg, and provides valuable clue for an in-depth study. As a simple example, let us consider the case of Brownian motion. English botanist Robert Brown in 1827 first observed the random motion of small smoke particles, which was not caused by the particle itself. Brownian motion refers to the motion of particles (suspended in a liquid such as water) observable under a microscope. This observation eventually led Einstein to develop a theory in 1906. According to this theory, the small random motions occur because atoms bombard the smoke particle in a haphazard manner, sometimes applying more force on one side than another. This random variation in the force causes the particle to move in a random fashion, sometimes called a *random walk*. Brownian motion thus illustrates how randomness (which is a form of uncertainty) stimulated a new research direction in history.

The role that uncertainty can play in data mining probably is more significant than those in many other research fields, because of the nature of data mining (which is to find hidden knowledge patterns from data). It is convenient to study data mining by starting from perfect data with perfect result. However, data are usually far from perfect, the regularity to be mined is far from perfect, and the mining process itself is full of various kinds of uncertainty.

Data mining incorporating uncertainty is important, because it puts the study of data mining in a more realistic setting. Equally important is *what the role of uncertainty can play*. Of course, we may want to get rid of uncertainty, such as cleansing the data during data preparation. However, uncertainty is important not because it is something we have to get rid of. In fact, uncertainty can play a much more *positive role* in data mining. In many cases, reasoning on data with uncertainty provides an excellent opportunity for us to reveal what is hidden underneath the uncertainty—and that is precisely what data mining is intended for! The indication of this exciting connection and related issues are discussed in the last three sections of this chapter.

## 4.3 SOURCES AND TYPES OF UNCERTAINTY IN INFORMATION SYSTEMS

### 4.3.1 Dealing with Missing or Inconsistent Data

***4.3.1.1 Dealing with Missing Data*** The term "missing values" usually refers to the situation where an underlying value was not captured. It may also indicate the value is empty because no corresponding real-world value (this could occur, e.g., if the data structure is poorly designed). Missing data can be filled in using imputation-based procedures, such as, mean imputation or regression imputation, model-based procedures, or some other methods. Replacing missing values, without elsewhere capturing the information that they were missing, actually removes information from the data set, because it obscures the fact that it was missing. The most predictive variable in a data set could be the missing-value pattern. The improved adequacy of a predictive model due to replacing missing values may not make real sense. In fact, *missing-value patterns* themselves should be captured first—the patterns in which the variables are missing their values. Once the information about the patterns of missing values is captured, the missing values themselves can be replaced with appropriate numeric values. The missing value can be replaced by estimating the value by preserving mean or variance as the estimate. Regression methods can be used to replace missing values while preserving between-variable relationships (Pyle 1999).

We need to consider what happens when some data values are missing. The tuple containing any missing data field can be simply discarded. But even with large data sets, the subset of cases with complete data may be relatively small. Future cases may also present themselves with missing values. Most prediction methods do not manage missing values very well; a missing value cannot be multiplied or compared (Weiss and Indurkhya 1998).

If the missing values can be isolated to only a few features, the prediction program can find several solutions: one solution using all features, other solutions not using the features with many expected missing values. Sufficient cases may remain when rows or columns in the database are ignored. However, by replacing all missing values with a single global constant or a view values (such as its feature mean), the data are biased. It is best to generate multiple solutions with and without features that have missing values or try to use logic methods.

***4.3.1.2   Inconsistent Data and Outliers***   Inconsistent data may be easy or difficult to identify, depending on the particular problem. For low-dimensional problems, we may consider to display the data in a graph and visually identify bad example patterns. In problems of hither dimensions, one may need to use thresholding or filtering of the data to automatically identify bad data values. Outliers are data points that lie outside of the normal region of interest in the input space. It is important to determine whether to include or exclude outliers, or whether to deal with them separately (Kennedy et al. 1997, Han and Kamber 2000). In discussion on the relationship between clustering methods and outliers can be found in Chapter 5.

### 4.3.2   Types of Error in Data and in Conclusion

In addition to dealing with errors in data, we should also consider errors in the conclusions. For this purpose, we can adopt concepts defined from statistics based on the different outcomes of some hypothesis, which is an assumption to be tested. A false positive or *type 1* error means accepting a hypothesis when it is not true. A false negative or *type 2* error means rejecting a hypothesis when it is true. Of course, when applied to data mining, such definitions are applicable only for confirmation type of data mining. For exploratory data mining, how to decide the errors in conclusion is a more complex issue, and depends on the actual algorithm used.

### 4.3.3   Objective and Subjective Uncertainty

Sources of uncertainties and errors may be grouped into categories of objective uncertainty and subjective uncertainty (Kasabov 1996):

- The *objective* uncertainties are mainly due to incomplete data and uncertain evidence.
- The *subjective* uncertainties are due to obscure (little-known) domain or unknown relations, functions, dependencies, and so on. Uncertainty can be a characteristic of data or of the problem knowledge, or both. Error in data can be due to acquisition of incorrect data, lack of precision and accuracy, or noise. Uncertainty in data may also mean uncertainty relating to the presence of an event, or uncertainty of the appearance of the event. Representing uncertainty in problem knowledge by using knowledge representation schemes (as briefly discussed in Chapter 5) is a more

complex problem than representing uncertainties in data. There are different types of errors resulting from incomplete and uncertain knowledge, including semantic, casual, systematic and logical. Since these specific topics are a topic more appropriately discussed in the context of AI, we will not provide detail here. Nevertheless, it is important to beware of these related issues.

## 4.4   DEALING WITH UNCERTAINTY IN DATA AND SCHEMA INTEGRATION

We now discussion how to handle uncertainty in integrated use of data, an important issue in the data preparation stage of data mining. Our primary consideration here is dealing with data from miscellaneous sources. Therefore, we start from fundamental issues such as schema integration and data cleansing, followed by issues more related to database semantics.

### 4.4.1   Schema Integration for Data Integration

Issues affecting warehouse creation, as identified by Srivastava and Chen (1999), include warehouse architecture selection (database conversion, synchronization), enterprise schema creation (enterprise data model, schema integration, constraints), and warehouse population (semantic issues, scalability, incremental updates). The following two aspects are related to uncertainty in affecting warehouse creation:

1. *Constraints*. In addition to the structural and semantic mismatches of schema entities, there is the problem of constraint mismatches, which are seldom evident from the definitions of entity types. For example, one database may have a constraint such as EMP.age $\Leftarrow$ 70, while another may have the constraint on age as EMP.age $\Leftarrow$ 62. In integrating such databases there seems to be in general no right approach to resolve such constraint incompatibilities.

2. *Scalability*. Since warehouses store information about the database as it progresses over time, they tend to grow much more rapidly than do online databases. It is quite common to start with an initial warehouse of size 10–100 gigabytes, and subsequently have a periodic (weekly or monthly) update rate of 1–10 gigabytes. The data integration tasks typically range in complexity from $O(n \log n)$ to $O(n^2)$ for $n$ data items. Given tens to hundreds of gigabytes of data, this can be very time-consuming, and hence there is a need for improved algorithms for integrated use of data. Furthermore, since these tasks are heavily set-oriented, data parallel computing techniques appear promising. Specific research issues to be addressed include: determining whether algorithmic improvements should require pairwise comparison

between all records; given the set-oriented nature of much of the data integration processing, data parallelization seems to be an attractive approach.

Reasoning involving uncertainty, due to inherit uncertainty (i.e., uncertainty is a way of life, no way to remove it), may take several forms, such as probability (e.g., thunderstorm this afternoon), vagueness in language (e.g., "rich" or "tall," thus also affecting thinking) or inconsistency. Emphasis of research in AI is in developing using mechanisms for reasoning. The size of data to be used could be as small as one, such as analogical reasoning or example-based reasoning.

### 4.4.2   Data Cleansing

*Data cleansing* (also called *data cleaning*) is a very early step of data preparation for data mining. The general requirement for data cleansing is removal or correct of questionable data so that data can be used for data mining or other purposes of data analysis. There are plenty of commercial tools for data cleansing; most of them, however, are application-specific. The term data cleansing is sometimes used in a loosely fashion; for example, some commercial products are claimed as data cleansing products, but their own function is simply dividing a long character string into tokens (name field, age field, etc.). From a theoretical perspective, the task of data cleaning can be formed as the problem of identifying *approximate duplicates*. The duplicate detection problem is also referred to in many academic papers as the *semantic integration problem*, *instance identification problem*, or *merge/purge problem* (Monge and Elkan 1997). Since there are misconceptions of data cleansing from a practical perspective, and since data cleansing is important but has not drawn enough attention from the research community, in the following paragraphs we provide a brief survey on some related aspects and existing work.

#### 4.4.2.1  *Domain Relevance*   Most duplicate detection methods can be classified as domain-dependent and domain-independent. Domain-dependent duplicate detection methods require some knowledge of the data source to be implemented. For instance, the person implementing the duplicate detection method may need to know what data fields would be the most distinguishing or uniquely identifying data fields because most of the domain-dependent methods require the data source to be sorted based on these fields.

In contrast, domain-independent methods do not require any familiarity with the data fields within the data source. Domain-independent methods use text strings within the records to search for matches. The text strings might consist of data from several of the text fields within the data source.

#### 4.4.2.2  *Sorted Neighborhood Duplicate Detection Method*   One of the most common duplicate detection methods is the *sorted neighborhood method*. The effectiveness of this approach depends on the quality of keys chosen to do the sorting. The data cleanser should choose sort keys that bring

the attributes that have the most distinguishing value among the records to the top of the sorting key. The steps involved in the sorted neighborhood method can be summarized as follows:

- *Create keys.* Compute a key for each record in the list by determining the most distinguishing field of data.
- *Sort data.* Sort the records in the data list using the key that was previously determined.
- *Merge.* Using a fixed-size window, advance the window through the list of records only searching for matching records within the window. Assuming that the size of the window is $w$, then the first record in the window will be compared to the next $w - 1$ records for matches. Then the window will be advanced one record and the record that was just compared will no longer be considered since it is now outside of the window.

### 4.4.2.3  *Multipass Sorted Neighborhood Duplicate Detection Method*
A variation to the sorted neighborhood method is the multipass sorted neighborhood method. The multipass sorted neighborhood method involves using multiple passes of the initial sorted neighborhood method. During each pass, the three steps, create keys, sort data, and merge, are performed selecting a different key field for each pass. Once the duplicate records are identified during a pass, all except one of the duplicates is eliminated from the data source. The output modified data source from any previous pass is used for any subsequent pass. It has been shown by that the multipass sorted neighborhood method provides better results. In general, several passes involving a small window size and cheap execution time and resource cost is better than performing one pass over the data with a large window size and expensive execution time and resource cost. Throughout the remainder of this discussion, the original sorted neighborhood duplicate detection method will be referred to as the "one-pass sorted neighborhood duplicate detection method" to clearly distinguish this method from the multipass sorted neighborhood method.

### 4.4.2.4  *Transitive Closure*   The idea of computing the transitive closure of duplicate relationships can be presented by utilizing a graph representing the relationships among the records and the union–find data structure to identify if any two records are already within the same path. If it can be determined that two records are already within the same path, then the record matching comparison can be avoided.

Assume that the starting state involves a graph G with $n$ vertices where each vertex represents one record in the database. Initially, all n vertices are unconnected to any other vertex. An undirected edge will be added between two vertices if it can be determined from the duplicate detection algorithm that the two records match. Before the duplicate detection algorithm does a record match comparison for any two records, the graph will be examined to see if the records belong to the same connected component. If they do, it is known that the records do match and do not need to be compared. If the records do not belong to the same connected component, a record match comparison will need to be performed. Then, if the records are determined to match, an edge between the two records will be added to the graph. The connected components within the graph represent the transitive closure of the previously detected "is a duplicate of" relationships.

Next, consider three nodes R1, R2, and R3 and their corresponding nodes N1, N2, and N3. If it is determined that R1 and R2 are duplicates, an edge is added to graph G between nodes N1 and N2. Once the edge has been added, N1 and N2 are in the same connected component. Then, if it is determined that R2 and R3 match, an edge is added to graph G between nodes N2 and N3. It can then be discovered through transitivity (R1 = R2 and R2 = R3, so R1 must = R3), that R1 and R3 are also duplicates. Therefore, an edge must exist between N1 and N3 as well.

**4.4.2.5 Union–Find Algorithms**    Union–find algorithms are used to track the sets of connected components. The algorithm has basic two operations (Weiss 1998):

- *Union(x,y)* combines the sets that contain nodes $x$ and $y$, say, sets $S_x$ and $S_y$, into a new set that is their union, $S_x \cup S_y$. A representative for the union is chosen, and the new set replaces $S_x$ and $S_y$ in the collection of disjoint sets.
- *Find(x)* returns the representative of the unique set containing $x$. If Find(x) is invoked twice without modifying the set between the requests, the answer is the same.

The algorithm begins with $n$ single sets containing only a single element. Then, for every edge (R1,R2) that exists in the set of edges within graph G, if Find(R1) is not equal to Find(R2), then the Union(R1,R2) will be computed. Two nodes R1 and R2 are in the same connected component only if their sets are the same, meaning Find(R1) = Find(R2). When this algorithm is applied to data cleansing, records differing in minor aspects will be accessed by the find operation, and grouped into one class using the union operation.

**4.4.2.6 Comments on Some Existing Methods**    Examining the sorted neighborhood method shows it is not very effective in detecting duplicate records in cases where the data source does not contain a primary key field of reference. For instance, consider a typical customer mailing list example containing first name, last name, street address, city, state, and zipcode data elements. The sorted neighborhood method would be much more effective if the customer mailing list had a data field which was similar to a primary key and provided a distinguishing characteristic. Then, by sorting on the primary key data element the duplicate records could be easily identified. However, the assumption of using a primary key may not always be realistic; for example, including a field of social security number in cleaning a customer mailing list, although makes things easy to handle, is unrealistic, because it is hard to imagine that people should provide their social security numbers when ordering magazines!

### 4.4.2.7 *k-Way Sorting Method*    The *k-way sort duplicate detection method* is designed to effectively detect duplicates in data sources that do not have any uniquely distinguishing data fields. *k*-Way sorting represents a new domain-independent duplicate detection method but the data sources it was designed for do have a common feature.

The concept behind the *k*-way sort method is as follows:

*Step 1.* Let *k* be the number of columns to be used for sorting.

*Step 2.* Select the *k* most meaningful combinations of sort keys based on the *k* selected columns.

*Step 3.* Assign a record identifier to each record.

*Step 4.* Sort records based on the selected sort key combinations.

*Step 5.* For each sorted set of data, compare adjacent rows within a given window size. If more than half of the *k* columns used for the sorting match, the records should be considered pairwise matches for that sort. Repeat with all subsequent windows of records, until all records have been examined.

*Step 6.* Draw *k* graphs, one for each sort, with undirected connectors between the record identifiers that were identified to be pairwise matches.

*Step 7.* Examine the *k* graphs collectively. For all pairwise matches, if the matches occur between the same record identifiers exceeds a certain predefined threshold (e.g., 0.5, which means that matches occur on more than half of the *k* graphs), then it should be mapped onto the summation graph. The summation graph should represent all pairwise matches that existed on certain number of the *k* sort graphs (determined by the threshold).

*Step 8.* The summation graph should then be handled by computing the transitive closure utilizing the find–union processes.

By examining the *k*-way sort methodology, one can see that it requires multiple sorting repetitions of the data source using a different multiple-data field sort key for each sort. In addition, the complexity of the method depends on the value chosen for *k*. By allowing the user to select the value for *k*, the accuracy and complexity of the data cleansing required can be adjusted.

As an example, let us consider the data set to be sorted in Table 4.1. The result of the third sort using the *k*-way sorting algorithm is shown in Table 4.2,

**Table 4.1 Input Records for _k_-Way Sort Conceptual Method Example**

| Last Name | First Name | Address | City | State | Zipcode |
|---|---|---|---|---|---|
| Brewer | BJ | 13961 William Circle | Omaha | NE | 68144 |
| Brewer | Bifford | 3242 Pederson Dr | Omaha | NE | 68144 |
| Brewer | BJ | 13961 William Circle | Omaha | NE | 68144 |
| Brewer | Clifford | 3242 Pederson Dr | Omaha | NE | 68144 |
| Brewer | Clifford | 3242 Pederson Dr | Omaha | NE | 68144 |
| Brewer | Patricia | 2430 Spaulding St | Omaha | NE | 68111 |
| Brewer | Patricia | 7609 Serum Av | Ralston | NE | 68127 |
| Brewer | Rev Cheryl | 407 Mary Mallory Kountze Mem Dr | Bellevue | NE | 68005 |
| Brewer | Rev Peter | 407 Mary Mallory Kountze Mem Dr | Bellevue | NE | 68005 |
| Brewer | Spencer Jr | 3827 Corby St | Omaha | NE | 68111 |
| Brewer | Spencer Jr | 4011 Corby St | Omaha | NE | 68111 |
| Brower | Dan | 16927 Holmes Circle | Omaha | NE | 68135 |
| Brower | Dan | 943 W Sunset Blvd | Omaha | NE | 68144 |
| Brower | K | 2040 N 50 Av | Omaha | NE | 68104 |
| Brower | M | 2040 N 50 Av | Omaha | NE | 68104 |
| Brower | Sam R | 838 S 93 St | Omaha | NE | 68114 |
| Brower | Sam R | 8805 Indian Hills Dr | Omaha | NE | 68114 |
| Brugler | Alan | 15711 Howard St | Omaha | NE | 68118 |
| Brunner | John | 6314 N 47 St | Omaha | NE | 68104 |
| Brunner | John M | 1315 N 38th St | Omaha | NE | 68131 |

which indicates how approximate duplicates are identified; for example, records with RID (record identifier) 7 and RID 8 are grouped together as a pair of approximate duplicates. For some other discussion related to this method, including a comparison between this method with other methods, see Feekin and Chen (2000).

Unlike the sorted neighborhood methods that use only one data field for each sort, the _k_-way sort method will sort with a key containing _k_ data fields. It can be seen by examining how the sorted neighborhood methods and the _k_-way sort method might handle a customer mailing list example, that the _k_-way sort method would be less likely to eliminate records that are not duplicates than the sorted neighborhood methods.

On examination of the k-way sort concept, one can see some areas of complexity that can be simplified. For example, the initial methodology suggested selecting _k_ most meaningful combinations of sort keys and then sorting the data _k_ times using these sort keys. The benefit of the sorting is that similar records would sort near or adjacent to each other. Then, only directly adjacent records are compared to determine whether the records are duplicates. Another concept presented was using a given window size to limit the number or record comparisons to be mapped on to each undirected graph.

**Table 4.2   Sorted Records for Third Sort of *k*-Way Sort Conceptual Method Example**

| Rid | Last Name | First Name | Address | CITY | ST | ZIP |
|---|---|---|---|---|---|---|
| 2 | Brewer | B J | 13961 William Circle | Omaha | NE | 68144 |
| 4 | Brewer | Bifford | 3242 Pederson Dr | Omaha | NE | 68144 |
| 1 | Brewer | BJ | 13961 William Circle | Omaha | NE | 68144 |
| 5 | Brewer | Clifford | 3242 Pederson Dr | Omaha | NE | 68144 |
| 6 | Brewer | Clifford | 3242 Pederson Dr | Omaha | NE | 68144 |
| 3 | Brewer | Patricia | 2430 Spaulding St | Omaha | NE | 68111 |
| 11 | Brewer | Patricia | 7609 Serum Av | Ralston | NE | 68127 |
| 9 | Brewer | Rev Cheryl | 407 Mary Mallory Kountze Mem Dr | Bellevue | NE | 68005 |
| 10 | Brewer | Rev Peter | 407 Mary Mallory Kountze Mem Dr | Bellevue | NE | 68005 |
| 7 | Brewer | Spencer Jr | 3827 Corby St | Omaha | NE | 68111 |
| 8 | Brewer | Spencer Jr | 4011 Corby St | Omaha | NE | 68111 |
| 12 | Brower | Dan | 16927 Holmes Circle | Omaha | NE | 68135 |
| 17 | Brower | Dan | 943 W Sunset Blvd | Omaha | NE | 68144 |
| 13 | Brower | K | 2040 N 50 Av | Omaha | NE | 68104 |
| 14 | Brower | M | 2040 N 50 Av | Omaha | NE | 68104 |
| 15 | Brower | Sam R | 838 S 93 St | Omaha | NE | 68114 |
| 16 | Brower | Sam R | 8805 Indian Hills Dr | Omaha | NE | 68114 |
| 18 | Brugler | Alan | 15711 Howard St | Omaha | NE | 68118 |
| 20 | Brunner | John | 6314 N 47 St | Omaha | NE | 68104 |
| 19 | Brunner | John M | 1315 N 38th St | Omaha | NE | 68131 |

Data are sorted so that similar records will be near each other after the sort. Nearness of duplicate records is needed if small comparison windows are used so that the duplicate records will be compared and one can be eliminated. If the data were not sorted, a record may be near the beginning of the array of records and a duplicate record may be near the end of the array of records. If the window size were chosen as $n/2$, where $n$ is the total number of data source records, the duplicate records would never be compared or detected by the duplicate detection method. Although these concepts limit the number of record comparisons necessary, the concepts require a great deal of memory tracking and recording of information in addition to $k$ sorts of the data.

By eliminating the $k$ sorts of the data and the window size from the algorithm and comparing all records against all other records in search of duplicates, one can minimize the $k$-way sort complexity. These changes require more enterrecord comparisons, but the need for the summation table and summation graph is eliminated and the amount of memory tracking and information recording is reduced.

The initial conceptual algorithm would have required $k$ different union–find graphs with $n$ elements to be maintained and compared to identify duplicate records, plus an additional union–find graph for the summation graph. Instead, the implementation of the algorithm follows a simplified version of the formal algorithm, which is outlined below.

### $k$-Way Sorting: The Implemented Algorithm

*Step 1.* Sort the $k$ most meaningful combinations of sort keys based on the $k$ selected columns.

*Step 2.* Compare the records. If more than the threshold percentage of $k$ fields match, the set containing the second record is unioned with the set containing the first record, and then the set that contained the second record is set equal to the empty set.

*Step 3.* Compare the Find function results for the records. If any of the record pairs have the same Find function result for more than the threshold percentage of sorts, then the final set containing the second record is unioned with the final set containing the first record, and then the final set containing the second record is set equal to the empty set.

*Step 4.* Eliminate all but one of the records in each final set.

The $k$-way algorithm indicates that the task of data cleansing is carried out as a process of dealing with uncertainty, and the method itself is not error-free. First, selection of $k$ data fields is subjective, which is based on the user's understanding of data. Second, approximate duplicate-ness is controlled by a threshold, which may influence the accuracy of the result. Nevertheless, experimental results have shown that in general, the $k$-way sort method outperformed other methods in identifying duplicates overall. Although for some of the test cases the results of the $k$-way and multipass sorted neighborhood methods were similar, for other test cases the multipass sorted neighborhood method proved to identify duplicates too aggressively. The multipass sorted neighborhood method identifies records as duplicates if any of the $k$ fields match. The $k$-way sort method only identifies records as duplicates if more than the threshold percentage of the $k$ fields match. Because the $k$-way sort method considers all the $k$ fields before trying to identify duplicates, it is more discriminating than the sorted neighborhood method. The one-pass sorted neighborhood method is limited to identifying duplicates based on only one data field. The test cases showed that for these data sources, without any uniquely identifying primary data element, the one-pass sorted neighborhood method was not accurate. In addition, the selection of the value of $k$ and the selection of the $k$ field elements seem to have a large affect on the accuracy of the $k$-way sort method. For more detail, see Feekin and Chen (2000), where some experimental results are also reported.

### 4.4.3  Data Inconsistency and Resolution Function in Multidatabase Systems

As indicated in Chapters 2 and 3, since data mining can be carried out in a multidatabase (or data warehousing environment), we should further consider data inconsistency and resolution function in multidatabase systems (Yu and Meng 1998), where independent management of component database system is the main reason for data inconsistency to occur. Usually, the schema integrator at the front end cannot modify the involved values in component databases to resolve the inconsistency because the integrator may not be authorized to do so or the integrator cannot be certain which values are incorrect. As a result, data inconsistency is often handled at the front end. To retain the ability to identify instances from different databases representing the same real-world object, we assume that data inconsistency does not occur on the ID attribute.

Sometimes an apparent inconsistency does not necessarily mean that one of the involved values must be incorrect. For example, suppose that a salary value of $25k$ ($25,000/year) is recorded for May in the first database while a value of $30k$ is recorded in the second database. This apparent inconsistency may have different explanations. It is possible that the apparent inconsistency is a real inconsistency in the sense that the two values should be the same but they are not. However, it is also possible that it is not a real inconsistency. For instance, it is possible that Mary has two different salary values in the two databases because she has two different part-time jobs. In this case, both salary values for Mary are correct and they should both be used to define the salary value for Mary in the integrated schema.

In general, when two values (either different or identical) exist for the same attribute of a real-world object in two databases, the following three cases exist:

1. There is no data inconsistency, and only one of the two values is needed;
2. There is a data inconsistency, but both values are needed to define the value of the object for the same attribute in the integrated schema.
3. There is no data inconsistency, but both values are needed (as the case illustrated above).

Different methods may be used to define the value of the object under an attribute in the integrated schema from the two corresponding values in the component databases.

In general, for cases 2 and 3 above, the global value in the integrated schema can be defined by a definition function. Since cases 2 and 3 can be handled uniformly through the use of definition functions, for the convenience of presentation, when an attribute is involved in either case 2 or 3, we say that there is a data inconsistency on the attribute and we call the corresponding definition function a resolution function.

### 4.4.4   Data Reduction

After schemas are integrated and data are cleaned, we are now closer to the task of data mining proper. Nevertheless, there is still some additional work we can do for data preparation. One particular concern must be addressed here is data reduction (which was discussed in Section 2.10). As frequently noted (Weiss and Indurkhya 1998), the data may be too big for some prediction programs. The expected time for inducing a solution may be too long. Therefore, reduction of big data, or shrinking the size of the database by eliminating both rows and columns, may be helpful for predictive data mining. In fact, better answers are sometimes found by using a reduced subset of the available data. Prediction programs can potentially fit their solutions to any size data. The bigger the data, the more exceptions that must be fit. Even with completely random data, many programs will first attempt to fit all the training data. By fitting so many exceptions, some prediction programs are more likely to err on the optimistic side, finding some concept that is not there.

The main theme for simplifying the data is dimension reduction. We can delete a column (viz., a feature), delete a row (which represents a case), or reduce the number of values in a column (smooth a feature). The emphasis here is to use simple techniques to implement and preserve the character of the original data, although advanced techniques, such as the method of principal components, can be used to replace the features with composite features.

Dimension reduction is the goal of the new process that mediates between data preparation and prediction methods. Methods that transform data into a new set of attributes (referred to as "features" in pattern recognition literature) can also be considered data preparation methods. Dimension reduction can be done by feature selection. The objective of feature selection is to find a subset of features with predictive performance comparable to the full set of features. This perspective on dimension reduction is independent of the prediction methods.

Data reduction techniques, along with prediction methods themselves, form the two types of tools that can contribute to the task of predictive data mining. Because data reduction is much faster than data modeling, the data are filtered to narrow the search space of the prediction methods. However, the reduction methods make assumptions that potentially could degrade results. These assumptions can be viewed as the sources of a kind of *uncertainty in data preprocessing*. In order to deal with this kind of uncertainty, the different data reduction techniques have been compared empirically. These techniques are then matched to the prediction methods to see which combinations work best. This kind of comparisons of different approaches to data reduction and mining should help us gain experience in picking the right tools for the job (Weiss and Indurkhya 1998). Data reduction and its relationship to discovery-type data mining are discussed in more detail in Chapter 7.

## 4.5 EXISTING WORK IN DEALING WITH DATA AND KNOWLEDGE UNCERTAINTY

### 4.5.1 Taxonomy of Data and Knowledge Uncertainty

It has been noted that the "norm" is to attempt to model the real world using some idealization by engineering out the inherent uncertainty. This means that one ends up with an elegant model, but one that can never give completely correct answers because it does not attempt to model precisely what is going on. Instead, one should take the uncertainty into account, trading the loss of elegance and simplicity for more accurate modeling (Parsons 1996). In this sense, uncertainty is handled as a sort of perturbation around the norm.

In order to build useful information systems, it is necessary to learn how to *represent* and *reason with* uncertain information. In general, uncertain information can be classified into the following categories:

- *Incompleteness.* This arises from the absence of a value (lack of relevant information).
- *Imprecision.* This arises from the existence of a value that cannot be measured with suitable precision, or arises from the granularity of the language used to make the imprecise statements; it may be disjunctive, existential or universal, but is distinguished from vagueness (see below).
- *Imperfect.* This arises from the fact that an agent has constructed a subjective opinion about the truth of a fact that it does not know for certain, or arises from a lack of information about the state of the world, and may be due to subjective error on the part of some observer.
- *Randomness.* In tossing a coin, the chance of a head or a landing upright tail is a typical example of randomness.
- *Vagueness.* This is a subcategory of imprecision (fuzzy valued imprecision).
- *Inconsistency.* This describes the situation in which there are two or more conflicting values for a variable (having too much information from too many sources);
- *Ignorance.* This is a lack of knowledge, particularly a lack of knowledge about the relative certainty of a number of statements.

Different approaches have been developed to deal with different types of uncertainty. For example, ignorance is handled by Dempster–Shafer theory.

### 4.5.2 Dealing with Uncertainty in Database Management Systems

DBMSs have tried to impose semantic consistency through an important concept called *integrity constraint* (IC), which is a condition that is specified on a database schema, and restricts the data that can be stored in an instance of the database. Integrity constraints may take various forms, including domain constraint, functional and other forms of dependencies, triggers, as well as others (Silberschatz et al. 1998).

Processing uncertain information in databases falls in three categories in domain constraints:

- *Incomplete Information.* Typical incomplete information in DBMS could take various forms, such as unknown, nonexistent, no information, undefined, or inapplicable. Values may be missing. Unknown values are replaced by variables. An incomplete set of rules should be considered to represent all the complete sets that may be established by replacing every missing value by every possible legal value.
- *Imprecise Information Due to Vagueness.* The incomplete information described above is concerned with DBMS proper. The DBMS functionality can be enhanced to deal with imprecise information due to vagueness. Typically, we can use fuzzy logic.
- *Vagueness.* Possibility theory is build on the idea of a fuzzy restriction. Consider a variable that is constrained to take its value from some fuzzy set of values. Any value within that set is a possible value for the variable. However, since the values have different degrees of membership in the set, they are possible to different degrees. A value that has a degree of membership of 1 will be completely possible as a value, while a value that has a degree of membership of 0.1 will be much less possible.
- *Randomness.* The simplest possible method for using probabilities to quantify the uncertainty in a database is that of attaching a probability to every member of a relation, and to use these values to provide the probability that a particular value is the correct answer to a particular query.

It has been noted that there are four basic ways in which we can handle imperfect information and all the methods developed so far are variations on one or more of them:

1. Use a number or symbol to indicate the *degree to which a given attribute is known to satisfy a relation.*
2. Use a number or symbol to indicate the *strength of the relation between attributes.*
3. Use a number or symbol to *indicate the strength of inheritance* (in an object-oriented system).
4. *Derive* the appropriate number or symbol to result from a query.

Different methods simply provide different mechanisms for one or more options sited above, and attach different meanings to the numbers or symbols

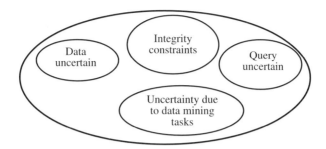

**Figure 4.1**    Dealing with different kinds of uncertainty in DBMSs.

that are provided. For instance, we can use null values to indicate that a given attribute within a relation has a value that is unknown, or we can use probability of 0.85 to indicate that a particular instantiation of an attribute in a given relation is known to be very likely to be correct. A choice of one way of modeling is likely to force the choice of others.

Various ways of dealing with uncertainty in database management systems can be briefly summarized in Figure 4.1.

### 4.5.3    Dealing with Uncertainty in Artificial Intelligence

Some background information of artificial intelligence (AI) will be provided in Chapter 5. In the context of AI, uncertainty handling can be discussed at different levels. At the higher level, in order to build a successful and quality knowledge base, domain experts should consider the following:

- *Identify gaps in the logic.* Human thinking may include skipping steps. Decision trees are very good at avoiding gaps in the logic of problem solving.
- *Identify conflicts.* Rules induced or obtained from different sources may conflict with each other.
- *Identify missing factors.* This overlaps the previous point. A clash between logical statements may suggest some missing factor failed to be incorporated into the knowledge base, and deserves some investigation.
- *Identify redundant factors and rules.* There could be overlap of rules, such as a rule is a subset (or superset) of one or more rules.

At a lower, concrete level, following the similar consideration in database management systems, approaches for processing imperfect information in AI fall in the following categories:

- *Incomplete Information.* There is a split in the AI community between those who deal *numerically* with the problem of imprecise and uncertain information and those who deal *symbolically* (i.e., nonnumerically) with the problem of incomplete information. This split is largely historical, and stems from the schism between mainstream practitioners of AI who scorned quantitative approaches and those who championed numerical methods of handling uncertainty. As a result of the split, work on incomplete information and that on uncertain information has largely taken place with no regard for the other, and it is only comparatively recently that work has begun on relating the two. As a result much of the work on combining the approaches is rather preliminary. Representative approaches include default logic and circumscription.

- *Imprecise Information Due to Vagueness*. We can use fuzzy logic (to be discussed in Chapter 7).
- *Uncertain Information Due to Randomness*
  - *Logical Approaches*. An obvious approach to handling deductive reasoning with uncertain information is to attach some measure of validity to every piece of information in the knowledge base. This measure can be probability, possibility, Dempster–Shafer belief, or something else. Possibilistic logic and probabilistic logic have been studied extensively. A variation on the logic-based scheme is the use of *augmented logic programming systems*. The basic idea behind argumentation is that it should be possible to say more about the certainty of a particular fact than may be expressed by quantifying it with a number between 0 and 1. In particular, it should be possible to assess the reason why a fact is thought to hold, and use this argument for the fact as its quantification. Note that argumentation is also somewhat related to the construction of Bayesian networks (also called *belief networks*; see remark below).
  - *Numerical Approaches*. Reasoning with Bayesian networks illustrates the use of numerical approaches. It also illustrates the connection between probability and logic-based approaches. We will revisit this issue in Section 4.6, and a discussion on Bayesian networks is provided in Chapter 6.

It has been observed (Parsons 1996) that with the handling of imperfect information in AI, there are four basic ways in which we can represent and reason with imperfect data:

- Use a number or symbol to given the *strength with which an attribute is known to take a given value*.
- Use a number or symbol to indicate the *strength of the relation between attribute values*.
- Use a number or symbol to indicate the *strength of inheritance between two objects* (in frame-based or object-oriented systems).

- Describe how to *derive* the number or symbol appropriate to a given attribute value from that known to be associated with some other attribute value.

In addition to uncertainty of data, we can also talk about imperfection in the *properties* of data; for example, we can talk about *vague* integrity constraints, or we may even talk about *uncertain queries*, since some users may not know exactly what they want. These are interesting issues, and can be incorporated into advanced data mining systems.

## 4.6 LOGIC AND NUMERICAL APPROACHES TO UNCERTAIN REASONING

Below we examine uncertainty in the reasoning process by providing a sketch on the relationship between logic and uncertainty.

### 4.6.1 Differences between Logical and Probabilistic Reasoning

We now use probability reasoning as an example to illustrate the difference between logic and uncertainty. In particular, we examine the case of probabilistic reasoning. Probabilistic reasoning systems have several important properties different from logical reasoning systems (Russell and Norvig 1995):

- *Nonmononotonicity*. We human beings perform reasoning in a nonmononotonic manner, meaning that we can withdraw our previous conclusion when new knowledge has arrived. For example, a presidential candidate may withdraw an earlier concession phone call to his openent when new information about election has obtained. First order predicate logic exhibits strict monotonicity, although commonsense reasoning exhibits nonmonotonicity. In contrast, in a probability reasoning system we can add or withdraw beliefs, which makes it nonmonotonic.
- *Global Solution*. In logical systems, when we have a rule of the form $A \rightarrow B$, we can conclude $B$ given evidence $A$, without worrying about any other rules. In contrast, probabilistic systems demonstrate a global feature, because we need to consider all of the available evidences.
- *Nondetachment*. In dealing with probabilities, the source of the evidence for a belief is important for subsequent reasoning. In contrast, in a logical system, when we have a rule of the form $A \rightarrow B$, once a logical proof is found for a proposition $B$, the proposition can be used regardless of how it was derived; in this sense, it is detached from its justification.

- *Nonadditivity*. In general, probability combination is a complex process, except under strong independence assumptions. This is quite different from logic, where the truth of complex sentences can be computed from the truth of the components.

### 4.6.2 Challenges in Dealing with Uncertainty

There are many difficulties encountered in dealing with uncertainty (Pearl 1988). Reasoning about any realistic domain always requires that some simplifications be made. The very act of preparing knowledge to support reasoning requires that we leave many facts unknown, unsaid, or crudely summarized. For example, if we choose to encode knowledge and behavior in rules such as "car is fast" or "every good student gets a good job," the rules will have many exceptions which we cannot afford to enumerate, and the conditions under which the rules apply (e.g., seeing a car or a good student) are usually either ambiguously defined, or difficult to satisfy precisely in real life. For example, uncertainty reasoning using probability theory performs reasoning globally and imposes severe restrictions (such as independence assumption).

Many approaches have been developed to deal with reasoning under uncertainty, each with its own strengths and restrictions. One way is to extend the logic-based approach summarized in the last section: in fact, the logicist school attempts to deal with uncertainty using non-numerical techniques, primarily nonmonotonic logic. Alternatively, one may use an informal, heuristic approach, in which uncertainties are not given explicit notation but are instead embedded in domain-specific procedures and data structures. A third approach is to stay with the traditional framework of probability theory, while attempting to buttress the theory with computational facilities needed to perform AI tasks. Pearl (1988) has described the relationship between logic and probability as "the strange connection." A fourth approach resorts to quantitative methods, regarding probability calculus as inadequate for the task and thus invents entirely new methods, such as the Dempster–Shafer calculus, and fuzzy logic.

Recall the discussion of dealing with uncertainty in AI (Section 4.5.3), a probabilistic logic provides a mechanism for implementing three out of the four ways: the first by associating probabilities with propositions, the second by associating probabilities with implications, and the last by specifying how to determine the probability of the consequent of an implication from the probabilities of its antecedent and the implication itself. Similarly, the use of a nonmonotonic logic provides a means of specifying (as true or false) the strength with which propositions and expressions relating propositions are known to hold, and given a set of formulae provides a means of determining whether various conclusions are true or false.

### 4.6.3  Taxonomy of Uncertain Reasoning

Extensions of classical logic have enriched the beauty of symbol-based reasoning. However, more fruitful results in real-world applications are found in other three approaches, particularly in the third and fourth approaches cited above. Various computational paradigms have been developed; while some of them have roots in centuries-old probability theory (such as Bayesian approach and causal networks, Dempster–Shafer theory), many others focus on more newly developed aspects of uncertainty (e.g., fuzzy logic, artificial neural networks, genetic algorithms, rough set theory). Some of these techniques are discussed in Chapters 6 and 7.

The wide spectrum of uncertain handling techniques and their relationship with several forms of information systems (including some systems to be briefly discussed in Chapter 5) is summarized in Figure 4.2. Note that the direction of the arrow indicates the increased uncertainty encountered by these various techniques.

## 4.7  INCORPORATING UNCERTAINTY HANDLING INTO DATA MINING

We now examine the impact of uncertainty in data mining process and results. In this section, we focus on predictive models, because they have been studied in pattern recognition literature for many years. However, we will also make certain remarks on dealing with uncertainty in descriptive approaches as well.

### 4.7.1  Uncertainty in Predictive Classification and Estimation

Some of the fields where data mining has received the most publicity and success are in database marketing and credit card fraud detection. For

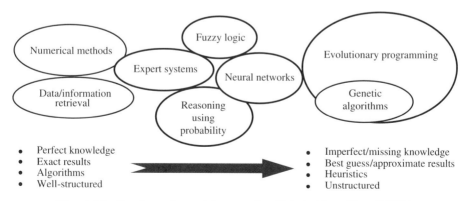

**Figure 4.2**  Spectrum of uncertain reasoning. [Adopted from Chen (1999).]

example, accomplishments in response modeling: predicting which prospects are likely to buy on the basis of previous purchase history, demographics, geographics, and lifestyle data. As already mentioned in Chapter 1, in many applications, the task of data mining can be conducted as a pattern recognition problem. Pattern recognition consists of classification, which is the process of assigning one of a finite set of labels to an observation, as well as estimation, which is the process of assigning one of a (typically infinite) number of numerical labels to an observation (Kennedy et al. 1997).

Uncertainty in predictive modeling can be discussed in terms of its two major categories: classification and estimation. Classification problems often entail decision-making in the face of uncertainty. For example, a handwriting character may look like either an A and an H. In a borderline case of this sort (and without additional contextual clues), either choice has some chance of being wrong. Thus a decision must be made in the face of uncertainty. In this event, the character should be categorized as the most probable class, even though there is some possibility the classification may be incorrect (i.e., the decision could not be made with high confidence).

The fundamental difference between estimation and classification is that "classes" in an estimation problem follow an explicit ordering (i.e., a sequence of values). In general, similar observations lead to estimates that are numerically close. Furthermore, in estimation problems, there is often an infinite continuum of classes, whereas in classification, the number of classes is finite.

Sequential relationships are typical to estimation problems, but nonexistent in classification. Classes in a classification problem have no clear concept of closeness or ordering among them. On the other hand, estimation problems offer a means of computing "closeness" or degree of error. Guessing a person's age as 25 years old is only "one off" if the person's age is 26. This would be a "better guess" than 29, which would be "four off." In classification, one wrong guess is generally as bad as another, while in estimation, a wrong guess close to the correct answer is generally better than a far one. The fact that estimation methods take advantage of ordinal features is the key distinction between estimation and classification.

As indicated earlier, estimates entails generating an approximation of some desired numerical values based on an observation. They often are prone to uncertainty. In some sense, the uncertainty inherent in estimation problems is worse than in classification problems. The slightest uncertainty in estimation can seriously affect the chance an estimate is exactly correct. This is certainly true for age estimation. However, estimates can be numerically close enough to true values to be useful. Classes in a classification problem have no clear concept of closeness or ordering among them (but hierarchical classification?). On the other hand, estimation problems offer a means of computing closeness or degree of error (Kennedy et al. 1997).

When there is uncertainty, no model can be error-free. It is thus important to point out how to characterize an optimal model: which is the one minimizing expected error.

### 4.7.2 Handling Modeling Errors

We now further discuss the issue of handling modeling errors, which will be followed by the modeling process with presence of uncertainty. First, we note the sources of error in modeling (Kennedy et al. 1997):

- *Modeling error.* This is the error due to differences between the model used and an optimal model.
- *Uncertainty.* An example would be rainfall prediction. Given a fixed set of input and output patterns, even the optimal model is imperfect (error-prone). However, this error might be reduced by redefining the estimation problem as a problem with additional inputs. In addition, although error may be reduced as more inputs are incorporated, as some point, additional inputs no longer improve the model's accuracy, and the model may still err. Uncertainty thus can be classified into two types: uncertainty due to (1) missing variables (problem features) and (2) inherently random noise. This distinction is important for developing estimation models. Uncertainty due to missing variables can be reduced by adding more information or input variables, while inherently random noise cannot be avoided.

In parallel to the discussion of various types in data modeling, a discussion of modeling *errors* should be handled differently for different kinds of models:

- *Fixed Models.* The development of an accurate fixed model requires a full understanding of the relationships between input and output variables.
- *Parametric Models.* Parametric modeling (such as liner regression) involves two stages. The first is similar to fixed modeling, and the second uses data to select numerical values for parameters. In general, the parameters are chosen to minimize error on a given data set. When at least one set of parameter values leads to a good model, parametric methods are extremely effective. However, the choice of effective parametric forms for many real-world estimation problems requires a degree of understanding which is not always available. The use of a parametric model can lead to poor models when the parametric model does not fit the underlying relationships. Determining whether inaccuracies of a parametric model are due to modeling error or noise is not a simple matter. A common approach is to try different parametric forms. However, flaws still exist in an iterative approach. If after a few attempts of parametric forms, the model is still not accurate, we cannot say that no accurate model exists.
- *Nonparametric Modeling.* This is a more challenging task. Since the problem of generating a mapping that fits a finite data set is ill-posed, we need heuristics, or "rules of thumb," for choosing one of the infinite number of candidate models that perform equally well on the data set.

The hope is the heuristics (such as analogy) will lead to models that will generalize well for most problems. The process of nonparametric modeling requires the generation of a large set of parametric forms (with varying complexity and smoothness) so that the most appropriate one will emerge or be selected.

Incorporating considerations related to error and uncertainty handling stated above, given a set of data, a top-level algorithm for applying nonparametric modeling can be summarized as below.

**Algorithm: Nonparametric Modeling**

*Step 1.* Reserve a portion of available data as an evaluation set of measure final performance.

*Step 2.* Divide the remaining data set into training and test sets.

*Step 3.* Generate multiple models with varying degrees of complexity and smoothness using different approximation architectures and turning parameters to fit the training set.

*Step 4.* Find the models that perform best on the test set.

*Step 5.* From the best performers, choose the model with lowest complexity and/or greatest smoothness.

*Step 6.* Assess performance of the final model using the evaluation set.

### 4.7.3   Data Modeling Process in Presence of Uncertainty

*4.7.3.1  Data Collection, Preparation, and Preprocessing*   We now re-examine the data mining cycle discussed in Chapter 2, with an emphasis on the impact of uncertainty handling at each stage of this cycle. We start with data collection. One important question should be answered is whether the data are adequate to describe the phenomena the data mining analysis is attempting to model. We also need to have a general understanding on the quality of data, such as whether the data sets being merged would consistent with each other, or the possibility of having redundancy in the data sets being merged. Again, these issues involve uncertainty.

As for data preparation, we need to answer questions such as how to handle missing data and noise or outliers. Part of preparing data should include a cursory inspection of the data to identify and discard erroneous data. Other steps in data preparation include cleansing the data, joining/merging data sources and the derivation of new attributes in the data through aggregation, calculations or text manipulation of existing data fields; all other them deal with uncertainty at various degrees.

As a critical (although often overlooked) step to the success of a model, data preprocessing is aimed to simplify the mining task without throwing away any important information. Reasons for preprocessing data include reducing noise, reducing the input space, feature extraction (typically, domain-specific knowledge is used to develop good features), and modifying prior probabilities. However, preprocessing should be handled with great care. One should not throw out too much data or information in an attempt to simplify the problem, because that may be inadvertently throwing away important features. A good approach to preprocessing is to start with minimal preprocessing and then incrementally add more preprocessing while evaluating the results. In addition, data mining techniques introduced in this book may be used to deal with uncertainty issues in preprocessing the data (such as for data cleansing).

### 4.7.3.2 *Taxonomy of Predictive Data Mining Methods*
We now turn to the data mining proper of the data mining cycle. Algorithms can be selected based on which category of model one is looking for. Table 4.3 groups several popular algorithms according to parameter/nonparameter and classification/estimation categories. Within each subcategory, such as parametric algorithms, several popular algorithms are shown, such as linear regression

**Table 4.3   Categories for Selection of Algorithms**

| General Category | Subcategory | Some Popular Algorithms |
|---|---|---|
| Parametric vs. nonparametric algorithms | Parametric algorithms | Linear regression<br>Logistic regression |
| | Nonparametric algorithms | MLP/BP<br>Radial basis functions<br>$k$ nearest neighbors<br>Nearest cluster<br>$k$ means clustering<br>Binary decision tree |
| Classification vs. estimation algorithms | Classification algorithms | Nearest clustering<br>Binary decision trees<br>Linear regression<br>Logistic regression<br>Backpropagation<br>Radial basis functions<br>$k$ nearest neighbors<br>$k$ means |
| | Estimation algorithms | Linear regression<br>Logistic regression<br>MLP/backpropagation<br>Radial basis functions<br>$k$ nearest neighbors<br>$k$ means |

or logistic regression. This table can help us to select appropriate algorithms to apply. For example, if the problem is appropriate for nonparametric algorithms, then several artificial neural network (ANN) algorithms (e.g., multilayer perception/back propagation (MLP/BP) or radial basis functions), along with $k$ nearest neighbors, etc., can be considered. Also note the general category of parametric versus nonparametric algorithms on one hand, and classification versus estimation algorithms on the other, are not mutually exclusive. So, suppose that the problem to be investigated is appropriate for nonparametric algorithms and also is of classification nature, then binary decision tree algorithm is appropriate, because it is in the intersection of two subcategories (Kennedy et al. 1997).

Here is a brief explanation for some of the terminology used in Table 4.3. A simple example of linear regression involving two variables, $x$ and $y$, is $y = 6x + 5$. Logistic regression generates a mapping between the input variables $x_i$ values and an output $y$ according to the logistic function in the form of $y = 1/(1 + e^{-\Sigma})$, where $\Sigma = w_0 + \Sigma_{i=1}^{N} w_j x_i$ (the $w_j$ values are free parameters). The concept of binary decision tree will be summarized in Chapter 5, and for more detail, see Chen (1999). Multilayer perceptron/backpropagation (MLP/BP) and radial basis functions are well-known ANN models and are summarized in Chapter 6. $k$ nearest neighbors, nearest cluster, and $k$-means clustering are well-known pattern recognition methods, and the basics of these methods (particularly $k$-means clustering) will be summarized in Chapter 5. For more detail of pattern recognition methods for data mining, see Kennedy et al. (1997).

### 4.7.3.3  Selecting a Data Mining Algorithm with Uncertainty Handling
The following can serve as guidelines for selecting a data modeling method for data mining:

- *Hard Constraints.* For example, estimation problem can only be solved using estimation algorithms.
- *Less Restrictive Constraints.* For example, one may have a dynamic situation where retraining needs to occur frequently, in which case training times may be an issue.
- *Factors to Consider.* These include how fast the model need to be, how long the models takes to train, memory requirements for the trained model, and how often the model should be retrained.
- *Prior Knowledge.* This is also important. The more we know about a problem, the less parameters must be fit using the data. If we know the form of the underlying relationships, then we can use a parametric algorithm which assumes that form. In this case, a parametric model is not only faster to train due to fewer free parameters, but also may provide better accuracy.
- *Parametric Algorithms.* These should be used where their form is known to fit the data well. If we do not know the underlying form of the data,

then it is usually best to use nonparametric algorithms. Binary decision trees are well suited for conjunctive problems. Gaussian mixture estimates probability density functions from data.

- *Practical Constraints*. Research has shown that often times, many modeling methods can achieve statistically equivalent error rates on the same pattern recognition problem, but may differ by orders of magnitude in other characteristics, such as memory requirements, training time, classification time, training problem complexity, and ability to adapt to new data. For example, for a $k$-means algorithm, the relative memory requirement is from medium to high, the training times is medium, while classification time ranges from medium to fast. On the other hand, for $k$ nearest neighbors, the memory requirement is high, relative training times is very fast, and relative classification time is slow.

### 4.7.3.4  *Post–Model Processing*    Post–model processing include troubleshooting to deal with various problems (Kennedy et al. 1997):

1. *Training error is poor* (performance on the training set is poor). Suggestions for dealing with this problem include to train incremental algorithms longer; increase complexity of the network; "normalizing" (i.e., "scaling") of the input data if not done so in the past; for estimation problems, normalize the output variables; examine the relationships between the model output and each input variable; try different output layers; collect more input variables; restructure an estimation model so there is a single output; turn off any data compression, etc.

2. *Test error is high*. The training error is good, but the test error is poor—the network does not generalize well to new data. Suggestions include reducing complexity of the network, using representative training data, and reducing the input space; for MLP/BP, stop training early.

3. A *classification model* performs accurately for some classes, but performs poorly on others. Suggestions include using more examples of the classes that are performing poorly and adjusting the prior probabilities of those classes.

4. Running the network in production mode with real data results in worse-than-expected error, or accuracy degrades over time. Suggestions include periodically retraining the model and making sure that training set data are representative of real-life data.

### 4.7.4  Measuring the Effectiveness of Data Mining

#### 4.7.4.1  *Measuring Models*    We first consider measuring effectiveness of predictive models, which are assessed on the accuracy of their predictions for previously unseen data. Different data mining tasks need two kinds of mea-

sures: Ways of assessing performance of the model as a whole, as well as ways of judging the accuracy for each particular record.

As indicated in the data preparation stage, a simple way to measure the classification error rate is to divide the available data into two mutually exclusive subsets of tuples, called the training set and the test set. (When data mining is conducted in a relational database, both sets are relations.) Only data in the former can be used to discover a relationship between the predicting attributes and the goal attribute. Data in the test set are used only for measuring the classification error rate of the knowledge discovered from the training set. This is done by selecting one of the discovered rules to predict the class of each of the tuples in the test data. For each tuple in the test set the class predicated by the selected rule is compared with the actual class of the tuple recorded in the test set. Note that sometimes the antecedents of more than one rule will be satisfied by a given test tuple. In this case the best rule is selected according to some criterion, often based on probability theory. After repeating this classification process for all the tuples in the test relation, the error rate of the discovered rules is simply the ratio of the number of tuples in the test set misclassified by the discovered rules over the total number of tuples in the test data (Freitas and Lavington 1998). In addition to these two sets, an evaluation set is used to evaluate the effective of the model.

Measuring descriptive models is a more challenging task, because it is more evasive to provide a criterion for the effectiveness of this kind of data mining. In addition, the effectiveness may vary from algorithm to algorithm. Nevertheless, this is not to say no common criterion can be developed at all. For example, we an use the so-called *minimum description length* (MDL) for a model to measure the expressive power of a rule, which is the number of bits it takes to encode both the rule and the list of all exceptions to the rule. The fewer bits required, the better the rule. This has been used in some data mining tools to decide which sets of rules to keep.

**4.7.4.2 *Measuring Results*** There is a general way to compare models without getting into their details. There most common way to compare the performance of classification models is to use a ration called *lift*. This technique can be adapted to compare models designed for other tasks as well. Lift measures the change in concentration of a particular class when the model is used to select a purposefully biased sample from the general population.

### 4.7.5 Summary of Data Mining Process with Uncertainty

The overall data mining lifecycle, as originally shown in Figure 2.7, is revised in Figure 4.3, where uncertainty issues are incorporated. For example, in step 5a, Selecting an algorithm, we may have more than one choice, may need try different methods, and may need to integrate results from different algorithms

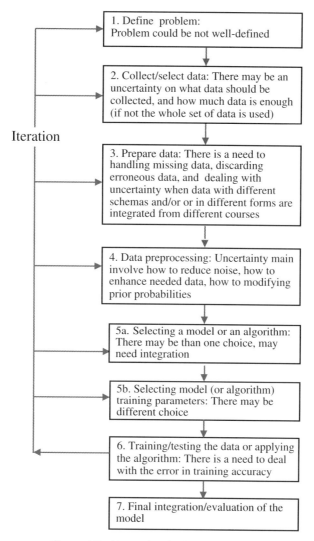

**Figure 4.3**   Uncertainty in data mining lifecycle.

which may provide different results. Note that although we have discussed this process in the context of predictive modeling, it is largely applicable in discovery type of data mining as well. Issues related to uncertainty may also involve maintenance of constructed models or discovered patterns or rules when new data has arrived. Intelligent agents developed for data mining should be able to handle various concerns related to uncertainty at all stages of the data mining cycle.

## 4.8   FEATURES OF UNCERTAINTY HANDLING IN KNOWLEDGE DISCOVERY

### 4.8.1   Overview

The overall data mining process incorporating uncertainty, as discussed in the previous section, was outgrown from predictive data mining, but it also covers discovery type of data mining. Nevertheless, there are unique features related to knowledge discovery and uncertainty, and this section will examine these features in some detail. Roughly speaking, uncertainty in knowledge discovery is associated with data used for mining, or the knowledge mined (the process of mining, the patterns mined, etc.), and a combination of both factors. Data mining, as an intelligent data analysis technique, has a very close relationship with reasoning as discussed in AI. Numerous challenges exist for data mining, including the following, which are related to uncertainty, including some factors related to data, as summarized in previous sections, including poor understanding of the problem, poor-quality data, and incomplete or incorrect data. The uncertainty may also be caused due to human error, such as selection of inappropriate mining methods, or inadequate training of analysts.

A more significant challenge of uncertainty for data mining, however, is in the technical side. Note that some discovery tasks, such as classification, have a root in pattern recognition or other traditional predictive methods. In general, however, comparing with predictive tasks, uncertainty in discovery-type data mining is a much trickier issue, and the following are some reasons:

1. There are unique features related to uncertainty due to different discovery paradigms, such as use of support and confidence for control the accuracy of association rules and use of vote in attribute-oriented induction to evaluate the strength of rules. We will discuss some of the issues in Chapter 5. Note that uncertainty issues like these directly depend on the actual steps in the algorithms, and ways used for dealing with uncertainty may affect the accuracy of the result, but in general they do not have profound impact on the behavior of the algorithms.

2. Another kind of challenge in discovery type data mining lies in the difficulties of measuring the result. Of course in some cases we may still divide data sets into training, test and evaluation sets, but in some other cases these concepts are not applicable. For example, in order to discover sales trends in a data warehousing environment, using a portion of historical data as test data to test the accuracy of rules discovered from another portion of historical data may not be a good idea; a more practical issue would be to apply the discovered rule to the new acquired data after daily or weekly refreshment. Should we still consider the rules discovered earlier are still effective, even the strength of these rules have been changed when applied to the new data? This

brings to the issue of incremental maintenance of discovered patterns for data acquired in the future. This discussion reminds us measuring accuracy of result now has a new meaning and uncertain reasoning may take many new forms which were nonexistent in the past.

3. However, the most important challenge knowledge discovery has brought to data mining is that the "freelance" style of discovery (that is, discovery of any interesting hidden pattern) has made the boundary among previously well-defined concepts blurred: First of all, *retrieval* is no long just to fetch the existing data, but implied knowledge as well, and this makes it looks like *reasoning*. In addition, it may not be easy to determine whether a piece of implied knowledge is trustable. For example, if in a transaction database we have found that in a certain day, there are 270 customers who used credit card, and 200 of them have spent more than $100 in one transaction; while for 304 non–credit card users, only 120 of them spent more than $100. Does this fact tell us anything useful for the store owners at all? In fact, this scenario may reveal more on *uncertainty* rather than *regularity*. The interesting question then comes: When we are dealing with data, we are dealing with uncertainty; and for the purpose of data mining, we want to identify useful patterns or regularity as well. So why don't we handle the task of discovery while doing uncertain reasoning, or vice versa?

In the remainder of this book we will discuss some issues raised here. Data mining paradigms will be studied in more detail in the remaining part of the book, particularly in Chapter 5. In the following, we provide an overview on one of the issues mentioned above, namely, the tighter integration of mining and uncertainty. A more detailed examination will then be continued in Chapter 6.

### 4.8.2 Relationship between Data Mining and Uncertain Reasoning

From a methodological and historical perspective, data mining and reasoning under uncertainty are two very different disciplines of research and have very different roots. Uncertain reasoning, as a subarea of artificial intelligence (AI), is aimed at developing methods to promote effective reasoning involving uncertainty. Data mining, on the other hand, is a new field focused on decision support queries within organizations. Data mining seeks to discover knowledge patterns hidden in data. Nevertheless, these two fields share several common interests. Data mining methods are designed to find regularity in databases. They achieve this by either removing uncertainty from data, or maintaining what is certain in the data. In addition, an interesting challenge is to utilize data mining techniques with missing and incomplete data. In many applications, there is a need to find unknown and interesting patterns even though the data may contain major flaws such as missing or inconsistent data values. Despite the uncertainty involved in the information stored in these systems, regularities can be found which characterize the intrinsic nature of the subject investigated. In other words, the study of uncertainty can be viewed as a study of discovering hidden "true" systems. The research of data mining from this perspective will thus enhance our understanding of uncertainty. This, in turn, will benefit the development of decision support systems. Note that reasoning under uncertainty is not necessarily aimed to discover new things, but can be used for this purpose.

Having discussed the impact of date mining on uncertain reasoning, let us now further consider how data mining can be affected by uncertain reasoning. Note that data mining is concerned with an in-depth analysis of entire sets of data at the semantic level; the emphasis here is to uncover the relationship of data in the overall contents (rather than individual pieces of data). Although in some cases what to be discovered could be scientific laws (such as Ohm's law), most likely this inherit relationship cannot be expressed using a mathematical function or any other kind of simple formula. Nevertheless by removing the dust, the golden nuggets could be shining. Various forms of uncertainty are the dust to be removed for finding the regularities of data.

We can also add a remark on data mining performed in a DBMS environment. In this case, we are encountering two kinds of uncertainty for data mining–related tasks: syntactic or semantic uncertainty on surface (as handled in traditional DBMS) versus semantic uncertainty in depth (as discussed in data mining context). In fact, we can view data mining as removal of uncertainty in depth. Traditionally, DBMSs *impose* exact integrity constraints (e.g., functional dependencies) in an *explicit* manner to guarantee data consistency; when data mining is carried out, the task is to *find implicit* knowledge patterns. Although the knowledge patterns are discovered rather than imposed, they reveal the mandatory relationship among data and thus can be viewed as an *extension* of integrity constraints. The knowledge patterns differ from integrity constraints also because they are usually *uncertain*. In addition, although integrity constraints may be both syntactic and semantic, knowledge patterns are normally semantic constraints. The task of data mining can be viewed as removing semantic uncertainty; in this sense, it should satisfy the following requirements—it must be goal-oriented (i.e., the user must have a clear idea of what need to be mined), and appropriate criteria must be established to determine what is considered as uncertain.

Note that similar to the case of machine learning, uncertain reasoning sets emphasis on the underlying mechanisms which are effective for reasoning processes, while data mining focuses on the data itself, as well as the result (which should be useful to users in various application domains). Although both deal with data, in the case of uncertain reasoning, the size of data may not necessarily be large, and usually data is assumed in the main memory. In contrast, in the case of data mining in DBMS environment, I/O access of data could become a critical issue of database operations. Nevertheless, the contribution of uncertain reasoning mechanisms to data mining should never be overlooked.

### 4.8.3 Uncertain Reasoning Techniques for Data Mining

Summarizing what we have discussed so far in this section, we have learned that besides various data mining paradigms summarized in Chapter 2 (and will be further discussed in Chapter 5), thanks to the blurred boundary between data mining and uncertain reasoning, we can also make use of traditional methods developed in artificial intelligence and related fields for uncertain reasoning, such as fuzzy logic, Bayesian networks, neural networks, as well as others, and extend their use for data mining. In addition, the preceding discussion also shed lights on how these uncertain reasoning methods can play in data mining. For example, discovery can be done by removing dust on the cover of the golden nuggets or by reconstructing the hidden system. In fact, each method in uncertain reasoning has its unique feature. For example

- Rough set theory views each set as confined in its upper and lower bounds. Rough set approach starts from the notion of approximation (that is, something unknown is described by using known upper and lower bounds) and can be used to explore the data in a reductionist fashion. A nice consequence of this is that it can live with inconsistency.
- Fuzzy logic puts emphasis on vagueness, and resorts to a numeric approach to represent the membership of belonging to a concept. As its original philosophy stands, fuzzy logic can capture vagueness and perform reasoning based on this vagueness, but it not useful for discovery of patterns hidden in the data.

As a result, it is extremely important to have answers to the following types of questions:

- Why does each of the uncertain reasoning method (e.g., ANN, fuzzy logic) works?
- Under what circumstances and how can these methods be extend for data mining?
- How do these methods play different roles in these two disciplines?
- When we have a data mining task in hand, where should we get started— starting from selecting a data mining paradigm or starting from an uncertain reasoning method?

Chapters 6 and 7 provide partial answers to these questions. In general, we can offer the following very general guideline for one of the questions, namely, when we have a data mining task in hand, where should we get started— starting from selecting a data mining paradigm or starting from an uncertain reasoning method? A reasonable answer could be like this:

1. If you think there should be some regularities in the data, and if you are interested in particular form of knowledge patterns, such as association or classification rules, you may select the one or more appropriate data mining paradigms and apply related algorithms accordingly. In this case, dealing with uncertainty is a secondary concern, and should be incorporated as a subtask of data mining. Results from applying different algorithms may need to be integrated. In Chapter 5 we discuss several popular data mining paradigms and related algorithms. We will also see how uncertainties can be handled in conducting these algorithms.

2. If you are not certain on the form of rules to be mined and if you want to explore the data to get a feeling about what to do next, then you may start with one or more uncertain reasoning methods to analyze the data. In order to carry out this analysis, you should understand the strength and limitation of each uncertain reasoning method. After this exploration, several options could be taken. If the analysis suggests some kind of affiliation could be discovered, you may try a formal data mining process using the association rule paradigm. On the other hand, instead of resorting a data mining paradigm, one may stay with the method used in exploration (e.g., ANN) to continue the discovery process. However, since uncertain reasoning methods are usually not developed for data mining, some additional steps should be taken, which are beyond the purpose of the original use of these methods. In Chapter 6 and Chapter 7, we examine several uncertain reasoning methods. We will first briefly review these methods as they are, and then discuss some sample situations where these methods can be extended for data mining. By so doing, we will also clarify some public misconception which may tend to believe any data analysis tool are also naturally candidate for data mining.

We summarize our discussion of various techniques for data mining in Figure 4.4.

## 4.9   DATA MINING METHODS FOR DATA PREPARATION

In the last two sections we how to incorporate uncertainty handling into predictive data mining and in knowledge discovery. Note that our emphasis has been using uncertain reasoning techniques for data mining. Nevertheless, data mining methods can also be used for uncertainty handling of data. Data mining techniques can be applied in back-end data processing.

In this short section, we take a look at issue through a brief re-examination of Figure 4.3. In fact, data mining methods can be incorporated into stages before the data mining proper (step 5 in Figure 4.3). In particular, here we take a look at how data mining methods can aid the task of data preparation (which was discussed in Chapter 2).

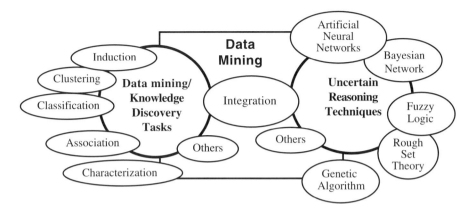

**Figure 4.4**   Data mining tasks, uncertain reasoning techniques, and their integration.

First we should note that of course not any method in data preparation is related to data mining. For example, for missing values, we may use a global constant to fill in the value, use the attribute mean to fill in the value or use attribute mean for samples belonging to the same class as the given tuple, or use the most probable value to fill in the missing value. None of them can be considered as using data mining techniques. However, there are some methods which do have features of data mining, such as

- *Binning*. Binning methods smooth a sorted data value be consulting the values around it.
- *Clustering*. Clustering methods (as to be discussed in Chapter 5) can be used to detect outliers, because values that fall outside of any clusters can be considered as noisy data.
- *Regression*. Data can be smoothed by fitting the data to a function using regression. This is to use predictive data mining for data cleaning.

For more discussion on this issue, see Han and Kamber (2000).

## 4.10  SUMMARY

Recapping our discussion in this chapter, we started a discussion on the inter-esting relationship between probability and logic. The following are some additional aspects related to these two directions. Sample aspects related to statistics and probability in data mining include discovery of probabilistic networks, discovery of exceptions and deviations, pattern recognition for data mining, statistical significance in large-scale search and the problems of over-fit. Sample aspects related to logic-based perspective on data mining include examining existing inference methods in logic, exploring different subcategories of first-order logic so that they are suitable for inference of knowledge from data, inductive logic programming for mining real databases, and the use of tolerance (similarity) relations in data mining. Intelligent agents used for data mining should be able to deal with various issues related to uncertainty handling, as demonstrated at various stages of the revised data mining cycle when uncertainty issues are incorporated.

The discussion on relationship between data mining and uncertain reasoning, as presented in this chapter, has a close tie with theoretical foundation of data mining, as discussed in Section 2.10. We now conclude this chapter by examining this connection through the development of *semantic approximation*. It has been recognized that similar issues, problems, and approaches underlie research on semantic approximation, partiality, granularity (abstraction, precisification), and vagueness in the following four fields (AAAI Workshop 2000):

- Knowledge representation in artificial intelligence (formalization of context, spatial and temporal knowledge bases)
- Formal modeling in computer science
- Formal ontology (which refers to the systematic study of being) in analytical philosophy
- Formal semantics and pragmatics in natural language (discourse interpretation, semantics of plurals, tense, aspect, underspecification, etc.)

Some commonalities include the use of various nonstandard forms of logic and possible worlds semantics for characterizing the dynamic interpretation of context, the employment of topological methods for modeling concepts and domains, theories of semantic abstraction and precisification, and domain modeling using structured formal constructs.

The notion of similarity suggests the concept of *semantic approximation*, which refers to locating on a scale from more precise (or concrete or specific) to less precise (or abstract or general), and this study is inherently multidimensional. In addition, the notion of a boundary region between conceptually approximate objects may have to be explicated. For example, how does one know that $A$ is approximately but not quite $B$; how should we interpret the formal constructs we use to characterize these notions of approximation, granularity, and abstraction, that is, linguistically (as technical vocabulary only) or ontologically (the formal objects have real existence); and what are the implications of how we interpret these, as well as other issues.

Specific techniques on uncertain reasoning will be discussed in Chapter 6, where we emphasize useful aspects of these techniques to support various paradigms of data mining tasks, which is discussed next (Chapter 5).

# 5

# DATA MINING TASKS FOR KNOWLEDGE DISCOVERY

## 5.1 OVERVIEW

So far in this book we have presented a nontechnical discussion of data mining and uncertain reasoning. Starting from this chapter, we will take a look at several specific techniques used in this integration. In this chapter we present some technical detail on several data mining tasks for knowledge discovery. Uncertain reasoning and its relevance to data mining, with some technical detail, will resume in Chapter 6.

In Chapter 2 we briefly discussed various kinds of data mining tasks (or functionalities) for knowledge discovery. For example

- *Characterization*. This is aimed to generalize, summarize, and possibly contrast data characteristics.
- *Data Classification*. This is the process that finds the common properties among a set of objects in a database and classifies them into different classes, according to a classification model.
- *Association Rules*. These are usually called market basket analysis (MBA) or affinity analysis in business applications, are intended to discover associations between the various attributes or transactions.

This chapter is organized as follows. Since many tasks in data mining are closely related to symbolic reasoning as discussed in artificial intelligence (AI), we start our discussion with a brief review of AI, with an emphasis on machine learning (Section 5.2). The rest of the chapter examines several important data mining tasks. The discussion starts with methods developed in inductive machine learning (including tree induction and rule induction) in Section 5.3. We then discuss attribute-oriented induction for characterization in Section 5.4, which employs inductive learning concepts. In the subsequent sections, we examine data classification (Section 5.5), clustering (Section 5.6), as well as association rules (Section 5.7). The formats and contents vary for different data mining tasks. For example, for inductive methods, we focus on semantics. For clustering algorithms, we put emphasis on varieties of algorithms. For association rules, because of their popularity and a well-developed literature, we discuss various aspects related to them, including semantics at both the regular (namely, primitive) level and aggregation levels, different implementation methods, and variations of association rules.

In addition to the discussion of algorithms, due to the importance of database-centric data mining, we also address implementation issues related to scalability and speedup. Section 5.8 and Section 5.9 contain a general discussion related to scaling up and speeding up of data mining, as well as other issues such as metarule-guided mining. We conclude the chapter in Section 5.10.

## 5.2   BASICS OF ARTIFICIAL INTELLIGENCE AND INDUCTIVE MACHINE LEARNING

### 5.2.1   Artificial Intelligence as Construction of Intelligent Agents

Artificial intelligence (AI), as the science of "making machine do things that would require intelligence if done by men," has introduced a new discipline for contemporary thinking, research, and practice in all walks of life. Artificial intelligence, *artificial evolution*, and *artificial life* are three distinct approaches to program computers in order to make them behave as if they were humans, more primitive animals, or other species. Comparing with AI, the other two disciplines are less ambitious in so far as they do not mimicking human, but only ore primitive, even prebiotic, intelligence, such as through collective or/and cooperative behavior of autonomous agents.

Artificial intelligence is now defined as the study and construction of intelligent *agents*. An agent is something that perceives and acts. The following important aspects of the concept of agent should be emphasized:

- *Agents are (semi)autonomous.* Each agent has certain responsibilities in problem solving with little or no knowledge of either what other agents do or how they do it.
- *Agents are "situated."* Each agent is sensitive to its own surrounding environments and usually has no knowledge of the full domain of all agents.
- *Agents are interactional and the society of agents is structured.* Agents cooperate on a particular task.

- *The phenomenon of intelligence in this environment is "emergent."* The overall cooperative result of the society of agents can be viewed as greater than the sum of its individual contributors.

Roughly speaking, these features indicate that an agent is able to conduct reasoning (namely, to derive conclusions and make decisions in its environment), learning (to improve its perform) and communication (with other agents) for decisionmaking and problem solving. An outline of an agent-based approach for data mining is outlined in Chapter 6.

From the very beginning, artificial intelligence has been considered as an empirical inquiry because of its exploratory nature. In terms of contents, much of AI can be discussed around the two major issues: state space search and knowledge representation. Intelligent agents can be developed using techniques developed around these two issues.

## 5.2.2  Basic Concepts of Artificial Intelligence

We now briefly review the basic concepts of search and knowledge representation in traditional AI, mainly from a logic-based perspective, which is based on the assumption of physical symbolism and representation. This assumption states that intelligent actions are demonstrated based on physical symbols. In the context of AI, a *symbol* is just a token to denote a thing which has a well-defined meaning. For example, "student" is a symbol denoting a concrete thing (an object), "thought" is a simple denoting an abstract object, and "take" is also a symbol denoting an activity. The use of symbols facilitates problem solving through *state space search*. A state space consists of states; intuitively, a state is represented by a set of related variables along with their values. Since a state space resembles a graph, various graph algorithms can be used to carry out state space search. However, in order to make search more effective and more efficient, it would be beneficial to develop some criteria to evaluate the "goodness" of each state. This is where *heuristic search* comes from. A heuristic is a rule of thumb, it may provide useful insight for problem solving, but it is fallible.

In addition to the notion of state space search, another basic concept in traditional AI is *knowledge representation*. In fact, without an effective way of representing knowledge involved in any specific problem to be solved, state space search will not be able to be conducted.

Because of the different needs in problem solving, various knowledge representation schemes (or methods) have been developed. One of the most fundamental knowledge representation scheme is *predicate logic*, which makes use of the notion of *predicate*. A predicate symbol has a truth value. In the simplest case, a *predicate* of arity $n$ consists of a predicate name and followed by $n$ ordered *arguments* (also referred to as *terms*) which are enclosed in parentheses and separated by commas. For example, "The fourth quarter profit of IBM is high" can be represented as "profit (ibm, 4Q, high)." Be more generally, one or more terms could be variables (instead of values), as in "profit (Company-name, Quarter, Degree)." (Here, following the convention of a logical programming language called *Prolog*, we use terms starting with lowercase letters to denote constants, terms starting with uppercase letters to denote variables.) The use of variables has extended the power of expression. Variables are used with *quantifiers*, which indicate the role of the variables in the expression. There are two quantifiers used in predicate logic: universal ∀ ("for all") and existential ∃ ("there exists"). First-order predicate calculus [also called *first-order predicate logic* (FOPL)] allows quantified variables and not to predicates or functions.

Predicates can be connected together to form *sentences* using *connectives* such as ∧ (and), ∨ (or), ¬ (not), → (implication) and = (equal). A sentence could be either a fact or a rule. A *knowledge base* consists of all the facts and rules that are valid at the same time.

The semantics of predicate calculus provide a basis for a formal theory of logical inference so that new expressions can be derived. Inference rules (or laws) have been developed to derive new expressions. An inference rule is *sound* with respect to semantics if everything that can be derived from a knowledge base is a logical consequence of the knowledge base. Intuitively, soundness requires the derived expression is "correct," and does not generate any dependencies that should not be generated. An inference rule is *complete* with respect to semantics if there is a proof of each logical consequence of the knowledge base. Informally, this is to say that using what should be derived will be derived (i.e., nothing is left out).

Two of the most important inference rules (or laws) in predicate logic are shown below (written in propositional logic, a simplified form of predicate logic):

$$\text{Modus ponens: } \{(p \rightarrow q) \wedge p\} \Rightarrow q$$

$$\text{Modus tonens: } \{(p \rightarrow q) \wedge \neg q\} \Rightarrow \neg p$$

The first law is to indicate: that, given $p \rightarrow q$ and $p$, we can infer $q$. Note that the double arrow $\Rightarrow$ works above the content level and denotes "to derive."

Laws such as this can be used in combination to perform *deductive inference*. For example, given $p \rightarrow q$, $\neg q$, and $\neg p \rightarrow r$, we can first use *modus tolens* to derive $\neg p$, and then use modus ponens to derive $r$. This is an example of simple *deductive reasoning*. A useful technique in deductive reasoning is *resolution proof*.

Other forms of reasoning also exist. For example, *induction* refers to the inference from the specific case to the general. The following is a simple example of induction. Suppose that we have observed the following facts: $p(a) \rightarrow q(a)$, $p(b) \rightarrow q(b)$, and so on. We may then attempt to conclude $\forall X$, $p(X) \rightarrow q(X)$. Note that in a sense, inductive reasoning can be considered as the "inverse" of modus ponens as used in deduction, because if we know $\forall X$, $p(X) \rightarrow q(X)$, then we can conclude $p(a) \rightarrow q(a)$, $p(b) \rightarrow q(b)$, and so on using modus ponens. Note that unlike deductive reasoning, inductive inference is not sound. Nevertheless, inductive inference let us discover new conclusions, and has served as a very effective vehicle for machine learning (see next subsection).

Another reasoning method called *abduction* can also be viewed as a different kind of "inverse" of modus ponens. The basic idea of abduction can be described by comparing it with modus ponens:

$$\text{Modus ponens: } (p \to q) \wedge p \Rightarrow q$$

$$\text{Abduction: } \quad (p \to q) \wedge q \Rightarrow p$$

Note that abduction is not sound because although $p$ implies $q$, the existence of $q$ does not necessarily imply that $p$ is true, because there may be some other reason to make $q$ true. Nevertheless, abduction is useful because it provides a clue for the possible cause.

First-order predicate logic is very basic, and its reasoning power is still limited. Nonstandard logic, such as nonmonotonic reasoning (which allows withdraw of a previous conclusion) has been developed to enhance the reasoning power. A result with significant philosophical evidence is from Kurt Godel; in 1929 he proved the completeness of first-order logic (FOPL). In 1931 he proved the incompleteness of any system of logic that was powerful enough to allow elementary arithmetic. That is, in any logical system allowing mathematics, one can construct statements that can neither be proved nor disproved within that system (Bender 1996).

Although predicate logic has served as theoretical foundation for "mainstream" AI, *production systems* provide a useful alternative for knowledge representation and reasoning in real-world problem solving. The knowledge base of a production system consists of production rules of the form "if (premise or antecedent) then (conclusion or consequent)." Production systems have been found very useful in building knowledge-rich *expert systems* in many application domains. In a rule-based expert system, the execution of production rules is handled by an *inference engine*.

Both predicate logic and production systems support modularity, because both predicates and production rules represent a piece of knowledge. On the other hand, in many other applications it is desirable to make use of *structured knowledge representation and reasoning schemes*, such as conceptual graphs and frame systems. In these knowledge representation schemes, relevant knowledge is grouped together as a unit. Note also structured knowledge representation schemes such as conceptual graphs have a close relationship with predicate logic.

### 5.2.3 Knowledge-Based Systems

There are many successful stories of AI, ranging from toy problems such as puzzles and games (particularly in early history of AI) to large-scale real-world applications.). One of the most successful area of AI applications is expert system, or more generally, knowledge-based systems. The rationale behind knowledge-based systems can be briefly explained as follows. Earlier we emphasized the importance of search in AI, because many AI problems are not well defined, and in order to solve such problems, we have to resort to search, because there are no alternatives. On the other hand, if we have plenty of knowledge to start with, this situation could be changed. In indeed, the more knowledge we have, the less search is needed. From this consideration, *knowledge-based systems* have been developed. In particular, expert systems have been developed. An *expert system*, as an interactive system, is able to demonstrate expertise (i.e., the expert level of knowledge) in a narrow, specific knowledge domain (e.g., disease diagnosis, car troubleshooting) and solve problems in this specific domain for consultation. The term expert system is closely related to the concept of *knowledge-based system*, and these two terms are usually used interchangeably. However, we should point out unlike an expert system, a knowledge-based system does not require expert-level knowledge. (In contrast to knowledge-based approach, a problem-solving method which does not use domain specific knowledge is called a *weak method*.)

A popular approach to building knowledge-based systems (including expert systems) is using the *production system model*. The following are important components in the production system model:

- Production rules (long-term memory)
- Working memory (short-term memory)
- Recognize–act cycle.

Let us take a brief look at the first two components. A production rule has the following format:

```
if antecedent (premise/condition) then consequence
(conclusion/action)
```

Here are some examples:

- If the color is dark and the temperature is hot, then take action A. (Note that in this example, the consequence is an action.)
- If the engine does not turn over, and the lights do not come on then the problem is battery or cables. (Note that in this example, the consequence is a conclusion.)

The set of production rules form the long-term memory (namely, the knowledge base). The case-specific data (i.e., data or facts directly used in the current session) are stored in the working memory. Contents in working memory are either conditions or actions of those rules that were fired in current session.

After the session ends, the content stored there are all gone. Working memory thus works like a buffer, and can be used to make the reasoning process efficient.

### 5.2.4   Symbol-Based Machine Learning

Although knowledge-based systems are powerful, we should keep in mind that such knowledge is usually static, and the systems are usually not able to acquire new knowledge or improve their behavior. This is not an ideal situation, because a very important feature an intelligent agent should posses is being able of learning. Machine learning is the field of AI to dealing with such kind of problems, and machine learning techniques can be incorporated into knowledge-based systems. (An interesting note must be made here is that the relationship between machine learning and knowledge-based approaches is mutually benefitial, because knowledge-based approaches can also be used to aid machine learning, as well as data mining.) Roughly speaking, learning refers to positive changes toward improved performance. When symbol-based machine learning is used, a learner must search the concept space to find the desired concept. Learning programs must commit to a direction and order of search, as well as to the use of available training data and heuristics to search efficiently.

The basic idea of machine learning can be demonstrated through *inductive reasoning*, which refers to the process of deriving conclusions from given facts (usually the facts used in inductive reasoning are referred to as samples, or the training set). For example, if you have observed your friend Mary has a Toyota, your uncle John has a Toyota, and your colleague at work also drives a Toyota, you may tend to think that everybody drives a Toyota. This is a simple but typical example of inductive reasoning; you have learned that "everybody drives a Toyota." Of course induction is not sound, because it does not guarantee the correctness of the conclusion. Nevertheless, induction is a useful approach to derive new conclusions from the given facts.

An important form of performing inductive reasoning is through *generalization.* There are several principles for generalization. A simple principle is replacing constants by variables. For example, consider the statement "Mary is a programmer," which is expressed in Prolog (a useful AI language) as "programmer (mary)." In order to perform generalization, we can replace the constant "mary" by a variable $X$, so "programmer(mary)" now becomes "programmer($X$)." This is to generalize the fact "Mary is a programmer" to derive the conclusion "Everybody is a programmer."

Another way of generalization is dropping conditions in conjunctive expressions in a rule so that less restriction will be imposed. For example, consider the following Prolog rule, which says "X is qualified if X has GPA greater than 3 and years of employment is greater than 5":

```
qualified(X):- gpa(X,G), G > 3, employment-year(X,Y), Y > 5
```

This rule can be generalized to

```
qualified(X):- gpa(X,G),  G > 3
```

where employment history requirement is dropped. Since the condition of the rule is relaxed, more people will be considered as qualified.

There are many other principles can be used for generalization and for induction. For example, in Section 5.4, we discuss attribute-oriented induction, which employs concept hierarchies. Induction can be carried out through replacing a property by its parent in a class hierarchy.

Since induction is not sound, it is important to decide how good a conclusion is. The *theory of learnability* has been established for quantifying the effectiveness of an inductive learning. Briefly, learnability is a property of concept spaces and is determined by the language required to represent concepts. The theory of learnability is important because it is concerned with two aspects which are both crucial for the success of learning: the quality of concepts learned and the size of the sample set.

Learnability can be measured in terms of probability as discussed in probability theory. Probability theory is concerned with how to handle randomness. A class of concepts is considered as *learnable* if an algorithm exists that executes efficiently and has a high probability of finding an approximately correct concept. (Note that this definition do not guarantee the correctness of learning.) The theory based on this definition, *probably approximately correct* (PAC) learning has been developed.

Extending the discussion on basic concepts of AI and machine learning to database management systems allows us to better understand where data mining is placed in a larger picture. According to Thuraisingham (1999), deductive database systems are database systems incorporating *deductive* logic programming, while data mining is database systems incorporating *inductive* logic programming. This viewpoint is consistent with the inductive database perspective of data mining, as discussed in Section 2.10.

For more detailed discussion on logic-based AI approach, see Chen (1999).

### 5.2.5   Other Approaches in Artificial Intelligence

The brief overview of AI presented so far has focused on symbol-based approaches. In fact, many other approaches have also been studied. Techniques to be discussed in Chapters 6 and 7 demonstrate this. For example, in artificial neural networks (ANNs), an artificial neuron may not necessarily denote a particular thing; rather, it could be simply a place holder in a learning process. In ANNs, the knowledge is represented through the connections of the artificial neurons and the strengths of these connections. For this reason, the approach of ANNs is referred to subsymbolic reasoning. Another approach, as outlined in Chapter 7, is called *genetic algorithms*. This approach employs a biological (instead of psychological) metaphor of human intelligence. ANNs, genetic algorithms, as well as many other approaches developed in AI, have important contributions in integrated data mining.

## 5.3 TREE AND RULE INDUCTION

On the basis of our brief summary of basic concepts in AI, in the balance of this chapter we will discuss various kinds of data mining tasks for knowledge discovery. We start with inductive learning methods developed in machine learning, and address the issue of scalability.

### 5.3.1 Basic Idea of Tree Induction

#### *5.3.1.1 ID3 and C4.5* A well-known tree induction algorithm adopted

from machine learning is ID3, which employs a process of constructing a decision tree in a top-down fashion. A *decision tree* is a hierarchical representation that can be used to determine the classification of an object by testing its values for certain properties. In a decision tree, a leaf node denotes a decision (or classification) while a non-leaf node denotes a property used for decision (color, size, etc.). We prefer the shortest path to reach a leaf, because it implies the fewest possible number of questions are needed. Note also that the role of examples is used to guide the construction of a decision tree.

The main algorithm is a recursive process. At each stage of this process, we select a property based on the *information gain* calculated from the training examples. The skeleton of the ID3 algorithm is shown below [following the presentation of Luger and Stubblefield (1998)]. A brief discussion on calculating the information gain will follow.

**Algorithm ID3**
*Input*: a set of examples
*Output*: a decision tree
*Method*:

```
ID3_tree (examples, properties)
 if all entries in examples are in the same category of
 decision variable
    Return a leaf node labeled with that category
else
    Calculate information gain;
    Select a property P with highest information gain;
    Assign root of the current tree = P;
    Assign properties = properties - P;
    for each value V of P
      Create a branch of the tree labeled with V;
      Assign examples_V = subset of examples with values V
      for property P;
      Append ID3_tree (examples_V, properties) to branch V
```

The information gain is calculated according to the notion of information *entropy*; roughly speaking, it involves a formula of the form $\Sigma k \log k$, where $k$ is the number of training examples pertaining to a particular property (such as color) or a particular value of the property (such as red).

To illustrate the basic idea of ID3, here we use a simple example. The training data are shown in Table 5.1. Our goal is to learn the concept of high or low profit.

First, we calculate the entropy in regard to all the possible outcomes (regardless of the properties): high or low profit. For example, we start with computing H (for overall training set):

$$H = -\tfrac{3}{8} * \log \tfrac{3}{8} - \tfrac{5}{8} * \log \tfrac{5}{8} = 0.955$$

The remaining process of computing can be captured using a table format [see Chen (1999) for details].

On the basis of our calculation, property color with the largest information gain, is selected. The first level of the ID3 tree is shown in Figure 5.1a, with color as the root, and values of color as leaves. Identifiers of examples are attached with the leaf nodes.

The recursive process continues for a leaf with training examples with mixed results of profits. At the nodes of "black," we have three properties to choose: "Size," "Made-in," and "On-sale." The training set involved here contains only three elements, namely, instances with ID 1, 5, and 7. Suppose the property "Made-in" was chosen after the information gain is calculated (please verify it). A subtree with root "made-in" is then constructed, as shown in Figure 5.1b. Since both instances 1 and 7 are made in the United States, and both have low profit, we have reached the leaf nodes, and no more subtrees should be further considered. At the node "white," there is only one instance 8, so it is a leaf node, and no subtree construction is needed. This is the same as in the case of node "Gray," where both instances 4 and 6 are in the same classification of profit "high." Finally, at the node "brown," the two instances 2 and 3 have different profit classifications, so a recursive process of subtree construction should be carried out. Suppose the property "Size" is chosen

**Table 5.1   Training Example for ID3**

| ID | Color (C) | Size (S) | Made in (M) | On sale (O) | Profit? |
|----|-----------|----------|-------------|-------------|---------|
| 1  | Black (Bl) | M | USA | Y | Low |
| 2  | Brown (Br) | L | USA | N | High |
| 3  | Brown (Br) | M | USA | Y | Low |
| 4  | Gray (G) | L | USA | Y | High |
| 5  | Black (Bl) | S | Foreign | Y | High |
| 6  | Gray (G) | M | Foreign | Y | High |
| 7  | Black (Bl) | S | USA | N | Low |
| 8  | White (W) | M | USA | N | High |

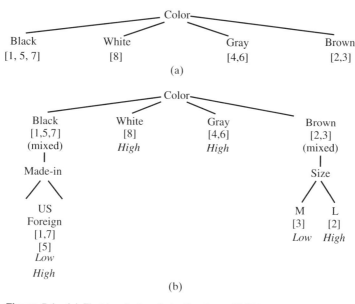

**Figure 5.1**   (a) First level of an induction tree; (b) ID3 tree constructed.

(please verify), the subtree can be constructed as shown in Figure 5.2b. Since sizes M and L can distinguish the profit, we have reached leaf nodes, and no further construction is needed.

The tabular format shown in Table 5.1 clearly indicates the step-by-step process of the ID3 algorithm. Note that there are only two classifications (profit high or low) are involved in the classification. However, the tabular format calculation can be generalized to the case where more than two classifications exist. In this case, more columns are needed.

ID3 has been proven a very useful method, yet there are many restrictions that make this algorithm not applicable in many real-world situations. For example, the data could be bad (when two or more identical attribute sets give different results), missing data, showing a continuous variable, as well as others. C4.5 was developed to deal with these problems, and can be considered as an enhancement of ID3. Issues considered include bad or missing data, continuous variables, as well as large data size. Specific techniques have been introduced to deal with these issues. For example, bagging produces replicate training sets by sampling with replacement from the training instances, and boosting uses all instances at each replication, but maintains a weight for each instance in the training set.

### 5.3.1.2   Scalability and Decision Tree Induction   Most decision tree algorithms assume that the training samples reside in the main memory. This restriction limits the scalability of data mining algorithms for data mining, because the decision tree construction becomes inefficient due to swapping of

the training samples between memory and disks. Early strategies for inducing decision trees from large databases include discretizing continuous attributes and sampling data at each node, or partitions the data into subsets that individually can fit into memory, and then builds a decision tree from each subset. More recently, algorithms have been developed to directly address the scalability issue. New algorithms, such as SLIQ and SPRING propose presorting techniques on disk-resident data sets that are too large to fit in memory, and both define the use of new data structures to facilitate the tree construction. Since the result of decision tree induction can be used for classification, the SLIQ algorithm will be briefly discussed in the context of data classification (Sections 5.5.1 and 5.10.2).

### 5.3.2 Variations of Decision Trees

Due to the popularity of decision trees, many useful forms have been developed, ranging from simple data structures without employing induction to rather complicated structures. The following is a brief outline of several variations:

- *Binary decision trees* are simple data structures for classification that draw decision region boundaries through constructing a binary tree. They make use of the search order property of binary search trees: when the tree is traversed, starting from the root, a comparison is made at each nonleaf node. If the search key value is smaller than the key, traverse the left subtree; otherwise, traverse the right subtree. Each leaf node contains a classification result.
- *Linear decision trees* are similar to binary decision trees, except that the inequality computed at each node takes on an arbitrary linear form that depend on multiple variables.
- *Classification and regression trees* (CARTs) are binary decision trees, which split a single variable at each node. As a unique feature, during the tree construction process, CART performs a recursively search on all variables to find an optimal splitting rule for each node.
- *Chi-squared automatic interaction detector* (CHAID) is a nonbinary decision tree. Just like in the case of binary trees, the decision or split made at each node is based on a single variable, but multiple branches can be produced. The decision of which variable and what split values to use is based on a chi-squared ($\chi^2$) analysis of the output/input variable.

### 5.3.3 Rule Induction

Another kind of induction useful to data mining is rule induction, which was introduced in Section 5.2. We have already seen simple examples of rule induction using generalization. In the next section (Section 5.4), we will discuss characterization rules, which demonstrate another way of rule induction.

In addition, rule induction can be used in conjunction with tree induction. In fact, rule induction can serve as a postprocessing of tree induction using ID3. For example, in our previous case, we can obtain the following rule: "If color is brown and size is medium, then profit is low." In general, a rule can be constructed by following a particular path from root to a leaf in the decision tree, with variables and their values involved in all the nonleaf nodes as the condition, and the classification variable as the consequence.

### 5.3.4  Inductive Learning and Knowledge Discovery

Although inductive learning is important, it has been noted that there are some problems with inductive machine learning for knowledge discovery (Cios et al. 1998). Disadvantages include the facts that generated hypotheses are not probabilistic in nature, methods cannot cope with inconsistent examples, the generated hypotheses are very sensitive to small changes in the training examples, and results of decision trees can be difficult to interpret for large training data.

Another particular problem is scaling up, which was addressed in Chapter 2. In order to deal with large size of database, we can split the data in the database into several disjoint subsets and generate rules for each subset, then combine the result. Another approach is to discretize values of continuous variables.

In order to deal with the problem with the large number of features recorded in a database, we can perform feature selection. Alternatively, we can randomly choose disjoint subsets of features and run machine learning algorithms on the databases after the features are reduced. A better approach is to rank the features and use only the features with highest rankings.

## 5.4  ATTRIBUTE-ORIENTED INDUCTION FOR CHARACTERIZATION

### 5.4.1  Concept Description and Attribute-Oriented Induction

If tree induction and rule induction are examples of extending machine learning techniques to data mining, then *attribute-oriented induction* (AOI) is a perfect example to illustrate algorithmic nature of the new breed of data mining methods. Attribute-oriented data mining employs the basic idea of inductive learning, but it also incorporates *concept hierarchies* as background knowledge. A hierarchy of appliances is shown in Figure 5.2, where items at the leaf level are primitive data, while items in the nonleaf nodes represent a more general (or more abstract) concept. For example, washer or dryer can be generalized to a more abstract concept called *laundry items*, while

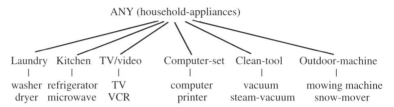

**Figure 5.2**   An appliance hierarchy.

refrigerator or microwave can be generalized to kitchen items, and so on. In addition, laundry items, kitchen items, as well as other items can be further generalized to "ANY (household-appliances)." Note that the level of the hierarchy could be arbitrary, and the tree does not have to be balanced.

In order to understand the role of attribute-oriented induction in data mining, recall that in Chapter 2 we noted that data mining could be classified into descriptive data mining and predictive data mining. Concept description is the most basic form of descriptive data mining. It describes a given set of task-relevant data in a concise and summarative manner, presenting interesting general properties of the data.

Concept description can take one of the two forms: characterization or comparison (or discrimination):

- *Characteristic rules* are assertions that characterize the concept satisfied by all the data stored in the database. A characteristic rule summarizes and describes a collection of data, called the *target class*. (Concept description is also called class description; however, as we will see soon, it should not be confused with classification rules.) For example, one may want to characterize what kind of people bought houses priced from upper $400,000 in West Omaha. Characteristic rules are the fundamental form of concept description.

- *Comparison rules* are assertions that discriminate one class from some other class(es). A comparison rule summarizes and distinguishes one collection of data, called the target class, from other collection(s) of data, collectively called the *contrasting class(es)*. For example, one may want to characterize what kind of people have bought houses from upper $400,000 in West Omaha, versus what kind of people bought BMWs in Nebraska. Since comparison rules can be viewed as a combination of two ore more characteristic rules, we will emphasize characteristic rules.

Attribute-oriented induction provides an effective mechanism to achieve characterization. The AOI approach consists of the various techniques, such as data focusing, data generalization by attribute removal or attribute generalization, count and aggregate value accumulation, attribute generalization control, and generalization data visualization.

The basic idea of using AOI for characterization can be illustrated using the following example. Suppose that we have a student relation in a sample university database consisting of the following attributes (fields): name, category, major, birth-place and grade point average (GPA). In addition, we have a concept hierarchy table which is a concept tree organized as an IS-A hierarchy (e.g., "music" and "history" can be generalized into "art," while "junior" and "senior" can be generalized into "undergraduate"). Now we want to find out something interesting about graduate students. A four-step algorithm for learning a characteristic rule can be performed as follows.

*Step 1.* The extraction of the task-relevant data by performing selection, projection, and join on the relevant relations (such as dropping the student name attributes, since we are not interested in individual students).

*Step 2.* The attribute-oriented induction process; generalization should be performed on attributes by substituting each attribute value with its higher-level concept (such as replacing "physics" by "science").

*Step 3.* The simplification of the generalized relation (e.g., removal of duplication).

*Step 4.* The transformation of the final relation into a logic formula.

The following is a sample rule that may be produced by the discovery process and can be used to produce an intensional answer:

> A graduate student is either a citizen born in this conutry with an excellent GPA or a foreign student majoring in science with a good GPA.

Note that this rule was not explicitly stated anywhere in the database. Rather, it is *derived* from the stored data. The most popular format of a database rule takes the format of "IF $C_1$ THEN $C_2$," or $C_1 \rightarrow C_2$. In fact, a rule is not necessary to cover all instances. If a rule is almost always correct, then it is called a strong rule.

Concept hierarchies are used as background knowledge for data mining. According to Han and Kamber (2000), there are four major types of concept hierarchies. The following two are quite basic:

- *Schema Hierarchy.* This is a partial order among attributes in the database schema, such as street, city, state, region, country. Typically, a schema hierarchy specifies a data warehouse dimension, and a set of schema hierarchies can play a very important role in OLAP, as well as data cube construction.

- *Set Grouping Hierarchy.* This organizes values for a given attribute or dimension into groups of constants orange values. For example, ages can be grouped to chidren-under-10, teenagers, and so on, which can further be grouped to young, middle-aged, and senior. Note that each level of this hierarchy has the purpose similar to discretizing values into ranges.

In addition, there are two other types of concept hierarchies:

- *Operation-Derived Hierarchy.* This is based on operations specified by users, experts, or the data mining system. Such hierarchies can be obtained through data clustering algorithms or other methods.
- *Rule-Based Hierarchy.* This is generated when a portion of the concept hierarchy is defined by a set of rules and is evaluated dynamically.

### 5.4.2   Remarks on Attribute-Oriented Induction

Because of the popularity of this method, we offer the following comments:

1. *Relationship with Machine Learning.* It is interesting to note the difference in philosophies and basic assumptions between AOI and learning-from-example learning paradigm. While both positive and negative samples are used in learning-from-example (positive used for generalization, negative for specialization or to avoid over-generalization), positive samples only are used in data mining (Han and Kamber 2000). But this is not to say data mining cannot use negative examples at all. There is just no need in most cases. Actually using negative example demonstrates nonmonotonic reasoning. Another difference noted by Han and Kamber (2000), concerning the methods of generalizations, is more technical: although machine learning methods (such as ID3) generalizes on a tuple by tuple basis, data mining generalizes on an attribute by attribute basis.

2. *Improvement of Attribute-Oriented Induction.* For example, Carter and Hamilton (1998) presented generalized database relation (GDBR) and fast, incremental generalization and regeneralization (FIGR) as two enhancements of attribute-oriented generalization. GDBR and FIGR are both $O(n)$ and, as such, are optimal. GDBR is an online algorithm and requires only a small, constant amount of space. FIGR also requires a constant amount of space that is generally reasonable (although under certain circumstances, may grow large). FIGR is incremental, allowing changes to the database to be reflected in the generalization results without rereading input data. FIGR also allows fast regeneralization to both higher and lower levels of generality without rereading input.

3. *Concept Description Using Data Cubes.* As noted by Chen et al. (1996), there are two general approaches to concept characterization; the data cube OLAP-based approach and the attribute-oriented induction approach. Both are attribute- or dimension-based generalization approaches. The attribute-oriented induction approach can be implemented using either relational or data cube structures. Similarly, concept comparison can be performed using the attribute-oriented induction or data cube approach. Generalized tuples from the target and contrasting classes can be quantitatively compared and contrasted. Both characterization and comparison descriptions (which form a concept description) can be visualized in the same generalized relation,

crosstab, or quantitative rule form, although they are displayed with different interestingness measures (which also indicate different aspects of uncertainty to be focused in these two kinds of concept description).

4. *Scalability and Efficiency of Concept Description.* In comparison with machine learning algorithms, database-oriented concept description leads to efficiency and scalability in large databases and data warehouses. Concept description mining can be performed incrementally, in parallel, or in a distributed manner, by making minor extensions to the basic methods involved.

5. *Wide Applications of Attribute-Oriented Induction.* Attribute-oriented induction is very useful, because it can be used as a stand-alone technique, or to be used in combination with other tasks. As we will see, attribute-oriented induction can be used by many data mining methods. For example, it can be used in multilevel association rules (as briefly discussed in Section 5.7.7). AOI can also be useful in clustering. Yet another example can be found in Chapter 9, where we discuss how AOI can be used to aid intelligent query answering.

### 5.4.3 Uncertainty and Attribute-Oriented Induction

An important issue is to examine the uncertainty involved in attribute-oriented data mining. For example, the measures used to indicate differences between characterization and comparison descriptions based on attribute-oriented include the t-weight (for tuple typicality) and d-weight (for tuple discriminability):

- The *t weight* for $q_a$ (a generalized tuple describing the target class) is the percentage of tuples of the target class from the initial working relation that are covered by $q_a$.
- The *d weight* for $q_a$ (a generalized tuple that covers some tuples of the target class) is the ratio of the number of tuples from the initial target class $C_j$ working relation (which is a generalized relation) that are covered by $q_a$ to the total number of tuples in both the initial target class and contrasting class working relations that are covered by $q_a$.

The connection between AOI and uncertainty also exists on a larger scope. For example, one particular aspect related to uncertainty is the difficulty of identifying incomplete, redundant or incorrect tuples in scientific and business applications. In order to support discovering processes in such databases, researchers have proposed various algorithms to derive rules using techniques of knowledge discovery and data mining. For example, Kawano and Hasegawa (1996) constructed a version space based on generalized relations, which are derived by an attribute-oriented induction algorithm. Furthermore, based on information-theoretic analysis, the quality of derived rules can be evaluated to decide the preferable sequence of generalizing path for attributes and the final abstract level. An attribute-oriented induction algorithm with entropy-based cost functions was proposed, and characteristics of derived optimum rules using an experimental model could then be explained.


## 5.5   DATA CLASSIFICATION

### 5.5.1   Basics of Data Classification

We now turn to the data mining task of classification. As indicated earlier, classification is similar to prediction as discussed in predictive data mining, although works on discrete variables. Classification involves associating an observation with one of several labels called classes. Data classification is the process that finds the common properties among a set of objects in a database and classifies them into different classes, according to a classification model (also called a *classifier*). To construct such a classification model, a sample database is treated as the training set. The objective of the classification is to first analyze the training data and develop an accurate description or a model for each class using the attributes (referred to as *features* in pattern recognition literature) available in the data, and then to use this model to classify the data based on the values of attributes (Chen et al. 1996). From this description, the task of classification is very similar to characterization as discussed in the previous section. However, characterization may be concerned with only some of the most important attributes, not necessarily all of them, as in the case classification. Another difference is that characterization usually employs symbolic reasoning techniques (such as attribute-oriented induction), while classification does not. Because of its close relationship with pattern recognition, which is concerned with many scientific applications, classification usually resorts to numeric measures (such as entropy) to control the model construction process, as well as its accuracy.

Another interesting connection is the relationship between data mining tasks of classification and induction. Classification models can be effectively constructed using some form of induction; for example, classification based on decision trees is popular. Note that the data mining task of tree induction or rule induction provides an effective way (but not the only way) for construction of models that can be used for classification. We should also note that the emphasis of classification is to classify the data, and the classifier may not necessarily be constructed using induction techniques. Since we have already discussed tree induction and rule induction, and since some other methods useful for classification (e.g., artificial neural networks) will be discussed later in Chapters 6 and 7, in the rest of this section, we will provide some remarks only on classification.

Data classification has been studied substantially in statistics, machine learning, neural networks and expert systems. However, most of the techniques developed in machine learning and statistics may encounter the problem of scaling-up. They may perform reasonably well in relatively small databases but may suffer the problem of either poor performance or the reduction of classification accuracy when the training data set grows very large, even though a database system has been taken as a component in some of the methods, such as neural networks. Methods for performance improvement have been proposed. For example, a fast data classifier, called *Supervised Learning In Quest* (SLIQ), was proposed for mining classification rules in large databases (Mehta et al. 1996). SLIQ is a decision tree classifier that can handle both numeric and categorical attributes. It uses a novel presorting technique in the tree growing phase. This sorting procedure is integrated with breadth-first tree-pruning algorithm that is inexpensive, and results in compact and accurate trees. The combination of these techniques enables it to scale for large data sets and classify data sets irrespective of the number of classes, attributes, and examples. An approach, called *metalearning*, was proposed, which is able to learn how to combine several base classifiers, which are learned from subsets of data. Efficient scaling-up to larger learning problems can hence be achieved (Chen et al. 1996).

Note that in most prior work on decision tree generation, a single attribute is considered at each level for the branching decision. However, in some classification tasks, the class identity in some cases is not so dependent on the value of a single attribute, but instead, depends on the combined values of a set of attributes. In this case, a two-phase method for multiattribute extraction can be used to improve the efficiency of deriving classification rules in a large training dataset. An attribute that is useful in inferring the group identity of a data tuple is said to have a good inference power to that group identity. Given a large training set of data tuples, the first phase (the feature extraction phase) is applied to a subset of the training database with the purpose of identifying useful features that have good inference power to group identities. In the second phase (feature combination phase), those features extracted form the first phase are evaluated together and multiattribute predicates with strong inference power are identified. It is noted that the inference power can be improved significantly by utilizing multiple attribute sin predicates, showing the advantage of using multiattribute predicates.

As an example of recent development in data classification, we can mention the approach of *support vector machines* (SVMs) for pattern classification (Burges 1998). Designed for two-group classification problems, the method attempts to separate points belonging to two given datasets in $n$-dimensional real space $R^n$ by a nonlinear surface defined by a kernel function. The nonlinear surface in $R^n$ is typically linear in its parameters and can be represented as a linear function in a higher-dimensional space. The original points of the two sets can be mapped into this dimensional space. The two sets can be linearly separated in this dimensional space by choosing a suitable kernel function. The main idea behind this method is to separate the classes with a surface that maximizes the margin between them.

## 5.5.2 Classification Accuracy

In order to estimate error rates for classification accuracy, we can use the partitioning method introduced in Chapter 2, where two independent data sets are used: a training set (consisting of two thirds of training samples), and a test set (containing the remaining training samples). This method is used for data set with large number of samples. Alternatively, we can use cross-validation: first, we divide the data set into $k$ subsets of samples, and use $k - 1$ subsets as training data and one subsample as test data. This is referred to as $k$-fold cross-validation. This method works well for data set with moderate size. Finally, for small size data, we can use the so-called bootstrapping technique, which works in a "leave-one-out" fashion.

In Chapter 6, we will discuss Bayesian networks. Bayesian networks can be viewed from several perspectives. In Chapter 6, Bayesian networks are treated as a structured representation. However, Bayesian networks can also be viewed as a classifier, and the probabilities propogated in a Bayesian network is related to classification accuracy.

## 5.5.3 Aggregation Semantics for Classification Rules

The discussion provided above are mainly concerned with how to carry out classification. We now turn to another aspect of classification, which is mainly concerned with a more fundamental issue of classification, namely, the semantics (or the meaning) of classification. In Chapter 3 we discussed aggregation semantics in integrated OLAP and data mining. We now apply the discussion of aggregation semantics to data classification rules. For the segment of sales table shown in Table 5.2, in order to obtain rules to characterize what kinds of prod-

**Table 5.2  A Simple Sales Table**

| RID | Quarter | Product | Product Color | Quantity | Profit |
|-----|---------|---------|---------------|----------|--------|
| 1 | 1st | Hat | Red | 62 | −100 |
| 2 | 1st | Scarf | Blue | 125 | 300 |
| 3 | 1st | Glove | Blue | 270 | 1000 |
| 4 | 2nd | Hat | Red | 116 | 100 |
| 5 | 2nd | Scarf | Blue | 34 | −200 |
| 6 | 2nd | Glove | Red | 52 | −100 |
| 7 | 3rd | Hat | Blue | 10 | −400 |
| 8 | 3rd | Scarf | Red | 37 | −300 |
| 9 | 3rd | Glove | Blue | 48 | −200 |
| 10 | 4th | Hat | Red | 412 | 6000 |
| 11 | 4th | Scarf | Blue | 206 | 200 |
| 12 | 4th | Glove | Blue | 149 | 300 |

ucts are profitable, we may first map the value of profit to a Boolean function "yes" or "no." (Of course, we may also use a more sophisticated multiple classification; e.g., profit 10,000 < profit < 20,000 will be classified as "low" profit).

Classification rules can be discovered at the primary level of data (which can also be called *granularity*). For example, we may have the following rule (Parsaye 1999):

```
Rule 1:
        If ProdColor = Blue
        then Profitable = No
        with confidence 0.75
```

Alternatively, we may apply aggregate functions on each particular kind of product, and then at aggregation level, there is only one result (tuple) per each particular aggregation, so confidence will no longer make any sense. For example, if we apply the aggregation operations as supported by DATA CUBE operator as proposed in Gray et al. (1996), we will get the following summary data as shown in Table 5.3.

The following rule can be obtained:

```
Rule 1′:
        If ProdColor = Blue
        then Profitable = Yes
```

Note that rules 1 and 1′ are not consistent with each other, because rule 1 indicates blue products are likely not profitable while rule 1′ indicates that they are. There is an inconsistency of knowledge discovered at the aggregation levels and at the granularity level. This is just an example of "anomalies" that may occur for data mining involving aggregation—knowledge discovered at the granularity level may not (and usually not) be able to correctly derive results obtained at aggregation level. Since knowledge discovered at different levels have different semantics, there is no general answer to the question of "which one is correct" when a kind of inconsistency exists. A careful study should be carried out for a deeper analysis before some meaningful insight can be reached. We will revisit this issue through a case study (to be presented in Chapter 8).

**Table 5.3    A Summary Sales Table**

| Quarter | Product | Product Color | Quantity | Profit |
|---------|---------|---------------|----------|--------|
| ALL | ALL | Blue | ALL | 640 |

## 5.6   CLUSTERING METHODS

### 5.6.1   General Aspects of Clustering Methods

If attribute-oriented data mining demonstrate something "new" from symbolic AI, then clustering analysis demonstrates the basic idea of using "old" techniques developed in pattern recognition for data mining. Here the term "pattern" is used in a narrow sense, although patterns can also be extended to conceptual patterns. Clustering algorithms can be viewed from different perspective, such as a mechanism for data reduction (as discussed in Chapter 2) and a mechanism for unsupervised learning (discussed further in Chapter 6).

*Clustering* refers to the process of grouping physical or abstract objects into classes of *similar* objects. It is a form of *unsupervised* classification (or learning). A *cluster* is a collection of data objects that are similar to one another within the collection and are dissimilar to the objects in other clusters. Clustering analysis helps construct meaningful partitioning of a large set of objects based on a "divide and conquer" methodology which decomposes a large scale system into smaller components to simplify design and implementation (Chen et al. 1996).

The quality of clustering can be assessed using a measure of dissimilarity of objects, which can be computed for various types of data, including interval-scaled, binary, nominal, ordinal, and ratio-scaled variables, or combinations of these variable types.

As the unsupervised classification of patterns (observations, data items, or feature vectors) into groups (clusters), clustering is a difficult problem combinatorially, and differences in assumptions and contexts in different communities have slowed down the occurrence of transfer of useful generic concepts and methodologies. Data clustering has been studied in statistics, machine learning, spatial databases, and data mining areas with different emphases. For example, clustering analysis, when studied as a branch of statistics, has focused mainly on distance-based clustering analysis. These approaches assume that all the data points are given in advance and can be scanned frequently. They do not have linear scalability with stable clustering quality. In the context of machine learning, *clustering analysis* often refers to unsupervised learning (since the classes that an object belongs to are not prespecified) or conceptual clustering (since the distance measurement may not be based on geometric distance). Classes are defined as collections of objects whose intracluster similarity is high and intercluster similarity is low. The method of clustering analysis in conceptual clustering is mainly based on probability analysis. Clustering analysis in large databases has been studied recently in the database community.

Data mining is one of four major application areas of clustering (the other three are image segmentation, object and character recognition, and document retrieval). As a data mining task, data clustering identifies clusters, or densely populated regions, according to some distance measurement, in a large,

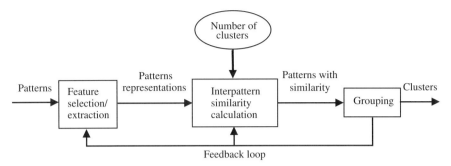

**Figure 5.3**  Stages in clustering.

multidimensional data set. Given a large set of multidimensional data points, the data space is rarely uniformly occupied by the data points. Data clustering identifies the sparse and the crowded places, and hence discovers the overall distribution patterns of the data set.

Stages of data clustering are depicted in Figure 5.3. There are three main steps, including attribute (feature) selection/extraction, interpattern similarity calculation (in many cases, this is done in accordance with the user specified number of clusters), and clustering. Note that there is an iterative process, where the clustering result is subject to further feature selection and extraction.

As a study developed in many other scientific fields (such as pattern recognition), the quality of a clustering result depends on both the similarity measure used by the method and its implementation. However, in the context of data mining, the quality of a clustering method is also measured by its ability to discover some or all of the hidden patterns.

Requirements of clustering in data mining are concerned with several crucial factors:

- *Scalability.* Many clustering algorithms were developed during the pre-data mining era, and most of them assume the entire data can reside in the main memory. It is extremely important to improve the efficiency of existing algorithms to deal with huge size of data. New algorithms have also been developed.

- *Uncertainty.* Clustering methods should be able to deal with noise and outliers. They should also be insensitive to order of input records. Therefore, clustering methods demonstrate many important concerns related to both data mining and uncertain reasoning.

- *Interpretability and usability.* In the context of data mining, clustering means much more than just grouping similar objects together. In order to make the obtained results actionable rules, it is extremely important to interpret the results so that they can be used for guiding future activities. This task is not covered in many traditional clustering methods, and it remains an important issue to be further explored for data mining.

- *Flexibility.* Due to the diversity of data and the diversity of user needs, clustering methods should be able to deal with different types of attributes, to discover clusters with arbitrary shape, to impose minimal requirements for domain knowledge to determine input parameters for modeling, to support high dimensionality, and to incorporate user-specified constraints.

Current clustering techniques do not address all the requirements adequately. Therefore, many problems and challenges still exist for clustering-based data mining methods.

## 5.6.2    Typical Clustering Algorithms

Two major types of clustering are hierarchical and partitioning. *Hierarchical* methods produce a nested series of partitions, whereas *partitioning* methods produce only one. Factors affecting clustering techniques include

- *Agglomerative versus Divisive.* An agglomerative approach begins with each pattern in a distinct singleton cluster, and successively merges clusters together until a stopping criterion is satisfied. A divisive method begins with all patterns in a single cluster and performs splitting until a stopping criterion is met.
- *Monothetic versus Polythetic.* This aspect relates to the sequential or simultaneous use of features in the clustering process.
- *Hard versus Fuzzy.* During the execution of the algorithm, each pattern can be allocated to a single cluster ("hard") or to several clusters ("fuzzy").

More remarks on several clustering algorithms follow. A *hierarchical* algorithm yields a dendrogram representing the nested grouping of patterns and similarity levels at which groupings change. Most hierarchical clustering algorithms are variants of the single-link, complete-link, and minimum-variance algorithms. The single and complete-link algorithms are most popular. These two algorithms differ in the way they characterize the similarity between a pair of clusters. In the single-link method, the distance between two clusters is the minimum of the distances between all pairs of patterns drawn from the two clusters, while in the complete-link algorithm, the distance between two clusters is the maximum of all pairwise between patterns in the two clusters. In either case, two clusters are merged to form a larger cluster according to minimum distance criteria. The complete-link algorithm produces tightly bound or compact clusters. The single-link algorithm, by contrast, suffers from a chain effect. The single-link algorithm is more versatile than the complete-link algorithm. The complete-link algorithm produce more compact result and more useful hierarchies in many applications.

A *partitioning* clustering algorithm obtains a single partition of the data instead of a clustering structure, such as the dendrogram produced by a hierarchical technique. A problem accompanying the use of a partitioning algorithm is the choice of the number of desired output clusters. The partitioning techniques usually produce clusters by optimizing a criterion function defined either locally (on a subset of the patterns) or globally (defined over all of the patterns). The most intuitive and frequently used criterion function used in this technique is the *objective function-based method* (or *squared-error criterion*). The *k-means algorithm* is the simplest and most commonly used algorithm employing such criterion. Clustering algorithms are used to find groups of similar data points among the input patterns. *k*-Means clustering is an effective algorithm to extract a given number of clusters of patterns from a training set. Once done, the cluster locations can be used to classify patterns into distinct classes. Alternatively, minimal spanning tree (MST) can be used for graph-theoretic clustering.

The following examples illustrate the wide variety of clustering algorithms.

1. *k-nearest-Neighbor Clustering.* This method illustrates the basic idea of using probability density estimation with variable-size regions. In this method, the number of patterns within a region is fixed, but the region size vary depending on the data. The method assigns each unlabeled pattern to the cluster of its nearest labeled neighbor patter, provided the distance to that labeled neighbor is below a threshold. The process continues until all patterns are labeled or no additional labeling occurs. This method is based on learning by analogy. Nearest-neighbor classifiers are instance-based. They are also called "lazy learners," because they store all training samples, but do not build a classifier until a new sample needs to be classified. In contrast, decision tree induction discussed earlier and artificial neural networks using backpropagation (to be discussed in Chapter 6) construct the classification structure in advance.

2. *Search-Based Techniques.* These are used to obtain the optimum value of the criterion function and are divided into deterministic and stochastic search techniques. Deterministic search techniques guarantee an optimal partition by performing exhaustive enumeration. On the other hand, the stochastic search techniques generate a near-optimal partition reasonable quickly, and guarantee convergence to optimal partition asymptotically. The deterministic approaches are typically greedy descent approaches, whereas the stochastic approaches permit perturbations to the solutions in non-locally optimal directions also with nonzero probabilities. The stochastic search techniques are either sequential or parallel, while evolutionary approaches are inherently parallel. The simulated annealing approach is a sequential stochastic search technique.

3. *Tabu Search.* Like simulated annealing, is a method designed to cross boundaries of feasibility or local optimality and to systematically impose and

release constraints to permit exploration of otherwise forbidden regions. Tabu search can be used to solve the clustering problem.

Other major categories of clustering methods are:

- *Density-Based Methods.* These algorithms cluster objects based on the notion of density. Clusters can grow according to the density of neighborhood objects (such as used in an algorithm called DBSCAN) or some density function (such as in algorithm DENCLUE).
- *Grid-Based Methods.* These algorithms first map the object space into a finite number of cells that form a grid structure, and then perform clustering on the grid structure. For example, STING is a typical example of a grid-based method based on statistical information stored in grid cells.
- *Model-Based Methods.* The objective of these methods is to optimize the fit between the given data and some mathematical model. When a model-based method is used, it hypothesizes a model for each cluster and finds the best fit of the data to that model. Statistics can be used for constructing the models, as in the case of conceptual clustering. In addition, artificial neural networks, as to be discussed in Chapter 6, can also be used for model construction.

### 5.6.3 Objective Function-Based Clustering

As a concrete approach of clustering, we now take a look at the case of portioning methods. A partitioning method first creates an initial set of $k$ partitions, where parameter $k$ is the number of partitions to construct; then it uses an iterative relocation technique that attempts to improve the partitioning by moving objects from one group to another. Typical partitioning methods include $k$ means, $k$ medoids, CLARANS, and their improvements. Below we study $k$-means and $k$-mode algorithms, which demonstrate the basic idea of objective function-based clustering.

*Algorithms using objective function-based clustering* are also called *squared-error algorithms*. In this category, the method hinges solely on a certain performance index $I$ whose minimization should reveal meaningful structures in the data. The common form used is

$$I = \sum_{i=1}^{n} \sum_{k=1}^{N} u_{ik}^m \|x_k - v_i\|^2 = \sum_{i=1}^{n} \sum_{k=1}^{N} u_{ik}^m d_{ik}^2$$

where $c$ denotes the number of clusters and $u_{ik}$ are elements in the partition matrix $U$, which is used to store all results of clustering (partitioning) the patterns into clusters.

#### 5.6.3.1 *General Aspects of k-Means and k-Mode Algorithms*    As an example of clustering algorithms, let us briefly examine a simple but useful algorithm, namely, the $k$-means algorithm and its generalized form, $k$-mode

algorithm. Both can be stated as an optimization problem, which can be considered as an alternative way of dealing with uncertainty, an aspect has not been examined in this book. $k$-Means algorithm is the simplest and most commonly used algorithm employing a squared error criterion. It starts with a random initial partition and keeps reassigning the patterns to clusters based on the similarity between the pattern and the cluster centers until a convergence criterion is met. The $k$-means algorithm is popular because it is easy to implement, and its time complexity is $O(n)$, where $n$ is the number of patterns. A major problem with this algorithm is that it is sensitive to the selection of the initial partition and may converge to a local minimum of the criterion function value if the initial partition is not properly chosen.

### Algorithm $k$-Means Clustering

*Step 1.* Choose $k$ cluster centers to coincide with $k$ randomly-chosen patterns or $k$ randomly defined points inside the hypervolumn containing the pattern set.

*Step 2.* Assign each pattern to the closest cluster center.

*Step 3.* Recompute the cluster centers using the current luster memberships.

*Step 4.* If a convergence criterion is not met, go to step 2. Typical convergence criteria are: no (or minimal) reassignment of patterns to new luster centers, or minimal decrease in squared error.

The $k$-means algorithm is well known for its efficiency in clustering data sets. However, working only on numeric values prohibits it from being used to cluster real world data containing categorical values. The $k$-modes algorithm (Huang 1998) extended the $k$-means algorithm to clustering categorical data set. The algorithm replaces the means of clusters with modes and uses a frequency-based method to update modes in the clustering process to minimize the clustering cost function.

Partitioning a set of objects in databases into *homogeneous groups or clusters* is a fundamental operation in data mining. Clustering is a popular approach to implementing the partitioning operation. The most distinct characteristic of data mining is that it deals with very large and complex data sets (gigabytes or even terabytes). The data sets often contain millions of objects described by tens, hundreds or even thousands of various types of attributes or variables (interval, ratio, binary, ordinal, nominal, etc.). This requires the data mining operations and algorithms to be scalable and capable of dealing with different types of attributes. In terms of clustering, we are interested in algorithms that can efficiently cluster large data sets containing both numeric and categorical values because such data sets are frequently encountered in applications.

However, the $k$-means algorithm works only on numeric data; that is, the variables are measured on a ratio scale, because it minimizes a cost function by changing the means of clusters. This prohibits it from being used in applications where categorical data are involved. The traditional approach to converting categorical data into numeric values does not necessarily produce meaningful results in the case where categorical domains are not ordered.

The $k$-modes algorithm (Huang 1998) extends the $k$-means method to cluster categorical data by using (1) a simple matching dissimilarity measure for categorical objects, (2) modes instead of means for clusters, and (3) a frequency-based method to update modes in the $k$-means fashion to minimize the clustering cost function of clustering. Because the $k$-modes algorithm uses the same clustering process as the $k$-means one, it preserves the efficiency of the $k$-means algorithm, which is highly desirable for data mining.

### 5.6.3.2 *k-Means Algorithm*   We present the algorithm based on Sun et al. (2000).

Let $X = \{X_1, X_2, \ldots, X_n\}$ denote a set of $n$ objects and $X_i = \{X_{i1}, X_{i2}, \ldots, X_{im}\}$ be an object represented by $m$ attribute values. Let $k$ be a positive integer. The objective of clustering $X$ is to find a partition that divides objects $X$ into $k$ disjoint clusters. For a given $n$, the number of possible partitions is definite but extremely large. It is impractical to investigate every partition in order to find a better one for a classification problem. A common solution is to choose a clustering criterion to guide the search for a partition.

The generalized $k$-means algorithm is to minimize the *cost function*. This can be formulated as the following mathematical programming problem $P(W,Q)$

$$\text{Minimize } P(W,Q) = \sum_{l=1}^{k} \sum_{i=1}^{n} w_{i,l} d(X_i, Q_l)$$

$$\text{Subject to } \sum_{l=1}^{k} w_{i,l} = 1, \ 1 \le i \le n;$$

$$w_{i,l} \in \{0,1\}, \ 1 \le i \le n, \ 1 \le l \le k$$

where $W$ is an $n \times k$ partition matrix, $Q = \{Q_1, Q_2, \ldots, Q_k\}$ is a set of objects in the same object domain, and $d(\cdot,\cdot)$ is the squared Euclidean distance between two objects. Problem $P(W,Q)$ can be solved by iteratively solving the following two problems:

1. Problem $P_1$. Fix $Q = \hat{Q}$ and solve the reduced problem $P(W,\hat{Q})$;
2. Problem $P_2$. Fix $W = \hat{W}$ and solve the reduced problem $P(\hat{W},Q)$.

Problem $P_1$ is solved by

$$w_{i,l} = 1 \ \text{if} \ d(X_i, Q_l) \le d(X_i, Q_t), \ \text{for} \ 1 \le t \le k;$$

or

$$w_{i,t} = 0 \ \text{for} \ t \ne l$$

and problem $P_2$ is solved by

$$q_{l,j} = \frac{\sum_{i=1}^{n} w_{i,l} x_{i,j}}{\sum_{i=1}^{n} w_{i,l}}$$

for $1 \le l \le k$, and $1 \le j \le m$.

Because $P(\cdot, \cdot)$ is nonconvex and the sequence $P(\cdot, \cdot)$ generated by the algorithm is strictly decreasing, after a finite number of iterations the algorithm converges to a local minimum point. The computational cost of the algorithm is $O(Tkn)$, where $T$ is the number of iterations and $n$ the number of objects in the input data set.

The convergent $k$-means algorithm and its ANN equivalent, the Kohonen net (see Chapter 6), have been used to cluster large data sets. The reasons behind the popularity of the $k$-means algorithm are as follows:

- Its time complexity is $O(nkl)$, where $n$ is the number of patterns, $k$ is the number of clusters, and $l$ is the number of iterations taken by the algorithm to converge. Typically, $k$ and $l$ are fixed in advance and so the algorithm is O($n$).
- Its space complexity is $O(k + n)$, because it requires additional space to store the data matrix.
- It is order-independent.

However, the $k$-means algorithm is sensitive to initial seed selection and even in the best case, it can produce only hyperspeherical clusters. Note also that the $k$-means algorithm presented above works only with numeric values. Because it often terminates at a local optimum, the initial partition often determines the quality of final results.

### 5.6.3.3  The k-Modes Algorithm

In principle, the formulation of problem $P$ as mentioned in a previous section is also valid for categorical and mixed-type objects. The cause that the $k$-means algorithm cannot cluster categorical objects is its dissimilarity measure and the method used to solve problem $P_2$. These barriers can be removed by making the following modifications to the $k$-means algorithm:

- Using a simple matching dissimilarity measure for categorical objects
- Replacing means of clusters by modes
- Using a frequency-based method to find the modes to solve problem $P_2$

Let $X,Y$ be two categorical objects described by $m$ categorical attributes. The dissimilarity measure between $X$ and $Y$ can be defined by the total mismatches of the corresponding attribute categories of the two objects. This measure is often referred to as simple matching. Formally, we have

$$d_1(X,Y) = \sum_{j=1}^{m} \delta(x_j, y_j)$$

where

$$\delta(x_j, y_j) = \begin{cases} 0 & (x_j = y_j) \\ 1 & (x_j \neq y_j) \end{cases}$$

Let $X$ be a set of categorical objects described by categorical attributes, $A_1, A_2, \ldots, A_m$; a mode of $X = \{X_1, X_2, \ldots, X_n\}$ is a vector $Q = [q_1, q_2, \ldots, q_m]$ that minimizes

$$D(X,Q) = \sum_{i=1}^{n} d_1(X_i, Q)$$

Here, $Q$ is not necessarily an element of $X$. Let $n_{c_{k,j}}$ be the number of objects having the $k$th category $c_{k,j}$ in attribute $A_j$, and $f_r(A_j = c_{k,j}|X) = n_{c_{k,j}}/n$ the relative frequency of category $c_{k,j}$ in $X$.

***Theorem 5.1***   The function $D(X,Q)$ is minimized if and only if

$$f_r(A_j = q_j|X) \geq f_r(A_j = c_{k,j}|X)$$

for $q_j \neq c_{k,j}$, for all $j = 1, \ldots, m$.

Theorem 5.1 defines a way to find $Q$ from a given $X$, and therefore is important because it allows the $k$-means method to be used to cluster categorical data. The theorem implies that the mode of a data set $X$ is not unique. For example, the mode of set $\{[a,b], [a,c], [c,b], [b,c]\}$ can be either $[a,b]$ or $[a,c]$.

When Theorem 5.1 is used as the dissimilarity measure for categorical objects, the cost function becomes

$$P(W,Q) = \sum_{l=1}^{k} \sum_{i=1}^{n} \sum_{j=1}^{m} w_{i,l} \delta(x_{i,j}, q_{l,j})$$

where $w_{i,l} \in W$ and $Q_l = [q_{l,1}, q_{l,2} \ldots, q_{l,m}] \in Q$.

To minimize the cost function, the basic $k$-means algorithm can be modified by (1) using the simple matching dissimilarity measure to solve $P_1$, and (2) using modes for clusters instead of means and selecting modes according to Theorem 5.1 to solve $P_2$.

As we will see in Section 5.6.5.1, the $k$-means method can be modified to the $k$-medoid algorithm to better dealing with outliers. Another refined *k*-means/*k*-mode algorithm will be presented in Chapter 8, where the algorithm is applied to a case study.

### 5.6.4  Scaling up Clustering Algorithms for Data Mining

Two aspects of clustering are crucial for data mining: the use of some prior knowledge, and the minimization of computational overhead associated with finding structures in high-dimensional data. Clustering with partial supervision is one way for exploiting prior knowledge. The modularization effect delivered by an original context-based clustering is an interesting way to reduce computational effort (Cios et al. 1998). This can be viewed as an instance of application-specific data mining systems discussed in Chapter 2. We can take advantage of the available information about data and apply it actively as part of the overall optimization procedures, because in many applications, a small fraction of the data is available, labeled by the data analysts as reflecting some domain knowledge. Such data mining tips are extremely valuable in the search for a global structure in the database by guiding the mechanisms of clustering (Cios et al. 1998).

As for the second aspect, namely, the minimization of computational overhead associated with finding structures in high-dimensional data, we turn to the issue of scalability. In fact, clustering algorithms are a typical showcase for the important issue of scaling up. Historically, they have been extensively studied in the pattern recognition literature for unsupervised learning. The classical algorithms developed in pattern recognition need to be upgraded to deal with the large-scale applications in data mining. Additional approaches to clustering based on genetic algorithms (to be discussed in Chapter 7), Tabu search and simulated annealing are optimization techniques, and are also restricted to reasonably small data sets. An analysis of complexity for each individual clustering algorithm would confirm this.

In the following, we offer a general remark (based on Jain et al. 1999) related to scalability of clustering algorithms (not necessarily restricted to partitioning methods). In the next two subsections, we will examine several methods for scalable partitioning clustering and scalable hierarchical clustering.

In the context of data mining, two things should be noted about clustering algorithms: (1) in order to make the clustering methods fully suitable for data mining purposes, one should think of a certain focusing of the activities therein to carry out more efficient data mining pursuits; and (2) there is a need for some back end of the method that develops some meaningful, non-numeric descriptors (summarization) of the revealed structure. The effort being expended to the design of the front end and back end of the specific clustering method depends heavily on the method itself (Cios et al. 1998). Implementations of conceptual clustering optimize some criterion functions and are typically computationally expensive.

The preceding discussion is concerned mainly with partitioning algorithms. Hierarchical algorithms are more versatile, and are facing various disadvantages as well. For example, the time complexity of hierarchical agglomerative algorithms is $O(n^2 \log n)$, while the space complexity of agglomerative algorithms is $O(n^2)$. A possible solution to the problem of clustering large data sets while only marginally sacrificing the versatility of clusters is to implement more efficient variants of clustering algorithms.

The emerging discipline of data mining has spurred the development of new algorithms for clustering large data sets. Two algorithms of note are the CLARANS algorithm for partitioning method and the BIRCH algorithm for hierarchical method. CLARANS identifies candidate cluster centroids through analysis of repeated random samples from the original data. Because of the use of random sampling, the time complexity is $O(n)$ for a pattern set of $n$ elements. The BIRCH algorithm stores summary information about candidate clusters in a dynamic tree data structure. This tree can be rebuilt when a threshold specifying cluster size is updated manually, or when memory constraints force a change in this threshold. Both algorithms have a time complexity linear in the number of patterns.

The preceding algorithms assume the main memory is able to accommodate the entire pattern set. However, there are applications where the entire data set cannot be stored in the main memory because of its size. There are currently three possible approaches to deal with this problem:

- *Divide and Conquer.* The pattern set can be stored in a secondary memory and subsets of this data clustered independently, followed by a merging step to yield a clustering of the entire pattern set.
- *Incremental Clustering.* The entire data matrix is stored in a secondary memory and data items are transferred to the main memory one at a time for clustering until the limit of main memory is reached. The basic incremental clustering method include the following steps:
  - Assign the first data item to a cluster;
  - Repeat. For the next data item, assign it to either one of the existing clusters or a new cluster using some criterion (e.g., the distance between the new item and the existing cluster centroids) until all the data items are clustered
- *Parallel Implementation.* A parallel implementation of a clustering algorithm may be used.

As an example of these approaches, we will discuss parallel implementation in Section 5.9. Below we will return to the issue of partitioning clustering algorithms, but this time we will focus on scalable algorithms only.

### 5.6.5  Scalable Partitioning Clustering Algorithms

Clustering large applications based upon randomized search consists several new algorithms.

### 5.6.5.1 *PAM (Partitioning around Medoids)*

The $k$-means algorithm is sensitive to outliers since an object with an extremely large value may substantially distort the distribution of data. To deal with this, instead of taking the mean value of the objects in a cluster as a reference point, the *medoid* can be used, which is the most centrally located object in a cluster. This forms the basis of the *k-medoids algorithms*.

The algorithm PAM finds $k$ clusters in $n$ objects by first finding a representative object (called *medoid*, which is the most centrally located point in a cluster) for each cluster. After selecting $k$ medoids, the alogirhtm repeatedly tries to make a better choice of medoids by analyzing all possible pairs of objects such that one object is a medoid and the other is not. Given a set of objects $X$ and the number of clusters $k$, PAM clusters $X$ by finding $k$ medoids (representative objects of clusters) that can minimize the average dissimilarity of objects to their closest medoids. Since PAM can use any dissimilarity measures, it is able to cluster objects with categorical attributes. Ng and Han (1984) have analyzed that the computational complexity of PAM in a single iteration is $O(k(n-k)^2)$ where $n$ is the number of objects in $X$. Obviously, PAM is not efficient when clustering large data set.

### 5.6.5.2 *CLARA (Clustering LARge Applications)*

CLARA utilizes sampling technique to achieve the goal of clustering. PAM is applied to a small subset of data. The idea is that if the sample is selected in a fairly random manner, then it should correctly represent the whole data set, and the representative objects chosen will thus be similar to those chosen from the whole data set. CLARA draws multiple samples and outputs the best clustering out of these samples. The problem with CLARA is that it cannot find the best clustering if any sampled medoid is not among the best $k$ medoids. CLARA (Clustering LARge Application) algorithm is a combination of a sampling procedure and the clustering program PAM. CLARA takes a small sample from a large data set, uses PAM to generate $k$ medoids from the sample, and uses the $k$ medoids to cluster the remaining objects by the rules $\{x \in S_i$ if $d(x, q_i) \le d(x, q_j) \wedge i \ne j\}$, where $1 \le i, j \le k$, $d$ is a dissimilarity measure, if $q_j$ is the medoid of cluster $j$ and $S_i$ is cluster $i$. Its computational complexity basically depends on the computational complexity of PAM that is decided by the size of sample set. In other words, CLARA is efficient in clustering large data sets only if the sample size used by PAM is small. However, for large and complex data sets in data mining application, small samples often cannot represent the genuine distributions of the data. The CLARA solution to this problem is to take several samples and cluster the whole data set several times. Then, the result with the minimal average dissimilarity is selected. Obviously, this increases computation cost.

### 5.6.5.3 CLARANS (Clustering Large Applications based on RANdomized Search)

CLARNS tries to integrate PAM and CLAR by searching only the subset of the data set but not confining itself to any sample at any given time. It draws a sample with some randomness in each step of the search. The clustering process can be presented as searching a graph where every node is a potential solution (i.e., a set of $k$ medoids). The clustering obtained after replacing a single medoid is called the *neighbor of the current clustering*. If a better neighbor is found, CLARANS moves to the neighbor's node and the process is started again, otherwise the current clustering produces a local optimum. If the local optimum is found, CLARANS starts with new randomly selected nodes in search for a new local optimum. CLARANS has been experimentally shown to be more effective than both PAM and CLARA. Several spatial data mining methods have been developed based on CLARANS.

Some drawbacks of CLARANS have been noticed, and focusing methods have been proposed as a remedy. A main problem for CLARANS is that it assumes that the objects to be clustered are all stored in main memory. The drawback is alleviated by integrating CLARANS with efficient spatial access methods, such as $R^*$ trees. [R tree is a data structure for handling spatial object. For a brief discussion on $R$ tree and its variations such as $R^*$ tree, as well as a way of implementation, see Schreck and Chen (2000).] The most computationally expensive step of CLARANS is calculating the total distances between the two clusters. To reduce the cost of this step, one may reduce the number of objects considered. A centroid query returns the most central object of a leaf node of the $R^*$ tree where neighboring points are stored. Only these objects are used to compute the medoids of the clusters. The number of objects taken for consideration is thus reduced. This technique, referred to as *focusing on representative objects*, has the drawback of not considering some objects that may be better medoids. A second technique to reduce computation is to restrict the access to certain objects that do not actually contribute to the computation, with two different focusing techniques: (1) focus on relevant clusters and (2) focus on a cluster. Using the $R^*$ tree structure, computation can be performed only on pairs of objects that can improve the quality of clustering instead of checking all pairs of objects as in the CLARANS algorithm.

### 5.6.6   BIRCH: A Scalable Hierarchical Clustering Algorithm

We use BIRCH (*Balanced Iterative Reducing and Clustering Using Hierarchies*) to illustrate hierarchical scalable clustering methods. A hierarchical clustering method works by grouping data objects into a tree of clusters. If the hierarchical decomposition is performed in a bottom-up fashion, we have *agglomerative* hierarchical clustering; if the decomposition is performed in a top-down fashion, we have *divisive* hierarchical clustering. To compensate for the rigidity of merge or split that becomes the source of high time and space complexity, the quality of hierarchical agglomeration can be improved by analyzing object linkages at each hierarchical partitioning (such as CURE and

Chameleon) or integrating other clustering techniques, such as iterative relocation (as in BIRCH).

Algorithm BIRCH was proposed for clustering large sets of points without using $R$ trees or their variants. The omission of R trees is a reasonable consideration because $R$ trees or their variants are not always available and their construction may be time-consuming. The method is an incremental one with the possibility of adjustment of memory requirements to the size of memory that is available. The algorithm makes use of two concepts: clustering feature (CF) and CF tree. A *clustering feature* (CF) is essentially a summary of the statistics for the given subclusters of points. The clustering features are sufficient for computing clusters and they constitute an efficient storage information method as they summarize information about the subclusters of points instead of storing all points.

A *CF tree* is an in-memory balanced tree with two parameters: branching factor $B$ and threshold $T$. The branching actor specifies the maximum number of children. The threshold parameter specifies the maximum diameter of subclusters stored at the leaves in the tree. By changing the threshold value, we can change the size of the tree. Then nonleaf nodes are storing sums of their children's CFs. The CF tree is built dynamically as data points are inserted. A point is inserted to the closest leaf entry (viz., the subcluster). If the diameter of the subcluster stored in the leaf node after insertion is larger than the threshold value, then the leaf node and possibly other nodes are split. After the insertion of the new point, the information about it is passed towards the root of the tree. Note that the size of the CF tree can be modified by changing the threshold $T$. If the size of the memory that is needed for storing the CF tree is larger than the size of the main memory, then a larger value of the threshold is specified and the CF tree is rebuilt. The rebuild process is performed by building a new tree in a bottom-up fashion, from the leaf nodes of the old tree. The rebuilding process can thus be carried out without the necessity of reading all the points. In fact, in order to build the CF tree, data has to be read just once.

Any clustering algorithm can be used with CF trees. The CPU and I/O costs of the BIRCH algorithm are of order $O(n)$, where $n$ is the total number of data points. A good number of experiments show linear scalability of the algorithm with respect to the number of points, insensibility of the input order, and good quality of clustering of data.

### 5.6.7 Issues of Clustering for Data Mining

In the preceding three subsections we have discussed how to scale up clustering algorithms for data mining. We now take a more general examination on the relationship between clustering and data mining. Jain et al. (1999) noted that since both clustering and data mining are exploratory activity, so clustering methods are well suited for data mining. In fact, clustering is often an important initial step in data mining process. Some of the data mining approaches that use clustering are

- *Database Segmentation.* Clustering methods are used in data mining to segment databases into homogeneous groups. A continuous $k$-means clustering algorithm has been developed for database segmentation.
- *Predictive Modeling.* Data mining can aid the user in discovering potential hypotheses prior to using statistical tools. Predictive modeling uses clustering to group items, then infers rules to characterize the groups and suggest models. In this sense, clustering methods may be integrated with classification.

To relate clustering methods to data mining, we should also note that the proactive role of a potential user in the process of data mining (Cios et al. 1998). In an interactive, goal-driven data mining environment, the following aspects should be considered in the clustering-related tasks.

- Clustering allows information granularity can be obtained at all levels for data mining. Regions of particular interest desire a high information granularity, while regions of low interest deserve coarse information granules. The variable level of information granularity provides a mechanism for expressing the idea of interestingness (one of the eight primitives discussed in Chapter 2).
- Clustering also supports transparency of generated summary of main associations revealed through data mining. The transparency is indicated by understandability of the summary as well as its relevancy to the data mining problem.

Therefore, clustering algorithms can be embedded in the auxiliary framework that implants these data mining requirements. As for the actual techniques employed, methods such as hierarchical clustering and objective function-based clustering are useful for data mining.

We now present some additional issues of using clustering methods for data mining.

1. *Visualization.* An obvious advantage of applying clustering analysis for data mining is related to visualization (particularly for two-dimensional case). In visualization, clusters in large databases can be used, in order to aid human analysts in identifying groups and subgroups that have similar characteristics. Visualization is also related to transparency (an aspect discussed above).

2. *Explanation.* One thing should be kept in mind, however, is that although graphical forms may be acceptable as the final result in engineering applications, they are only visual aids for business applications. It is reasonable to require that the result of clustering should be expressed into logical forms. Additional work is needed for explanation the result. In fact, partly because

of the data normalization usually required in clustering algorithms, the impact of factors on the result should be mapped back before normalization. Work still need to be done in this area.

3. *Spatial Data Mining.* In addition to these basic applications, clustering can aid various specific forms of data mining, such as mining large unstructured databases and spatial data mining. For example, clustering techniques may serve as an important foundation for spatial data mining, which is the process of applying data mining methods on spatial objects. To be more specific, it refers to the extraction of knowledge, spatial relationships, or other interesting patterns not explicitly stored in spatial databases. Discussion on spatial data mining and related issues can be found in Ng and Han (1994), Roddick and Spiliopoulou (1999), and Han and Kamber (2000). In order to perform spatial data mining, spatial data cube construction and spatial OLAP techniques can be used to build a spatial data warehouse so that spatial data mining can be performed in this environment.

### 5.6.8  Clustering and Uncertainty Handling

In addition to the preceding discussions, clustering methods are important to data mining in terms of dealing with uncertainty. The following are some remarks related to this aspect.

1. *Evaluation of Clustering.* Several measures have been developed for evaluating and comparing the effectiveness of various clustering methods. A popular measure is *classifier accuracy*; methods for classifier accuracy include *stratified k-fold cross-validation* (the recommended method for estimating classifier accuracy), as well as "bagging" and "boosting" methods (which can be used to increase overall classification accuracy by learning and combining a series of individual classifiers). Other measures, such as *sensitivity, specificity*, and *precision* are also useful for evaluation of clustering, particularly when the main class of interest is in the minority. (A more general discussion on imbalanced data set was provided in Section 3.5.5.)

2. *Outlier Analysis.* In real-world applications, some data objects do not comply with the general behavior or model of the data. The data objects that are grossly different from, or inconsistent with, the majority of the data, are usually referred to as *outliers* (as originally used in statistics). Outliers can be caused by measurement or execution error; thus they are treated as noise. They may also be the result of inherent data variability. Data mining algorithms tend to minimize the influence of outliers or eliminate them all together. However, this should be done with great care, because from one perspective, the outlier could be noise, but from some other perspective, it could be a piece of treasure. Therefore, outlier detection and analysis becomes a data mining problem, and is referred to as *outlier mining.* The objective of outlier mining is as follows. Given a set of $n$ data points or objects, and $k$ (the expected number of

outliers), find the top $k$ objects that are considerably dissimilar, exceptional, or inconsistent with respect to the remaining data. In order to solve an outlier mining problem, two issues should be dealt with: (1) how to define outlier for a given data set and (2) how to find these outliers efficiently. Outlier analysis is an interesting example of data mining integrated with uncertain reasoning. Methods developed from statistics, as well as OLAP data cube techniques, can be used for outlier mining (Han and Kamber 2000).

3. *Fuzzy Clustering for Data Mining.* Clustering can be aided by uncertain reasoning techniques for data mining, such as fuzzy logic (to be further discussed in Chapter 7), as illustrated in the case of *context-oriented fuzzy clustering* (Cios et al. 1998). Roughly speaking, the term context used here refers to linguistic expressions whose semantics will be incorporated into the clustering process. According to a taxonomy of linguistic contexts exploited in data mining, contexts could be either generic or composite, which could be logical, relational, or regression. An example of composite logical context is "visibility is poor and temperature is low or rain is heavy." An example of composite relational context is "prices of VCR and discount prices of 13-inch TV are similar." An example of composite regression context is "error of linear model $y = f(x, a)$ is negative small."

A context-oriented clustering algorithm is presented in Cios et al. (1998). The conditioning aspect (context sensitivity) of the clustering mechanism has been introduced to a context-oriented clustering algorithm for data mining. However, context-oriented clustering leaves us with a number of contexts and induced clusters. The links (associations) between these entities are assumed by the method but not quantified at all. Quantification of the associations between information granules can be achieved in various ways, as discussed in Cios et al. (1998).

## 5.7  ASSOCIATION RULES

### 5.7.1  Importance of Mining Association Rules

*5.7.1.1  Understanding Associations*    In the business world, association rules are also called *affinity grouping* or *market basket analysis* (MBA). In order to take more precise marketing actions, we should find out why products occur together more (or less) frequently than by random chance. For example, there could be at least two underlying reasons why products "repel" each other. One is that they are substitutes, meaning that they compete in the same market segment. Another is that they serve different market segments, and thus do not compete. In addition, two products may "attach" each other either because they are complements, or because a third product complements both. These distinct reasons can lead to very different marketing strategies (Groth 2000).

### 5.7.1.2 *Actionable and Effective Market Basket Analysis* Market
basket analysis can be very effective in generating actionable information
that leads to strategic marketing decisions. However, subtle and surprising
patterns may emerge when this kind of analysis is carefully applied to
real-world data.

1. We must be careful when considering associations of the type "If customers buy product A, they also tend to buy product B, 40% of the time."
   While looking at these types of associations is common practice, such
   kind of mining tends to generate many useless associations that occur by
   random chance. We should limit our search to only those associations
   that are different from what would happen by random chance, because
   these associations have the best likelihood of leading to actionable marketing decisions. One of the most effective ways of detecting statistically
   significant nonrandom associations (or dependencies) is by using the
   chi-squared test in the context of the dependence framework of market
   basket analysis.

2. We must not blindly discard associations that have "low support" (viz.,
   low frequency of concurrence in the database). The reason is that, while
   low support might be a manifestation of low statistical significance, it can
   also be the result of items that "repel" each other with a very high statistical significance. These associations can be very valuable (Think, for
   example, about the competition between Coke and Pepsi products). The
   focus should be on high statistical significance, and not necessarily on
   high support.

Once we have found groups of items that exhibit statistically significant nonrandom associations, we must further analyze these groups of items to determine exactly what causes their nonrandom associations. For example, if we
know that two products "repel" each other, we need to know why they do; are
they substitutes, or do they address totally different market segments (Groth
2000)? A careful analysis is an important step after the result of data mining
has been obtained.

## 5.7.2 Basics of Association Rules

We now take a closer look at the association rules. Barcode technology has
made it possible for retail organizations to collect and store massive amounts
of sales data, referred to as "basket data." Here we talk about transaction
databases; a *transaction database* is usually a relation consisting of transactions
as tuples (each transaction is a list of items purchased by a customer in one
shopping activity—so just think about your sales receipt). Given a database of
sales transactions (each transaction in the transaction databases has a transaction ID called TID), it is desirable to discover the important associations
among items such that the presence of some items in a transaction will imply

the presence of other items in the same transaction. (*Note*: Here we are not talking about transaction processing!) Association rules are statements of the form "70% of customers that purchase 2% milk will also purchase bread." Finding customer purchase patterns is an important task for many organizations (such as for supermarkets to promote sales).

The constructed association rules take the format of Prolog rule "Head :- Body" (or equivalently: "Body → Head"), which means that *a customer who buys items in the body, also buys the head*. It may also written as LHS → RHS (lefthand side → righthand side).

Two important measures used to indicate the strength of association rules are support and confidence. These two concepts are defined below.

- *Support.* The support for a set is the percentage of transactions that contain all of these items. The support for a rule LHS → RHS (or Body → Head*)* is the support for the set of items LHS ∪ RHS ("LHS and RHS appear together"). The formula used for calculation is as follows:

$$s = \frac{N \text{ transactions involving all items in LHS and RHS of this rule}}{N \text{ total transactions}}$$

  Where $N$ is the number of transactions. This rule is satisfied in the set of transactions $T$ with the support $s$ if and only if at least $s\%$ of transactions in $T$ contain all items appearing in either LHS or RHS. The support is the joint probability of finding LHS and RHS in the same transaction. In other words, support = probability (LHS ∪ RHS).

- *Confidence.* The confidence for a rule LHS → RHS is the percentage of such transactions that also contain all items in RHS. It indicates the degree of correlation between purchases of these sets of items. The formula used for calculation is

$$c = \frac{N \text{ transactions involving all items in LHS and RHS of rule}}{N \text{ transactions involving all items in LHS}}$$

  This rule is satisfied in the set of transactions $T$ with the confidence factor $c$ if and only if at least $c\%$ of transactions in $T$ that satisfy (contain) LHS also satisfy (contain) the RHS. The confidence is the conditional probability in the same transaction of finding RHS having found LHS. In other words, confidence = probability (RHS | LHS).

Both $s$ (i.e., support) and $c$ (i.e., confidence) are represented by a number between 0 and 1 (the percentage involved in the calculation). A threshold (such as 0.1) is used as a cutoff point for support, and a (different) threshold (such as 0.2) is used as a cutoff point for confidence. An association rule can be typically presented as LHS → RHS [*s,c*].

Some authors use the number of transactions as support, confidence, and threshold. It is straightforward to convert from one method to another. For example, if threshold is 0.1 and total transactions are 1000, then the threshold can be converted to 100 (in terms of number of transactions). A rule with support or confidence below threshold is considered as not strong enough to be accepted. The meaning of support and confidence can be studied from an example with initial transaction data shown in Table 5.4.

For convenience of use, the purchase table is grouped by transactions. Some simple association rules can be found as shown in Table 5.5 ($S$ stands for support; $C$, for confidence).

Now let us verify $S$ and $C$ for rule 3. Item in LHS, "color bags," appears in TID = 2, TID = 4; item in RHS, "brown boots," appears in TID = 2. So only TID = 2 involve all items in LHS and RHS. We have the following results (the vertical bars are used to indicate the cardinality of the set, or the number of elements in the set):

$$S = \frac{|\{TID2\}|}{|\{TID1,2,3,4\}|} = 0.25$$

$$C = \frac{|\{TID2\}|}{|\{TID2, \; TID4\}|} = 0.5$$

As another example, let us verify $S$ and $C$ for rule 7 (LHS "jackets" in TIDs 2, 3, 4; RHS "color bags" in TID 2, 4):

**Table 5.4  The Purchase Table for a Large Store**

| TID | Customer | Item | Date | Price, $ | Quantity |
|-----|----------|------|------|----------|----------|
| 100 | C1 | Ski pants | 01/11/99 | 150 | 2 |
| 100 | C1 | Hiking boots | 01/11/99 | 180 | 1 |
| 200 | C2 | Colored shirts | 01/12/99 | 28 | 3 |
| 200 | C2 | Brown boots | 01/12/99 | 160 | 2 |
| 200 | C2 | Jackets | 01/12/99 | 250 | 2 |
| 300 | C3 | Jackets | 01/14/99 | 260 | 1 |
| 400 | C4 | Colored shirts | 01/14/99 | 28 | 2 |
| 400 | C4 | Jackets | 01/14/99 | 260 | 3 |

*Source*: Revised from Meo et al. (1998a,b).

**Table 5.5  Some Association Rules Mined**

| Rule | Body | Head | Support $S$ | Confidence $C$ |
|------|------|------|-------------|----------------|
| 1 | Ski pants | Hiking boots | 0.25 | 1 |
| 2 | Hiking boots | Ski pants | 0.25 | 1 |
| 3 | Colored bags | Brown boots | 0.25 | 0.5 |
| 4 | Colored bags | Jackets | 0.5 | 1 |
| 5 | Brown boots | Colored bags | 0.25 | 0.5 |
| 6 | Brown boots | Jackets | 0.25 | 1 |
| 7 | Jackets | Colored bags | 0.5 | 0.66 |

$$S = \frac{|\{TID2, \ TID4\}|}{|\{TID1, TID2, \ TID3, \ TID4\}|} = 0.5$$

$$C = \frac{|\{TID2, \ TID4\}|}{|\{TID2, \ TID3, \ TID4\}|} = \frac{2}{3} = 0.667$$

Additional measures for association rules have also been proposed. For example, Carter et al. (1997) introduced the measures share, concidence, and dominance as alternatives to the standard itemset methodology measure of support. Lin and Kedem (1998) noticed that discovering frequent itermsets typically entails a bottom-up breadth-first search and performance drastically decreases when some of the maximal frequent itemsets are relatively long. A new algorithm is proposed that is still bottom-up, but a restricted search is also conducted in the top-down direction. This search is used for maintaining and updating a data structure called the *maximum frequent candidate set*.

### 5.7.3  Finding Association Rules Using the Apriori Algorithm

#### 5.7.3.1  *Basic Ideas of Apriori*    The Apriori algorithm constructs a candidate set of large itemsets, counts the number of occurrences of each candidate itemset, and then determines large itemsets based on a predetermined minimum support. The trick of the algorithm is the *a priori property*, where every subset of a frequent itemset must also be a frequent itemset. The following is some basic terminology:

- *Itemset*—a set of items
- *k itemset*—an itemset having $k$ items
- *Frequent itemset* (also called *large itemset*)—an itemset with minimum support
- $L_k$— a set of large $k$ itemsets
- $_{Ck}$—a set of condidate $k$ itemsets

The following example illustrates the process of large itemset generation [taken from Chen et al. (1996)] (assuming that minimum transaction support required is two). Consider the transaction database shown in Table 5.6.

We now illustrate how to process to generate candidate itemsets and large itemsets. Scanning $D$, we have the data mining process shown in Tables 5.7–5.9.

Note that the Apriori algorithm has a *prune* phase which is best illustrated in the last pass in Table 5.9. (It is also used in previous passes, but to no significant effect.) Why do we not consider $ABC$ or $ABE$? Because, for example, $AB$ (the subset of $ABC$) is not a large 2-itemset, so $ABC$ is not qualified in frequent 3-itemset. Now you should be able to answer the following question: "Why should we stop at 3-itemset?" Or: "Why don't we consider 4-itemsets at all?" For more discussion on the prune phase, see Agrawal and Srikant (1994). The Apriori algorithm is now sketched below.

**Table 5.6   Transaction Database *D***

| TID | Items |
|-----|-------|
| 1000 | *A C D* |
| 2000 | *B C E* |
| 3000 | *A B C E* |
| 4000 | *B E* |

**Table 5.7   First Pass: $C_1$ and $L_1$**

| $C_1$ | | $L_1$ | |
|-------|---------|-------|---------|
| Itemset | Support | Itemset | Support |
| *A* | 2 | *A* | 2 |
| *B* | 3 | *B* | 3 |
| *C* | 3 | *C* | 3 |
| *D* | 2 | *D* | 3 |
| *E* | 3 | | |

**Table 5.8   Second Pass: $C_2$ and $L_2$**

| $C_2$ | | $L_2$ | |
|-------|---------|-------|---------|
| Itemset | Support | Itemset | Support |
| *AB* | 1 | *AC* | 2 |
| *AC* | 2 | *BC B* | 2 |
| *AE* | 1 | *E* | 3 |
| *BC* | 2 | *CE* | 2 |
| *BE* | 3 | | |
| *CE* | 2 | | |

**Table 5.9   Third Pass: $C_2$ and $L_2$**

| $C_3$ | | $L_3$ | |
|-------|---------|-------|---------|
| Itemset | Support | Itemset | Support |
| *BCE* | 2 | *BCE* | 2 |

**Algorithm Aprioi**

```
L(1) = {large singular item sets};
for (k = 2; L(k - 1) k++) do begin
  C(k) = Apriori-generation(L(k - 1)); // new candidates
    for each transaction t ∈ D begin
      C(t) = subset(C(k),t); // Candidates contained in t
        for each candidate c ∈ C(t) do
          c-count ++;
        end;
L(k) = {c C(k) | c-count ≥ minimum support}
end
∪ₖ L(k)
return
```

The A priori-generation function takes as argument $L(k - 1)$, the set of all large $(k - 1)$-itemsets. It returns a superset of the set of al large $k$-itemsets. The function works as follows. First, in the join step, we join $L(k - 1)$ with $L(k - 1)$:

```
insert into C(k)
  select p-item(1), p-item(1), ... p-item(k - 1),
q-item(k - 1),
  from L(k - 1) as p, L(k - 1) as q
  where p-item(1) = q-item(1), ...,
        p-item(k - 2) = q-item(k - 2),
        p-item(k - 1) < q-item(k - 1)
```

Next, in the prune step, we delete all the item sets $c$ in $C(k)$ such that some $(k - 1)$-subset of $c$ is not in $L(k - 1)$:

```
For each item sets c in C(k) do
  For each (k - 1)-subsets s of c do
    If (s not in L(k - 1)) then
      delete c from C(k);
```

The subset($C(k),t$) function can be sketched as follows. Candidate itemsets $C(k)$ can be stored in a *hash tree*. A node of the hash tree contains either a list of itemsets (a leaf node) or a hash table (an interior node). In order to add to the $c$ itemset, the hash tree is scanned from root to leaf. In an interior node of depth $d$, the branch to follow is the result of the hash function applied to $c[d]$. All nodes are initially created as leaf nodes. When the number of itemsets in a leaf node exceeds a specified threshold, the leaf node is converted to an interior node.

In order to find all itemsets contained in transaction $t$, the itemssets contained in a leaf node are found and added to the answer set. In an interior node that has been reached by hashing on $t[j]$; all $t[k](kj)$ will be hashed and this procedure will be recursively applied to the node in the corresponding bucket. At the root node, every itemset is hashed.

### 5.7.3.2 Remarks on Apriori Algorithm

*Analysis of Complexity* The discussion presented above indicates that we should generate all association rules in the database that have a support greater than min_sup (which indicates that the rules are frequent), and that have a confidence greater than min_con (which indicates that the rules are strong). We can examine the complexity of executing this algorithm through the following two basic steps involved in this process:

1. Find all frequent itemsets having minmum support. The search space for enumeration of all frequent itemset is $2^m$, which is exponential in $m$, the number of items. However, if we assume that the transaction length has a bound, it can be shown that association data mining is essentially linear in data size.
2. Generate strong rules having minimum confidence, from the frequent itemsets. We generate and test the confidence of all rules of the form $X \mid Y \Rightarrow Y$, where $Y \subset X$ and $X$ is frequent. Because we must consider each subset of $X$ as the consequent, the rule-generation step's complexity is $O(r;2')$, where $r$ is the number of frequent itemsets and $l$ is the longest frequent itemset.

*Lattice of the Itemsets* The two important aspects of association rule mining are

1. The subset relation $\subseteq$ defines a partial order on the set of itemsets.
2. The subset relation $\subseteq$ is monotonic with respect to the frequency; that is, for any frequent itemset, all its subsets are also frequent.

Note that 1-itemset, 2-itemset, ..., k-itemset form a lattice, as shown in Figure 5.4 for the case of $k = 3$.

*Remark on Upward-Closed and Downward-Closed Property* The Apriori algorithm property is a downward-closed property. In general, consider the

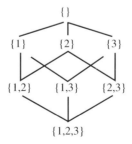

**Figure 5.4** A lattice of frequent itemset ($k = 3$).

lattice $L$ of all possible itemsets from the universe of items $I$. A property $P$ is said to be *upward-closed* with respect to the lattice $L$ if for every set with property $P$, all its supersets also have property $P$. Similarly, property $P$ is said to be *downward-closed* if for every set with property $P$, all its subsets also have property $P$. It is clear that the upward and downward closures are two faces of the same coin. In particular, if a property $P$ is upward-closed, then not having the property is downward-closed. Downward closure is a pruning property; it is capable of identifying objects that cannot have a property of interest. In contrast, upward closure is constructive, in that it identifies objects that must have a property of interest.

### 5.7.4 Implementation Aspects of Association Rules

*5.7.4.1 Aspects of Implementation*   Implementation of association rules has been determined largely by two factors: traversing the search space for the large itemset and determining itemset supports (Hipp et al. 2000, Zaki 1999, 2000b).

*Traversing the Search Space*   Algorithms differ in the manner in which they search the itemset lattice spanned by the subset relation. Most approaches use a breadth-first search (or levelwise; sometimes also called *bottom-up search*) of the lattice to enumerate the frequent itemsets. If long frequent itemsets are expected, a pure depth-first (or top-down) approach might be preferred. A hybrid search has also been proposed.

- *Breadth-First Search* (*BFS*). The support values of all $(k-1)$ itemsets are determined before counting the support values of the $k$ itemset. This approach is sometimes referred to as *bottom-up*.
- *Depth-First Search* (*DFS*). Search recursively descends following the tree structure obtained from the itemset lattice. This approach is sometimes referred to as *top-down*.

*Horizontal versus Vertical Data Layout*   This is concerned with the method for determining itemset supports. Most algorithms assume a horizontal database layout, which stores each customer's TID along with the items contained in the transaction. Some methods also use a vertical database layout, associating with each item $X$ its TID list, which is a list of all TIDs containing the item. Two common approaches to determine the support value of an intemset are

- *Horizontal*, or *Direct Count Occurrences of the Itemsets in the Database*. A counter is set up and initialized to zero. Then all transactions are scanned and the counter is incremented whenever one of the candidates is recognized as a subset of a transaction. Typically subset generation and candidate lookup are integrated and implemented on a hash tree or a similar data structure. Only those subsets that are contained in the candidates or that have a prefix in common with at least one of the candidates are generated.

- *Vertical, or Set Intersections.* The TID-list of a candidate $C = X \cup Y$ is obtained by C.TID-list = X.TID-list $\cap$ Y.TID-list. The TID-lists are sorted in ascending order to allow efficient intersections.

As can be seen from the common algorithm presented in Section 5.7.4.2, an advantage of counting is that only candidates that actually occur in the transactions cause any effort. In contrast, an intersection means at least passing though all TIDs of the smaller of the two TID-lists, even if the candidate is not contained in the database at all. But intersections do have their own merit; when using intersections, the size of the candidate under investigation does not have any influence.

### 5.7.4.2 Common Algorithms

Using the two factors introduced above, the main algorithms for implementing association rules can be categorized as shown in Table 5.10.

Below we will briefly describe each algorithm. For surveys on implementation of association rules, see Hipp et al. (2000) and Zaki (2000a).

### 5.7.4.3 Algorithms Using Breadth-First Search (BFS)

*Using Counting Occurrences*   The Apriori algorithm employs the a priori property. In addition, it prunes those candidates that have an infrequent subset before counting their supports. This can be done, because BFS ensures that the support values of all subsets of a candidate are known in advance. Apriori counts all candidates of a cardinality $k$ together in one scan over the database. The critical part is looking up the candidates in each transaction. As mentioned in Section 5.7.3.1, a data structure called *hash tree* can be used; the items in each transaction are used to descend in the hash tree. From an implementation perspective, Apriori is an iterative algorithm, using a complete, bottom-up search with a horizontal association, and enumerating all frequent itemsets. The algrorithm counts itemsets of a specific length in a given database pass. The process starts by canning all transactions in the database and computing the frequent items. Then a set of potentially frequent candidate 2-itemsets is formed from the frequent items. Another database scan obtains their supports. The frequent 2-itemsets are retained for the next pass, and the process

**Table 5.10   Implementation of Association Rules**

|  | Search: BFS | Search: DFS |
|---|---|---|
| Horizontal (counting occurrences) | A priori; A priori TID; DIC | FP-growth |
| Vertical (set intersecting) | Partition | Eclat |

is repeated until all frequent itemsets have been enumerated. The algorithm has three main steps:

1. Generate candiates of length $k$ from the frequent $k - 1$ length itemsets, by a self-join on $F_{k-1}$.
2. Prune any candidate that has at least one infrequent subset. (This is very important step.)
3. Scan all transactions to obtain candidate supports. Apriori stores the candidates in a hash tree for fast support counting. In a hash tree, itemsets are stored in the leaves, while internal nodes contain hash tables (hashed by items) to direct the search for a candidate.

The *dynamic hashing and pruning algorithm* extends the Apriori approach by using a hash table to precompute approximate support of 2-itemsets during the first iteration. The second iteration need count only those candidates falling in hash cells with minimum support. This hash table technique can successfully remove many candidate pairs that would eventually have become infrequent.

The two-pass partition algorithm logically divides the horizontal database into nonoverlapping partitions. Each partition is read, and vertical TID-lists (which are lists of all TIDs where the item appears) are formed for each item. Partition then generates all locally frequent itemsets through TID-list intersections. Locally frequent itemsets from all partitions merge to form a global candidate set. Partition then makes a second pass through candidates' global counts through TID-list intersections.

The *sequential efficient association rules algorithm* (SEAR) is identical to the a priori algorithm, except that the algorithm stores candidates in a prefix tree instead of a hash tree. In a prefix tree (also called a *trie*), each edge is labeled by items; common prefixes are represented by tree branches, and the unique suffixes are stored at the leaves. This algorithm also uses a so-called pass bundling optimization, where it generates candidates for multiple passes if the candidates will fit in main memory.

*AprioriTID* is an extension of the basic Apriori algorithm. Instead of relying on the original database, this method internally represents each transaction by the current candidates that it contains. AprioriHybrid combines the two approaches described above.

*DIC* is a further improvement of the Apriori algorithm. It softens the strict separation between counting and generating candidates. Whenever a candidate reaches minimum support, the algirhtm starts generating additional candidates based on it. A data structure called *prefix tree* is employed.

*Using TID-List Intersections*   In the original Apriori algorithm the size of intermediate results (which involve all $k - 1$ itemsets for generation of $k$-itemset) easily grows beyond the physical memory limitations of main memory. To deal with this, the Partition algoirhtm splits the database into several chunks that are treated independently. The size of each chunk is chosen in such a way that all intermediate TID-lists fit into the main memory. Locally frequent itemsets can be determined for each database chunk, from which a globally frequent interest can be selected through an extra scan.

### 5.7.4.4   Algorithms Using Depth-First Search (DFS)

*Using Counting Occurrences*   Unlike the case of BFS, the search direction (DFS) and counting occurrences do not blend in a straightforward manner. FP-growth algorithm handles this relationship in a novel way. In a preprocessing step, the FT-growth algorithm derives a highly condensed representation of the transaction data, called *FP-tree*. The generation of the FP-tree is done by counting occurrences and DFS. The algorithm directly descends to some part of the itemsets in the search space. In a second step the algorithm uses the FP-tree to derive the support values of all frequent itemsets.

*Using TID-List Intersections*   When using DFS it suffices to keep the TID-lists on the path from the root down to the class currently investigated in the main memory. Therefore, splitting the database as done by the Partition algorithm in the case of BFS is no longer needed.

Eclat optimizes the itemset generation using a technique called *fast intersections*. We can break off each intersection as soon as it is known that it will not achieve the minimum support. Eclat and its family use a vertical database format, complete search, and a mix of bottom-up and hybrid approach, and they generate a mix of maximal and nonmaximal frequent itemsets. The main advantage of using a vertical format is that we can determine the support of any $k$-itemset by simply intersecting the TID-lists of the lexicographically first two $(k - 1)$-length subsets that share a common prefix (the generating itemsets). These methods break the large search space into small, independent, manageable chunks. These chunks can be processed in memory through the prefix- or clique-based equivalence class; the clique-based approach produces much smaller classes. Each class is independent in that it has complete information for generating all frequent itemsets that share the same prefix.

The *dynamic itemset counting algorithm* (Brin et al. 1997) is a generalization of Apriori. The database is divided into $p$ equal-sized partitions so that each partition fits in memory. For partition 1, the algorithm gathers the supports of single items. Items found to be locally frequent (only in this partition) generate candidate 2-itemsets. Then partition 2 is read in and supports for all current candidates (i.e., the single items and the candidate 2-itemsets) are obtained. The process repeats for the remaining partitions. The algorithm starts counting candidate $k$-itemsets while processing partition $k$ in the first database scan. After the last partition $p$ has been processed, the processing wraps around to partition 1 again. A candidate's global support is obtained after the processing wraps around the database and reaches the partition where it was first generated. In general, this method is effective in reducing the number of database scans if most partitions are homogeneous (viz., have similar frequent itemset distributions); otherwise the algorithm may generate many false positives (viz., itemsets that are locally frequent but not globally frequent), and scan the database more than Apriori does. Nevertheless, the dynamic itemset counting algorithm proposes a random partitioning technique to reduce the data–partition skew.

***5.7.4.5  Other Factors***   There are other factors that affect implementation, as briefly described below.

- *Complete versus Heuristic Candidate Generation*. Heuristic generation trades in completeness for speed. This is a teaching step; it examines only a limited number of "good" branches.
- *All versus Maximal Frequent Itemset Enumeration*. The majority of algorithms list all frequent itemsets, although only the maximal ones can be generated.
- *Number of Scans*. A very important concern for association rule implementation in a database environment is the number of database scans. Although many methods require the number of scans to be $k$ (where $k$ is the largest number of items in an itemset), some methods have managed to use a much smaller one (such as 2 or 3).

In summary, we have summarized different implementation methods based on two factors. If we also incorporate factors other than search direction and database layout, we can use various implementation methods, such as those listed in Table 5.11.

Other methods for implementing association rule mining also exist. For example, the concept of closed frequent itemset for generating nonredundant association rules has been proposed (Zaki 2000b). Hidber (1999) presents an algorithm to compute large itemsets online. The user is free to change the support threshold any time during the first scan of the transaction sequence.

**Table 5.11   Summary of Implementation Methods**

| Database Layout | Algorithm | Data Structure | Search Direction | Enumeration | Number of Database Scans | Note |
|---|---|---|---|---|---|---|
| Horizontal | Apriori | Hash tree | BFS | All | $k$ | |
| | DHP | Hash tree | BFS | All | $k$ | |
| | SEAR | Prefix tree | BFS | All | $k$ | |
| | DIC | Prefix tree | BFS | All | $\leq k$ | |
| Vertical | Partition | None | BFS | All | 2 | |
| | Eclat | None | BFS | All | $\geq 3$ | |
| | MaxEclat | None | Hybrid | Max/nonmax | $\geq 3$ | |

The algorithm maintains a superset of all large itemsets and for each itemset, a shrinking, deterministic interval on its support. After at most two scans, the algorithm terminates with the precise support for each large itemset.

### 5.7.4.6 Avoiding Candidate Generation through FP Trees

The bottleneck of Apriori is at the process of candidate generation. It would be desirable for mining frequent patterns without candidate generation. The frequent-pattern tree (FP-tree) technique compresses a large database into a compact FP-tree structure. It is highly condensed, but complete for frequent pattern mining; it also avoids costly database scans. By decomposing mining tasks into smaller ones, the FP-tree-based frequent pattern mining method is an efficient, divide-and-conquer methodology.

The general steps of constructing FP-tree from a transaction database DB are the following:

*Step 1.* Scan DB once, find frequent 1-itemset (single item pattern);

*Step 2.* Order frequent items in frequency descending order;

*Step 3.* Scan DB again, construct the FP-tree.

This method is complete, meaning that it never breaks a long pattern of any transaction and preserves complete information for frequent pattern mining. The method is also compact, such as to reduce irrelevant information, since infrequent items are eliminated. The method uses frequency descending ordering, so that more frequent items are more likely to be shared.

Mining frequent patterns using FP-tree is carried out in a manner of divide-and-conquer: the FP-tree is used to recursively construct a growing frequent pattern path. More discussion on FP-tree can be found in Han et al. (2000).

### 5.7.5 Semantic Aspects of Association Rules

Research activities in finding association rules have been quite active since the late 1990s. In this section, we discuss some advanced studies on this topic. Our discussion is not intended to be complete, but to be representative. For references related to these aspects, see Chapter 10 of Chen (1999).

### 5.7.5.1 Template Design and Constraints for Mining Association Rules

An effective way for the users to guide the process of data mining is providing semantics through templates, which utilize metaknowledge for data mining. For example, Fu and Han (1995) employ a rule template to describe what forms of rules are expected to be found from the database, and such a rule template is used as a guidance or constraint in the data mining process. A classification of association rule types has been proposed (Baralis and Psaila 1997) that provides a general framework for the design of association rule mining applications. Dimensions of rule types include the mining condition,

the clustering condition, and the filtering condition. According to the identified association rule types, predefined templates can be introduced as a means
to capture the user specification of mining applications. A general language to
design templates has also been proposed for the extraction of arbitrary association rule types.

The following are two kinds of rule constraints to improve the efficiency of
association rule mining (Han and Kamber 2000):

- *Rule Form Constraints*. This is to perform metarule guided mining. A
  metarule works like a template to indicate how the resulting rule should
  look like. For example,

$$p(X,Y) \wedge q(X,W) \rightarrow \text{makes}(x, \text{"high profit"}).$$

  This metarule specifies that the resulting rule should involve two predicates $p$ and $q$ which results in a predicate concerning "high profits."
- *Rule Content Constraint*. This is to perform constraint-based query optimization. For example, the following constraint indicates the conditions
  should be satisfied in left hand side (LHS) and right hand side (RHS):

$$(\text{sum(LHS)} > 100) \wedge (\text{max(LHS)} < 30) \wedge$$
$$(\text{count(LHS)} > 4) \wedge (\text{sum(RHS)} > 500).$$

### 5.7.5.2 Sampling Techniques in Finding Association Rules   In
Chapter 3 we discussed sampling techniques in general. As a concrete
approach for sampling, we can apply it to find association rules. Remember
that sampling large databases in mining association rules is based on a portion
of the database from the whole database in order to decrease the operation
of disk I/O. The tradeoff for this method is the possibility of missing the real
frequency sets. The following techniques can be used to avoid missing the frequency sets: (1) decrease the frequency threshold during mining of the sample,
(2) use negative borders to further increase the supersets that are likely to be
the real frequent sets, and (3) keep the sample size large enough to represent
the whole database. The paper by Toivonen (1996) is a on the use of sampling
techniques for association rules well known.

### 5.7.5.3 Aggregation Semantics for Association Rules   In Chapter 3 we
addressed the issue of integrated OLAP and data mining. A very important
task for this integration is to discover rules at the aggregation level (rather than
the original level consisting of primitive data). However, we should note that
although association rules can still make sense at the aggregation level, the
semantics may be different from finding association rules at the primitive
(namely, nonaggregation) level. Consider the summarized data in Table 5.12.

The primary key at the granularity level (OrderID) disappeared. We may
be interested in how the sales data are related to the new primary key (year
and month). Although the granularity-level TID serves only the purpose of

**Table 5.12  A Summary Table**

| Year | Month | Sum (OrderID) | Sum (Milk) | Sum (Bread) | Sum (Cigarettes) | Sum (Beer) |
|------|-------|---------------|------------|-------------|------------------|------------|
| 1998 | 01 | 18,000 | 7000 | 8000 | 900 | 1000 |
| 1998 | 07 | 21,000 | 8500 | 9200 | 1700 | 5000 |

the identifier (i.e., surrogate), the primary key in the summary table may bear more meaning, and may be used for explanation purposes. For example, the sale of beer is much higher in July than in January because there were more outdoor social events at that time because of the weather.

The association between the sum of milk orders and the sum of bread orders is now examined in the orders involved in whole month, not in each individual orders (viz., transactions). Therefore, in an extreme case, 7000 orders of milk may be from the same 8000 transactions that ordered bread, while in another extreme case, the purchase of milk and bread may be from 15,000 completely disjoint transactions.

This is not to say that association rules will not make any sense at aggregation levels. The summary data obtained from different states may reveal some connections of attributes that can be found only at the aggregation level of the state. For example, we may have the following (hypocritical) rule discovered:

> *Rule 2*. States that have high amount of sales in milk and eggs are likely to have a high amount of cheese sales in winter.

Note that what this rule says is different from saying that the same customer who purchased milk and eggs is likely to purchase cheese in winter. Therefore, association rules have different semantics between granularity and aggregation levels.

#### 5.7.5.4  *Different Assumptions or Heuristics Possibly Needed at Different Levels*  Assumptions and heuristics are frequently needed to make the data mining process more effective. For example, in order to discover rules characterizing graduate students at the granularity level, the names of students can be dropped. Assumptions and heuristics are also important for data mining at aggregation levels, but they may be quite different from those at the granularity level.

Consider association rules at aggregation levels. We may compute the rate (percentage) of total orders for one product over some other products in each month. The following heuristic may be used:

> If for two products, the rate of orders is relatively stable over time, it may imply some kind of association between them; on the other hand, if the rate highly fluctuates, it may indicate little or no association between two products.

For example, applying this heuristic to Table 5.12, we may find out that the total purchase of milk and total sale of bread is associated more closely than the total purchase of milk and total purchase of beer, because the total orders of milk changed very little from January to July (7000 to 8500), which is not proportional to the change of total orders for beer (from 1000 to 5000).

***5.7.5.6 Other Semantic Issues***   There are various other issues related to semantics of association data mining. One aspect is on to maintain mined association rules. For example, in a data warehouse, when new sales data is flushed at the end of the day, how to maintain previous mined rules? Cheung et al. (1996) presented an approach using an incremental updating technique.

### 5.7.6   Association Rules and Database Functions

Association rules discovery process has also spawned research work related to the basic data mining mechanism. For example, Holsheimer et al. (1995) discusses how general-purpose database management systems can be used for data mining. Meo et al. (1996, 1998a) proposed extending SQL for mining association rules. A more recent paper by Meo et al. (1998b) discussed related issues in more depth. In Agrawal and Shafer (1996), issues related to loosely and tightly-coupled data mining techniques are discussed. An extended study of Agrawal and Shafer (1996) can be found in Sarawagi et al. (1998).

### 5.7.7   Extension or Variations of Association Rules

***5.7.7.1 Overview***   Association rules have been extended in many ways. For example, Srikant and Agrawal (1995) consider generalized association rules involving hierarchies. Srikant and Agrawal (1996) extends association rules to handle intervals as well as categories. Srikant et al. (1997) discusses how to incorporate user-specified constraints to find rules containing a specific item or rules that contain children of a specific item in a hierarchy. Bayardo et al. (1999) is a further study of using user-specified constraints for mining association rules. In addition, dense databases are considered; they are different from transaction databases which consist of itemsets that are "sparse" (as studied in earlier literature).

Srikant and Agrawal (1996) extend association rules to handle intervals as well as categories. Srikant et al. (1997) discuss how to incorporate user-specified constraints to find rules containing a specific item or rules that contain children of a specific item in a hierarchy.

***5.7.7.2 Variations of Association Rules***   Han and Kamber (2000) provide the following roadmap for variations of association rule mining:

- Based on the types of values handled in the rule:
  - *Boolean.* A Boolean association rule is a rule concerning the presence of absence of items.
  - *Quantitative.* A *quantitative* association rule is an association rule concerned with discretized quantitative values for items.
- Based on the dimensions of data involved in the rule:
  - *Single-Dimensional.* A *single-dimensional* association rule involves only one dimension of data in both LHS and RHS, such as "buying this also buying that." Single-dimensional rules are the starting point of association rule study.
  - *Multidimensional.* A *multidimensional* association rule extends the original association rule in that it allows different dimensions to appear in the LHS and RHS. For example, "Rich and young people buy fancy sports cars." Here "richness," "age," and "cars" are three different dimensions. There are two important things to note: (1) since these dimensions are actually different attributes, these rules have extended association rules from "items" to attributes; and (2) these rules also resemble characterization rules, because LHS conditions characterize the scenarios under which the RHS would happen.
- Based on the levels of abstractions involved in the rule set:
  - *Single-Level. Single-level* association rules find rules at the same abstract level of RHS. For example, rules may be concerned with original product items (e.g., milk).
  - *Multilevel. Multilevel* association rules find rules at the different abstract levels of RHS. Such abstraction is usually carried out through a concept hierarchy (as discussed in Section 5.4). For example, some rules may be concerned with a particular product items (e.g., milk), while others are concerned with more abstract concepts (such as dairy product).
- Based on various extensions to association mining, such as:
  - *Correlation Analysis.* A *correlate rule* is of the form $\{i_1, i_2, \ldots, I_n\}$, where the occurrences of these items are correlated (viz., statistically significant using $\chi^2$ test).
  - *Mining Maxpatterns.* A *maxpattern* is a frequent pattern that any proper superpattern of that pattern is not frequent.
  - *Frequent Closed Itemsets.* An itemset is *closed* if there eexists no proper superset of $c,c'$, such that every transaction containing $c$ also contains $c'$.

In addition to discovery of associations between the fields of case data (i.e., association for items, or more generally, attributes), there is another type of discovery: discovery of associations between business events or transactions, such as a certain type of transactions accompanied by other types of transactions.

***5.7.7.3   Clustering and Representative Association Rules***   Since many association rules may be found in the same transaction database, it makes sense to ask where there are any important findings shared by these rules. Different criteria have been developed. *Representative association rules* are defined as a minimum set of rules that covers all association rules satisfying certain user-specified constraints. A user may be provided with a set of representative association rules instead of the whole set of association rules. The nonrepresentative association rules may be generated on demand by means of the cover operator Kryszkiewicz (1998) and Lent et al. (1997) discuss how to cluster two-dimensional association rules in large databases.

***5.7.7.4   Association Rules Extended with Quantities***   In most cases, quantities of purchased items are not a concern of association rules. A transaction with 1 bottle of milk along with one dozen of eggs is treated in the same way as a transaction with 10 bottles of milk with 5–10 dozen eggs. However, one may argue that in some situations quantities may be a factor to be considered. For example, take a look at Tables 5.13 and 5.14. Even though both sets of tables show the same number of transactions, in Table 5.14 (TID 1), there is information that is not accounted for in the *Apriori* algorithm. In fact, TID 1 indicates a strong relationship that could be eliminated by Apriori. With the purchase quantity equaling 10, TID 1 could have an effect equivalent to 10 individual TIDs. This is not accounted for in Apriori.

Using the Apriori algorithm, Table 5.15 depicts the result of large itemset using support = 2 transanctions, which eliminates TID 1. In Table 5.16 instead

**Table 5.13   Sample Basket Data**

| TID | Item | Item |
|-----|------|------|
| 1 | *A* | *B* |
| 2 | *C* | *D* |
| 3 | *C* | *D* |
| 4 | *E* | *F* |
| 5 | *E* | *F* |

**Table 5.14   Sample Basket Data with Quantity**

| TID | Item | Quantity | Item | Quantity |
|-----|------|----------|------|----------|
| 1 | *A* | 5 | *B* | 5 |
| 2 | *C* | 1 | *D* | 1 |
| 3 | *C* | 1 | *D* | 1 |
| 4 | *E* | 1 | *F* | 1 |
| 5 | *E* | 1 | *F* | 1 |

**Table 5.15  Using Apriori with Support = 2**

| $C(1)$ | |
| --- | --- |
| $A$ | 1 |
| $B$ | 1 |
| $C$ | 2 |
| $D$ | 2 |
| $E$ | 2 |
| $F$ | 2 |

| $L(1)$ | |
| --- | --- |
| $C$ | 2 |
| $D$ | 2 |
| $E$ | 2 |
| $F$ | 2 |

| $C(2)$ | |
| --- | --- |
| $CD$ | 2 |
| $CE$ | 0 |
| $CF$ | 0 |
| $DE$ | 0 |
| $DF$ | 0 |
| $EF$ | 2 |

| $L(2)$ | |
| --- | --- |
| $CD$ | 2 |
| $EF$ | 2 |

of calculating whether an attribute exists, we also take into account the quantity of the attribute being considered. Again we use support = 2 transactions.

The result shown in Table 5.16 is not without problems, however; several issues need to be studied. One problem with this method is in the definition of support changes. Interested users may explore more aspects of this approach as well as its limitations.

**5.7.7.5  *Dissociation Rules***  A dissociation rule is similar to an association rule except that it allows "not" in its premise, conclusion, or both. The following are examples of dissociation rules (Berry and Linoff 1997):

IF $A$ and not $B$ THEN $C$.

IF not $A$ and not $B$ THEN not $C$.

Dissociation rules can be generated by adapting algorithms for generating association rules. The adaptation can be made by introducing a new set

**Table 5.16   Using Aprori Including Quantity with Support = 2**

| $C(1)$ | |
| --- | --- |
| $A$ | 5 |
| $B$ | 5 |
| $C$ | 2 |
| $D$ | 2 |
| $E$ | 2 |
| $F$ | 2 |

| $L(1)$ | |
| --- | --- |
| $A$ | 5 |
| $B$ | 5 |
| $C$ | 2 |
| $D$ | 2 |
| $E$ | 2 |
| $F$ | 2 |

| $C(2)$ | |
| --- | --- |
| $AB$ | 10 |
| . . . | 0 |
| $BC$ | 0 |
| . . . | 0 |
| $CD$ | 4 |
| . . . | 0 |
| $EF$ | 4 |

| $L(2)$ | |
| --- | --- |
| $AB$ | 10 |
| $CD$ | 4 |
| $EF$ | 4 |

of items that are the inverses of each of the original items. Each transactions is modified so that it includes an inverse item if and only if the transaction does not contain the original item. For example, if $A,B,C$ are the only items under consideration, and a rule "IF $A$ THEN ..." can be replaced by "IF $A$ and not $B$ and not $C$ THEN ..." Note that inclusion of inverted items not only doubles the number of items but also significantly increases the size of individual transactions. Therefore, although dissociation rules may make sense in certain applications to emphasize the existence of inverse items, they should be used only when they have to. A useful technique to reduce the overhead is to invert only the most frequent items in the set for analysis.

#### 5.7.7.6 *Dependence Rules*

Motivated partly by the goal of generalizing beyond market basket data and partly by the goal of ironing out some problems in the definition of association rules, Silverstein et al. (1998) proposed the notion of *dependence rules* that identify statistical dependence in both the presence and absence of items in itemsets. The chi-squared test for independence from classical statistics has been used to measure significance of dependence. This leads to a measure that is upward-closed in the itemset lattice, enabling the reduction of the mining problem to the search for a border between dependent and independent itemsets in the lattice. Pruning strategies are proposed on the basis of the closure property, and thereby an efficient algorithm for discovering dependence rules was proposed.

#### 5.7.7.7 *Correlation and Causality Analysis*

It has been noted that even strong association rules (i.e., rules with high support and confidence measures) can be uninteresting and misleading. The confidence of a rule "Buying $A$ also buying $B$" can be deceiving in that it is only an estimate of the conditional probability of itemset $B$ given itemset $A$. It does not measure the real strength of the implication between $A$ and $B$. For this reason, correlation analysis has been proposed as an alternative, which has the basis in probability theory. A correlation rule is of the form $\{i_1, i_2, \ldots, i_m\}$, where the occurrences of the mentioned items are related. The chi-squared statistic is used to determine the correlation (Han and Kamber 2000).

In contrast to correlation analysis, causality analysis is concerned with the following query: "If two items appear together, does one cause the appearance of the other?" The interesting thing to note is that although it is easy to *define* these two problems, it is difficult to distinguish causality from correlation. Yet researchers have started to attack this issue (Silverstein et al. 2000). We will present a study dealing with some aspects of causality in Chapter 6.

#### 5.7.7.8 *Constraint-Based Data Mining*

In constraint-based association mining, mining is performed under the guidance of various kinds of constraints provided by the user. Constraints could be knowledge-type constraints, interestingness constraints, metarule-guided mining, as well as others. In fact, constraint-based mining is not restricted to association mining. We have already seen constraint-based association rule mining in Section 5.7.5.1. A discussion of constraint-based, multidimensional data mining can be found in Han et al. (1999).

### 5.8 INTERPLAY OF DATA MINING TASKS

#### 5.8.1 Selecting Appropriate Data Mining Tasks

Since there are so many data mining tasks available, it is important to select an appropriate task (or tasks) for problem solving in real-world applications.

Although some data mining software supports several kinds of data mining tasks (e.g., DBMiner, as to be briefly introduced in Section 8.4, can accommodate classification, association, or other types of mining), in most cases, we need to carefully identify the appropriate tasks before data mining is carried out. This can be done by a study of the data mining problem specification, a study of the data features, and so on. Sampling techniques can also be applied to a subset of data for selection of tasks.

### 5.8.2 On the Boundary of Data Mining Tasks

The main focus of this section is on integrated use of data mining tasks. However, we also offer a negative note regarding misconception about data mining tasks (Freitas 2000). Boundary among data mining tasks is blurred at times. In fact, we have already noticed the similarity between classification and characterization (Section 5.4), as well as multidimensional association rules and characterization rules (Section 5.5). The following are some additional examples.

1. *Classification versus Association.* Freitas (2000) addressed the issue of misconceptions between classification and discovery of association rules. In fact, these two are very different in many aspects, not just syntactically (e.g., asymmetry of attributes in classification rules but not in association rules) and semantically (e.g., classification is an ill-defined, nondeterministic task involving prediction, while association rules are not).

2. *Clustering versus Classification.* Although conceptually they share some of the same considerations, technically they are very different. In clustering, similar objects are grouped in a class called *cluster*, and the similarity is usually determined using some measure (such as a certain form of distance).

Misconception is an indication of how different tasks are related to each other. Although close relationship among different tasks is a good sign for integrated use of these tasks, the misconceptions of these tasks may lead to inappropriate use of these methods. Therefore, a good understanding of the meaning of each task is a crucial factor for successful data mining.

### 5.8.3 Integrated Use of Data Mining Tasks

On a positive note, we now discuss the need for integrated use of these tasks. In fact, there is no universally best data mining algorithm across all application domains. One approach to increasing the robustness of data mining algorithms is to use an integrated data mining architecture, applying different kinds of algorithms and/or hybrid algorithms to a given data set, to try to get better results (Freitas and Lavington 1998). As an example, below we consider classification based on concepts from association rule mining. Several algorithms have been developed for this purpose.

> *Association Rule Clustering System* (*ARCS*). This method mines association rules of the form $A_{q1} \wedge A_{q2} \Rightarrow$ Cat, where $A_{q1}$ and $A_{q2}$ are tests on quantitative attribute ranges dynamically determined, and Cat assigns a class label for a categorical attribute from the given training data. Association rules are plotted on a two dimensional grid, which is then scanned in searching for rectangular cluster of rules. Adjacent ranges of the quantitative attributes occurring within a rule cluster may then be combined. Associative classification mines rules of the form AVpair-set $\Rightarrow$ Cat, where AVpair-set is a set of attribute–value pairs and Cat is a class label. The method consists of two steps: (1) using an iterative approach to find the set of all possible rules that are both frequent and accurate (i.e., satisfying minimum confidence) and (2) using a heuristic method to construct the classifier, where the discovered rules are organized according to decreasing precedence based on their confidence and support.
>
> *Classification by Aggregating Emerging Patterns* (*CAEPs*). This method uses the notion of itemset support to mine emerging patterns, which are used to construct a classifier. Here "emerging patterns" refer to the itemsets whose support increases significantly from one class to another. Mining emerging patterns is based on minimum support and growth rate.

These methods have also been experimentally compared with C4.5 with impressive results (Han and Kamber 2000).

### 5.8.4   Tools Supporting Integrated Data Mining Tasks

As for the actual systems developed, we can note the following. The loosest coupling is found in "toolbox" architectures, where several algorithms are collected into a toolbox, from which the most suitable algorithm for the target problem is somehow chose. An example is the MLC++ Machine Learning Library. Although effective, the system is very time-consuming in dealing very large data sets. A slightly higher degree of coupling is found in the Machine Learning Toolbox system, where a consultant expert system asks the user about the characteristics of the problem and automatically chooses the most suitable data mining algorithm for the target problem. This avoids the efficiency problem at the expense of some loss in robustness and autonomy. A much tighter coupling is achieved when a single hybrid data mining algorithm uses methods derived from different tasks or different algorithms to solve the target problem. Note that this architecture can be regarded as a kind of intraalgorithm integration, unlike the interalgorithm integration of the previous architectures. A particularly promising approach seems to be the integration of the rule induction and the instance-based learning methods, since these tasks have largely complementary strengths and weaknesses.

In addition, integrated use of data mining methods can be carried out in the overall data mining process. This can be explained through the process of modeling as depicted in Figure 4.2. Note that in the iteration of the modeling process, the algorithm selected for data mining may not necessarily be same, and the result of mining obtained in the previous iteration may be incorporated to the next iteration. Suppose, for example, that in the first round of execution, a basic classification algorithm did not produce a good result. Then in the second iteration, we may use a more advanced classification algorithm, or incorporate fuzzy logic techniques into the original classification algorithm.

## 5.9   DISTRIBUTED AND PARALLEL DATA MINING

Integration of data mining tasks also needs architectural support. In Chapter 3, we discussed several approaches to make data mining faster. Having discussed data mining algorithms, we can take a more detailed look at one aspect, namely, distributed and parallel data mining for scalability.

### 5.9.1   Distributed Data Mining

In essence, distributed data mining consists of three phases (Freitas and Lavington 1998):

1. Divide the data to be mined into $p$ data subsets (where $p$ is the number of available processors) and send each subset to a distinct processor.
2. Each processor runs a (same or different) data mining algorithm on its local data subset.
3. Combine the local knowledge discovered by each data mining algorithm into a global, consistent discovered knowledge.

Note that the combination in phase 3 can be done in a number of different ways. The simplest way would be to use some kind of voting scheme. For instance, in one scheme a new tuple to be classified is presented to all the local models (e.g., rule sets, neural networks) and each of them predicts a class for the tuple. The class with the largest number of predications is then the final prediction. This scheme can usually be somewhat improved by using a weighted voting scheme. In this approach the prediction of each model is weighted by the estimated accuracy of the model. For instance, if the model is a rule set, the weight of the prediction would be a measure of the classification accuracy of the particular rule used for prediction. More sophisticated approaches include:

1. *Model Integration.* This involves merging the local models discovered by each data mining algorithm (from its local data subset) into a global, consistent model. For example, a system that integrates local rule sets into a global rule set could work as follows. Initially a decision tree building algorithm is applied to several random samples of the data being minded, in order to quickly build a decision tree from each sample. These local decision trees are then converted into local rule sets, and the quality of each rule is evaluated by a statistical significance test. This test is applied to each condition in the rule antecedent, in order to identify conditions that are statistically irrelevant for predicting the class specified in the rule consequent. Irrelevant conditions are then removed from the rule antecedent. This statistical significant test is also applied to the antecedent of the rule as a whole, in order to identify and remove statistically irrelevant rules. Finally, the pruned local rule sets are combined into a global rule set by a separate algorithm. This algorithm selects a minimal subset of rules that achieves a complete coverage of the data being mined. Apparently model integration is easier if all the local models are homogeneous.

2. *Metalearning.* This approach employs a metalearner that combines the predictions of the models discovered by local data mining algorithms, rather than combining the models themselves. Each local data mining algorithm is treated as a black box. Hence, in this scheme the local data mining algorithms can be either the same or completely different.

3. *Interprocessor Cooperation.* This approach guarantees to avoid the reduction of prediction accuracy in distributed data mining as demonstrated in the previous two approaches. In essence, this approach consists of using an invariant partitioning rule quality measure. Measures of this kind have the property that any rule that would be discovered by a given data mining algorithm in the entire data being mined is guaranteed to be discovered by that algorithm in at least one partition of the data. This approach makes use of the fact that every rule that would be discovered by a global version of that algorithm will be discovered by some local data mining algorithm. Since a rule discovered by a local algorithm might not hold for the global data, processors have to cooperate with each other to validate rules. Note that the use of interprocessor communication to globally validate locally discovered rules suggests that this approach might be considered as a form of parallel (rather than distributed) processing.

### 5.9.2 Parallel Data Mining

***5.9.2.1 Basic Aspects*** In contrast to distributed data mining, in principle a parallel data mining algorithm discovers exactly the same knowledge as its sequential counterpart. Parallel processing can be used to speed up data mining in several ways, mainly in two groups:

- *Interalgorithm Parallelization*. Each algorithm is run in sequential mode on a single processor, but several data mining algorithms run in parallel with each other on multiple processors. A typical use for this approach is a toolboxlike architecture, where several data mining algorithms are applied to a database to determine the best algorithm for the target KDD task and available data. As another example, we may want to run several instances of a data mining algorithm, each with a different set of parameters. A typical example is the training of a neural network in parallel for different network topologies to determine the best topology. Interalgorithm parallelization has the advantage that it is straightforward to implement. However, although the degree of parallelism scales up with the number of data mining algorithms implemented, it does not scale up with an increase in database size. In addition, interalgorithm parallelization assumes that all the data being mined can be directly accessed by all processors, thus distinguishing itself from distributed data mining. Since each algorithm run is independently of the others, as in distributed data mining, the algorithms are loosely coupled.
- *Intraalgorithm Parallelization*. A given data mining algorithm is run in parallel on several processors. The processors somehow communicate and cooperate with each other during the execution of the data mining algorithm.

### 5.9.2.2  *Parallel Data Mining without DBMS Facilities*

*Parallel Rule Induction*   A rule induction algorithm can be viewed as an iterative heuristic search in a rule space. Some heuristic criterion is used to guide the search toward the most promising regions of the rule space.

Consider a *candidate rule*, which is a partially constructed rule and can be further expanded (specialized or generalized) by the rule induction algorithm. In essence, each search iteration consists of the three steps, until a satisfactory set of candidate rules is found:

*Step 1.*  Select the best candidate rules according to an evaluation function.

*Step 2.*  Expand the selected candidate rules, generating new candidate rules.

*Step 3.*  Evaluate the new candidate rules, according to evaluation function.

Steps 1 and 2 are associated with control parallelism (which refers to the concurrent execution of multiple operations or instructions), while steps 3 offers potential for both control and data parallelism (data parallelism refers to the execution of the same operation or instruction on multiple large data subsets at the same time).

*Parallel Decision Tree Building*   These are a particular kind of rule induction algorithm. There are three basic levels of parallelism in these algorithms:

- *Internode Parallelism*. Multiple trees nodes are processed at the same time, in parallel, by multiple processors. Each processor computes a partitioning quality measure for all candidate attributes in its decision tree nodes. (*Partition quality measure* refers to a measure of quality for each candidate attribute used to select the best partitioning attribute in a given tree node.)
- *Interattribute Evaluation Parallelism*. Candidate attributes in a given decision tree node are distributed among available processors, so that each processor computes a partitioning quality measure for each attribute in its subset of candidate attributes.
- *Attribute Evaluation Parallelism*. Computation of the partitioning quality measure for a single attribute is performed in parallel by multiple processors.

*Parallel Generation of C4.5 Rules*   As indicated in Section 5.3, C4.5 is a specific decision tree building algorithm. A parallel implementation transforms a decision tree into a set of rules and prunes this set. C4.5 rules are generated in several phases: (1) pruning rule conditions, (2) selecting a subset of rules for each set of rules predicting the same class (value of the goal attribute) using control parallel approach, and (3) evaluating the rule set as a whole on the data being mined by removing one rule at a time as this process does not reduce the estimated classification accuracy.

*Parallel Discovery of Association Rules*   The core step consists of finding all itemsets having a support count greater than or equal to a user-specific value. Algorithms proposed by Agrawal and Shafer (1996) include the following.

- *Count Distribution Algorithm*. In each iteration of this data parallel algorithm, each processor generates the complete set of candidate itemsets of a given size. This redundant, replicated computation is done to avoid exchange of data among processors. Let #Cand be the number of generated candidate itemsets. Then each processor independently computes local support counts for all the #Cand candidate itemsets, by accessing only database tuples in memory. These partial counts are then exchanged among processors, so that processors do not need to exchange any database tuple.
- *Data Distribution Algorithm*. In each step of this control parallel algorithm, each processor computes support counts for only #Cand/p of the candidate itemsets, where #Cand is the number of candidate itemsets and p is the number of processors. In each iteration of the algorithm, each

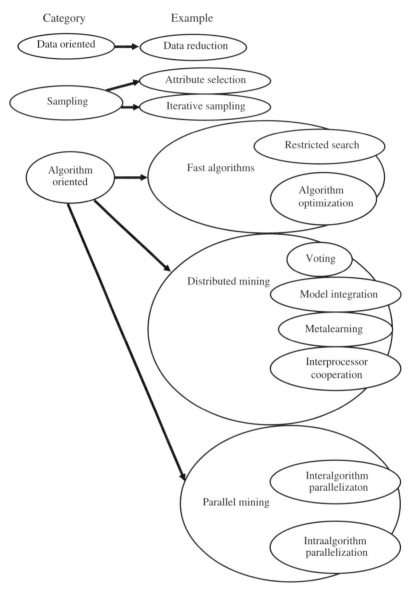

**Figure 5.5** Approaches to speed up data mining.

processor has to broadcast its local data to all the other processors. This algorithm can be further improved by too wordy using a more efficient interprocessor communication scheme to improve the data distribution algorithm to achieve an intelligent data distribution algorithm, and furthermore, it can be combined with count distribution algorithm.

**Table 5.17 Speedup Approaches**

| | | Reduce rule space to be searched? | |
|---|---|---|---|
| | | Yes | No |
| Reduce amount of data to be mined? | Yes | Attribute selection | Sampling distributed mining |
| | No | Discretization-restricted search | Algorithm optimization parallel mining |

*Source*: Based on Freitas and Lavington, (1998).

#### 5.9.2.3 *Database-Centric Parallel Data Mining*   Parallel data mining can take advantage of integrated data mining and data warehouse frameworks. One is server-based, where the data mining algorithm is run on the parallel database server. The other is hybrid client/server-based, where some procedures of the data mining algorithm are performed on the client but other procedures (the data-intensive, time-consuming ones) are performed on the parallel database server.

### 5.9.3   A Sample Taxonomy of Approaches to Speed up Data Mining

Approaches to speed up data mining are depicted in Figure 5.5, which summarizes methods described above, along with some other approaches.

Several approaches for speeding up data mining are compared in Table 5.17.

## 5.10   SAMPLING AND DATA MINING TASKS

As we have seen earlier in this chapter, scalability has been a focal concern of various data mining tasks. As noted in Chapter 3, sampling techniques could be an effective way of approach scalability. We should also note that various data mining tasks require different sampling methods. In other words, sampling techniques could be built into various data mining tasks. In Section 5.6, we discussed the use of sampling in clustering. In this section, we briefly examine two other cases of sampling for data mining: association rule mining and classification.

### 5.10.1   Sampling for Association Rule Mining

As indicated in Section 5.7, for association rule mining, several passes are need over the analyzed database, and the role of input/output overhead is significant for very large databases. Sampling and other techniques have been used to deal with this problem. For example, Toivonen (1996) presented the idea of picking a random sample to find all association rules that probably hold in the whole database and then to verify the results with the rest of the database.

The algorithms thus produce exact association rules, not approximations based on a sample. In case the sampling method does not produce all association rules, the missing rules can be found in a second pass. In a more recent report, Domingo et al. (1999) presented a sequential sampling approach to deal with the difficulty of determining appropriate sample size needed in random sampling, and proposed an adaptive sampling algorithm. The algorithm obtains examples sequentially in an on-line fashion, and it determines from those obtained examples whether it has already seen enough number of examples. Thus, sample size is not determined in advance; rather it is adaptive to the actual situation encountered.

### 5.10.2   Sampling in Classification

Sampling is also an important issue in discovery of classification rules. Many methods for learning classification rules have been developed from machine learning research community. Most of these algorithms have the restriction that the training data should fit in the main memory. Even at mid-1990s, the largest dataset in a well-known machine learning repository is only 700 KB with 20,000 examples. The ideal of modifying tree classifiers to enable them to classify large datasets has been explored extensively, including sampling of data at each decision tree node, and discretization of numeric attributes. These methods decreases classification time significantly but also reduce the classification accuracy. The SLIQ algorithm (Mehta et al. 1996), as briefly discussed in Section 5.5.1, has been developed to improve learning time for the decision tree induction classifier, without loss in accuracy. The developed techniques allow classification to be performed on large disk-resident training data. SLIQ uses a presorting technique in the tree-growing phase, and it is integrated with a breadth-first tree growing strategy to enable classification of disk resident datasets. SLIQ also uses a nonexpensive tree-pruning algorithm to construct compact and accurate trees.

The idea behind sampling is to trade accuracy for speed. For classification problems, sampling tends to be effective in problems with low class dispersion (i.e., tuples belonging in each class are concentrated in the tuple space), and tends to be ineffective in problems with high class dispersion (i.e., small disjuncts, there are small clusters of points in the tuple space, where each cluster is located far from the others) (Freitas and Lavington 1998). Loosely speaking, one can say that a classification problem is easy when there is a small number of classes with high cardinality (i.e., the number of members in the same class), and a classification problem is hard when there is a large number of small classes.

The effectiveness of sampling also depends on the size of the tuple space in the database. Intuitively, the larger the size of the tuple space, the higher the risk of prediction-accuracy degradation associated with sampling. This is related to the topic of overfitting (Freitas and Lavington 1998). Consider a data set with three binary predicting attributes $A$, $B$, and $C$, and two

**Table 5.18   Example of Sampling**

| Entire Data Set | | | | Sample Data Set | | | |
| --- | --- | --- | --- | --- | --- | --- | --- |
| A | B | C | class | A | B | C | class |
| b | b | b | + | b | b | b | + |
| b | b | a | + | | | | |
| b | a | b | + | b | a | b | + |
| b | a | a | + | | | | |
| a | b | b | − | | | | |
| a | b | a | − | a | b | a | − |
| a | a | b | − | | | | |
| a | a | a | − | a | a | a | − |

classes denoted + and −, as shown in the left hand side of Table 5.18. It shows the eight possible cases to be considered in this problem, each with its corresponding class. From the data a rule induction algorithm could easily discover the rules:

If $A = b$ then class = +;
If $A = a$ then class = −.

Now suppose we extract a sample of three tuples, as shown in the RHS of Table 5.18. We observe that both attributes $A$ and $C$ seem to be perfect class discriminators. Sampling has led to a loss of the information necessary to tell the algorithm that $C$ is not a perfect class discriminator. In this example, sampling might lead a rule induction algorithm to overfit the data by discovering the two spurious rules:

If $C = b$ then class = +;
If $C = a$ then class = −.

## 5.11  SUMMARY

In this chapter we have examined several important data mining tasks. The main ideas of various mining algorithms have been discussed for the tasks of tree induction, characterization, classification, clustering, and association, and their variants. These tasks form the core of the functionality possessed by intelligent data mining agents. We have also examined several issues related to implementation. Although this chapter does not emphasize uncertainty itself, it does incorporate uncertainty-related concerns into various algorithms, such as measuring criteria in clustering, support and confidence in association rules, and use of entropy in tree induction. In the next chapter, uncertainty issues will again be back on center stage of our discussion.

This chapter started with a brief review of AI concepts. The relevance of AI to data mining has been recently discussed by McCarthy (1999). At the end of this chapter, recapping basic AI issues such as search, data and knowledge representation, we present the following future directions for data mining:

- Explore data and knowledge representation beyond relational databases, such as text, multimedia, and Web data models.
- Explore issues related to preprocessing, such as data mining–motivated data reduction and discretization.
- Explore the prior domain knowledge and use of the discovered knowledge.
- Integrate data and knowledge management, including knowledge representation for enterprise databases.
- Explore a better way to mode knowledge uncertainty.
- Combine query systems with discovery capabilities.
- Explore better ways to represent knowledge and hypotheses spaces.
- Study complexities of search for knowledge.
- Explore how to integrate multiple search methods in one system.
- Explore prediction and intervention use of knowledge.
- Explore data mining in distributed and multiagent systems.

# 6

# BAYESIAN NETWORKS AND ARTIFICIAL NEURAL NETWORKS

## 6.1 OVERVIEW

In this chapter, we examine two specific approaches: Bayesian networks and artificial neural networks, for a better understanding of the connection between data mining and uncertain reasoning. Note that although both employ a netlike structure, these two approaches are inherently very different. Bayesian networks, where the nodes denote physical symbols and arcs reflect probabilities, can be considered as a structured knowledge representation, similar to frame systems and conceptual graphs (Chen 1999). On the other hand, artificial neural networks (ANNs) are a well-known subsymbolic structure for dealing with the reasoning process tampered with uncertainty. Nevertheless, both approaches demonstrate a common theme: dealing with uncertainty. For example, for ANN, the architecture itself contains uncertainty, which is represented by the weights indicating the strength of connections between neurons. In Bayesian networks, uncertainty is captured by probability through propagation. In addition, by dealing with uncertainty, both approaches are able to uncover underlying regularities hidden in the data.

An examination of these two approaches reminds us to take a fresh look at existing approaches originally developed for uncertain reasoning, and sheds light on the general relationship between data mining and uncertainty. Indeed, a main difference between using soft computing computing techniques discussed in this chapter and the next chapter, such as fuzzy sets, neural networks, and genetic algorithms, for uncertain reasoning versus their role in data mining is that for uncertain reasoning, we just want the technique to "do the job" (viz., solve the particular problem at hand, such as in the case of fuzzy controller), with the existence of uncertainty. Although being able to explain the problem-solving process is always welcome, the explanation is not used as the starting point of some other business decisions. On the other hand, for data mining, the acquired result should be understandable, because depending on which important decisions will be made innovated steps could be taken (e.g., change of an investment strategy). Another difference between uncertain reasoning and data mining is the amount of data used. For example, in the case of a fuzzy controller (which can be viewed as an expert system using fuzzy logic techniques), the size of data used could be small, while in the case of stockmarket analysis, the size of data could be huge. Therefore, although we may employ the same technique of fuzzy logic in both problems, the outcome of the studies could be very different.

This chapter, as the title suggests, consists of two parts. The first part consists of Sections 6.2 to Section 6.5. In Section 6.2, we examine the relationship among probability, logic, and uncertainty. In Section 6.3 we review basics of probability theory. In Section 6.4 we discuss Bayesian networks. In Section 6.5, we examine the issue of using Bayesian networks for data mining. The second part of the chapter consists of Sections 6.6–6.8. The general characteristics of artificial neural networks as well as their relationship with data mining are discussed in Sections 6.6. In the consecutive two sections, Sections 6.7 and 6.8, we discuss neural network models of supervised and unsupervised learning, as well as their role in data mining. In Section 6.9, we examine some theoretical and practical issues about artificial neural networks. We summarize the whole chapter in Section 6.10.

## 6.2 PROBABILITY, LOGIC, AND UNCERTAINTY

Historically, in order to deal with uncertainty, various approaches have been tried. Two major camps of dealing with uncertainty are using logic and using probability. Their connection can be examined through what Pearl (1988) called "softened logic versus hardened probabilities." According to this observation, lacking an appropriate logical device for conditionalization, the natural tendency is to interpret the English sentence "IF $A$ THEN $B$" as a softened version of the material implication constraint $A \supset B$. A useful consequence of such softening is the freedom from outright contradictions. For example, while the classical interpretation of the three rules "Penguins do not fly," "Penguins are birds," and "Birds fly" yields a blatant contradiction, attaching uncertainties to these rules renders them manageable. They are still not managed in the correct way, however, because the material implication interpretation of IF/THEN rules is so fundamentally wrong that its maladies cannot be rectified simply by allowing exceptions in the form of shaded truth values.

George Polya (1887–1985) was one of the first mathematicians to attempt a formal characterization of qualitative human reasoning. In his 1954 book *Patterns of Plausible Inference*, Polya argued that the process of discovery, even in as formal a field as mathematics, is guided by nondeductive inference mechanisms, entailing a lot of guesswork. "Patterns of plausible inference" was his term for the principles governing this guesswork.

The conspicuous patterns listed by Polya include the following four, which clearly indicate the intrinsic connections between logic and probability:

1. *Inductive Patterns.* "The verification of a consequence renders a conjecture more credible." For example, the conjecture "John lost his job" becomes more credible when we verify the consequence "John looks quite depressed."

2. *Successive Verification of Several Consequences.* "The verification of a new consequence counts more or less if the new consequence differs more or less from the former, verified consequences." For example, if in trying to substantiate the conjecture "All employees drive light-colored cars," we observe $n$ employee cars, all of them are light-colored, and all of them are Toyota, our subsequent confidence in the conjecture will be increased substantially if the $(n + 1)$-th car is a Chevy and is light-colored, rather than another Toyota.

3. *Verification of Improbable Consequences.* "The verification of a consequence counts more or less according as the consequence is more or less improbable in itself." For example, the conjecture "John lost his job" obtains more support from "John bought a gun and shot his boss" than from the more common observation "John looks depressed."

4. *Inference from Analogy.* "A conjecture becomes more credible when an analogous conjecture turns out to be true." For example, the conjecture "Of all objects displacing the same volume, the sphere has the smallest surface" becomes more credible when we prove the related theorem "Of all curves enclosing the same area, the circle has the shortest perimeter."

Nevertheless, Polya preferred probabilities over logic. Polya's influence is interesting, because the heuristic thinking has a strong impact on Newell for symbolic reasoning (Groner et al. 1983), while Polya's specific observation on probability has simulated another line of thinking in AI, which resorts to numerical solutions.

## 6.3  BASICS OF PROBABILITY THEORY

The basic properties of probability theory can be described as follows. Let $A$ and $B$ be two events (such as tossing a coin or running out of gas) and $P$ be the probability. The following are the basic properties of probability theory:

$$\text{IF } A \subseteq B \text{ THEN } p(A) \leq p(B) \tag{6.1}$$

$$P(\neg A) = 1 - p(A) \tag{6.2}$$

$$P(A \cup B) = P(A) + p(B) - p(A \cap B) \tag{6.3}$$

Note that property (6.1) can be generalized to more than two events. In addition, in case $A$ and $B$ are independent events, property (6.3) is simplified to

$$P(A \cup B) = p(A) + p(B) \tag{6.3'}$$

In general, the assumption of independence may greatly simplify the calculation related to probability. However, in many cases, the independence assumption is not realistic. The independence assumption is a major hurdle of applying probability theory in some real-world assumptions.

Probability theory can be defined as the study of *how knowledge affects belief*. Belief in some proposition, $f$, can be measured in terms of a number between 0 and 1. The probability $f$ is 0 means that $f$ is believed to be definitely false (no new evidence will shift that belief), and a probability of 1 means that $f$ is believed to be definitely true. Statistics of what has happened in the past is knowledge that be conditioned on and used to update belief.

Various approaches to uncertain reasoning have been developed on the basis of probability theory. Because of space limitation, in the following we very briefly sketch only for one of them, namely, the Bayesian approach to deal with causality. Another theory, the Dempster–Shafer theory, also rooted in probability theory, has a profound theoretical impact because of its relationship with other uncertain reasoning techniques.

## 6.4   BAYESIAN NETWORKS

In this section we review some basic features of Bayesian networks. Our presentation follows the discussion of Glymour and Cooper (1999), Pearl (1998, 2000) and Parsons (1996). Useful information can also be found in Neapolitan (1990). Note that these references mainly address reasoning aspects of Bayesian networks.

### 6.4.1   Basics of Bayesian Networks

We start with the notion of conditional probability $P(A|B)$, which states the probability of event A given that event $B$ occurred. The inverse problem is to find the inverse probability that states that the probability of an earlier event given that a later one occurred. This type of probability occurs very often. For example, in medical diagnosis or various mechanical troubleshooting problems, we want to find the most likely cause for the observed symptoms. The solution for this problem is stated as Bayes' theorem (or Bayes' rule), which serves as the basis of a well-known approach in probability theory called the *Bayesian approach*. More formally, Bayes theorem is stated as

$$P(H \mid X) = \frac{P(X \mid H)P(H)}{P(X)},$$

where $P(H|X)$ is the posterior probability of $X$ conditioned on hypothesis $H$.

*Bayesian networks* (also called *belief networks*) relax several constraints of the full Bayesian approach. These networks are also referred to as causal networks, because of their ability of dealing with causality. This approach takes advantage of the assumption that the modularity of a problem domain causes many of the dependence/independence constraints required for Bayes approach to become relaxed.

The links between the nodes of the belief network are represented by conditioned probabilities. For example, the link between two nodes $A$ and $B$, denoted $A \rightarrow B(c)$, reflects evidence of $A$'s support for the belief in $B$ with confidence $c$, sometimes referred to as a *causal influence measure*.

Coherent patterns of reasoning may be reflected as paths through cause–symptom (or cause–effect) relationships. The cause–symptom relationships of the problem domain will be reflected in a network. Paths within this network represent the use of different possible arguments.

Naive Bayesian classifiers assume that the effect of an attribute value on a given class is independent of the values of the other attributes. In theory, such classifiers have a lower error rate than do all other classifiers. However, the assumption of class conditional independence is unrealistic in many situations. Unlike naive Bayesian classifiers, Bayesian belief networks are graphical models that allow the representation of dependencies among subsets of attributes. In addition to the graph itself, a conditional probability table is assigned for each variable. The conditional probability table for a variable $X$ specifies the conditional probability distribution $P(X|\texttt{Parents}(X))$, where $\texttt{Parents}(X)$ are the parents of $X$ in the graph.

### 6.4.2 Reasoning with Bayesian Networks

It is important to note that the kind of links over which the probabilities are propagated are not logical implications, but a form of *causal* relation as discussed by Pearl (1988). A belief network should not be viewed merely as a passive code for storing factual knowledge but also as a computational architecture for reasoning about that knowledge. This means that the links in the network should be treated as the only mechanisms that direct and propel the flow of data through the process of querying and updating beliefs. Indeed, we may view each node in the network as associated with a separate processor, which maintains the parameters of belief for the host variable and manages the communication links to and from neighboring, conceptually related variables. The communication lines are assumed to be open at all times; that is, each processor may, at any time, interrogate its neighbors and compare their parameters to its own. If the compared quantities satisfy some local constraints, no activity takes place. However, if any constraint is violated, the responsible node is activated and the violating parameter corrected. Therefore, it activates similar revisions at neighboring nodes and initiates a multidirectional propagation that will continue until a new equilibrium is reached (Pearl 1988).

The early reluctance of using probabilistic methods by the AI community was due mainly to the complexity. If we have a system that involves $n$ variables, we need $2n$ probabilities to fully specify the probabilistic relationships between those variables. What Pearl realized is that although this is true in general, in practice one often needs many fewer probabilities. This is because the kind of knowledge that is represented in AI systems seldom involves interrelationships between many variables. The relationships that do exist, and thus the probabilities that are required, may be exposed by the construction of a network in which variables are represented by nodes and the explicit dependencies between them by arcs. When two nodes are not connected, it is because the value of one node is known to be conditionally independent of that of the other. The resulting structure not only identifies the necessary probabilities but may also be used as the basis for computing the updated values during inference.

### 6.4.3 Dynamic Construction of Bayesian Networks

In order to apply Bayesian reasoning for data mining in a database context, a number of problems are entailed in applying Bayesian networks in the kind of dynamic environment that exists within a database. The first is that to perform inference with a Bayesian network, we need a network. We have to provide a means of constructing the network automatically. There has been a considerable amount of work on this issue. One of the earliest attempts to provide for automated construction was to take a number of different types of qualitative information, such as "$A$ is a cause of $B$" or "$A$ is independent of $B$ given $C$" and use these, along with a blackbox that tests for independence, to create networks.

An algorithm has been developed to deduce the most likely structure of a belief network linking a set of variables given a database of cases of the form "in case 1, $A$ is present, $B$ is absent, and $C$ is present." The derivation of the network is based on the assumptions that the database explicitly mentions all the relevant variables, the cases mentioned in the database are independent, and all the cases are complete.

In a slightly different approach, starting from a database that records statistical data of the form "$D$ and $E$ occur with $A$, $B$, and $C$ on 2048 occasions." Issues to be discussed include how to reduce sets of relations into fourth normal form corresponding to the cliques of the equivalent belief network, and from which the necessary conditional probabilities may be learned.

In addition, methods for dynamically constructing networks have been addressed, as in a tool called *Pulcinella*. Facts and relations are represented in first-order logic, and resolution used to build a proof path from which a network can be constructed. The network may then be fed to Pulcinella for evaluation. A similar approach uses first-order Horn clause logic to represent the variables in a belief network and the relationships between them, attaching an associated probability to each. The logical clauses are then used to deduce various facts such that the probability associated with the facts is the probability that would be established for them using the equivalent network. This network is never built, but is implicit in the computation. Alternatively, a specialized network construction language can be used.

Given the dynamic nature of databases, it is important to remember that all the network construction techniques mentioned so far build networks that are correct at a particular instant in time, but do not allow for changes in the network. Sensitivity analysis has been used to determine when better decisions would have been taken using a different model, and gives an algorithm for performing the updating. The need to update networks is often due to the fact that the problem being diagnosed changes over time, and so the history of the problem becomes important.

Another factor that has been disregarded in all the systems considered so far is the problem of separating model construction from evaluation. In a resource-bound environment this could lead to the query-driven construction of a network that could not be evaluated in reasonable time. This difficulty can be alleviated by integrating the two stages to give an "anytime algorithm" for query evaluation that gives successively better approximations of the answer. In addition to always providing a solution, the method allows useless solutions to be identified at an early stage, and its deductive style brings the use of numerical methods almost full circle and back to the logical methods discussed above (Parsons 1996).

### 6.4.4  Bayesian Networks and Relational Databases

It should also be noted that there are some striking similarities between the representation of data in probabilistic networks and that in relational databases. Probabilistic databases should allow the computation of the same probability distributions as belief networks given information about the dependencies between different data. In other words, if the graphical structure is known, then the probabilistic information that is stored in the system is sufficient to establish a unique joint probability distribution for all the pieces of data in the database.

In addition, Bayesian networks can be represented as relational databases. If a probability distribution is given over a set of relational tables, it is possible to perform correct probabilistic inference using only the project and join operations that one would expect of a relational database. Thus, when new evidence is obtained, its effects may be propagated through the database in a manner consistent with the underlying dependencies but without building a network. However, the method does rely on the prior structuring of the relations in order to represent the conditional independencies.

## 6.5    BAYESIAN NETWORKS AND DATA MINING

Having described the basic features of Bayesian networks, we now present two examples to illustrate how Bayesian networks can benefit data mining. Major issues need to be addressed including how to deal with computational challenges for huge amount of data, how to accommodate Bayesian networks for various kinds of data mining tasks (or functionalities), as well as others.

### 6.5.1    Belief Network Inductor

Musick (1999) describes BNI (belief network inductor), a tool that automatically induces a belief network from a database, and thus may benefit data mining. The fundamental thrust of this research program has been to provide a theoretically sound method of inducing a model from data, and performing inference over that model. Based on probability theory, BNI has been designed to be a quick, practical, and accurate method of inducing data models. The results include a belief network that stores beta distributions in the conditional probability tables, coupled with theorems demonstrating how to maintain these distributions through inference. An interesting aspect of this approach is that techniques have been developed for applying neural networks and other learning techniques to the task of conditional probability table learning, thus combining these two very different kinds of net structures. In addition, a decision theoretic sampling theory that addresses scalability issues by characterizing the size of the sample needed to produce high quality inferences.

### 6.5.2    An Agent-Based Model for Data Mining Using Bayesian Networks

We now examine another approach that emphasizes the role of Bayesian networks can play in the overall data mining process. A high-level agent-based model for data mining using Bayesian networks is depicted in Figure 6.1, where $G$ denotes the goal, $B$ (or BN) denotes the Bayesian network, $A$ denotes the agents, $D$ denotes the database, and $K$ denotes the knowledge discovered. In the following we provide a brief discussion of this model. More details can be found in Chen and Zhu (1998).

In this model, a knowledge pattern is defined as a construct consisting of the goals, the relations among the goals, and the functions defined in them. A causal network can be used to represent the knowledge patterns that are explored at the initial, intermediate, and final stages of a knowledge discovery process.

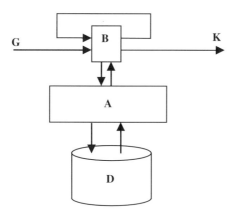

**Figure 6.1**   A data mining model.

In a knowledge discovery process, new nodes and links associated with the relevant data attributes in exploration could be added to the BN conveniently. A structural analysis that traces the nodes and links of the whole or partial BN identifies the dependency relations and the network structure to be updated. The BN could thus serve as a control mechanism to guide the generation and evaluation of the subsequent subgoals, as well as a representation of the intermediate and final knowledge patterns. In this sense, the belief network is used as both a reasoning tool and a memory structure for the knowledge applied and deducted.

### 6.5.3   Mining Causal Patterns from Frequent Itemsets

To make our discussion more concrete, we now take a look at a study of mining causal patterns from frequent itemsets using a Bayesian approach. Mining association rules in transaction databases has received much attention in the field of data mining. Although progress has been made in developing techniques of mining association rules, the results often indicate only the mutual correlative relationships among the frequent items, paying little attention to the directional, or causal, relations. For example, when a data set indicates an association between items $A$ and $B$, it is rarely clear whether the access of $A$ caused the access of $B$, or the converse. In real-world applications, however, knowing such causal relations is extremely useful for decision support. People would be interested not only in whether the facts that $A$ and $B$ are related but also in the possible sequences and directions among the items. Mining transaction databases for this kind of knowledge offers the potential for deep analysis of business situations and finding strategies of operation. In this section, we describe a Bayesian approach to mining causal relations from frequent itemsets (Xiao et al. 2001). As noted in Chapter 5, Silverstein et al. (2000) studied the problem of determining causal relationships, instead of mere associations, when mining market basket data. The study presented in this section continues this research direction. The results of the research described below include two algorithms based on Bayesian statistics model: a serial and diverging connection discovery algorithm (SDCD) and a converging connection discovery (CCD) algorithm. Experimental results indicate that the performance of the algorithms is scalable.

**6.5.3.1  Overview**   Data mining is motivated by the decision support problems faced by many large businesses and industrial organizations. For example, progresses in barcode technology have made it possible for retail organizations to collect and store massive amounts of sales data, referred to as "basket" data. A record in such data typically consists of the transaction data and the items purchased in the transaction. Successful organizations view such database as important information source of the market analysis. In the field of data mining, there are several research directions that focus on finding the correlations among the basket data, such as mining association rules and clustering analysis.

The problem of mining association rules over basket data, as discussed in Chapter 5, was introduced in Agrawal and Srikant (1993). Association rule mining techniques discover unordered correlations among items found in a database of transactions. An example of such a rule might be that 98% of customers who purchase tires and auto accessories also have automotive services done. Finding all such rules is valuable for cross-marketing and attached mailing advertises. Mining Website access logs to find Web page associations also became an interesting research topic in the 1990s for promoting effectiveness of Web design and related e-commerce implementations (Chen et al. 1996).

A common problem existing in the research and development mentioned above is that rules discovered from these algorithms indicate only the mutual correlative relationships among the data items. They do not specify the "cause–effect" nature of the relationship, namely, the direction of influence between the items. For example, if there is a relationship between $A$ and $B$, these algorithms cannot indicate whether the presence of item $A$ causes the presence of item $B$, or the converse. In real-world data mining applications, however, knowing such causal relations is very important and useful for decision support.

As indicated earlier, Bayesian networks (Pearl 1988) provide a well-known technique of representing the complete causal model from the data. A Bayesian network (BN) consists of a structural model and a set of probabilities. The structural model is a directed acyclic graph in which nodes represent random variables and arcs represent probabilistic dependences. The possible number of causal network topology is exponential in the number of the random variables. For example, if the number of measured variables is 10, the numbers of causal Bayesian network structure will reach up to $4.2 \times 10^{18}$ (Glymour and Cooper 1999). It is impossible to deal with all these causal relationships in mining of a full causal model from very large databases. In order to make efficient use of Bayesian networks in decision support, it is necessary to have some algorithms that effectively determine the directions of the causal relations in the probabilistic model space, so as to reduce the network size and make the probability propagation function efficiently.

The remaining part of this section describes a Bayesian approach to mining causal relationships embedded in frequent itemsets. An important concept for causal discovery, called *d-separation* [originally defined in Pearl (1988)], is further specified by incorporating two new definitions, and is used as the basic constraint in our approach. Note that d-separation can be expressed through three nodes, and the causal relationship patterns can be discovered through our algorithms when every two to three frequent itemsets are considered (which represent two to three itemsets brought together). Two algorithms are presented. The performance results of both algorithms have shown that they are scalable as the size of transaction database increases. This research would shed light on investigation of more general causal relationships using Bayesian network representations.

### 6.5.3.2  *Problem to Be Investigated*

We now describe the problem to be investigated in more detail. Let $I = \{i_1, i_2, \ldots, i_m\}$ be a set of literals, where $i_j$ is an item and $1 \leq j \leq m$. Let $D$ be a set of transactions, where each transaction $T$ is a set of items such that $T \subset I$. Associated with each transaction is a unique identifier, called *TID*. We say that a transaction $T$ *contains* $X$, a set of items in $I$, if $X \subseteq T$. An association rule is an implication of the form $X \Rightarrow Y$, where $X \subset I, Y \subset I$, and $X \cap Y = \Phi$ (Agrawal and Srikant 1993).

An itemset $s$ is usually measured by two indicators: support and confidence. In this section, we will focus on the notion of *support*, which is defined as the fraction of total items in the database that contains the itemset $s$. The *frequent itemset* is the itemset that has a certain user-specified minimum support.

In this approach, an important concept is a causal pattern, which is a set of event classes connected by arrows in a BN representation, where the direction of the arrow indicates the direction of influence or causality. A more formal definition is given below.

A *causal pattern* is a directed acyclic graph $(N,A)$, where $N$ is a set of event classes and $A$ is a set of labeled directed arcs. Each node represents an event class. The direction of each arc indicates the direction of influence or causality. As to causal pattern $A \rightarrow B$, the event class $A$ is the antecedent and the event class $B$ is the consequent.

Consider, for instance, causal patterns $\alpha, \beta, \gamma$ in Figure 6.2. Causal pattern $\alpha(A \rightarrow B \rightarrow C)$ is a *serial connection*; event $A$ has an influence on $B$, which, in turn, has influence on $C$. Obviously, evidence on $A$ will influence the certainty of $B$, which then influences the certainty of $C$. Causal pattern $\beta(A \leftarrow B \rightarrow C)$ is a *diverging connection*; event $B$ has an influence on $A$ and

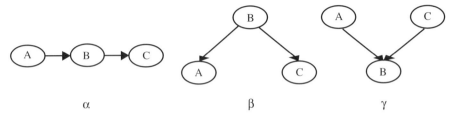

**Figure 6.2**    The three patterns of causal relations.

*C* and influence can pass between all the children (*A* and *C*) of *B* unless the state of *B* is known. Causal pattern γ(A → B ← C) is a converging connection; event *A* and event *C* influence event *B*, but not the reverse.

A primitive version of our problem statement can be stated as follows. Given a transaction database *D*, the problem of mining causal patterns is to find the three causal relations: serial, diverging, and converging connections among all frequent itemsets. Any one of the three connections discovered is a causal pattern.

Consider a database D of Web logs as an example. Each log consists of the following fields: user-id, log time, and the Web server accessed in this log transaction. Here the user-id serves as the TID as described in the beginning of this section. In the data shown in Figure 6.3, there are four users, and the log time is the time of user accessing the different Web page. For simplicity, we denote the log (access event) with respect to the same Web server by a map code. We call one map code an *item*, such as item (*A*) indicating an access of the URL www.microsoft.com/search.

The data in Figure 6.3 have been sorted on user-id and log access time. With the minimum support set to 25%, the itemset {(*A*)(*B*)(*C*)} is a frequent itemset, which satisfies the user-specified minimum support. We then try to discover the causal pattern on the basis of the frequent itemset {(*A*)(*B*)(*C*)}. The result should be one of the following three patterns:

$$\alpha:(A){\rightarrow}(B){\rightarrow}(C), \qquad \beta:(B){\leftarrow}(A){\rightarrow}(C), \qquad \gamma:(A){\rightarrow}(C){\leftarrow}(B)$$

The causal pattern α shows that the event of user accessing URL www.microsoft.com/search will cause the event of user accessing URL www.microsoft.com/msdownload, which, in turn, cause the event of user accessing www.microsoft.com/ie. The causal pattern β shows that the event of user accessing www.microsoft.com/search will cause both of the event of user accessing www.microsoft.com/msdownload and the event of user accessing www.microsoft.com/ie. While the causal pattern γ shows that both of the event of user accessing www.microsoft.com/search and the event of user accessing www.microsoft.com/msdownload will cause the event of user accessing www.microsoft.com/ie.

***Definition 6.1*** A path *p* is said to be *d-separated* (or *blocked*) by a set of nodes Z iff *p* contains (1) a serial connection *i* → *m* → *j* or a diverging con-

| User Id | Time | Method/URL/Protocol | Map Code (Item) |
|---|---|---|---|
| 1 | [25/March/1999:04:33:22] | http://www.microsoft.com/search | (A) |
| 1 | [25/March/1999:04:38:43] | http://www.microsoft.com/msdownload | (B) |
| 1 | [25/March/1999:04:49:14] | http://www.microsoft.com/ie | (C) |
| 2 | [26/March/1999:03:13:12] | http://www.microsoft.com/search | (A) |
| 2 | [26/March/1999:03:21:42] | http://www.microsoft.com/msdownload | (B) |
| 2 | [26/March/1999:03:33:15] | http://www.microsoft.com/msofficesupport | (D) |
| 2 | [26/March/1999:03:39:44] | http://www.microsoft.com/ie | (C) |
| 3 | [24/March/1999:12:34:22] | http://www.microsoft.com/sql | (E) |
| 4 | [27/March/1999:06:37:18] | http://www.microsoft.com/search | (A) |
| 4 | [27/March/1999:06:49:28] | http://www.microsoft.com/msdownload | (B) |

**Figure 6.3**  Web logs database sorted by user ID and time.

nection $i \leftarrow m \rightarrow j$ such that the middle node $m$ is in $Z$ or (2) a converging connection $i \rightarrow m \leftarrow j$ such that the middle node m is not in $Z$ and such that no descendant of $m$ is in $Z$.

A set of nodes $Z$ is said to *d-separate* $X$ from $Y$ if and only if $Z$ blocks every path from a node in $X$ to a node in $Y$.

In the serial connection $i \rightarrow m \rightarrow j$ and diverging connection $i \leftarrow m \rightarrow j$, the variables $i$ and $j$ are marginally dependent but become independent of each other (i.e., blocked) once we apply condition on the middle variable $m$. Figuratively, conditioning on $m$ appears to "block" the flow of information along the path, since learning about $i$ has no effect on the probability of $j$, given $m$.

A converging connection $i \rightarrow m \leftarrow j$ represents two causes having a common effect, but acting in the opposite way. If the variables $i$ and $j$ are (marginally) independent, they will become dependent once we apply condition on the middle variable $m$.

As an example, consider given a transaction database about the access logs on the Web pages $\{A,B,C,D,E,F\}$. According to the conditional probability that accessing one Web page influences accessing of another Web page, a hypothetical network such as that shown in Figure 6.4 is built. The resulting Bayesian network is concerned with the causal relationships among the Web pages accessed.

In Figure 6.4, each node $X$ represents the event of the Web page $X$ being visited. For example, as to the serial connection $D \rightarrow E \rightarrow F$, the event of Web page $D$ being accessed influences the event of Web page $E$ being accessed and, in turn, influences the event of Web page $F$ being accessed. If the knowledge about $E$ being accessed is confirmed, the information that $D$ being accessed

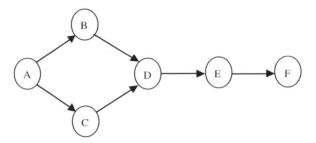

**Figure 6.4**   A hypothetical Bayesian network structure.

will not influence, in terms of probability dependency, the information that $F$ being accessed. In other words, the evidence that $E$ has been accessed *blocks* the information that $D$ being accessed passes to $F$. Therefore, $D$ is d-separated from $F$ by $E$.

As shown above, the definition of d-separation is closely related to conditional probability. Conditional probability is a far too strong requirement in many real-world applications. In order to capture the causal relationship among variables in a more realistic manner, we propose to extend the concept of independence and conditional independence. In particular, we introduce two parameters $\Delta$ and $\delta$, to be defined in Definitions 6.2 and Definition 6.3, to describe the *independence* and *conditional independence* of item sets in transaction databases in an *approximate* manner.

Recall that in the field of mining association rules, a number of frequent itemsets should be obtained, such as 1-frequent itemsets: $A,B,C$; 2-frequent itemsets: $AB$, $AC$, $BC$; and 3-frequent itemsets: $ABC$. The support of these frequent items can be calculated through approximations $p(B) = \text{support}(B)$, and $p(A,B) = \text{support}(A,B)$. Note that we also use the shorthand notation support($AB$) to denote support($A,B$). Therefore, support obtained from the transaction databases can be used for approximate probability calculations. Definitions 6.2 and 6.3 are two major definitions.

***Definition 6.2***   Consider three items $A$, $B$, and $C$. We say that $A$ and $B$ are blocked by C, denoted $(A,B) \perp C$, iff $\Delta = |p(A|B,C) - p(A|C)|$ is less than a predefined small value min_$\Delta$.

The parameter $\Delta$ is useful in handling serial and diverging connections. As an example, consider the serial connection of the form $D \rightarrow E \rightarrow F$; we say that $(D,F) \perp E$ and $D$ and $F$ are independent given $E$. That means there is a $\Delta = |p(D|F,E) - p(D|E)|$ such that the $\Delta$ is less than the min_$\Delta$.

The diverging connection $B \leftarrow A \rightarrow C$ has a casual effect similar to that of the serial connection, that is, $B$ is d-separated from $C$ by $A$. We have $(B,C) \perp A$. This means that there is a $\Delta = |p(B|A, C) - p(B|A)|$ and the $\Delta$ is less than the min_$\Delta$. It shows that the event of $A$ being accessed is a causation of $B$ and $C$ being accessed.

***Definition 6.3*** Consider a variable

$$\delta = \left| \frac{\text{support}(A,B,C)}{\text{support}(B)} \right|$$

and three items $A$, $B$, and $C$. We say that $A$ and $C$ are *conditionally dependent* on $B$ if and only if $\delta$ is larger than the predefined min_$\delta$.

The parameter of $\delta$ is useful in dealing with converging connections. Suppose that there are two items $A,B$ and the itemset $AB$ has support above the minimum support; then item $A$ and $B$ are dependent. Consider three items $A$, $B,C$, where the support of itemset $AC$ under the condition of item $B$ is the value $\delta$. If $\delta$ is above min_$\delta$, then $A$ and $C$ are conditionally dependent on $B$.

The converging connection $B \rightarrow D \leftarrow C$ shows that the event $B$ being accessed and the event $C$ being accessed represent two different causations of the event of $D$ being accessed. The event $B$ being accessed and the event $C$ being accessed are independent; in other words, the itemset $BC$ is not a frequent itemset. But if, under the condition of the event $D$ being accessed, the event $B$ being accessed and the event $C$ being accessed are somehow related,

$$\delta = \left| \frac{P(B,C,D)}{P(D)} \right|$$

and the $\delta$ is larger than the min_$\delta$, then the event $B$ being accessed and the event $C$ being accessed are conditionally dependent on $D$.

Based on definitions presented in this section, we are now ready to provide a more specific problem statement. Given a transaction database $D$, the problem of mining causal patterns is to find (1) the serial connections and diverging connections among the frequent itemsets using a user-specified min_$\Delta$ and (2) the converging connections among the frequent itemsets using a user-specified min_$\delta$, under the assumptions that the 2- and 3-itemsets with certain minimum support can be readily extracted from the databases. The serial connections, the diverging connections, and the converging connections of the frequent itemsets serve as the causal patterns (defined in Definition 6.1) to be mined from the transaction databases.

Two algorithms for mining the abovementioned causal pattern sets from the transaction databases have been developed in our research:

- *Serial and diverging connection discovery* (SDCD) *algorithm*—algorithm used to discover the causal patterns according to the value of $\Delta$, where the resulting causal patterns are in the form of serial and diverging connections

- *Converging connection discovery* (CCD) *algorithm*—an algorithm used to discover the causal patterns according to the value of δ, where the resulting causal patterns are in the form of converging connections

### 6.5.3.3 *Two Algorithms*   We now describe these two algorithms (SDCD and CCD).

*Serial and Diverging Connection Discovery (SDCD) Algorithm*   The SDCD algorithm first retrieves the 3-itemsets from the transaction database. It then applies a preselected Δ on the 3-itemsets to verify the conditionally independent relationships among the three items in the 3-itemsets. Finally, it uses the concept of d-separation to obtain the causal patterns of the 3-itemset. In the itemsets described below, only the frequent counts of the items are considered.

The first pass of the algorithm simply counts item occurrences to determine the frequent 1-itemsets. The data structure of each itemset is a record that contains two members. One is the $item_i$, which is used to construct the itemset; the other is the *support* of the itemset. In the subsequent passes, the frequent 2-itemsets and frequent 3-itemsets are identified. We make use of the functions `apriori-gen` and `subset` as described by Agrawal et al. (1993) in the algorithm. The `apriori-gen` function takes as argument $L_{k-1}$, the set of all frequent $(k - 1)$-itemsets, and returns a superset of all frequent $k$ itemsets. The `subset` function searches $C_k$ and takes a count for $C_k$, where $C_k$ is the set of candidate $k$-itemsets.

The 3-frequent itemset is then used to discover causal patterns among the three items. Consider all the permutations; six forms of these could be constructed by any three items: $item_1item_2item_3$, $item_1item_3item_2$, $item_2item_1item_3$, $item_2item_3item_1$, $item_3item_1item_2$, and $item_3item_2item_1$.

We need to find the combination that best satisfies the conditions for the causal patterns. According to Definition 6.2, different Δ values can be calculated for the six possible forms. In step 12 of algorithm SDCD, $r$ is the 3-frequent itemset. The function of $\varphi(r)$ gets the six forms for each 3-item frequent itemset. The function sort $(\Delta_{\varphi(r)})$ sorts the six Δ values. We then select the minimum Δ of the six Δ values and put it into a set $\Psi'_\Delta$. If the selected Δ is less than the min_Δ, then put it into the set $\xi_1$. By using the set $\xi_1$, we can verify that the items in the first and third position of the 3-frequent item are conditionally independent, given the item in the second position as a condition. The function $\text{Change}_1$ ($\xi_1$) returns the partial causal in the form of serial and diverging connections.

As an example to illustrate the algorithm, suppose that $ABC$ is a 3-frequent itemset. By $\varphi(r)$, we have six forms about $ABC$: $ABC, ACB, BAC, BCA, CAB$, and $CBA$. Calculating $\Delta_{\varphi(r)}$ means calculating $\Delta_{(A,C)\perp B}, \Delta_{(A,B)\perp C}, \Delta_{(B,C)\perp A}, \Delta_{(B,A)\perp C}, \Delta_{(C,B)\perp A}$ and $\Delta_{(C,A)\perp B}$. Suppose that the results are $0.5, 0.2, 0.3, 0.24, 0.01$, and $0.25$.

In selecting the minimum $\Delta$ from the $\{\Delta_{\varphi(r)}\}$, also assume min_$\Delta = 0.05$. Since $\Delta_{(C,B)\perp A}$ is the minimum $\Delta$, and $\Delta_{(C,B)\perp A}$ is less than min_$\Delta$, we can say that $(C,B) \perp A$. After getting the $(C,B) \perp A$, according to Definitions 6.1 we can get the causal patterns $B \to A \to C$ and $B \leftarrow A \to C$.

*Converging Connection Discovery (CCD) Algorithm*   The CCD algorithm uses two 2-item frequent itemsets to construct a 3-itemset that contains causal relation annotations, under a given condition that the two 2-item frequent itemsets contain one common item between the pair. The item that is common to both sets is referred to as a *common-item*, and the other two items are referred to as *noncommon-items*. Use the *noncommon-items* between the two pairs of 2-frequent itemsets, the CCD algorithm tries to construct a new itemset. We will refer the new itemset as *template-itemset*.

In the following, we use $L_i$ to denote the set that contains all the $i$-item itemsets, use $l_i$ to denote a single itemset, and use $l_i.item$ to a particular item in an item set $l_i$. The function GetTemplateItem $(l_1, l_2)$ takes argument $l_1$ and $l_2$, the two frequent itemsets, and returns a *template-itemset* $l_t$. If the *template-itemset* $l_t$ is not a 2-item frequent itemset, it means that the two itemsets from which the *template-itemset* is constructed are independent.

The function Construct takes three argument $l_1$, $l_2$, $l_t$ to construct a 3-itemset called *goal-itemset*. All the *goal-itemsets* are put into a set $L_g$. The process of the function Construct is described as follows.

insertinto $L_g$
select $1_t.item_1$, $l_1.item_i$, $l_t.item_2$
from $L_2l_1$, $L_2l_2$, $L_tl_t$
where $l_1.item_i = l_2.item_j$  $(1 \le i, j \le 3)$

The description $l_1.item_i = l_2.item_j$ means that $l_1.item_i$ and $l_2.item_j$ are the common-item of $l_1$ and $l_2$. In the CCD algorithm, the transaction database is scanned and every $\delta(l_g) = |l_g.\text{sup}/l_c.\text{sup}|$ is calculated, where $l_i.\text{sup}$ is the support value of $l_i$. If $\delta(l_g)$ is larger than the minimum $\delta$, according to Definition 6.3, the two items that form the template-itemset are conditionally dependent with respect to the common-item. The function change$_2$ ($\xi_2$) converts the itemset to causal pattern and insert it into set *CausalSet$_2$*. The algorithm is presented below.

As an example, consider two 2-frequent itemsets: *AB* and *BC*. Here *B* is the common-item, *A* and *C* are non-common-items. The function Get-TemplateItem $(AB, BC)$ returns the template-itemset *AC*. If the support of template-itemset *AC* is less than the minsup, we say that *A* and *C* are independent. We then construct the goal-itemset *ABC* and calculate $\delta = |\text{support}(ABC)/\text{support}(B)|$. If $\delta$ is larger than the minimum $\delta$, according to previous definitions, *A* and *C* are conditionally dependent on *B* and the causal pattern $A \to B \leftarrow C$ is resulted.

### 6.5.3.4  *Experiments on the Real Data for Discovery of Causal Patterns*

The above algorithms have been implemented, and some test experiments have been carried out. The algorithms were first tested on synthetic data that were used to verify the programs are scalable. As the testing of real data sets, the public real data from the Microsoft anonymous website http://kdd.ics.uci.edu/databases/msWeb/msWeb.html have been used. The data set was created by sampling and processing the www.microsoft.com logs (in 1996). Examples of the data set are shown in Figure 6.5. The data set records the visits of www.microsoft.com by 38,000 anonymous, randomly selected users. Each instance represents a visit to the Website.

Each attribute is an area ("vroot") of the www.microsoft.com Website. For each user, the data lists all the areas of the Website (Vroots) that the user visited in a one-week timeframe. The 294 Vroots are identified by their title (e.g., "Netshow for PowerPoint") and URL (e.g., "/stream"). The data shown in Figure 6.5 are for one week in February 1998.

Using minsup 0.016 and min_$\Delta$ 0.0065, we applied the SDCD algorithm to the data set and calculated the *CausalSet*$_1$ which has a size of 527. Some of the itemsets are shown in Figure 6.6. For example, in the *CausalSet*$_1$ we have obtained the following causal pattern: *"Microsoft.com Search"* $\rightarrow$ *"isapi"* $\rightarrow$ *"Free Downloads."* This means that a visit to Website http://www.microsoft.com/search caused a visit of Website http://www.microsoft.com/isapi and then the Website http://www.microsoft.com/msdownload. The structure of a pattern in *CausalSet*$_1$ is $A \rightarrow B \rightarrow C$ or $A \leftarrow B \rightarrow C$.

Using minsup 0.016 and min_$\delta$ 0.80 in our CCD algorithm, we get *CausalSet*$_2$. The size of *CausalSet*$_2$ is 418. Some of the samples of *CausalSet*$_2$ are shown in Figure 6.6. The structure of a pattern in *CausalSet*$_2$ is $A \rightarrow B \leftarrow C$. For example, *"Microsoft.com Search"* $\rightarrow$ *"Knowledge Base"* $\leftarrow$ *"Windows95 Support"* is obtained. This means that the visits to Websites http://www.microsoft.com/search and http://www.microsoft.com/windowssupport result in visits to Website http://www.microsoft.com/kb.

| Item | Title | URL | $\Delta$ |
|------|-------|-----|----------|
| A | "Internet Explorer" | http://www.microsoft.com/ie | |
| B | "Support Desktop" | http://www.microsoft.com/support | 0.00149 |
| C | "Knowledge Base" | http://www.microsoft.com/kb | |
| A | "Microsoft.com Search" | http://www.microsoft.com/search | |
| B | "isapi" | http://www.microsoft.com/isapi | 0.00426 |
| C | "Free Downloads" | http://www.microsoft.com/msdownload | |
| A | "Free Downloads" | http://www.microsoft.com/msdownload | |
| B | "Developer Workshop" | http://www.microsoft.com/workshop | 0.00622 |
| C | "Internet Site Construction for Developers" | http://www.microsoft.com/sitebuilder | |

**Figure 6.5**  Samples of *CausalSet*$_1$.

| Items | Title | URL | $\delta$ |
|-------|-------|-----|----------|
| A | "Microsoft.com Search" | http://www.microsoft.com/search | |
| B | "Knowledge Base" | http://www.microsoft.com/kb | 0.08061 |
| C | "Windows95 Support" | http://www.microsoft.com/windowssupport | |
| A | "Free Downloads" | http://www.microsoft.com/msdownload | |
| B | "Windows Family of OSs" | http://www.microsoft.com/windows | 0.118827 |
| C | "Windows 95" | http://www.microsoft.com/windows95 | |
| A | "Internet Explorer" | http://www.microsoft.com/ie | |
| B | "Internet Site Construction for Developers" | http://www.microsoft.com/sitebuild | 0.111765 |
| C | "SiteBuilder Network Membership" | http://www.microsoft.com/sbnmember | |

**Figure 6.6**   Samples of *CausalSet₂*.

**6.5.3.5  *Summary of Mining Causal Patterns***   In this section we described a particular approach for discovery of causality using a Bayesian network approach. Discovery of causality is a complex issue. An excellent discussion on causality can be found in Pearl (2000). Causality can be considered as a deep analysis related to association rules. There are many important aspects of causality, and many of them are yet to be explored. For example, an interesting aspect is how to distinguish a "causing" (causual) factor from a *contributing factor*—a factor that, when combined with other factors, may cause the phenomenon, but does not itself cause the result. For example, in the 2000 U.S. presidential election, the uncertainty as to who won the election was a contributing factor of the stockmarket in November 2000, although it was not a causing factor. However, this conclusion is observed by human experts. Issues such as how to automatically discover contributing factors and distinguish them from causing factors, remain to be explored.

## 6.6  ARTIFICIAL NEURAL NETWORKS

In this section we review some basic features of artificial neural networks. Further discussion is continued in Sections 6.7 and 6.8. The discussion of these three sections follow the presentations in Fanelli et al. (1999) and Chen et al. (2000).

### 6.6.1  Overview

*Artificial neural networks* serve as a well-known example illustrating what subsymbolism is and how it differs from symbolism. The basic feature of subsymbolism is to deemphasize the use of symbols to denote objects and relations; intelligence is viewed as arising from the collective behavior of large numbers of simple, interacting components. Unlike symbol-based computational intelligence, a neural network system assumes no correspondence between the units of computation and objects or relations in the world. ANNs contain electronic processing elements (PEs) connected in a particular fashion. There is a distributed representation: to represent knowledge implicitly in patterns of interactions between components (weights). For this reason, the term *connectionism* has been used to describe neural networks. Connectionism signals another departure of ANNs from mainstream AI, because the assumption of sequential processing is now replaced by massive parallelism.

ANNs mimic biological information processing mechanisms. They are typically designed to perform a nonlinear mapping from a set of inputs to a set of outputs. They have been developed to attempt biological system type performance using a dense interconnection of simple processing elements analogous to biological neurons. They are nonprogrammed adaptive information processing systems that can autonomously develop operational capabilities in response to an information environment. ANNs learn from experience and generalize from previous examples. They modify their behavior in response to the environment, and are ideal in cases where the required mapping algorithm is not known and tolerance to faulty input information is required. Therefore, ANNs offer certain advantages over many conventional techniques. These advantages are generalization capability, parallelism, distributed memory, redundancy, and learning.

### 6.6.2  Fundamental Concepts of Neural Networks

Neural networks constitute a class of predictive modeling system that works by iterative parameter adjustment. Structurally, a neural network consists of a number of interconnected elements (called *neurons*) organized in layers that learn by modifying the connection strengths (i.e., the parameters) connecting the layers.

Neural networks usually construct complex equational surfaces through repeated iterations, each time adjusting the parameters that define the surface. After many iterations, a surface may be "internally" defined that approximates many of the points within the data set (Parsaye 1999).

Each neuron usually has a set of weights that determine how it evaluates the combined strength of the input signals. Inputs coming into a neuron can be either positive (excitatory) or negative (inhibitory). Learning takes place by changing the weights used by the neuron in accordance with classification errors that were made by the net as a whole. The inputs are usually scaled and normalized to produce a smooth behavior.

Despite the apparent diversity among various models, any ANN model can be described by specifying the following basic components:

- Neuron model
- Network structure
- Learning rule

The structure of connectionist models can be described in greater detail according to their *network*, *cell*, *dynamic*, and *learning* properties (discussed further in Section 6.7).

**6.6.2.1  *Neuron Model***   A neuron is an information processing unit that is fundamental to the operation of a neural network. All models of artificial neurons try to resemble their biological counterparts that have a very complex structure and functionality. Although different types of neurons are known in neurophysiology, the biological neurons share a common capability to receive, process, and transmit electrochemical signals over the neural pathways that comprise the communication system of the brain.

The basic function of each neuron is to (1) evaluate input values, (2) calculate a total for the combined input values, (3) compare the total with a threshold value, and (4) determine what its own output will be. Although the operation of each neuron is fairly simple, complex behavior can be created by connecting a number of neurons together. Typically, the input neurons are connected to a middle layer (or several intermediate layers), which is then connected to an outer layer (Parsaye 1997).

In the context of artificial neural networks, the neuron is usually represented by the model shown in Figure 6.7. The general artificial neuron has a set of *n inputs* $\{x_1, x_2, \ldots, x_n\}$ representing the synaptic contacts between its cell body and the axons of the neurons it is connected with, and a single *output y* representing the neuron's axon. Each input $x_i$ is multiplied by an associated *weight* $w_i$ to indicate the strength of the synapse before it is applied to the summation block labeled by $\Sigma$. In addition, it has a *threshold* value $\theta$ that has to be reached or exceeded for the neuron to produce a signal. The summation block, corresponding roughly to the biological cell body, adds all the weighted inputs algebraically, producing an overall unit *activation u*. This activation is then processed by an *activation function F* to produce the neuron's output *y*. The function *F* is usually nonlinear to simulate the property of biological neurons to require a minimum activation above the threshold $\theta$ before firing and to reach a certain level of saturation with increasing activation.

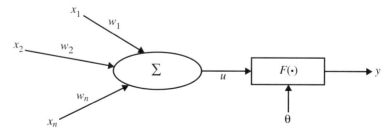

**Figure 6.7**   Basic neuron model.

Formally, the activity of a neuron is described completely by means of the following pair of equations:

$$u = \sum_{i=1}^{n} w_i x_i \qquad \text{activation}$$

$$y = F(u - \theta) \qquad \text{output}$$

where $(u - \theta)$ is named the *net input* of the neuron.

By viewing the threshold as a weight $w_0 = \theta$ associated with an input $x_0$ that is permanently set to $-1$, the equations can be reformulated as

$$Net = w_0 x_0 + \sum_{i=1}^{n} w_i x_i = \sum_{i=0}^{n} w_i x_i \qquad (6.1)$$

$$y = F(Net)$$

Regarding the use of different net input forms, the simple linear relation defining the neuron's input net can be extended to include high-order terms that are a polynomial combination of the input values. These neurons are called *high-order* or *also sigma–pi* neurons because the net input is a sum of products of $x_i$. The net input of the $k$th-order neurons is determined by

$$Net^{(k)} = x_{i_1} x_{i_2} x_{i_k}, \qquad i_{i=1,2,\ldots,w_k} \qquad j = 1, 2, \ldots k$$

where $n_k$ is the number of the $k$th-order neurons, $1 \leq n_k \leq n$.

Some examples of nonlinear activation functions are depicted in Figure 6.8.

### 6.6.2.2 Network Structure

Once a model for the neurons has been defined, the combined structure of neurons and connections of the network must be specified. The network structure, also called *topology* or *architecture*, includes the neural framework (number of neurons, number of layers, neuron model type, etc.) and the interconnection structure, describing how the neurons are connected to form the network.

The simplest topologies are the fully connected ones, where all possible connections are present. However, depending on the neural framework and learning rule, different schemes of interconnection can be used.

One common interconnection structure groups neurons having the same characteristics into layers, and allows all possible interlayer connections, but no intra- or supralayer ones. Layered topologies can be single-layer or multilayer. A *single-layer network* has only an input layer and an output (computational) layer. In a *multilayer network*, one or more hidden layers are inserted between the input and the output layer.

Besides the common layered topologies, there are a variety of other topologies, which are not necessarily layered or at least not homogeneously layered. Moreover, depending on how the network processes the flow of information,

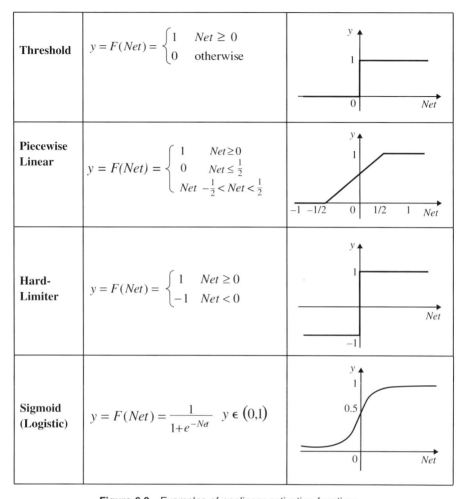

| Threshold | $y = F(Net) = \begin{cases} 1 & Net \geq 0 \\ 0 & \text{otherwise} \end{cases}$ | |
| --- | --- | --- |
| **Piecewise Linear** | $y = F(Net) = \begin{cases} 1 & Net \geq 0 \\ 0 & Net \leq \frac{1}{2} \\ Net & -\frac{1}{2} < Net < \frac{1}{2} \end{cases}$ | |
| **Hard-Limiter** | $y = F(Net) = \begin{cases} 1 & Net \geq 0 \\ -1 & Net < 0 \end{cases}$ | |
| **Sigmoid (Logistic)** | $y = F(Net) = \dfrac{1}{1+e^{-Na}} \quad y \in (0,1)$ | |

**Figure 6.8**  Examples of nonlinear activation functions.

neural network topologies can be roughly divided into feedforward and recurrent networks. In a *feedforward network* the information signal propagates only in a forward direction from input neurons through possible intermediate (hidden) neurons to output neurons, with no loops back to previous neurons (Figure 6.9a). Conversely, a *recurrent network* contains at least one feedback loop and hence allows the information signal to flow from a neuron back to itself either directly or through other neurons, as depicted in Figure 6.9b.

### 6.6.2.3  *Connectionist Machine Learning*  A key property of an artificial neural network is its ability to incorporate knowledge in the weights through

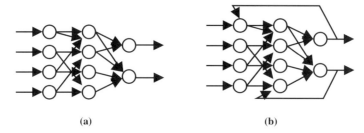

(a)                           (b)

**Figure 6.9**   Examples of (a) feedforward and (b) recurrent neural network.

learning. Generally speaking, in the context of neural networks, learning is an iterative process of adjustment applied to the synaptic weights (free parameters) of the network in response to an external stimulus. The process used to perform the learning process is called a *learning algorithm*, the function of which is to modify the synaptic weights so as to obtain a desired design objective. A learning algorithm generally goes through the following three steps:

*Step 1.*  Presentation of an external stimulus to the network.

*Step 2.*  Change in the weights as a result of this stimulation.

*Step 3.*  Evaluation of the new response of the network due to the changes that have occurred in its structure.

The manner in which the weight changes take place is described by a *learning rule* that is formulated by mathematical expressions called *weight updates*. There are a few basic categories of learning rules, depending on the external environment in which the network operates. These can be grouped into two main categories of learning methods, namely, supervised (or directed) learning and unsupervised learning.

### 6.6.3   Using Artificial Neural Networks for Data Mining

In general, artificial neural networks are especially useful for analytical problems in which

- A large amount of example data (in some cases, 30 gigabytes or more) is available and it is difficult to specify a parametric model for the data
- High input dimension and relationships exist within the data that are not fully understood, with many potential models that could be specified
- There are potentially stable patterns in the data that are subtle or deeply hidden
- The data exhibit significant uncharacterizable nonlinearity
- Iterative use of the data is required to detect patterns

- Problems are solved by generating predictions of complicated phenomena rather than by generating explanations

Common applications of neural networks include credit risk analysis, market segmentation, and sales prediction.

ANNs provide useful mechanism for various data mining tasks described in Chapter 5. For example, some of the features of the ANNs are important in pattern clustering (Jain et al. 1999):

- ANNs process numerical vectors and require patterns to be represented using quantitative features.
- ANNs may learn their interconnection weights adaptively.

The architectures of ANNs for clustering are simple because they are single-layered. Patterns are presented at the input and are associated with the output nodes. The weights between the input nodes and the output odes are iteratively changed until a termination criterion is satisfied.

In contrast to some misconception caused by some articles or books with misleading titles, ANNs are not necessarily a natural choice for data mining. In many applications the aim of ANNs technology is to discover and predict relationships in the data. A major problem with ANNs is that, although symbolic rules are suitable for verification or interpretation by humans, usually it is difficult for ANNs to explicitly state how classifications were made using such rules.

Nevertheless, there are many nice features of ANN, which make them attractive for data mining. As noted by Cios et al. (1998), these features include learning and generalization ability, adaptivity, content addressability, fault tolerance, self-organization, robustness, and simplicity of basic parallel computations. In terms of the knowledge discovery perspective, ANNs have been used for the following areas:

- *Clustering*—the unsupervised learning technique is useful for exploratory data analysis and data compression. A typical example is the self-organizing feature map (SOFM) network (see Section 6.8.2).
- *Prediction*—a typical example is a radial basis function (RBF) network.
- *Function approximation*—RBF and other ANNs are useful.
- *Associative memories*—contents stored in an ANN can be recalled correctly even when only distorted input is provided.
- *Image recognition* and *reduction* for pattern recognition

Artificial neural networks employ massive parallel computing. There are two basic approaches to exploiting parallelism in neural networks for data mining:

• Exploitation of control parallelism by distributing the neural network among the available processors
• Exploitation of data parallelism by distributing the data being mined among the available processors

## 6.7 NEURAL NETWORK MODELS OF SUPERVISED LEARNING

We now take a closer look on supervised learning, where both the input stimulus and the desired response to that stimulus are provided to the network by the external environment. In supervised learning, a *training set*, which contains both input patterns and the corresponding desired outputs (or target patterns), is presented iteratively to the network that is trained to implement a mapping that matches the training examples as closely as possible. During the training phase of learning, the network sets the weights that determine the behavior of the intermediate layer. Incorrect guesses reduce the thresholds for the appropriate connections. The learning rule derives from a combination of the current input stimulus and the *error signal*, defined as difference between the actual response of the network and the desired response. During the learning process, the network adjusts its parameters in response to an input stimulus so that its actual output response converges to the desired output response. When the actual output response is the same as the desired one, the network has completed the learning phase; in other words, it has "acquired knowledge." The task is to learn a mapping function, in terms of the set of network weights, that approximates the input–output relation. The best known examples of this technique occur in the Backpropagation algorithm, the delta rule, and the perceptron rule. Within the framework of supervised learning, there is also the *reinforcement learning*, where instead of correct responses for given inputs, the environment provides an indication about the correctness of the outputs, indicating whether these are right or wrong, which is called *reinforcement signal*. Reinforcement learning is sometimes called "learning with a critic," as opposed to supervised learning, also called "learning with a teacher."

### 6.7.1 Single-Layer Networks

Perceptron and Adaline are two models of single-layer networks which are simple but influential in the development of the field. Both networks basically consist of an input layer of $n$ neurons and a single output neuron, whose weights are adjusted by means of a learning rule that takes into account the error made by the single neuron for the current pattern, in an attempt to minimize a global error function that is a scalar measure of the extent of deviation of the neuron's output from the desired output on the whole training set.

The difference between Perceptron and Adaline consists mainly in the form of the activation function. As a consequence, the weight updates are performed according to different learning rules—Perceptron rule and delta rule, respectively. The *Perceptron rule* guarantees that the Perceptron will learn to correctly classify two classes of input patterns provided that the classes posses an important property called linearly separable. The *delta rule*, on the other hand, leads the Adaline to converge quite fast to a good solution regardless of linear separability.

A general scheme of the learning algorithm for both Perceptron and Adaline is shown below. Usually the stopping condition for determining the end of training is based on the magnitude of the gradient or on the minimal value of $E(\overline{w})$ (below a certain threshold).

**Algorithm for Perception and Adaline** Given a set of $P$ training patterns $(\overline{x}^{(p)}, t^{(p)})$, $\overline{x}^{(p)} = (x_1^p, \ldots, x_n^p)$:

*Step 1.* Initialize randomly the weights $w_i$, for $i = 1, \ldots, n$

*Step 2.* Repeat. For $p = 1, \ldots, P$ compute:

$$y^{(p)} = F(Net)^{(p)}$$

$$\delta^{(p)} = t^{(p)} - y^{(p)}$$

$$w_i = w_i + \eta \delta^{(p)} x_i^{(p)} \qquad \text{for } i = 1, \ldots, n$$

until (*Stopping Condition*).

## 6.7.2  Multilayer Networks and Backpropagation

The single-layer network models described previously can implement only a very limited class of mappings. Instead, multilayer feedforward neural networks, usually referred to as *multilayer perceptrons* (MLPs), can implement nonlinear input–output mappings of general nature. This property of *universal approximation* refers to the mapping capability of the MLP network that lays a mathematical foundation for its application to a wide variety of classification or function estimation problems.

MLP networks are built by combining simple perceptrons in a hierarchical structure forming a feedforward topology (see Figure 6.9a) with one or more layers of hidden neurons, between the input and the output neurons. In general, all neurons in a layer are connected to all neurons in the adjacent layers through unidirectional links. Using enough hidden neurons, and provided the activation functions of hidden neurons are nonlinear, any input–output relationship can be approximated arbitrarily well. In most applications, a single hidden layer is used with a sigmoid activation function for the neurons.

The Backpropagation (BP) algorithm, based on the chain rule and the gradient descent, is the simplest and the most widely used learning algorithm for feedforward multilayer neural networks. The BP algorithm is based on an iterative process. Each step of the this process involves two passes through the different layers of the network. During the first pass, referred as *forward pass*, an input $\bar{x}$ is presented and propagated forward through the network to compute the output value $y_j$ for each output neuron. The second phase involves a *backward pass* through the network during which the error signal is passed leftward through the network, layer by layer, and appropriate weight changes are calculated. The basic idea behind both of the weight update formulas involved in these phases, commonly referred to as *generalized delta rule*, is to determine a way to make the appropriate correction to a weight in proportion to the error that it causes. Weight updates can be applied after the presentation of each training pattern (*online* or *pattern training mode*) or after all training patterns have been presented to the network (*offline or batch training mode*). In the former case the BP algorithm is termed *stochastic*, while in the latter case it is classified as *deterministic*.

Several improvements of backpropagation have been developed in an attempt to overcome deficiencies of the standard BP algorithm. The most troublesome comes from the length of the training process, which depends on the number of iteration (passes through the training data) that are needed to minimize the error over the training set. The length of the training process also depends on the selected value of the learning rate.

Multilayer perceptrons (MLPs) and MLPs using backpropagation, or backpropagation networks (BPNs), are compared in Figure 6.10.

### 6.7.3  Radial Basis Function Networks

An alternative to the MLP network in many applications involving supervised learning is the *radial basis function* (RBF) network, which makes use of a family of radial basis functions to approximate and interpolate functions in multidimensional space. RBF networks can perform both classification and function approximation. As shown in Figure 6.11, an RBF network is a two-layer feedforward neural network. RBF networks are as an example of *composite network*, since the neuron models are different for each layer. Output nodes form a linear combination of the radial basis functions computed by hidden nodes.

The input layer simply feeds the input signals to the next layer. Neurons at the first layer (hidden layer) are activated by a radial basis function, which simulates a *localized receptive field* described by a center and eventually by a radius. The (nonlinear) basis function produces a significant nonzero response to input stimulus only when the input falls within the small region covered by the receptive field. The connections between the input layer and the hidden layer are not weighted, so each hidden neuron receives inputs unaltered. Neurons in the second layer (output layer) are simple linear units. The connections between the hidden layer and the output layer are weighted. The output layer of the network forms linear combinations of the input nonlinear transformation provided by the hidden layer. In contrast to multilayer perceptrons, which construct a global approximation to nonlinear input–output

| Multilayer perceptrons (MLP's) | Backpropagation networks (BPN's) |
|---|---|
| *Network properties*: Arbitrary feedforward networks. Cells are numbered so that the p input cells are indexed 1 through $p$, and so that if cell $u_j$ is connected to $u_i$, then $j < i$. | *Network properties*: Same as MLP's. |
| *Cell properties*: Cell inputs and activations are *discrete*, assuming values of {1, 0, -1}, with 1, 0, -1 representing true, false and unknown, respectively. Every cell computes its activation as a linear discriminant (or threshold logic function) of $S_i = \sum_{j=0}^{i-1} u_i$, where $u_i = 1$, -1 or 0, for $S_i > 0$, $S_i < 0$, or $S_i = 0$, respectively. | *Cell properties*: Inputs and activations are continuous, assuming values on [0, 1] or [-1, 1]. Activations are computed as $S_i = \sum_{j=0}^{i-1} u_i$, where $u_i = 1/(1 + e^{-S_i})$ if activations in [0, 1] are used (thus $u_i$ approaches 1 for large positive $S_i$ and approaches 0 for large negative $S_i$), or $u_i = -1 + 2/(1 + e^{-S_i})$ if activations in [-1, 1] are used (thus $u_i$ approaches 1 for large positive $S_i$ and approaches -1 for large negative $S_i$). |
| *Dynamic properties*: Evaluation of the network proceeds according to the cell ordering, with each cell computing and posting its new activation value before the next cell is examined. One pass through the network brings it to steady state, and the output cell activations are interpreted as the outputs for the entire network. | *Dynamic properties*: Same as MLP's. |
| *Learning properties*: Various algorithms. | *Learning properties*: Various algorithms using backpropagation. |

**Figure 6.10**   MLP versus BPN. [Revised from Gallent (1993).]

mapping, a RBF network constructs a local approximation using localized nonlinearities.

A sufficient condition for valid basis functions in RBF networks is that they must be conditionally or strictly positive definite. This can be determined based on its relationship with monotonic functions. Recall in mathematical analysis, a function $f(x)$ is monotonic on $(0,\infty)$ if it is positive for even derivatives and negative for odd derivatives, or $f(x) \geq 0$, $f'(x) \leq 0$, $f''(x) \geq 0$, etc., for $x \in (0,\infty)$. A function $f(x)$ is monotonic on $(0,\infty)$ if and only if $f(x^2)$ is positive. Therefore, if $f(x)$ is monotonic, then $f(x^2)$ can be used as a basis function.

Training in RBF networks involves finding centers, radii and weights. Precisely, the connection weights can be computed in different ways, depending on how the centers of radial basis functions are specified. A simple but expensive way is *weight computation without center selection*. To overcome this computational difficulty, schemes of *weight computation with center selection* can be used.

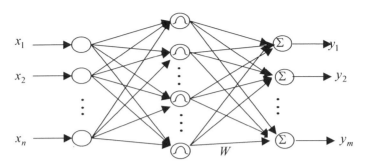

**Figure 6.11**   Schematic of a radial basis function network.

The popularity of the RBF network is due partly to the fact that, unlike most supervised learning ANN algorithms, it is able to find the global optimum. In contrast, using a feedforward ANN with backpropagation learning usually only the local optimum can be found. The popularity is also due to the shorter training time, most notably using backpropagation for adjustment of weights. In addition, the topology of the RBF network is very simple to set up, and requires no guesswork as with backpropagation. We will revisit RBF when we discuss the issue of supervised artificial neural networks and data mining.

As a final remark, recall that the RBF network is a composite network. Another kind of composite neural network, called a *probabilistic neural network* (PNN; also known as a *kernel neural network*), was first proposed as a neural implementation of the kernel-based probability density estimation and optimal Bayesian classification rule.

### 6.7.4   Supervised Artificial Neural Networks and Data Mining

#### 6.7.4.1   *Artificial Neural Networks and Interpretability*   A major disadvantage of neural networks lies in their knowledge representation. Acquired knowledge in the form of a network of unites connected by weighted links is difficult for humans to interpret. Various algorithms for the extraction of rules have been proposed. The methods typically impose restrictions regarding procedures used in training the given neural network, the network topology, and the discretization of input values (Han and Kamber 2000).

Fully connected networks are difficult to articulate, Hence, the first step toward extracting rules from neural networks is often network pruning. This consists of removing weighted links that do not result in a decrease in the classification accuracy of the given network. Once the training network has been pruned, some approaches will then perform link, unit, or activation value clustering. For example, clustering can be used to find the set of common activation values for each hidden unit in a given trained two-layer neural network. The combinations of these activation values for each hidden uit are analyzed. Rules are derided relating combinations of activation values with corresponding output unit values. Similarly, the sets of input values and activation values are studied to derive rules describing the relationship between the input and hidden unit layers. Finally, the two sets of rules may be combined to form IF/THEN rules. Other algorithms may derive rules of other forms including $M$-of-$N$ rules (where $M$ out of a given $N$ conditions in the rule antecedent must be true in order for the rule consequent to be applied), decision trees with $M$-of-$N$ tests, fuzzy rules, and finite automata.

Lu et al. (1996) presented an approach to discover symbolic classification rules using neural networks. With the proposed approach, concise symbolic rules with high accuracy can be extracted from a neural network. The network is first trained to achieve the required accuracy rate. Redundant connections of the network are then removed by a network pruning algorithm. The activation values of the hidden units in the network are analyzed, and classification rules are generated using the result of this analysis. The effectiveness of the proposed approach is clearly demonstrated by the experimental results on a set of standard data mining test problems. The rule extraction (RX) algorithm is shown below.

**Algorithm Rule Extraction from Neural Network**

*Step 1. Clustering.* Apply a clustering algorithm to find clusters of hidden node activation values.

*Step 2. Rule Generation*:

    a. *Output Rule Generation.* Enumerate the discretized activation values and compute the network outputs. Generate rules that describe the network outputs in terms of the discretized hidden unit activation values.

    b. *Input Rule Generation.* For each hidden unit, enumerate the input values that lead to them and generate a set of rules to describe the hidden units' discretized values in terms of the inputs.

*Step 3. Rule Merging.* Merge the two sets of rules obtained in step 3 to obtain rules that relate the inputs and outputs.

Sensitivity analysis can be used to assess the impact that a given input variable has on a network output. The output to the variable is varied while the remaining input variables are fixed at some value. Meanwhile, changes in the network output are monitored. The knowledge gained from this form of analysis can be represented in rules such as "IF $X$ decreases by $a\%$ THEN $Y$ increases by $b\%$."

***6.7.4.2 Using RBF Networks for Data Mining*** Cios et al. (1998) suggested that feedforward ANN in general and RBF networks in particular be used for data mining. Most ANN require the availability of a training data set,

However, even if we use an unsupervised ANN such as Knhonen's net (see Section 6.8), there is a problem with interpreting the results of the clustering operation it performs. The RBF network can be used in conduction with fuzzy logic for data mining. The RBF network is attractive because of its robustness and ability to work with large data sets when the radial basis centers are selected via clustering.

Under some weak conditions, the RBF network is equivalent to a system of fuzzy production rules. It has been demonstrated that a fuzzy system, as well as feedforward ANN, can approximate any continuous function. Therefore the approximation problem can be seen as a problem of designing a fuzzy system expressed in terms of fuzzy production rules from training data pairs. We can take advantage of this fact, because if we can quickly find a certain trend in the data using an RBF network, we can also find a corresponding set of fuzzy rules that describe the same trend.

We want to construct an ANN topology that is easy to interpret. The hidden layer in the RBF network is formed by a series of radial basis functions. The output neuron with a linear transfer function combines the outputs of the hidden layer neurons via its weights. When fuzzy context RBF networks are used, all connections are fuzzy sets, and not numbers (weights) as in the standard RBF network. In addition, these fuzzy sets are the fuzzy contexts already specified for the purpose of clustering. This makes it possible to eliminate the need for training for the output layer. One advantage of using fuzzy context is shorter training time. More important is that the network can now be interpreted in the form of the IF/THEN production rules. Since the connections between the neurons are now defined as fuzzy sets, the result is also a fuzzy set. The computations involve fuzzy arithmetic.

Finally, we can construct a collection of rules from the fuzzy context RBF network. The condition part of each rule is represented by the hidden layer cluster prototype, and the conclusion of the rule is formed by the associated fuzzy set of the context.

## 6.8 NEURAL NETWORK MODELS OF UNSUPERVISED LEARNING

A major problem encountered in supervised learning is that a set of learning examples is not always available, and the only information about the problem is provided by a set of input data. Examples of such problems are clustering, vector quantization, dimensionality reduction, and feature extraction. In these cases, learning is performed in an *unsupervised or self-organized* manner, without benefit of an external teacher response, and the learning algorithm should lead to the discovery of relevant information within the (redundant) training data. The basic learning rules to perform unsupervised learning are the Hebbian and the competitive rules, both inspired by neurobiological considerations.

### 6.8.1 Competitive Learning Networks

One of the most basic schemes of self-organizing networks is the *competitive learning network*, which can be described as a process in which output layer neurons compete among themselves to acquire the ability to fire in response to given input patterns. A simple competitive learning network for *clustering* data is a single-layer network composed of neurons, each fully connected to the input layer via excitatory connections. When an input pattern is presented, a winning output neuron $k$ is selected and activations are reset such that $y_k = 1$ and $y_{j \neq k} = 0$. This is the competitive aspect of the network, and we refer to the output layer as the "winner take all" layer.

The consequence of such competitive learning rules is the *clustering* of the input data. Each time an input vector is presented to the network, the weight vector most similar to this input vector is selected and made still more similar to this input. As a result, weight vectors are moved so as to locate them in the center as clusters in the input data. An almost identical procedure of moving cluster centers is used in a large family of conventional clustering algorithms such as the well-known $k$-means clustering algorithm (discussed in Chapter 5). One problem with the clustering based on competitive learning is that, if the weight vectors are randomly initialized, some neurons will never be chosen as winners and thus their weight vectors will never be moved. To distribute the weight vectors according to the density of input vectors that must be clustered, several techniques have been proposed such as initializing the weights to samples from the input itself or updating the weights of the winners as well as all of the losers but with a much smaller learning factor ("leaky" learning).

### 6.8.2 Self-Organizing Feature Map Networks

Another network that relies on the use of competitive learning but with different emergent properties is the *Kohonen self-organizing feature map* (SOFM), as shown in Figure 6.12. It is interesting to note that Kohonen net can be considered as ANN equivalent of the $k$-means algorithm. The topology and the learning process of a SOFM are intended to map a continuous high-dimensional space into a discrete one- or two-dimensional space, preserving the topology of the input space. A SOFM network is characterized by the formation of a topographic map of the input patterns, in which the spatial locations of the neurons, arranged in a one- or two-dimensional grid, correspond to intrinsic features of the input patterns; hence the name "self-organizing feature map."

This type of network tries to capture the essential features of the topologically ordered computational maps found in the brain. For the development of these maps, *localized lateral feedback* is established within the output layer by means of a set of connections and associated weights among output layer neurons. The magnitude and type (excitatory or inhibitory) of these weights

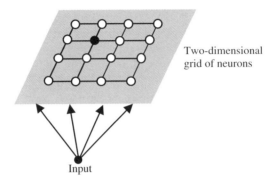

Two-dimensional grid of neurons

Input

**Figure 6.12** The SOFM network.

are functions of the geometric distance between neurons on the output grid. Hence, lateral connections serve to excite neurons in close physical proximity and to inhibit those farther away. Specifically, negative weights tend to inhibit the firing of other output neurons. Such lateral inhibition can be seen as contributing to the winner-take-all strategy described previously.

To induce topological organization among neurons, a SOFM network includes two types of connections: a set of *feedforward connections* between the external input and output layer, and a set of lateral connections within the output layer, which are *feedback connections*. The weights of such intralayer connections are fixed according to a well-suited function.

### 6.8.3 Adaptive Resonance Theory Networks

The *adaptive resonance theory* (ART) is a recurrent self-organizing network (see Figure 6.9b for architecture of recurrent network in general). The ART model was developed to solve the problem of instability in feedforward systems, particularly the *stability–plasticity dilemma*. ART networks solve this dilemma by embedding a self-regulating control structure into a competitive learning scheme. The models of these networks are consistent with cognitive and behavioral models. A family of ART neural network architectures has been progressively developed.

As shown in Figure 6.13, the architecture of the ART network has two layers of binary neurons: the input/comparison layer with a number of neurons equal to the dimension of the input pattern, and the output/classification layer with a number of neurons that is dynamically adapted during the learning process. The two layers interact through forward and backward connections having different types of weights. In addition, for each layer, there are signals that control the data flow.

The novelty of this approach is that the network is able to adapt to new incoming patterns but the previous memory is not corrupted. On the contrary,

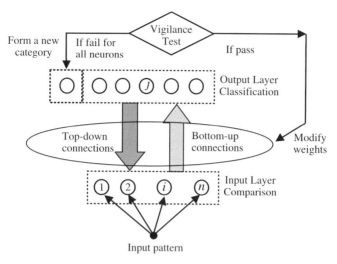

**Figure 6.13**    Architecture of the ART network.

in most neural networks, such as MLP networks, the teaching of new patterns may corrupt the weights for all previously learned patterns.

### 6.8.4  Principal-Component Networks

The main task performed by the networks presented in the previous sections is *clustering* or *classification* of patterns. Here, we briefly describe some self-organized network models, whose aim is to extract the most representative low-dimensional subspace from a high-dimensional pattern vector space; thus, they can perform the principal-component analysis (PCA) of input data. Single-layer models of these networks are able to measure familiarity or projecting the input data onto the principal components, and may be used for data compression or dimensionality reduction. Moreover, in a network with a multilayer structure this can lead to some *feature extraction* properties.

All learning rules for principal-component networks can be considered as a variant of the *Hebbian learning rule*. The basic idea is that if two neurons $j$ and $k$ are active simultaneously, their interconnection must be strengthened. The Hebb postulate, in its simplest version, prescribes modification of the weight $w_{jk}$ of the connection from neuron $j$ to neuron $k$, with the learning rule, where the change in the synaptic weight $w_{jk}$ is computed as a product of the incoming signal $x_j$ and the outgoing signal $j_k$. This rule emphasizes the correlation nature of the Hebbian interconnection and is often referred to as the *activity product rule*. However, this basic learning rule would make the weights grow exponentially if there were correlations in the input patterns. To avoid such a saturation, different modifications of the Hebbian rule have been proposed.

The principal-component network that consists of a single-linear neuron can evolve into a filter for the first principal component of the input pattern distribution by adapting its weights using a modified Hebbian rule. In other words, the weight vector of a single neuron can converge to the eigenvector of the correlation matrix with maximum eigenvalue, where the weights of the neuron are directed in the direction of highest energy of variance of the input patterns.

Another neural network that performs PCA has both forward and feedback connections. The strength of forward connections is modified by Hebbian rule, whereas the (lateral) feedback connections follow an anti-Hebbian rule (this rule tries to decorrelate the neuron activities). The learning algorithm, called *adaptive principal-component extraction* (APEX), performs a recursive computation of the principal components.

### 6.8.5   Unsupervised Artificial Neural Networks and Data Mining

The SOFM has several beneficial features that make it a useful methodology for exploratory phase in KDD (Vesanto 1997). It follows the probability density function of the underlying data and is readily explainable, simple and (perhaps most importantly) highly visual. It is most useful as a data exploration tool. The SOFM provides excellent visualization capabilities, including techniques to give an informative picture of the data space, and techniques to compare data vectors or whole data sets with each other. The SOFM can also be used for clustering, classification, and modeling. SOFM is very effective in clustering (withougt being told the number of clusters) and data reduction, but it can also be used for data cleaning and preprocessing. Integrated with other methods, it can be used for rules extraction and regression.

As a feature related to uncertain reasoning, it is interesting to note how the SOFM deals with errors in data. The SOFM suffers from the presence of any kind of flaws in the data, but the degradation of performance is gradual. An outlier in the data only effects one map unit and its neighbors. The outlier is also easy to detect from the map, since its distance in the input space from other units is large. An important property of the SOFM is that it can be used even on partial data, or data with missing data component values. Only a simple change to the algorithm is needed, namely, if the sample input vector on a specific training step has missing components, they are simply omitted from the distance calculations and the updating procedure. The algorithm remains statistically valid unless the number of missing components in the vector is large.

### 6.9   THEORETICAL AND PRACTICAL ISSUES ABOUT ARTIFICIAL NEURAL NETWORKS

Although significant progress has been made in artificial neural networks, the foundation of its theory is not without questions. A debate about how the brain learns is discussed in Roy (2000), which starts from a discussion on the distinction between memory and learning. It has been noticed that there are various problems of connectionism, or the so-called misconceptions:

- The connectionist conjecture that no other physical entity directly signals changes in a cell's behavior is a major misconceptions about the brain.
- The brain does not collect or store any information about the problem prior to actual learning.
- The brain learns instantly from each and every learning example presented to it.
- The networks are predesigned and externally supplied to the brain and the learning parameters are externally supplied as well.

Therefore, connectionism's autonomous learners, in the end, are directed and controlled by other sources after all! As a conclusion, there are subsystems within the brain that control other subsystems. This discussion reveals inconsistency of foundations of artificial neural networks. How to deal with misconceptions or how to fix the problems remains a research challenge. (An earlier, but similar, criticism of the foundation of fuzzy logic is sketched in Chapter 7.)

Challenging issues also exist in the practice of neural networks (Parsaye 1999). Remember that neural networks are opaque equational techniques since they compute surfaces internally within a numeric space. As data is repeatedly fed into the network, the parameters are changed so that the surface becomes closer to the data point.

Neural networks can be trained to reasonably approximate the behavior of functions on small and medium-sized data sets since they are universal approximators. However, in practice they work only on subsets and samples of data and at times run into problems when dealing with larger data sets, such as failure to converge or being stuck in a local minimum.

It is well known that backpropagation networks are similar to regression. There are several other network training methods that go beyond backpropagation, but still have problems in dealing with large data sets. One key problem for applying neural nets to large data sets is the preparation problem. If the data reside in a data warehouse environment, the data has to be mapped into real numbers before the network can use it. This is a difficult task for commercial data with many nonnumeric values.

Since input to a neural network has to be numeric (and normalized), interfacing to a large data warehouse may become a problem. For each data field used in a neural net, we need to perform scaling and coding. The numeric (and date) fields are normalized (or *scaled*). They are mapped into a scale that makes them uniform. This can be done through normalization (as discussed in Chapter 2). However, nonnumeric values cannot be easily mapped to numbers in a direct manner since this will introduce "unexpected relationships" into the data, leading to errors later. For instance, if we have 100 cities, and assign 100 numbers to them, cities with values 98 and 99 will seem more related together than those with numbers 2 and 79.

To be used in a neural network, values for nonscalar fields such as city, state, or product need to be coded and mapped into "new attributes," taking the values 0 or 1, in a way similar to bitmap index (as briefly discussed in Chapter 3). This means that the attribute "North Plain State" which may have five values: {MN, SD, ND, NE, IA} is no longer used. Instead, we have five new attributes, called MN, SD, ND, NE, IA, each taking the value 0 or 1, depending on the value in the record. For each tuple, only one of these attributes has the value 1, and the others have the value 0.

The solution introduced here is apparently questionable when the values of an attribute are big. Some systems try to overcome this problem by grouping the large number of values (say, $M = 2000$) into a smaller number of groups (say, $N = 100$), so that each group will contain 100 cities values. However, this may introduce bias into the system, since in practice it is hard to know what the optimal groups are, and for large warehouses this requires too much human intervention.

The distinguishing power of neural networks comes from their ability to deal with smooth surfaces that can be expressed in equations. These suitable application areas are varied and include fingerprint identification and facial pattern recognition. However, with suitable analytical effort neural network models can also succeed in many other areas such as financial analysis and adaptive control.

## 6.10  SUMMARY

In this chapter we studied two approaches using symbolism and subsymbolism. We now summarize our discussion with a specific remark on their integration as reflected in knowledge-based neural networks.

An interesting connection between symbolic reasoning and subsymbolic reasoning is through connectionist expert systems. There are several practical reasons for this. First we want to solve the problem of automatic constructing knowledge bases for expert systems. In addition, a network can make inferences from partial information, suggest useful pieces of information that are not yet known, and justify inferences by producing IF/THEN rules (even though there are no IF/THEN rules explicitly in the knowledge base (Gallent 1993).

A shortcoming of neural networks is their negligence of background knowledge and compilaitons with the search for the ideal topology. A knowledge-based ANN system was developed to learn in logic and then tune the acquired knowledge by way of neurl network training (Kubat et al. 1998). Two steps characterize the system. First, the knowledge is translated into the network where the supporting facts are modeled by input units; intermediate concepts, by hidden units; and the final concepts, by output units. The dependencies between units in different layers are represented by weights. At this stage, all weights have the same absolute value. In the second step, the network is enlarged to also give a chance to those predicates and facts that have not explicitly appeared in the background knowledge. Then, the weights ar slightly perturbed by radom numbers and the net is trained by the backpropagation algoirthm.

The concept of using a number to denote a kind of uncertainty, such as in the case of probability theory, has been adopted by may other theories on uncertain reasoning. In the next chapter, we will discuss some numerical approaches to deal with uncertainty, and examine how they can be used in various tasks of data mining.

# 7

# UNCERTAIN REASONING TECHNIQUES FOR DATA MINING

## 7.1 OVERVIEW

In Chapter 6, we examined two specific approaches to explore the relationship between data mining and uncertain reasoning. In this chapter, we take a further look at several other reasoning methods in uncertainty. The term *uncertain reasoning* focuses on the mechanisms (or means) used in deriving new knowledge when uncertainty is present, while the term *data mining* puts emphasis on the results derived from data in various applications. However, as we pointed out in the last section of Chapter 4, uncertain reasoning can effectively achieve the goal of data mining. This chapter exploits this perspective. Since there are many books available on uncertain reasoning, our focus here is not on the techniques themselves; rather, we want to use this discussion to show why and how each individual approach is able to deal with uncertainty, under which conditions each approach is most appropriate, what the most important features of each approach are, and, most importantly, why and how each approach can (in its own way) contribute to data mining. Note also that these uncertain reasoning techniques have been developed to analyze data sets, and seldom assume any database environment.

In general, uncertain reasoning methods discussed in Chapters 6 and 7 can serve as *techniques* for tasks of data mining as discussed in Chapter 5. In particular, they can significantly facilitate the classification task as described in Chapter 5. However, we should also keep in mind that they are *not* necessary components of the data mining process, because data mining tasks have been developed in their own right. We should also be aware that performing uncertain reasoning on a set of data does not necessarily mean that we are doing data mining, because data analysis could be only a minor step in a large task that is unrelated to data mining. Therefore, a very important theme of this chapter is to identify aspects of various uncertain reasoning methods that are useful for data mining.

Each approach discussed in this chapter deals with uncertain reasoning and data mining in a unique manner. Fuzzy logic, as discussed in Section 7.2, representing a mathematical approach, deals with vagueness. As a mathematical theory, it is aimed to capture uncertainty by proving a quantitative description, in a way similar to probability theory (as outlined in Chapters 4 and 6). However, the type of uncertainty to be captured is very different from that handled by probability theory. In Section 7.3, we discuss genetic algorithm and evolutionary algorithms literature. Another mathematical theory called *rough set theory* (discussed in Section 7.4) takes a reductionist approach to reveal the true systems by removing uncertainty. Unlike the two approaches mentioned above, rough set theory does not rely on a specific measure (as in the case of probability theory and fuzzy set theory, which use probability and fuzzy membership function, respectively).

Another issue to be addressed is scalability. Approaches based on genetic algorithms, Tabu search, and simulated annealing are optimization techniques and are restricted to reasonably small data sets.

## 7.2  FUZZY LOGIC

### 7.2.1  Basics

Whereas probability theory is aimed at coping with randomness in reasoning, fuzzy logic deals with a different kind of uncertainty, namely, vagueness. Fuzzy logic, first developed by Lotfi Zadeh, provides an approximate but effective means of describing the behavior of systems that are too complex, ill-defined, or not easily analyzed mathematically. The traditional Boolean algebra has no provision for approximate reasoning. Fuzzy logic is an extension of Boolean logic in the sense that it also provides a platform for handling uncertain and imprecise knowledge. Fuzzy logic uses fuzzy set theory, in which a variable is a member of one or more sets, with a specified degree of membership, usually denoted by $\mu$.

As noted in Cios et al. (1998), a fuzzy set can be regarded as an elastic constraint imposed on the elements of a universe or a domain. An interesting analogy is an elastic rubberband and the membership value can be viewed as inversely proportional to the force needed to stretch the rubber band.

Advocates of fuzzy set theory have argued that the attempts to automate various types of activities from assembling hardware to medical diagnosis have been impeded by the gap between the way human beings reason and how computers are programmed. Fuzzy logic uses graded statements rather than ones that are strictly true or false. It attempts to incorporate the "rule of thumb" approach generally used by human beings for decisionmaking. Thus, fuzzy logic provides an approximate but effective way of describing the behavior of systems that are not easy to describe precisely. Fuzzy logic controllers, for example, are extensions of the common expert systems that use production rules like "IF/THEN." With fuzzy controllers, however, linguistic variables like "tall" and "very tall" might be incorporated in a traditional expert system. The result is that fuzzy logic can be used in controllers that are capable of making intelligent control decisions in sometimes volatile and rapidly changing problem environments.

The most commonly used fuzzy logic functions for implementing complement, logical AND (min), and logical OR (max) are defined as follows:

$$\mu_{(-A)} = 1 - \mu_A$$

$$\mu_{(A \wedge B)} = \min(\mu_A, \mu_B)$$

$$\mu_{(A \vee B)} = \max(\mu_A, \mu_B)$$

Fuzzy variables are processed using a system called a *fuzzy logic controller*. It involves fuzzification, fuzzy inference, and defuzzification. The fuzzification process converts a crisp input value to a fuzzy value. The fuzzy inference is responsible for drawing conclusions from the knowledge base. The defuzzification process converts the fuzzy control actions into a crisp control action. The basic structure of a fuzzy controller is shown in Figure 7.1.

As an example, consider a fuzzy control system that uses the value of room temperature (temp.) as input to control an air conditioner:

$$\text{Room temp (crisp)} = 30°C \Rightarrow \text{room temp. (fuzzy)} = \text{HIGH}$$

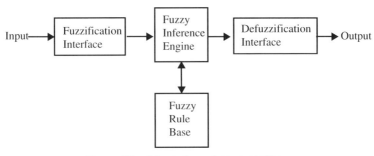

**Figure 7.1**  A basic fuzzy logic controller.

The conversion of crisp input values to fuzzy values is performed using membership functions that, in a sense, provide fuzzy terms with a definite meaning. Every fuzzy set that is used to specify a certain variable in terms of fuzzy values is defined by means of a membership function. The degree of membership of a crisp input value to a certain fuzzy set represents the confidence, expressed as a number from 0 to 1, which a particular (crisp) value belongs to this fuzzy set.

The fuzzy knowledge base usually contains a set of rules. A rule is a condition statement taking the form of IF/THEN rules. As an example, the following rule for manipulating the air conditioner in an automobile is given:

> IF day temperature is high AND motor speed is high THEN switch on the air conditioner.

The fuzzy inference engine is responsible for drawing conclusions from the knowledge base, thereby generating fuzzy control actions in response to fuzzified inputs.

Figure 7.2 is an example showing the calculation of the degree of membership of temperature $T^*$ to the fuzzy sets MED and HIGH. In this example a simple fuzzy logic controller is used to control an airconditioner, based on measurements of the room temperature.

The defuzzification unit converts the fuzzy control actions, as generated by the fuzzy inference engine into a nonfuzzy (crisp) control action. And, this is an important point. Fuzzy systems can provide crisp, exact control actions. Thus, they can be used to effectively manipulate systems that require precise actions. A commonly used defuzzification technique uses the centroid method, which defines the crisp output as the center of gravity of the distribution of possible actions. The equation for calculating the center of gravity is

$$\Delta\eta = \frac{\int x\mu(x)\,dx}{\int \mu(x)\,dx}$$

where $\mu(x)$ = grade of membership of an element $x$ to a function $\mu$.

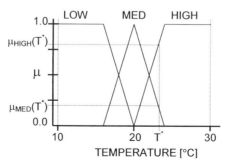

**Figure 7.2**  Fuzzy membership.

## 7.2.2 Fuzzy Inference Laws

*Fuzzy inference* refers to an inference method that uses fuzzy implication relations, fuzzy composition operators, and an operator to link the fuzzy rules. The result of the inference process is some new facts based on the fuzzy rules and the input information supplied. A popular reasoning strategy is generalized modus ponens. When this law is applied over a simple fuzzy rule, it works in the following manner:

$$\text{IF } x \text{ is } A, \quad \text{THEN } y \text{ is } B,$$
$$\text{Now } x \text{ is } A' \underline{\hspace{2cm}}$$
$$\text{so } y \text{ is } B'.$$

The most important difference between the fuzzy logic and the conventional two state logic must be their inference techniques. Consider the simple rule of the form.

| IF $A$ THEN $C$ | $A$ is the antecedent of the rule |
| $A'$ | $A'$ is the matching fact in the fact database |
| $C'$ | $C$ is the consequent of the rule |
| | $C'$ is the actual consequent calculated |

In the two-state logic, the antecedent $A$ and fact $A'$ have to be exactly the same to issue the conclusion $C'$ referring to consequent $C$. On the other hand, in the fuzzy logic, the rule can issue the actual consequent $C'$ as long as the matching fact $A'$ is somewhat belongs to the antecedent $A$. Four types of rules can be considered, as shown in Table 7.1.

For more detail on fuzzy rule evaluation, see Chen (1999).

## 7.2.3 Remark on the Nature of Fuzzy Logic

Fuzzy logic may be viewed with two different meanings: (1) a narrow interpretation, in which fuzzy logic is basically a logic of approximate reasoning; and (2) a wide interpretation, in terms of which fuzzy logic is coextensive with the theory of fuzzy sets, that is, classes of objects in which the transition from membership to nonmembership is gradual rather than abrupt. In its wide sense, fuzzy logic is a very broad theory with many branches.

**Table 7.1 Types of Inference Rules**

| Antecedent | Consequent | Type of Rule |
|---|---|---|
| CRISP | CRISP | CRISP–CRISP |
| CRISP | FUZZY | CRISP–CRISP |
| FUZZY | CRISP | FUZZY–CRISP |
| FUZZY | FUZZY | FUZZY–FUZZY |

The resurgence of interest in fuzzy logic since the late 1990s is due to a number of factors:

- Fuzzy logic provides an approximate but effective means of describing the behavior of the systems that are too complex or ill-defined and not easy to tackle mathematically. As the complexity of a system increases, our ability to make precise yet significant statements about its behavior diminishes until a threshold is reached beyond which precision and relevance become almost mutually exclusive characteristics.
- Attempts to automate various types of activities from assembling a personal computer to diagnosing a patient have been impeded by the gap between how human reasons and how computers are generally programmed. Thus, fuzzy logic is a step forward toward automation.

A large number of commercial applications have appeared. These applications have helped to reinforce the idea that fuzzy logic can reduce the time needed to develop many complex systems. Nevertheless, just as the case of artificial neural networks (as discussed in Chapter 6), fuzzy logic has been a controversial topic since its inception, and many researchers in mainstream AI remain skeptical about the significance of fuzzy logic and its potential for providing answers to some of the enduring problems in knowledge representation, commonsense reasoning, as well as others. A heated debate, surrounding Charles Elkan's well-known paper on the paradoxical success of fuzzy logic, can be found in Shastri (1994). Note that this debate has little impact on the popularity of fuzzy logic; rather, it has raised interesting philosophical issues related to fuzzy logic for further exploration.

### 7.2.4    Fuzzy Logic for Data Mining

There are various explanations on the role of fuzzy logic in data mining. We summarize some of them here.

1. *Knowledge Granulation.* As noted by Cios et al. (1998), fuzzy sets are conceptual extensions of the generic set theoretic framework, and as such, are predominantly geared toward various aspects of knowledge representation and, predetermining most of activities of data mining, especially knowledge granulation. Fuzzy set theory can thus assist data mining in dealing with knowledge granulation. Fuzzy sets are linguistic information granules capturing concepts with continuous boundaries. They naturally fit as one among contributing technologies of data mining. Humans operate on information granules rather than on numbers. The size of the information granules implies a certain point of view at data, and help to make associations at this level of specificity (granularity) of information (Negoita 2000).

2. *Better Tolerance.* Fuzzy sets exploit uncertainty in an attempt to make system complexity manageable. Fuzzy logic is not only able to deal with incomplete, noisy or imprecise data but may also be helpful in developing uncertain models of the data that provide smarter and smoother performance than do traditional systems. Since fuzzy systems can tolerate uncertainty and can even utilize languagelike vagueness to smooth data, they may offer robust, noise-tolerant models or predictions in situations where precise input is unavailable or too expensive (Goebel and Gruenwald 1999).

3. *Data Classification.* Related to knowledge granularity, fuzzy logic provides the advantage of working at a high level of abstraction. Consequently, fuzzy logic is useful for data mining systems performing classification (Han and Kamber 2000). When fuzzy logic is used for classification, attribute values are converted to fuzzy values; for example, the attribute "age" can be mapped into the discrete categories {young, mid-aged, old} with fuzzy values calculated. Note that for a given new sample, more than one fuzzy value may apply, each applicable rule contributes a vote for membership in the categories and truth values for each predicted category are typically summed.

4. *"Indirect" Contribution to Data Mining through Its Relationship with Artificial Neural Networks.* Fuzzy set theory by itself is neither a machine learning nor a data mining technique; however, fuzzy set theory has close ties with the weights used in artificial neural networks, which are well known for their learning abilities.

5. *Increased Chance of Knowledge Discovery Due to Vagueness.* Fuzzy set theory can also be combined with other data mining and uncertain reasoning approaches; by allowing vagueness, the chance of uncovering hidden knowledge using these methods can be enhanced. Therefore, fuzzy logic may still play an active role in data mining, even though it is not a data mining method itself. For example, the concepts of support and confidence in association rules are related to uncertainty, which are mainly probability but not necessarily fuzzy. However, we can extend association rules to fuzzy association rules along several directions, such as "young females who buy skim milk are very likely to buy diet food as well", where here "young" and "very likely" are fuzzy concepts. (Note that "very likely" is not the same as confidence.)

## 7.3 EVOLUTIONARY COMPUTING AND GENETIC ALGORITHMS

### 7.3.1 Evolutionary Computing

*Evolutionary computing* refers to the task consisting of a collection of algorithms based on the evolution of a population toward a solution of a certain problem. These algorithms can be used successfully in many applications requiring the optimization of a certain multidimensional function. The population of possible solutions evolves from one generation to the next, ultimately arriving at a satisfactory solution to the problem. These algorithms differ in the way in which a new population is generated from the present one, and in how the members are represented within the algorithm. Three types of evolutionary computing techniques have been widely reported: *genetic algorithms* (GAs), *genetic programming* (GP), and *evolutionary algorithms* (EAs). The EAs can be divided into evolutionary strategies (ESs) and evolutionary programming (EP). All three of these algorithms are modeled in some way after the evolutionary processes occurring in nature. In the following, we will briefly examine genetic algorithms (GAs).

## 7.3.2   Genetic Algorithms

Genetic algorithms are general-purpose search algorithms that use principles inspired by natural genetic populations to evolve solutions to problems. The basic idea is to maintain a population of knowledge structures that evolves over time through a process of competition and controlled variation. Each structure in the population represents a candidate solution to the concrete problem and has an associated fitness to determine which structures are sued to form new ones in the competition process. The new ones are created using genetic operators such as crossover and mutation. Genetic algorithms have had a great measure of success in search and optimization problems. The reason for a great part of their success is their ability to exploit the information accumulated about an initially unknown search space in order to bias subsequent searches into useful subspaces, namely, their robustness. This is their key feature, particularly in large, complex, and poorly understood search spaces, where classical search tools, such as enumerative or heuristic methods, are inappropriate, offering a valid approach to problems requiring efficient and effective search techniques. Genetic algorithms are most appropriate for optimization-type problems.

Genetic algorithms were envisaged in the 1970s as an algorithmic concept based on a Darwinian-type survival-of-the-fittest strategy with sexual reproduction, where stronger individuals in the population have a higher chance of creating an offspring. A genetic algorithm is implemented as a computerized search and optimization procedure that uses principles of natural genetics and natural selection. The basic approach is to model the possible solutions to the search problem as strings of ones and zeros. Various portions of these bitstrings represent parameters in the search problem. If a problem-solving mechanism can be represented in a reasonably compact form, then GA techniques can be applied using procedures to maintain a population of knowledge structure that represent candidate solutions, and then let that population evolve over time through competition (survival of the fittest and controlled variation). The GA applies genetic operations (e.g., selection, crossover and mutation to be discussed below) to modify the chosen solutions and select the most appropriate offspring to pass on to succeeding generations. GAs consider many points in the search space simultaneously and have been found to provide a rapid convergence to a near-optimum solution in many types of problems; in other words, they usually exhibit a reduced chance of converging to local minima. It is important to note that GAs show promise but suffer from the problem of excessive complexity if used on problems that are too large. Therefore, scalability is a key factor for applying GAs for data mining.

Generic algorithms are an iterative procedure consisting of a constant-sized population of individuals, each one represented by a finite linear string of symbols, known as the *genome*, encoding a possible solution in a given problem space. This space, referred to as the GA search space, comprises all possible solutions to the optimization problem at hand. Standard genetic algorithms are implemented where the initial population of individuals is generated at random. At every evolutionary step, also known as *generation*, the individuals in the current population are decoded and evaluated according to a *fitness function* set for a given problem. The expected number of times an individual is chosen is approximately proportional to its relative performance in the population. Crossover is performed between two selected individuals by exchanging part of their genomes to form new individuals. The mutation operator is introduced to prevent premature convergence.

Every member of a population has a certain fitness value associated with it, which represents the degree of correctness of that particular solution or the quality of solution it represents. The initial population of strings is randomly chosen. The strings are manipulated by the GA using genetic operators, to finally arrive at a quality solution to the given problem. GAs converge rapidly to quality solutions. Although they do not guarantee convergence to the single best solution to the problem, the processing leverage associated with GAs make them efficient search techniques. The main advantage of a GA is that it is able to manipulate numerous strings simultaneously, where each string represents a different solution to a given problem. Thus, the possibility of the GA getting stuck in local minima is greatly reduced because the whole space of possible solutions can be searched simultaneously. A basic genetic algorithm makes use of three genetic operators, namely, selection, crossover, and mutation.

The basic idea of GA can be summarized as follows. Starting from an initial population of strings (representing possible solutions), the GA uses these operators to calculate successive generations. First, pairs of individuals of the current population are selected to mate with each other to form the offspring, which then form the next generation. *Selection* is based on the survival-of-the-fittest strategy, but the key idea is to select the better individuals of the population, as in tournament selection, where the participants compete with each other to remain in the population. A commonly used strategy to select pairs of individuals is the method of *roulette-wheel selection*, in which every string is assigned a slot in a simulated wheel sized in proportion to the string's relative fitness. This ensures that highly fit strings have a greater probability to be selected to form the next generation through crossover and mutation.

After selection of the pairs of parent strings, the *crossover* operator is applied to each of these pairs. The crossover operator involves the swapping of genetic material (bit values) between the two parent strings. In single-point crossover, a bit position along the two strings is selected at random and the two parent strings exchange their genetic material.

The *mutation* operator alters one or more bit values at randomly selected locations in randomly selected strings. Mutation takes place with a certain probability, which, in accordance with its biological equivalent, typically occurs with a very low probability. The mutation operator enhances the ability of the GA to find a near-optimal solution to a given problem by maintaining a sufficient level of genetic variety in the population, which is needed to make sure that the entire solution space is used in the search for the best solution. In a sense, it serves as an insurance policy; it helps prevent the loss of genetic material.

The following is a simple example of rule encoding in GA. It also illustrates how GA can be used for optimization (Cios et al. 1998). Consider a classification rule with the structure of

IF p(Color) and q(Temperature) and r(Size)
THEN Positive conclusion.

Let us consider the structure of the condition. Assume that there are three possible colors, c1, c2, and c3; two possible temperature, t1 and t2; and two possible sizes, s1 and s2. The predicates p, q, r describe any OR combinations of the values of attributes Color, Temperature and Size, respectively. If we use a single bit to represent a particular value of a predicate, the "c1 or c3" can be represented as 101.

Therefore, to encode a rule involving all the possible values of variables require $3 + 2 + 2 = 9$ bits. For example, the string 1100110 denotes the rule IF c1 or c2 and t2 and s1 THEN Positive conclusion.

We can define fitness function as $f = e_+ + (1 - e_-)$, where

$$e_+ = \frac{n_p}{n_+}$$

$$e_- = \frac{n_n}{n_-}$$

where $n_p$ = the number of all data identified as belong to the class (Positive conclusion)

$n_+$ = the number of all positive instances encountered in the population of the patterns

$n_n$ = the number of all data identified as belonging to the class (Positive conclusion)

$n_-$ = the number of all negative instances encountered in the population of the patterns

The crossover mechanism swaps the content of two binary strings, thus contributing to the increased diversity in the population of the strings. For example, consider the crossover applied to the following strings of (1) and (2):

1. 1100110 ("IF c1 or c2 and t2 and s1 THEN Positive conclusion")
2. 1010001 ("IF c1 or c3 and s2 THEN Positive conclusion")

If we apply crossover at the position after the fourth bit, we get two new strings standing for two new rules:

1. 1100001 ("IF c1 or c2 and t3 THEN Positive conclusion")
2. 1010110 ("IF c1 or c3 and t2 and s1 THEN Positive conclusion").

The fitness function can be used to evaluate the quality of each rule obtained. Note that the search space in this example is $2^7$.

Genetic data mining can also be carried out through induction techniques (as discussed in Chapter 5). The rules to be generated are of the IF/THEN form. It consists of a collection of predicate—value pairs. For example, if we want to express "a personal computer product that which is made in Korea and is of color yellow is profitable," we can first write it in predicate form: "Product (p) $\land$ made_in(p, Korea) $\land$ color (p, yellow) $\Rightarrow$ profitable." Then we can encode it as a string shown below:

| PC | p | made_in | p | Korea | Color | p | Yellow |
|---|---|---|---|---|---|---|---|

After rules are encoded, standard techniques of genetic algorithms can be used. In addition, we can generalize predicates as well as the values. For example, suppose that PC is generalized to electronic appliance, Korea is generalized to East Asia, and yellow is generalized to light color, we will end up the rule like below:

| Electronic appliance | p | made_in | p | East Asia | Color | p | Light color |
|---|---|---|---|---|---|---|---|

If no more generalization is possible, then predicate is dropped, replacing the previous predicate by an empty symbol.

The fitness function can be defined to reflect the criteria of completeness and complexity, where consistency is defined as $(N_- - n_-)/N$, while completeness is defined as $n_+/N_+$, where $N_+$, $N_-$ are positive and negative examples, respectively, while $n_+$ and $n_-$ are positive and negative examples covered by the rules, respectively.

Genetic algorithms are used for a number of different application areas. An example is multidimensional optimization problems in which the character string of the chromosome can be used to encode the values for the different parameters being optimized. Mathematically, it can be shown that the process of fitness proportionate reproduction is near optimal in some senses.

In practice, therefore, we can implement the genetic model of computation by having arrays of bits or characters to represent the chromosomes. Simple bit manipulation operations allow the implementation of crossover, mutation, and other operations. Although a substantial amount of research has been performed on variable-length strings and other structures, the majority of work with genetic algorithms is focused on fixed-length character strings.

In addressing real-world problems the following features are required from a genetic algorithm (beyond the standard GA functionality):

1. The user should be able to represent the parameters of the problem as numeric variables (phenotype or feature genes). Mapping these numeric variables into genotype genes (in bits) is carried out by the algorithm, which should be transparent to the user.

2. The algorithm should allow the number of genes to be a variable that is determined at runtime.

3. The algorithm should allow the genes to be structured into a number of chromosomes (which are groups of genes). The genetic operators (such as crossover and mutation) should work on each chromosome independently.

4. The algorithm should support different types of phenotype genes, numeric, index, and sequence. Numeric genes are used to represent numeric parameters (real or integer numbers), and the developer should be able to define the minimum and maximum allowable values for each gene. Index genes are used to represent selections from lists of options, and each gene can have a defined maximum value. Sequence genes are used to return an ordered list of index genes.

5. The genetic operators (mutation and crossover) should ensure that only valid gene values are generated, that is, numeric or index gene values falling within the minimum and maximum allowable values, and sequence genes having unique values within a chromosome. The algorithm should have a strategy for repairing genes in order to meet the value constraints.

6. An additional genetic operator is often needed to fine tune the genetic search in the later stages of the evolution cycle. This operator named as *adaptation* by Al-Attar (1994) is inspired by the principles of Lamarkian adaptation. The operator is very similar to mutation, except that it would only retain mutations which improve the individual.

7. It is beneficial for the algorithm to support an optional crossover operator for sequence genes which functions at phenotype gene level.

Evolutionary approaches can be used for clustering (discussed in Chapter 5). An evolutionary algorithm for clustering is summarized below.

**Algorithm: Evolutionary Algorithm for Clustering**

*Step 1.* Choose a random population of solutions. Each solution corresponds to a valid $k$-partition of the data. Associate a fitness value with each solution. Typically, fitness is inversely proportional to the squared error value. A solution with a small squared error will have a larger fitness value.

*Step 2.* Use the evolutionary operators selection, recombination, and mutation to generate the next population of solutions. Evaluate the fitness values of these solutions.

*Step 3.* Repeat step until some termination condition is satisfied (Jain et al. 1999).

Regarding performance issues, we point out the nature of genetic algorithms leaves plenty of room for *parallel genetic algorithms*. There are two broad sources of parallelism in genetic algorithms:

- Exploit parallelism in the application of genetic operators (e.g., selection, crossover and mutation)
- More importantly, exploit parallelism in the computation of the fitness (quality measure) of the population individuals (candidate rules).

### 7.3.3  Evolutionary Algorithms

The evolutionary algorithm is an umbrella term used to describe computer-based problem solving systems that use computational models of evolutionary processes as key elements in their design and implementation. Various evolutionary algorithms have been proposed. In addition to genetic algorithms, evolutionary algorithms include evolutionary programming, evolution strategies, classifier systems, and genetic programming. They all share a common conceptual base of simulating the evolution of individual structures via processes of selection, mutation, and reproduction. The processes depend on the perceived performance of the individual structures as defined by an environment.

More precisely, EAs maintain a population of structures, that evolve according to rules of selection and other operators, that are referred to as "search operators" (or genetic operators), such as recommendation and mutation. Each individual in the population receives a measure of its fitness in the environment. Reproduction focuses attention on high fitness individuals, thus exploiting the available fitness information. Recombination and mutation perturb those individuals, providing general heuristics for exploration. Although simplistic from a biologist's viewpoint, these algorithms are sufficiently complex to provide robust and powerful adaptive search mechanisms.

## Algorithm EA

```
t ← 0; // start with an initial time
init_population P (t); // initialize a usually random
population of individuals
evaluate P (t); // evaluate fitness of all initial
individuals in population
while not done do // test for termination criterion (time,
fitness, etc.)
  {t ← t + 1; // increase the time counter
  P' ← selectparents P (t); // select sub-population for
  offspring production
  recombine P' (t); // recombine the "genes" of selected
  parents
  mutate P' (t); // mutate the mated population
  stochastically
  evaluate P' (t); // evaluate it's new fitness
  P ← survive P,P' (t); // select the survivors from actual
  fitness}
```

The genetic algorithm is a model of machine learning that derives its behavior from a metaphor of the processes of evolution in nature. This is done by the creation within a machine of a population of individuals represented by chromosomes. The individuals in the population then go through a process of evolution.

We should note that evolution (in nature or anywhere else) is not a purposive or directed process. That is, there is no evidence to support the assertion that the goal of evolution is to produce humankind. Indeed, the processes of nature seem to boil down to different individuals competing for resources in the environment. Some are better than others. Those that are better are more likely to survive and propagate their genetic material.

In nature, we see that the encoding for our genetic information (genome) is done in a way that admits asexual reproduction (e.g., by budding) typically results in offspring that are genetically identical to the parent. Sexual reproduction allows the creation of genetically radically different offspring that are still of the same general flavor (species).

Earlier in Section 7.3.2 we discussed operators in GAs. We now review these operators in a more general context of EAs.

The crossover operation happens in an environment where the selection of who gets to mate is a function of the fitness of the individual; namely, how good the individual is at competing in its environment. Some genetic algorithms use a simple function of the fitness measure to select individuals (probabilistically) to undergo genetic operations such as crossover or asexual reproduction (the propagation of genetic material unaltered). This is fitness-proportionate selection. Other implementations use a model in which certain randomly selected individuals in a subgroup compete and the fittest is selected. This is called *tournament selection* and is the form of selection we see in nature when stags rut to vie for the privilege of mating with a herd of hinds (a female deer breed). The two processes that most contribute to evolution are crossover and fitness-based selection/reproduction.

Mutation also plays a role in this process, although how important its role is still arguable, because for some researchers, it is merely a background operator, while others view it as playing the dominant role in the evolutionary process.

### 7.3.4  Remark on Evolutionary Computing for Data Mining

It has been noted (Cios et al. 1998) that there are two key facts of evolutionary computing:

- As already noted, evolutionary computing is useful to data mining in that it can be used to solve optimization problems. The optimization processes are based on a population of potential solutions rather than relying on a single search point being moved according to some gradient based or probabilistic search rules. This is an example of *search for solutions*: It is a more general class of search for paths. The idea is to efficiently find a solution to a problem in a large space of candidate solutions. However, in order to make this kind of search possible, a GA search space should be constructed.
- From a mathematical perspective, the problems being solved do not require any differentiable (or even smooth) objective functions (performance indexes). Therefore, one can handle problems in which fitness function may assume a highly complex format with respect to the parameters that need to be optimized. For data mining tasks requiring constructing a mathematical model, GA provides more useful mechanism to achieve this goal.

According to Negoita (2000), one may wonder how much evolutionary methods are suitable as an optimization vehicle for data mining. On one hand, the computational intensity of evolutionary computing could be easily prohibitive. On the other hand, the aspect of structural optimization supported therein is highly attractive, especially in a highly heterogeneous environment that begs for a variety of patterns to be explored and eventually discovered in the database. On the whole, once some fundamental dimensionality problems have been tackled, this avenue will rapidly grow in importance as one among the basic tools in the data mining toolbox.

Genetic algorithms and evolutionary programming are used in data mining to formulate hypotheses about dependencies between variables, in the form of association rules or some other internal formalism (Goebel and Gruenwald 1999).

## 7.4  REDUCTION APPROACHES AND ROUGH SET THEORY

Rough set theory has several outstanding aspects. Our discussion of rough sets will focus mainly on one particular aspect: reduction. But first, we will provide a more general discussion on data reduction.

### 7.4.1  Data Reduction Approaches for Data Mining

#### 7.4.1.1  *Dimension Reduction for Data Preparation*    In Chapter 2 we discussed data reduction for data preprocessing. We now take a closer look at this issue. Weiss and Indurkhya (1998) distinguish data reduction from predictive methods. In general, reducing the number features (attributes) or the number of values is a relatively efficient process, bypassing the prediction methods. Dimension reduction is the goal of the process that mediates between data preparation and prediction methods. This process can be further decomposed into subprocesses that manipulate either triples or attributes of the data set.

Deleting an attribute has a more dramatic effect on data reduction than deleting a triple. In dimension reduction, irrelevant, weakly relevant or redundant attributes of dimensions are detected and removed. Dimension reduction is thus similar to attribute selection (as discussed in Chapter 5), although the latter term is more frequently used in knowledge discovery. This perspective of dimension reduction is independent of the prediction methods. Some prediction methods have embedded feature selection techniques that are inseparable from the prediction method. Careful attention must be paid to the evaluation of intermediate experimental results so that wise selections can be made from the many alternative approaches.

Feature selection in data preparation is part of a larger task for dimension reduction. Feature selection employs the following techniques to reduce dimensions and pass the reduced data to the prediction programs:

- *Feature Selection from Means and Variance*. In the classical statistical model, the cases are a sample from some distribution. The data can be used to summarize the key characteristics of the distribution in terms of means and variance. By replacing the data set by mans and variances, the dimensions are greatly reduced. The main weakness in this approach is that the distribution is not known. Nevertheless, the means and variances can be viewed as heuristics that guide the feature selection process.

- *Principal Components*. As a well-known method in statistics, this is used to reduce feature dimensions by merging features, resulting in a new set of fewer columns with new values.

- *Feature Selection by Decision Trees*. Unlike the methods described above, feature selection can be considered a task that is integrated with the search for solutions. Using a decision tree for feature selection (as discussed in Chapter 5) is particularly advantageous in large feature spaces.

In contrast to the other techniques of feature selection, decision tree induction, as a recursive partitioning process, is directly performed with error measures.

### 7.4.1.2  *Value Reduction*

Another important technique is to reduce the possible values of the domain taken by an attribute. Within a column of a table, the number of distinct values can be counted, and if this number can be reduced, there would be a valuable data reduction. In particular, we may use the following techniques.

- Value reduction by rounding using a controlling parameter $k$; for example, the number 164 is rounded to 170 with $k = 1$, and rounded to 200 with $k = 2$.
- $k$-Means clustering. The value reduction problem can be stated as an optimization problem. Given $k$ bins (which are containers for holding data), distribute the values in the bins to minimize the average distance of a value from its bin mean. The mean of a bin's values replaces the values in the bin. $k$-means clustering (as discussed in Chapter 5) can do a good job of approximating and smoothing the original values.
- Both rounding and $k$-means clustering concentrate on approximation, but do not look at the goals of reduction. This can be remedied by value reduction through class entropy clustering, which is briefly discussed in Weiss and Indurkhya (1998).

Value reduction can be considered as a special case of *numerosity reduction* (Han and Kamber 2000), where the data are replaced or estimated by smaller data representations.

### 7.4.1.3  *Case Reduction*

Deleting a tuple in the data set is more closely tied to a prediction method. Each tuple represents a sample, or a case, in the data set. Case reduction is the most complex form of data reduction, because the computationally expensive prediction methods must be invoked more often to determine the effectiveness of case reduction.

The relationship between training all the cases and training a random subset is quite interesting. In practice, the results of training in all cases should be near the best, but not nessarliy be better, and can be slightly worse because of the much larger space of solutions that are examined, some of which may look more promising but fail to hold onto new cases.

Sampling can be used as an effective case reduction technique, because it allows a large data set to be reduced to a much smaller set of data. In many cases, the sample set is a subset of the original data; this happens when simple random sample without replacement strategy is used. In case replacement is allowed (for example, age 29 is rounded to 30), the sample set is no longer a subset of the original data set. Note, however, in general, the result of data reduction may not necessarily be a subset of the original data. Therefore, reduction has a broader sense comparing with sampling.

A major concern of case reduction through random sampling is how to use the samples in a controled manner. Two basic forms of random sampling are effective for this purpose: incremental samples and average samples. Understanding the expected relationships and trends among error complexity and multiple random samples is the key to effective data reduction along the case dimension. These two forms of sampling are summarized below.

*Incremental Samples*    This is to train on increasingly larger random subsets of cases, observer the trends and stop when no progress is made. The general expectation is that substantial amounts of new data should lead to better performance, and that the complexity of the solution should be acceptable. Before moving to a larger subset, the net changes in error and complexity are examined. If error is not decreasing much when sample size is increased, we should determine whether, the increased complexity worth it, particularly when the population may change in the future.

*Average Samples*    A data warehouse may contain huge numbers of cases beyond its processing ability. Data are then mined not from a single random sample of $N$ cases, but from $k$ random samples of $N$ cases. As discussed in Chapter 3, segmentation can be used. Instead of finding a solution for the samples of all cases in the warehouse, solutions for samples from different segmentations can be averaged. Average or voted solutions usually have less error than do single solutions. Note that the mean error can be described in terms of three factors: the error of the best solution, bias, and variance. Averaging or voting solutions may eliminate most of the error due to variance. If answers averaged or voted from many samples are the same as the answers for pooling those samples, then no additional bias is introduced with smaller samples. Experience shows that averaged solutions for sample samples can be as effective as those for large samples. In addition, the potential of averaging solutions for minimizing error is also highly significant. If the error due to variance is eliminated, and no bias is introduced into the solutions, then the averaged solutions can approach the performance of the best solution.

#### 7.4.1.4  *Summary of Data Reduction*    There are some other forms of data reduction. For example, continuous variables may need a process of discretization so that qualitative reasoning for data mining techniques can be used. In this process, raw data values for attributes are replaced by range variables. In addition, concept hierarchy generation, such as attribute-oriented induction (discussed in Section 5.2), can also be viewed as a kind of data reduction, where raw data values of attributes are replaced by attribute values at higher conceptual levels.

Data reduction can also be carried out through specific form or functions. For example, data reduction can be done through data cube aggregation, where aggregation operations are applied to the data in the construction of a data cube. Another example is data compression, where encoding mechanisms are used to reduce the data set size.

So far we have treated data reduction mainly as part of data preparation, instead of the data mining proper. However, the concept of reduction can be used as a mining technique. In fact, a very important step in many pattern recognition tasks is identifying most important features, or feature selection. The $k$-means clustering algorithm usually is as a form of performing pattern recognition; however, the preceding discussion has treated it as part of data preparation. Reductionism for data mining is also strongly indicated when using the rough set approach, as discussed in Section 7.4.2. Therefore, the boundary between data preparation and data mining (as discussed in Chapter 2) is blurred.

### 7.4.2    Basic Concepts of Rough Set Theory

Different from many other tasks in dealing with uncertainty, the theory based on the notion of rough set handles the uncertainty issue through a reductionist approach and is lenient with inconsistent data.

Rough set theory has found many interesting applications. It seems of particular importance to decision support systems. The main advantage of rough set theory is that it does not need any preliminary or additional information about data, such as probability in statistics, basic probability in Dempster–Shafer theory, or grade of membership in fuzzy set theory (Pawlak 1997).

Rough set theory makes use of some additional information (knowledge or data) about elements of a universe of discourse. This kind of information could be presented in an *information system* (which may take the form of a decision table consisting of several attributes along with one or more decision attributes). Elements that exhibit the same information are *indiscernible* (similar) and form blocks that can be understood as elementary granules of knowledge about the universe. These granules are called *elementary sets* (concepts), and can be considered as elementary building blocks of knowledge. Elementary concepts can be combined into compound concepts, namely, concepts that are uniquely determined in terms of elementary concepts. Any union of elementary sets is called a crisp set, and any other sets are referred to as "rough."

With a rough set $B$, we associate two crisp sets, called its *lower approximation* and *upper approximation*, denoted as $\underline{B}$ and $\bar{B}$, respectively. Intuitively, the lower approximation of a set consists of all elements that definitely belong to the set, whereas the upper approximation of the set constitutes of all elements that possibly belong to the set. The difference between the upper and the lower approximations is a boundary region, which consists of all elements that cannot be classified uniquely for the set or its complement using available knowledge.

Note that approximations are interior and closure operations in a topology generated by the indiscernibility relation. Consequently, the popular definition of the rough set concept has its roots in topology. However, rough sets can also be defined using rough membership functions ($\mu_X^B(x) \in [0,1]$):

$$\mu_X^B(x) = \frac{|X \cap B(x)|}{|B(x)|}$$

Approximations and the boundary region of a set can be defined in both ways, as shown in Table 7.2, where $U$ denotes the universe of discourse.

Rough set theory has demonstrated several advantages in applications. It provides efficient algorithms for finding hidden patterns in data. It finds minimal sets of data, and generates minimal sets of decision rules from data and valuates significance of data. In addition, most algorithms based on the rough set theory are particularly suited for parallel processing, but in order to exploit this feature fully, new hardware is needed.

Although the rough membership function resembles a fuzzy membership function, it differs the latter due to the following properties:

$$\mu_{U-X}^B = 1 - \mu_X^B(X) \qquad \text{for any } x \in U$$

$$\mu_{X \cup Y}(X) \geq \max\ (\mu_X, \mu_Y) \quad \text{for any } x \in U$$

$$\mu_{X \cap Y}(X) \leq \min\ (\mu_X, \mu_Y) \quad \text{for any } x \in U$$

In addition, it has been observed that rough sets embody the idea of indiscernibility between objects in a set, while fuzzy sets model the ill-definition of the boundary of a subclass of this set. Rough sets are a calculus of partitions, while fuzzy sets are a continuous generalization of set-characteristic functions.

We now use a different example to present another way to view a rough set. Consider a 30-element universe $U = \{x_1, \ldots, x_{30}\}$ as shown in Figure 7.3.

Suppose that each equivalent class in the partition induced from equivalence relation $P$ is depicted as a cell in the figure. For example, $\{x_1, x_2\}$ is an equivalent class, and $\{x_7, x_{13}\}$ is another equivalent class. Now consider $X = \{x_2, x_3, x_4, x_6, x_7, x_{10}, x_{12}, x_{13}, x_{14}\}$. In Figure 7.3, all the elements involved in $X$ are circled in a big oval. The lower approximation of $X$ consists of subsets that are entirely falling in the oval, namely, $\{x_7, x_{13}\}$ and $\{x_{12}, x_{14}\}$.

**Table 7.2  Comparison of Two Definitions of Rule Set**

| Original Definition | Using Rough Membership Function |
|---|---|
| $B = \{x \in U: B(x) \subseteq X\}$ | $B = \{x \in U: \mu_X^B(x) = 1\}$ |
| $\bar{B} = \{x \in U: B(x) \cap X \neq \emptyset\}$ | $\bar{B} = \{x \in U: \mu_X^B(x) > 0\}$ |
| Boundary $(X) = \bar{B} - B$ | Boundary $(X) = \{x \in U: 0 < \mu_X^B(x) < 1\}$ |

There is an interesting connection between rough set theory and probability theory. In fact, in contrast to fuzzy membership, rough set membership has been interpreted as a kind of conditional probability. Therefore, there are two ways of defining rough sets: by using topological or probabilistic methods. However, it can be shown that both definitions are not equivalent.

There is also a relationship between the rough set theory and the Dempster–Shafer theory of evidence. Some relations exist also between the rough set theory and discriminant analysis, the Boolean reasoning methods, decision theory, and others.

### 7.4.3 Using Rough Sets for Data Mining

In the following paragraphs, we illustrate rule induction using a rough set approach for classification problems.

We use the following example to illustrate rule induction using rough set approach. Suppose we are given the decision table as shown in Table 7.3. In the context of rough set theory, a *decision table* is a relation consisting of several condition attributes and one or more decision variables. They can be viewed as a schema of a relation. Each tuple of the decision table indicates a specific case in the problem domain.

The partition generated *by decision* (I) is

$$X = \{\{0,1,3,5,6\}, \{2,4,7,8,9\}\}$$

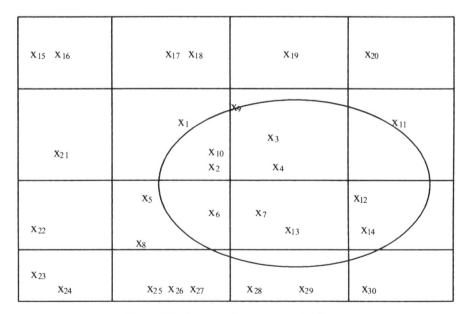

**Figure 7.3** Lower and upper approximations.

**Table 7.3   A Decision Table**

| Tuple | $T$ | $D$ | $M$ | $H$ | $I$ |
|-------|-----|-----|-----|-----|-----|
| 0 | $n$ | $a$ | $a$ | $a$ | $a$ |
| 1 | $n$ | $a$ | $b$ | $b$ | $a$ |
| 2 | $s$ | $a$ | $b$ | $b$ | $b$ |
| 3 | $s$ | $b$ | $a$ | $a$ | $a$ |
| 4 | $s$ | $b$ | $a$ | $a$ | $b$ |
| 5 | $h$ | $a$ | $a$ | $a$ | $a$ |
| 6 | $h$ | $b$ | $a$ | $a$ | $a$ |
| 7 | $h$ | $b$ | $a$ | $a$ | $b$ |
| 8 | $h$ | $b$ | $b$ | $b$ | $b$ |
| 9 | $h$ | $b$ | $b$ | $b$ | $b$ |

Partition generated *by attributes* is

$$\{T,D,H,M\} = \{T,D,H\} = \{\{0\},\{1\},\{2\},\{3,4\},\{5\},\{6,7\},\{8,9\}\}$$

The set $P$ of attributes is the *reduct* (or *covering*) of another set $Q$ of attributes if $P$ is minimal and the indiscernibility relations defined by $P$ and $Q$ are the same. Here the set $\{T,D,H\}$ is a reduct by removing $M$, which has no effect on the partition. Also

- For $X_1 = \{0,1,3,5,6\}$:
  - Since $\{0\} \subseteq X_1, \{1\} \subseteq X_1, \{5\} \subseteq X_1$, we have $\underline{P}X_1 = \{0\} \cup \{1\} \cup \{5\} = \{0,1,5\}$.
  - Since $X_1 \subseteq \{0\} \cup \{1\} \cup \{3,4\} \cup \{5\} \cup \{6,7\} = \{0,1,3,4,5,6,7\}$, we have $\bar{P}X_1 = \{0,1,3,4,5,6,7\}$.
- For $X_2 = \{2,4,7,8,9\}$:
  - Since $\{0\} \subseteq X_2, \{8,9\} \subseteq X_2$, we have $\underline{P}X_2 = \{2\} \cup \{8,9\} = \{2,8,9\}$.
  - Since $X_2 \subseteq \{2\} \cup \{3,4\} \cup \{6,7\} \cup \{8,9\} = \{2,3,4,6,7,8,9\}$, we have $\bar{P}X_2 = \{2,3,4,6,7,8,9\}$.

Certain rules from set $\underline{P}X_1 = \{0,1,5\}$ are

$$(T = n) \wedge (D = a) \wedge (H = a) \to I = a$$
$$(T = n) \wedge (D = b) \wedge (H = a) \to I = a$$
$$(T = n) \wedge (D = b) \wedge (H = a) \to I = a$$

$$(T = h) \wedge (D = a) \wedge (H = a) \to I = a$$

After simplification, the first two rules become

$$(T = n) \wedge (H = a) \to I = a$$

Certain rules after simplification from set $\underline{P}X_2 = \{2,8,9\}$ are

$$(T = n) \wedge (H = b) \rightarrow I = b$$

Possible rules after simplification from $\bar{P}X_1 = \{0,1,3,4,5,6,7\}$ are

$$T = n \rightarrow I = a$$

$$H = a \rightarrow I = a$$

Possible rules after simplification from $\bar{P}X_2 = \{2,3,4,5,6,7,8,9\}$ are

$$T = s \rightarrow I = b$$

$$D = b \rightarrow I = b$$

Rough set theory is a discrete technique, requiring discrete types of attributes and providing granular computations of approximations, classifications, and so on (Cios et al. 1998).

In general, rough set theory is a deterministic methodology useful not only for large data sets but also for small amounts of data for which statistical methods may not be adequate. However, this is not to say that rough set theory guarantees scalability. Using core and reduct computation, rough sets can be applied to feature reduction/selection and attribute relevancy evaluation. Rough sets are computationally intensive. Specifically, reduct computation is an NP-hard problem. Thus, for large data sets with large numbers of attributes, users should resort to heuristic methods (rather than the rough set method) for feasible computations. One problem with the reduct idea is that a reduct defines a minimal set of attributes for which classification accuracy of a given data set is identical for the entire original attribute set. However, a reduct does not ensure that it will be satisfactory for new objects. Selection of the best reduct is generally an optimization problem that requires applicable methodologies.

Rough sets can be used to approximately or "roughly" define classes that cannot be distinguished in terms of the available attributes. Rough sets can also be used for feature reduction and relevance analysis. The problem of finding the minimal subsets (reducts) of attributes that can describe all the concepts in the given data sets is NP-hard. However, algorithms to reduce the computation intensity have been proposed. For example, a discernibility matrix can be used that stores the differences between attribute values for each pair of data samples (Han and Kamber 2000).

Like fuzzy sets, rough sets are seldom used as a standalone solution for data mining. Insetead, they are usually combined with other methods such as rule induction, classification, or clustering methods (Goebel and Gruenwald 1999). Rough sets have been successfully applied for feature reduction and expert system design. There have been also attempts to merge rough sets with probabilistic methods and fuzzy sets.

From an examination from uncertainty perspective, reduction is related to dealing with inconsistency (i.e., reduction can be carried out despite the presence of inconsistency). Note that data mining is also achieved due to reduction.

As an example of how rough set theory can be used for data mining, consider the work reported in Hu (1995), which describes knowledge discovery in databases using rough set theory in three aspects:

1. First, develop an attribute-oriented rough set approach for knowledge discovery in databases. The method adopts the "learning from examples" task combined with rough set theory and database operations. The learning procedure consists of two phases: data generalization and data reduction. In data generalization, the method generalizes the data by performing attribute-oriented concept tree ascension; thus some undesirable attributes are removed and a set of tuples may be generalized to the same generalized tuple. The generalized relation contains only a small number of tuples, thus substantially reducing the computational complexity of the learning process; furthermore, it is feasible to apply the rough set technique to eliminate the irrelevant or unimportant attributes and choose the "best" minimal attribute set. The goal of data reduction is to find a minimal subset of interesting attributes that have all the essential information of the generalized relation; thus the minimal subset of the attributes can be used rather than the entire attribute set of the generalized relation. By removing those attributes that are not important and/or essential, the rules generated become more concise and efficacious.

2. A generalized rough set model is formally defined with the ability to handle statistical information and also consider the importance of attributes and objects in the databases. A theoretical model is constructed to explain the mechanism of multiple knowledge bases (or redundant knowledge) in the context of rough set theory. A decision matrix is used to construct a multiple knowledge-based system in a dynamic environment.

3. The method integrates a variety of knowledge discovery algorithms, such as DBChar for deriving characteristic rules, DBClass for classification rules, DBDeci for decision rules, DBMaxi for maximal generalized rules, DBMkbs for multiple sets of knowledge rules, and DBTrend for data trend regularities, which permit a user to discover various kinds of relationships and regularities in the data. This integration inherits the advantages of the attribute-oriented induction model and rough set theory.

Further details related to the approach introduced by Cercone et al. (1997) will be examined in a case study in Chapter 8. In addition, rough set theory can incorporate basic concepts of fuzzy logic, as discussed in Dubois and Prade (1992).

## 7.5 INTEGRATION OF UNCERTAIN REASONING METHODS FOR DATA MINING

### 7.5.1 Introduction

Summarizing the tasks discussed so far, we can notice some key aspects supported by each of the task. For example

- Fuzzy sets concentrate on a number of knowledge representation aspects (including a specification of a relevant information granularity and providing tools necessary in uncertainty management).
- Artificial neural networks are concentrated on approximating nonlinear mappings.
- Evolutionary computing is focused on a broad class of structural and parametric optimization tasks omnipresent in system design.

However, we can also notice that each task also has its limitations. For example, genetic algorithms can solve complex problems that other technologies may be difficult to deal with. However, genetic algorithms are the least understood of the approaches as well as the most "open." For example, fitness functions can vary widely. The main requirement is that a fitness function have certain properties that allow for convergence to minimal error, yet that leaves wide room for varying implementations. In addition, systems based on predicate logic are good at dealing with horn clauses but pay the price of high computational demands; neural networks are excellent at pattern recognition but suffer from their sensitivity to the initial topology and weights, as well as proper selection of attributes; and genetic algorithms, albeit surprisingly powerful, require smart encoding into chromosomes and can be very slow learners (Kubat et al. 1998).

Integrated use of various computational tasks as discussed in previous sections, or the *fusion* of these techniques (as it is sometimes called), has drawn much attention from researchers and practitioners. In this section, we briefly examine several examples. There are at least two main reasons for using hybrid systems for problem solving and knowledge engineering: (1) some requirements for solution of a problem might not be met by using a single method; and (2) there exist models for AI problem solving that cannot be implemented by using a single method, or they would be implemented better if more than one task were used.

One approach of integration advocates a two-level hierarchical model, in which the lower level communicates with the environment, and deals with recognition, classification, identification, and pattern matching, while the higher level takes a rule-based approach for strategic reasoning. Each level can consist of several sublevels. Examples of multimodular, multitask systems could be a feedforward structure, or a recurrent structure allowing feedback.

Various tasks are complementary for several reasons: (1) they facilitate dealing with different kinds of knowledge representation, different inference, different accuracy, and fault tolerance, as well as other features; (2) each of them may be superior to the others when solving a concrete subtask at different levels; and (3) one task may be applied to improve the performance of another. We take a closer look of some examples below.

### 7.5.2 Synergy of Fuzzy Sets and Neural Networks

As the first example of synergy of different tasks, we note that fuzzy sets and neural networks can assist each other (Cios et al. 1998, Kasabove 1996). For example, fuzzy rules can be used to "prewire" a neural network structure for faster training and better generalization; fuzzy rule scan also can be used for initialization of connection weights. On the other hand, neural networks can be used for learning fuzzy rules and to refine fuzzy rules and membership functions.

Fuzzy sets are focused on knowledge representation issues, including the way in which various factors of vagueness are taken care of. Primarily normative in essence, fuzzy sets cannot cope with the prescriptive aspects of phenomena to be modeled and accommodate efficacies implied by the underlying data. On the other hand, neural networks tend to be more efficient when it comes to learning, and therefore are naturally inclined to address the descriptive factors of the problem at hand. The two technologies are ideally geared for handling the evident duality in the prescriptive–descriptive approach accompanying any problem statement. Fuzzy sets can be used to enhance neural networks by incorporating knowledge-oriented mechanisms. These knowledge-based enhancements fall into three categories:

- Preprocessing of training data that could easily lead to improvement in learning and/or enhanced robustness characteristics of the network
- Enhancements of specific training procedures through knowledge-based learning schemes, including learning metarules (which are rules about rules)
- Linguistic interpretation of results produced by neural networks

In addition, fuzzy sets and neural networks can be integrated to form *fuzzy neural networks*. These are highly heterogeneous neural architectures seemingly combining the learning abilities residing within neural networks while enjoying an explicit format of knowledge representation. This leads to systems with lower level of arithmetical precision with a higher level of logical reliability. In particular, basic concepts of OR/AND *logic neurons* have been developed, and their logic-driven characteristics, learning, and result interpretation have been studied.

### 7.5.3   Synergy of Fuzzy Logic and Genetic Algorithms

Another typical example of synergy involves fuzzy logic and genetic algorithms. Genetic algorithms (and other kinds of evolutionary algorithms) can be used to create, modify, improve, and update fuzzy systems. One way to combine them is to first generate the initial fuzzy logical rules or predicates. Genetic or evolutionary algorithms are then used to evolve rule sets, modify the set membership parameters, or update the fuzzy logic systems as the domain changes. When the two techniques are combined in this way, the results can be better than if either is applied to the problem. According to a classified review of the combination fuzzy logic–genetic algorithms bibliography (Cordon et al. 1997), almost half of them are related to fuzzy logic controllers (design, learning, tuning, applications), while others fall into fuzzy genetic algorithms, fuzzy clustering, fuzzy optimization, fuzzy neural networks, fuzzy relational equations, fuzzy expert systems, fuzzy classifier systems, fuzzy information retrieval and database querying, fuzzy decisionmaking, financial and economic models, fuzzy regression analysis, fuzzy pattern recognition and image processing, fuzzy classification–concept learning, and other categories.

For fuzzy genetic algorithms, sample topics include fuzzy tools to improve genetic algorithms and adjusting parameters of genetic algorithms by fuzzy control rules. An example of fuzzy regression analysis could be a fuzzy regression analysis of data (with error) using the genetic algorithm. An example of fuzzy classification–concept learning could be selection of fuzzy IF/THEN rules by genetic algorithm for classification problems. Figure 7.4 illustrates the role of fuzzy encoding and decoding for conversion between a traditional search space and a GA search space.

### 7.5.4   Clustering with Fuzzy or Evolutionary Approaches

Fuzzy clustering extends traditional clustering to associate each pattern with every cluster using a membership function. Clustering can also take advantage of ANNs. Some of the features of the ANNs that are important in pattern clustering are

1. ANNs processes numerical vectors and so require patterns to be represented using quantitative features only.
2. ANNs are inherently parallel and distributed processing architectures.
3. ANNs may learn their interconnection weights adaptively. They can act as pattern normalizers and feature selectors by appropriate selection of weights.

Competitive (or winner-take-all) ANNs are often used to cluser input data, where similar patterns are grouped by the network and represented by a

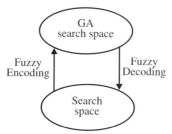

**Figure 7.4**  Mapping between search space and GA search space.

single unit (neuron). This grouping is done automatically according to data correlations.

**A High-Level Algorithm: Evolutional Approaches for Clustering**

*Step 1.*  Choose a random population of solutions. Each solution corresponds to a valid $k$ partition of the data. Associate a fitness value with each solution. Typically, fitness is inversely proportional to the squared-error value. A solution with a small squared error will have a larger fitness value.

*Step 2.*  Repeat use the evolutionary operators selection, recombination and mutation to generate the next population of solutions. Evaluate the fitness values of these solutions. Until some termination condition is satisfied.

### 7.5.5  Comparison between Clustering Algorithms

As an alternative of integration of different techniques, we now compare clustering algorithms using different approaches. Various deterministic and stochastic search techniques used to approach the clustering problem can be examined as an optimization problem, where the cases (or objects) are grouped into most appropriate clusters. A majority of these methods use the squared-error criterion function, and the partitions generated by these approaches are not as versatile as those generated by hierarchical algorithms. The clusters generated are typically hyperspherical in shape. Evolutionary approaches are globalized search techniques, whereas other approaches for clustering are localized search techniques. ANNs and GAs are inherently parallel, so they can be implemented using parallel hardware to improve their speed. Evolutionary approaches are population-based because they search using more than one solution at a time, while other methods are based on using a single solution at a time. ANNs, GAs, and Tabu search are all sensitive to the selection of various learning and control parameters. In theory, all of these methods are *weak methods* in that they do not use explicit domain knowledge.

Some empirical studies of the performance of various clustering methods have been carried out. The following are some observations:

- Only the $k$-means algorithm and its ANN equivalent, the Kohonen net (see Chapter 6), have been applied on large data sets; other approaches have typically been tested on small data sets. This is because obtaining suitable learning and control parameters for ANNs and GAs is difficult and their execution times are very high for large data sets.
- It has been shown that $k$-means method converges to a locally optimal solution. This behavior is linked with the initial seed selection in the $k$-means algorithm.
- Although none of the methods mentioned above is strong enough in dealing with data mining, experimental studies suggested that *combining domain knowledge* would improve their performance. For example (1) ANNs work better in classifying images represented using extracted features than with raw images, and hybrid classifiers work better than ANNs; and (2) using domain knowledge to hybridize a GA improves its performance.
- Approaches utilizing domain knowledge tend to generate a partition of hyperspherical clusters, and this could be a limitation.

### 7.5.6   Integration Involving Genetic Algorithms

Finally, we provide several brief remarks on integration involving genetic algorithms. First, we mention the synergy of neural networks and genetic algorithms. Genetic algorithms have often been used in conjunction with neural networks to provide a higher level of model understanding. While neural networks have often been said to be "blackboxes," genetic algorithms in conjunction with neural networks can record groups of input variables that impact an outcome directly into a database, providing more detailed documentation of each neural network model. After experimenting with various models, a final model can be built by reading one of the earlier model's variable sets.

As a second example, we consider the ICET algorithm (Turney 1995) for cost-sensitive classification, which uses a genetic algorithm to evolve a population of biases for a decision tree induction algorithm. The fitness function of the genetic algorithm is the average cost of classification when using the decision tree, including both the costs of tests (features, measurements) and the costs of classification errors. ICET is compared here with three other algorithms for cost-sensitive classification (EG2, CS-ID3, and IDX) and also with C4.5, which classifies without regard to cost. The five algorithms are evaluated empirically on five real-world medical data sets. Three sets of experiments are performed. The first set examines the baseline performance of the five algorithms on the five data sets and establishes that ICET performs significantly better than its competitors. The second set tests the robustness of ICET under a variety of conditions and shows that ICET maintains its advantage. The third set looks at ICET's search in bias space and discovers a way to improve the search.

In addition, Al-Attar (1994) described a hybrid GA-heuristic search strategy. It is noted that there is currently wide interest in genetic algorithms among the AI community worldwide. This interest is driven mainly by the inadequacy of linear programming and rule-based (heuristic) systems in solving complex resource planning and scheduling problems, and more generally by the desire to have an effective search algorithm that is independent of the nature of the solution domain. The GA concepts are very appealing since they appear to offer the ultimate "free lunch" scenario of good solutions evolving without a problem-solving strategy, once the requirements and constraints are defined.

However, developers are often faced with having to use a very large number of genes to represent real problems and, as a result, hours or days to evolve solutions that may not be of acceptable quality. So, how does one reconcile the hype (hyperbole) and the reality? The lack of heuristics in searching for good solutions would account for the large number of genes required and the slowness of the evolution process.

The basic concept behind the hybrid methodology is that instead of using the GA to directly optimize the parameters of the solution, the GA should be used to optimize the parameters of a simple heuristic problem solving strategy. This approach is depicted in Figure 7.5. In addition to the GA engine, a heuristic problem solver is used to produce candidate solution. The acceptable answer produced from the iterative process is further processed by a synthesizer to get the final result.

Finally, we briefly remark on GAs for data mining and clustering addressed by GARAGe (Genetic Algorithms Research and Applications Group) at Michigan State University. The goal was clustering of large, noisy data sets via parallel GAs. More specifically, the goal was to take a large data set of objects, each described by a set of features and a known classification and

- Select those features most important for discriminating between the different classes of the objects.
- For those selected features, weight them (relatively) per their importance to the classification.
- Apply these weighted features to determine the classification of unknown (not used in creating the weightings) objects.

We can optimize the effectiveness of a *k nearest neighbor* (*k*NN) *decision rule* using a GA. For each dimension in the *k*NN, we create a weight that multiplies the values in that dimension. These weights are modified by the GA such

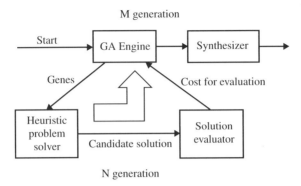

**Figure 7.5**   Hybrid GA optimizer.

that we get optimal separation between the different classes. Features with a 0 weight are unimportant (feature selection); those remaining are weighted relative to their importance (classification).

## 7.6   UNCERTAIN REASONING TECHNIQUES AS DATA MINING TASKS

The tasks reviewed in this chapter demonstrates a wide spectrum of uncertain reasoning techniques. Note that unlike the data mining tasks discussed in Chapter 5, they have been developed for uncertain reasoning rather than for data mining. Yet they can also be very useful in data mining. It is important to examine what makes them useful in data mining. The following are some observations from an agent-based approach. In fact, they can play a role of an agent with a wide range of qualifications:

1. *As an Assistant.* They perform various duties at various stages of data mining. In fact, at each stage, different uncertain reasoning methods can be used, and the tasks of these methods may not be related to each other. Nevertheless, uncertain reasoning methods are invoked in the overall data mining process and integrated in a coherent manner. This is a tight conceptual coupling, where uncertain reasoning performs a humble duty. For example, in many applications, clustering and classification tasks can be appropriately assisted by neural networks or some other uncertain reasoning techniques.

2. *As an Equal Partner.* Part of the overall data mining task can be done by one or more of the data mining methods described in Chapter 5, while the remaining part can be done using uncertain reasoning. The results, of course, should be combined. For example, the same data mining problem may be investigated independently using genetic algo-

rithms and rough set approaches, and the results obtained from each approach are then compared or combined. This is a loosely coupled approach.

3. *As a Participant in a Relay.* An uncertain reasoning method can be used as a preprocessor or postprocessor of a data mining method described in Chapter 5. For example, a rough set approach can be used for reduction in data preparation and preprocessing stages, and the result will be used for association rule mining.

4. *As a Boss.* An uncertain reasoning method can be the main technique to accomplish data mining, while maintaining one or more data mining methods as its assistants. This is the reverse picture of role 1 described above. For example, Bayesian networks can be used to provide the major framework for causal relationship mining, which may incorporate algorithms developed for association rule mining. A study described in Chapter 6 will illustrate this.

5. *As a Standalone Method.* In an extreme case a data mining task can be performed by a method usually categorized as uncertain reasoning. It could be a sole player, without any significant involvement of the data mining methods described in Chapter 5. In fact, data analysis using statistic methods illustrate this. Since it does not take advantage of new development in data mining, the power of this approach is limited.

## 7.7  SUMMARY

Uncertain reasoning techniques offer rich computational mechanisms for building intelligent agents. In this chapter, we examined some of them. We also discussed the need for integration of these techniques, and how they can serve the main data mining tasks (as discussed in Chapter 5). Note that our discussion of these techniques has been focused mainly on their roles in the step of data mining proper. In fact, uncertain reasoning techniques can play an equally important role in other stages of data mining, such as in data preparation or data processing.

Because of space limitations, our presentation for each uncertain reasoning technique has been very brief. For each technique, we selected only several important aspects that are more or less related to data mining. For more aspects of each technique, and their integration, the readers are referred to Chen (1999), Chen et al. (2000), Katayama et al. (1996), Kasabov (1996), and Pedrycz (1998).

Summarizing materials discussed in Chapters 6 and 7, we can point out the following:

- Each specific uncertain reasoning technique should be evaluated individually for its relevance to data mining. For example, for fuzzy logic, we know that this method is not effective for performing machine learning by itself, but it can assist data mining when used with other methods (e.g., artificial neural networks). If a concept is conjectured, fuzzy theory can offer much help, because it allows us to perform perturbation around a norm. Fuzzy logic is appropriate to be used along with rules.

- Use of artificial neural networks (ANNs) or genetic algorithms (GAs) can be considered when a symbol-based approach does not fit well in problem solving. They can be used when the number of factors is not too small yet their interrelationship is complex or when users are not too concerned with an explanation of the process. They are good for performing machine learning tasks. Although the behavior of these algorithms is similar to that of a black- (or gray-) box, the result can still be symbolized.

- It is important to integrate different approaches. There are numerous ways to integrate various data mining and uncertain reasoning tasks. We have already seen many examples, such as the interplay of association rules and Bayesian networks, which bridge uncertain reasoning and data mining (Section 6.5). As another example, consider the case of fuzzy set theory and rough set theory. The synergy of these two tasks leads to consider rough approximation of fuzzy sets, as well as approximations of sets by means of fuzzy similarity relations or fuzzy partitions.

# 8

# DATA MINING LIFECYCLE WITH UNCERTAINTY HANDLING: CASE STUDIES AND SOFTWARE TOOLS

## 8.1 OVERVIEW

So far we have examined several major data mining tasks as well as several useful uncertain reasoning techniques for data mining. In order to demonstrate how these methods can be used for problem solving, in the last two chapters of this book, we present several case studies. The case studies in this chapter demonstrate basic aspects of integrated data mining, while the case studies presented in the next chapter cover a wider scope of data mining applications.

The aim of this chapter is to wrap up key ideas presented so far in this book, and to illustrate how data mining cycle with uncertainty is handled in various applications. In Section 8.2, we provide a summary of various aspects (as presented in previous chapters) of integrated data mining and uncertain reasoning, an outline of data mining lifecycle with uncertainty, which covers all the major stages of data mining, including data preparation, data modeling, and post–model processing. We use the term uncertainty handling in a sense broader than uncertainty reasoning, because it also deals with uncertainty in data.

Section 8.3 consists of several case studies of applications of data mining methods. These case studies are selected to represent some unique features, and are organized in such a way that they represent different stages and various aspects of data mining. Each case study described in this chapter has a unique focus. The first case study, bank credit applications, is concerned mainly with the overall data mining process. The second case study is also concerned with the overall mining process, but with an emphasis on incorporating OLAP-related aspects into integrated data mining. The next two case studies illustrate application of basic data mining tasks: The third case study demonstrates how to OLAP-related considerations into mining of association rules, and the fourth study presents an application of a revised clustering algorithm. Finally, in the fifth case study we show how a reduction approach (originated from rough set theory) for uncertain reasoning can be used for data mining.

Complementary to our own studies is a discussion on commercially available software for data mining. We examine these tools from the integrated data mining perspective; in particular, we discuss how uncertain reasoning techniques have been used in these tools for data mining, and what is still lacking. This discussion, as presented in Section 8.4, leads to a general discussion of some important features of the software, as well as a brief description of sample products. This section ends with a discussion of issues that should be resolved for future data mining software, echoing the research issues addressed at the end of Chapter 2.

This chapter concludes with Section 8.5, where we include several observations from these case studies.

## 8.2 REVIEW OF UNCERTAIN REASONING IN DATA MINING LIFECYCLE

In Chapter 4 we provided an overview of uncertainty issues related to data mining. On the basis of technical discussions presented in Chapters 5–7, we can review the data mining lifecycle in Chapter 4 in more depth, by incorporating technical considerations into our main interest of data mining with uncertainty. There are numerous factors of uncertainty that impact data mining. In particular, we note the following:

1. Uncertain reasoning is an element that should be incorporated into each step of data mining. The following are some questions to be answered:

   • The quality of the data (or, how clean the data is)
   • Which kind of uncertainty (e.g., vagueness or randomness) is involved in the data
   • Which kind of rule should be discovered (e.g., classification or discrimination)
   • As for the data mining proper, which one is more appropriate: directly apply an algorithm in data mining (e.g., Apriori algorithm for association rule discovery) or initiate our task by applying some technique in uncertain reasoning (e.g., ANN)

- How to determine the strength of a discovered knowledge pattern (e.g., use of support or confidence in association rules, or other measures such as $t$-weight, $d$-weight, and vote in attribute-oriented induction, as discussed in Chapter 5 and to be discussed in Chapter 9)
- How to decide whether we should keep a previously discovered knowledge pattern after the database update
- Whether we should use any measure (e.g., using entropy or something else) as a guideline to control the degree of uncertainty in the data mining process (such as in the ID3 algorithm);

2. We should take advantage of the data mining infrastructure as discussed in Chapters 2 and 3. In addition, the process of data mining itself should assist in the development of a better infrastructure. Take a look at the case of metadata. As discussed in Chapter 3, we can take advantage of metadata in a data warehouse to aid data mining. We can also consider the issue of mining the metadata. This refers to conducting data mining on the metadata, because the data in the database may be incomplete and inaccurate, and the metadata could provide more meaningful information. For example, if the metadata contains the information about statistics about queries submitted by various users, we may be able to derive rules about which queries are frequently associated with other queries submitted by the same user.

3. The overall data mining process is an iteration process. For example, as indicated in Chapters 2 and 4, data cleansing is usually considered as a preparation for data mining. However, data mining itself may be part of data cleansing, because data cleansing may incorporate data mining techniques to first find some implicit regularity hidden in the dirty data and then fix the data accordingly. For a similar reason, data mining techniques can also be applied on incomplete data (such as data with missing or inconsistent values).

4. A careful study should be carried out to determine whether to start with a data mining paradigm directly or start from data analysis by focusing on uncertainty.

5. Integrated data mining is a multifacet phenomenon, which includes integration of different data mining tasks, integration of different uncertain reasoning methods, integrated use of data mining paradigms, and uncertain reasoning techniques. Uncertain reasoning can be followed by data mining, or vice versa.

6. There are some additional aspects of data mining that may be important in some circumstances. For example, as indicated in Chapter 4, data are not the only source of uncertainty. The problem of data mining itself may be uncertain. In Chapter 2 we discussed some data mining issues related to the contents of database management systems environment (Freitas and Lavington 1998), such as discovery of semantic query optimization, discovery of database dependencies, dependence modeling, and causation modeling. All these tasks may involve uncertainty. For example, we may set up a threshold for discov-

ery of database dependencies so that if the tuples in a relation demonstrating a certain dependence achieve a certain percentage, we will accept the conjectured dependency a is true. Apparently there is a kind of uncertainty when a threshold is used; however, this uncertainty is introduced by this conjecture, and may not be caused by the data itself.

7. There are additional issues related to uncertainty in data mining process but were not discussed (or emphasized) in previous chapters. For example, the process of querying may be uncertain. Queries themselves may be uncertain. Uncertainty may also be involved in query refinement. Uncertainty in conventional query processing (e.g., fuzzy queries) can also be applied to query processing involved in data mining.

The remaining part of this chapter demonstrates various aspects in the integrated data mining, as well as the wide diversity of data mining applications.

## 8.3   CASE STUDIES

### 8.3.1   Case Study 1: Data Mining Process in Bank Credit Applications

Our first case study is used to illustrate the general process of data mining, where the data mining process in bank credit applications is described. The case study also illustrates how to preprocess the data in different ways for different data mining needs, as well as how to circumvent the missing data problem.

Preparing data for bank credit application involves all the steps of the data mining process: goal definition, data selection, data preparation and transformation, data exploration, pattern discovery, and pattern deployment.

*Goal Definition.* The goal of this study is to find the most important factors (viz., attributes) that may contribute to credit card bankruptcy.

*Data Selection.* The raw data are related to credit card processing. The data have 150 columns of daily records. In order to select the data, we identify the source data as the applications data and the monthly payments database. Furthermore, we focus on historic mortgage applications, for example, those made in 1996 and 1997 and all payments records from 1996 until present date.

*Data Preparation.* We have extracted application records from 1996 and 1999, extracted history of credit card usage information, and performed join on these two kinds of tables. We have normalized data by first calculating maximum value and minimum value of each attribute. Furthermore, the data are clustered into 297 clusters. Different forms of data have been prepared, such as binary or text files for use for different ways of further processing. As the result, 150 attributes are reduced to 20. The number of attributes can be further reduced later in the step of data mining proper using rough set theory. If next month is higher than this month, then the change rate is 1; if it is lower, the change rate is −1; if there is no change, the rate is 0. The average rate is the sum of these numbers. If the sum is greater than 0, the final rate is 1; if the sum is less than 0, the final rate is −1; if the sum is 0, the final rate is 0. Using this procedure, it is easy to deal with missing values, because if a value for a month is missing, it is simply skipped over. The resulting schema of the data used for mining is shown in Table 8.1.

*Data Exploration.* Various choices are available, such as to explore the frequency distribution of data attributes, explore the correlation between data attributes, and plot the goal against other attributes.

*Pattern Discovery.* Using neural networks with different architectures and different training algorithms such as backpropagation and radial basis function (RBF), the result is compared with the approach of using rough set theory. Testing of the discovered results.

*Pattern Deployment.* Generate the patterns as SQL, which is used to generate regular reports on the proportion of newly acquired data matching of each pattern discovered.

**Table 8.1  Schema of Data to Be Mined**

| Attribute Number | Attribute Name | Attribute Description |
|---|---|---|
| 0 | bankrupt | Bankruptcy flag (0,1) |
| 1 | line98 | Credit line at month 11/97–10/98 |
| 2 | avg_cash98 | Average cash advance during 11/97–10/98 |
| 3 | rate_cash98 | Rate cash advance during 11/97–10/98 |
| 4 | avg_sales98 | Average purchase during 11/97–10/98 |
| 5 | rate_sales98 | Rate purchase during 11/97–10/98 |
| 6 | avg_pay98 | Average payment during 11/97–10/98 |
| 7 | rate_pay98 | Rate payment during 11/97–10/98 |
| 8 | avg_balance98 | Average balance during 11/97–10/98 |
| 9 | rate_balance98 | Rate balance during 11/97–10/98 |
| 10 | sum_delinquency98 | Sum delinquency during 11/97–10/98 |
| 11 | avg_balance97 | Average balance during 11/96–10/97 |
| 12 | rate_balance97 | Rate balance during 11/96–10/97 |
| 13 | avg_cash97 | Average cash advance during 11/96–10/97 |
| 14 | rate_cash97 | Rate cash advance during 11/96–10/97 |
| 15 | avg_pay97 | Average payment during 11/96–10/97 |
| 16 | rate_pay97 | Rate payment during 11/96–10/97 |
| 17 | avg_sales97 | Average purchase during 11/96–10/97 |
| 18 | rate_sales97 | Rate purchase during 11/96–10/97 |
| 19 | avg_min | Average minimum payment due at 96 |
| 20 | rate_min | Rate minimum payment due at 96 |

## 8.3.2 Case Study 2: Incorporating Rollup Operation in Data Mining

This case study starts with the same data used in case study 1, but with a different focus in mind. The objective of this study is to find the difference of cash advance habits between bankrupted credit card members in regions 1 and 2. To achieve this, we explore some aspects of integrating OLAP-related considerations into data mining. In the following, we discuss one aspect, namely, discovery of knowledge patterns by applying the rollup operation along the time dimension, which is characterized by the "month, season, year" hierarchy.

Since this case study has its own focus, the data are processed in a differently from that described in case study 1. Each table used in this case study can be viewed as a materialized view (as discussed in Chapter 3) produced from the original data by applying relational database operators such as join, projection, and selection. These tables (viz., materialized views), labeled as R$i$, are constructed in a way so that each frequently used query accesses one table in the database:

- R1: a table with all the information of each credit card member
- R2: a table with only the information relevant to the project purpose of each credit card member
- R3: the average amount of cash advance per month of bankrupted and nonbankrupted members in region 1 by month for the whole year
- R4: the average amount of cash advance per month of bankrupted and nonbankrupted members in region 2 by month for the whole year
- R5: the average amount of cash advance per month of bankrupted and nonbankrupted members in region 1 by season for the whole year
- R6: the average amount of cash advance per month of bankrupted and nonbankrupted members in region 2 by season for the whole year
- R7: the average amount of cash advance per month of bankrupted and nonbankrupted members in region 1 by for the whole year
- R8: the average amount of cash advance per month of bankrupted and nonbankrupted members in region 2 by year for the whole year

The high cash advance is more than twice the average cash advance per person per month grouped by all members in the whole base data. The amount of cash advance per person per month of all members is $17.32, so if a certain group of people receives $34.64 or more per person per month, it will be considered to be a high cash advance.

As stated earlier, the purpose of this study is to find the difference between bankrupted credit card members in regions 1 and 2. To do this, first the OLAP operations are performed for credit card members using the dimension level of time on a monthly based is; then dimension place of state of region 1 and region 2 are executed. The results are shown in Table 8.2. The unit of numbers

**Table 8.2 Monthly Data for Regions 1 and 2**

| Jan. | Feb. | Mar. | Apr. | May | June | July | Aug. | Sept. | Oct. | Nov. | Dec. | Bankrupt |
|------|------|------|------|------|------|------|------|-------|------|------|------|----------|
| Region 1 | | | | | | | | | | | | |
| 18.33 | 13.45 | 23.34 | 13.24 | 12.22 | 14.46 | 10.43 | 8.65 | 11.01 | 18.91 | 16.35 | 27.48 | 0 |
| 53.42 | 67.86 | 84.32 | 66.33 | 92.34 | 72.53 | 57.34 | 64.57 | 49.32 | 46.78 | 80.32 | 90.01 | 1 |
| Region 2 | | | | | | | | | | | | |
| 13.22 | 11.48 | 8.24 | 12.67 | 9.72 | 9.64 | 5.32 | 8.77 | 11.36 | 18.42 | 19.69 | 21.35 | 0 |
| 23.89 | 20.66 | 19.38 | 11.45 | 18.57 | 17.63 | 20.58 | 31.37 | 18.44 | 177.45 | 207.32 | 310.46 | 1 |

is the U.S. dollar. The represent average cash advance amount per individual per month. In addition, B stands for bankrupt status of credit card member: 0 represents nonbankrupted members, and 1 indicates bankrupted members. Monthly data for regions 1 and 2 are shown in Table 8.2.

The result shows that for bankrupted credit card members who had high ($34.42) cash advances every month in 12 months of year 1996, the confidence calculation equals 1.00.

Furthermore, we can calculate measures of the result. In particular, we can calculate confidence for confidence (which is the percentage of true case) for monthly bankrupted credit card members for region 1. We use subscripts to denote this, where the first character indicates the level in the dimension ($m$ for month, $s$ for season, and $y$ for year, as to be used later), the second character in the subscript indicates the region (1 for region 1 and 2 for region 2), and the third character in the subscript indicates bankrupt situation (1 for bankruptcy, 0 for nonbankruptcy). The calculation results in confidence for monthly data for region 1 with bankruptcy is $C_{m11} = 12/12 = 1.00$.

Likewise, the confidence of high cash advance of nonbankrupted credit card members in region 1 is $C_{m10} = 0.00$; the confidence of high cash advance of bankrupted credit card members in R2 is $C_{m21} = 3/12 = 0.25$; the confidence of high cash advance of nonbankrupted credit card members in region 2 is $C_{m20} = 0.00$.

From the above results, it is sufficient to establish the rule that credit card bankrupted members in both regions 1 and 2 had high cash advances in some of the months in 1996, whereas no nonbankrupted members in region 2 had high cash advance in any month in 1996. In addition, region 1 bankrupted credit card members had high cash advances in every month in 1996, while in only 3 months out of 12 months of region 2 bankrupted credit card members had high cash advances. Comparing $C_{m11} = 1$ versus $C_{m21} = 0.25$, apparently region 1 bankrupted credit card members had higher cash advances in 1996 compared to region 2 bankrupted credit card members.

We now apply the rollup operation of OLAP at the time dimension. Suppose that we roll up from month to year (the highest level in the hierarchy), for bankrupted and nonbankrupted credit card members in regions 1 and 2, for the year 1996. The results are shown in Table 8.3.

**Table 8.3  Yearly Data for Regions 1 and 2[a]**

| Cash Advances per Member per Month | Bankruptcy Status |
|---|---|
| Region 1 | |
| 12.55 | 0 |
| 68.86 | 1 |
| | |
| Region 2 | |
| 15.04 | 0 |
| 70.93 | 1 |

[a] Thus we have $C_{y11} = 1/1 = 1$; $C_{y10} = 0/1 = 0$; $C_{y21} = 1/1 = 1$; $C_{y20} = 0/1 = 0$.

**Table 8.4  Seasonal Data for Regions 1 and 2[a]**

| Spring | Summer | Fall | Winter | Bankruptcy Status |
|---|---|---|---|---|
| Region 1 | | | | |
| 17.31 | 13.89 | 9.81 | 19.06 | 0 |
| 70.09 | 81.3 | 58.38 | 73.93 | 1 |
| | | | | |
| Region 2 | | | | |
| 11.93 | 10.63 | 8.57 | 19.05 | 0 |
| 20.15 | 15.47 | 24.47 | 218.69 | 1 |

[a] Thus we have $C_{s11} = 4/4 = 1$; $C_{s10} = 0/4 = 0$; $C_{s21} = 1/4 = 0.25$; $C_{s20} = 0/4 = 0$.

The average amount of cash advance for bankrupted members in region 1 was $68.8 per member per month in 1996, while the average amount for bankrupted members in region 2 was $70.93 per member per month in 1996. This indicates that at the year level there is no significant difference between these two groups in cash advance habit if OLAP and data mining are conducted at the time dimension level of *year*. The amount of average cash advance ($70.93) of bankrupted region 2 members was even a little higher than the amount of average cash advance ($68.8) of bankrupted region 1 members.

These results suggest that we need to refine our mining process by either OLAP rollup at the dimension level of month, or OLAP drilldown at the dimension level of year. Either operation will yield the OLAP at the dimensional level of season.

Analysis of the time dimension at the level of season brings the results shown in Table 8.4.

The result from Table 8.4 seems to be the same as that obtained using the monthly dimensional OLAP rule, but the rollup provides a clearer picture of the difference between the profiles of bankrupted credit card users in regions 1 and 2 in the year 1996. The region 1 bankrupted members had high cash advances in all four seasons in the year 1996, while the region 2 bankrupted credit card members had no high cash advances in the first, second, and third seasons, but had very high ($218.69) cash advances at the fourth season (winter) in 1996. The extreme high cash advance of region 2 bankrupted members during the winter covered the low cash advances in the rest three seasons, while the high cash advance in region 1 had evened out in every season, so the yearly time dimensional level–based OLAP showed that there was no difference between cash advance habits between the regions 1 and 2 bankrupted credit card members.

The discrepancy between regions 1 and 2 cash advance habits among bankrupted credit card members might reflect the different economical and culture backgrounds of the credit card members in these two regions. The region 1 bankrupted credit card members, who were living in a more expensive coastal area, might have been tempted by the expensive commodities in the department stores every month, and spent the money recklessly for their own benefits, while the bankrupted credit card members living in region 2, a largely agricultural region, had very high cash advances only in winter, perhaps because to celebrate the Thanksgiving–Christmas holiday season. These observations are just hypotheses, and are subject to further investigation.

In this case we used an integrated OLAP–data mining process to compare the cash advance habits between bankrupted credit card members in regions 1 and 2 in 1996. The result showed that region 1 bankrupted credit card members had almost uniformly high cash advance in all four seasons in 1996, while region 2 bankrupted credit card members had an average cash advance in the first three seasons in 1996, but had very high cash advances in the fourth season. The further knowledge recovery may embrace economic and cultural differences between the two regions.

We conclude this case study with a brief description of how the implemented prototype system works. The configuration is shown in Figure 8.1. The user interface is done through an HTML file. Once the "Submit Query" button is pressed, the Web page will pass the query to a servlet on the Web server; then the servlet will process query and send SQL string to database via the JDBC–ODBC (Java–object database connectivity) bridge. The result of query will be returned in the form of HTML. JDBC allows Java serlvets to be connected to the database, while the Java serlvet processes the request sent form an HTML file on a Website accessible from the Internet. The Java serlvet responds to the request by sending the result from SQL execution in the database in the form of an HTML file to the user.

### 8.3.3 Case Study 3: Mining Association Rules at Multiple Levels

In case study 2, we discussed incorporating OLAP aspects into integrated data mining. Case study 3 is also related to OLAP, but this time we pay attention to one particular data mining task: association rules. We show how to discover association rules at different levels of a dimension. We note that this process is of nonmonotonic nature. The term *nonmonotonic*, adopted from

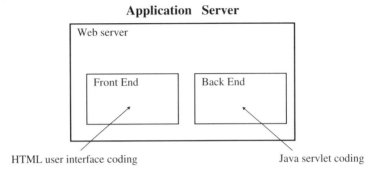

**Figure 8.1**  System configuration for bankrupted credit card case study.

nonstandard logic, refers to an important aspect of reasoning; reasoning is not a monotonic process, because sometimes we have to withdraw our previous conclusion when new knowledge becomes available. When we perform OLAP operations such as drilldown or rollup, the conclusion we made at the lower level (e.g., the level of primitive data) may have to be withdrawn at a high level of granularity, because knowledge patterns mined at different levels have different semantics, and they are not isolated from each other. Understanding the nonmonotonic nature of reasoning from one level to another level (such as in moving from the granularity level to an aggregating level, and vice versa) is important for us to establish a comprehensive picture of data analysis, and thus has great business value.

Nonmonotonic data mining reflects the logical impact of numerical uncertainty. Nonmonotonic data mining introduced another cycle (local mainly at data mining step), independent to the general cycle as discussed in Chapter 4. Since revision of discovered rules can be viewed as a kind of post–model processing (where the model consists of all the discovered rules), this case study also shows another variation of the general mining cycle, namely, that post–model processing can sometimes be absorbed into the modeling process itself.

Influential association rules demonstrate the idea of nonmonotonic reasoning. They represent the influence pattern of influencing items $X$ on influenced targets $Y$. In the form of $X \Rightarrow Y$, an influential association rule is expressed as condition part $X$ has a influential association relationship with assertion part $Y$ and $X \cap Y = \emptyset$. The condition part $X$ is composed of a set of dimension items and the assertion part $Y$ is composed of a set of measure items. Influential association rules concern data patterns in two levels, granularity and aggregation. In granularity level, the frequency of $X$ and $X \cup Y$ is concerned. In the aggregation level, the summarized value of $Y$ in the transactions $X \cup Y$ is concerned. The support $s$ of the rule in granularity level is the percentage $s\%$ of item sets in the whole analytical scope containing the set $X$. The confidence $c$ of the rule in granularity level is the fraction $c$ in item sets containing $X$ that also contain item set $Y$. The aggregation value $v$ of the rule in aggregated level is the sum on $Y$ for all item sets containing both $X$ and $Y$.

Thus, to an analytical target of relation view $R$, influence association rules are stated as $X \Rightarrow Y$ with support $s$, confidence $c$, aggregation value $v$, where $X$ is the condition part composed of a dimension item set and $Y$ is the assertion part composed of a measure item set. There are at least $s\%$ tuples of all tuples in view $R$ containing $X$, and a fraction $c$ of all tuples containing $X$ fall into the category of $Y$. The aggregated value $v$ is the accumulation on measure attributes for all tuples containing $X$ and falling into category $Y$. Item set $Y$ is derived from these measure attributes.

Influential association rules can be viewed as a special form of conventional association rules. In addition to frequent set computation, another challenge for discovery of association rules is to prune and refine the discovered candidate rules so that only meaningful rules are presented and maintained. Redundancy should be removed. Pruning and refining is a time-consuming and expensive for analysis of a massive data set. Constraints imposed in candidate association rule computation will greatly reduce the computation cost and rule redundancy. Influential association rules can be considered as conventional association rules in a special formal and restricted with quantitative measurement constrains. Thus, influential association rules present useful information with less redundancy.

In the data warehousing environment where a multidimensional data model is used, the association patterns along dimensions may not be primary larger for analysis in decision support processing. Only when the dimension context plays a significant role on numeric measure, are the association patterns of dimensions and their impacts on target numeric measures meaningful to a decision support system. Therefore, discovery of influential association rules is of great interest to decision support processing in the context of data warehouses.

Due to the massive data volume and multiple dimensions of a data warehouse, the following issues must be dealt with for discovery of influential association rules in the data warehousing environment.

- Multiple dimensions of data warehouses suggest that the length of dimensions for an influential association rules could be substantially long. In contrast, length of frequent sets is usually short because of the sparsity of item sets within operational databases.
- Influence of dimensions on numeric measures are expressed in the association patterns of dimensions with categories of the numeric measures considered. The effects of categorization of the target numeric measures on discovery of influential association rules must be scrutinized.
- In addition to the granularity level in which occurring frequencies of association patterns are considered, the influence of dimensions on aggregation of numeric measures is an integral part of influential association rules.

- Massive volume of data warehouses suggest that algorithms for discovery of influential association rules be efficient and scalable.

Conventional association rules are the association patterns of items in a set of records. The main difference between influential association rules and conventional association rules is that influential association rules emphasize the influential effects of a set of dimensions on a set of numeric measures. The set of dimensions are, to some extent, equivalent to the frequent sets of conventional association rules. Therefore, it is necessary to reviews the strategies used to discovering conventional association rules before we discuss the methodology of discovering influential association rules.

Discovery of influential association rules can be applied to a decision support system in two types of context. First, a conventional association rule is carried over further to analyze the influential effects of this association pattern on numeric measure. In this situation, each item in the frequent set of the association rule is considered a dimension. Let us use association rule *Bread* ⇒ *Butter*, as an example. The frequent set of this association rule is {*Bread, Butter*}. In the context of influential association rule, *Bread* and *Butter* are treated as two dimensions. The influential effects of the two dimensions on numeric measures, such sale quantity and profitability, are analyzed to discover influential association patterns.

In the other situation where data warehouses and OLAP are integral parts of decision systems, influential association rules are computed on selected dimensions and numeric measures within multidimensional data model. In addition to the influential associations of different items as dimensions with target numeric measures, one item and its features and characteristics can also be considered as dimensions. For instance, we may be interested in the sale patterns of television sets with other dimensions such as store location, brand name model, sizes.

Given a set of dimensions and a set of numeric measures, the problem of mining influential association rules is to discover the influential association patterns between the set of dimensions and the set of numeric, such that, the set of dimensions has the highest influential effects on the set of numeric measures. The final rules must have support and confidence grater than the user-specified support (minimum support) and confidence (minimum confidence). The *highest influential effects* means that the final rules have the highest confidence and highest absolute aggregation value among all candidate rules with the same value of dimension set.

The goal of discovering the association patterns hidden within data in the form of conventional association rules, which is an important and successful data mining technique, is to help marketing managers to design information-driven marketing processes and strategies. For instance, associated items can be arranged onto the same shelf in a supermarket. The convenience for customers provides better service and may potentially increase sales.

We have built a prototypical system to carry out several experiments on an analysis of sales data in a retail sales transaction database. Because of space limitations details of the implementation are not discussed here. Below we only describe an example to illustrate how integrated OLAP and data mining take place in the derivation of the influential association rules (as discussed in Chapter 3).

Suppose that the task is to analyze "how profits are influenced by states" on the basis of sales data. The data records are grouped in terms of the time period when the sales occurred. Table 8.5 depicts a portion of the sales data in the first quarter of 1997 (where the notations are as the follows: Q.: QUARTER, Y.: YEAR, S.: STORE, ST.: STATE, QU.: QUANTITY). Such data are obtained as a materialized view constructed from the primitive data provided by individual stores located in various states, and will be used as the starting point of this example.

We make use of the following algorithm to extract the influential association rules that depict the coherent relationships of the sales data records to the profitability of the merchandise.

**Algorithm Influence Analysis**

*Input*: A relational view that contains a set of records and the questions for influence analysis.
*Output*: An influential association rule.

*Step 1.* Specify the dimension attribute and the measure attribute.

*Step 2.* Identify the dimension itemsets and calculate support counts.

*Step 3.* Identify the measure itemsets and calculate support counts.

*Step 4.* Construct sets of candidate rules, and compute the confidence and aggregate value.

*Step 5.* Form a rule at the granularity level with greatest confidence, and form a rule at the aggregation level with largest abstract value of the measure attribute.

*Step 6.* Compare the assertions at different levels, exit if comparable (i.e., there is no inconsistency found in semantics at different levels).

*Step 7.* For the case where the discovered rules are not comparable, and derive the refined measure itemset and the framework of the rule.

*Step 8.* If the value of the measure consists of both negative and positive values, form a rule indicating the summary value; otherwise, form a rule concerning average value.

*Step 9.* Construct the final rule.

The dimension attribute to be analyzed in the query is STATE. The measure attribute to be analyzed is PROFIT. The dimension itemsets of STATE are KS, IA, NE, and MO. The support counts of the dimension attribute STATE is then calculated. In this instance, the calculated result is 19, 20, 22, and 19, respectively. The generated category set of PROFIT consists of five categories that are "very_high" (from 419 to 1545), "high" (from 213 to 418), and so forth.

**Table 8.5  A Portion of the Sales Table**

| RID | Q. | Y. | S. | ST. | CITY | PRODUCT | BRAND | COLOR | SIZE | QU. | SALES | PROFIT |
|---|---|---|---|---|---|---|---|---|---|---|---|---|
| 01 | 1st | 97 | #1 | KS | Topeka | ActiveWear | FadedGlory | Red | Medium | 48 | 1101.12 | −275.78 |
| 02 | 1st | 97 | #1 | KS | Topeka | Jeans | Jordache | Stonewash | Large | 54 | 1350 | 311.54 |
| 03 | 1st | 97 | #3 | KS | Lawrence | ActiveWear | FadedGlory | Yellow | Medium | 27 | 619.38 | 176.97 |
| 04 | 1st | 97 | #3 | KS | Lawrence | ActiveWear | Jerzees | Red | Small | 35 | 523.6 | 87.27 |
| 05 | 1st | 97 | #1 | IA | DesMoines | Jacket | Jordache | Blue | Large | 92 | 2391.08 | −1024.75 |
| 06 | 1st | 97 | #2 | IA | DesMoines | Jacket | FadedGlory | Black | Medium | 24 | 1197.6 | 342.17 |
| 07 | 1st | 97 | #2 | IA | Davenport | Jacket | FadedGlory | Blue | Small | 40 | 1996 | 570.29 |
| 08 | 1st | 97 | #2 | IA | Davenport | Jacket | FadedGlory | Blue | Medium | 33 | 1646.7 | 470.49 |
| 09 | 1st | 97 | #3 | IA | Davenport | Jacket | Wrangler | Black | X-Large | 37 | 2256.63 | 752.21 |
| 10 | 1st | 97 | #2 | NE | Lincoln | ActiveWear | Jerzees | Yellow | Medium | 36 | 825.84 | 235.95 |
| 11 | 1st | 97 | #2 | NE | Lincoln | ActiveWear | FadedGlory | Yellow | X-Large | 31 | 463.76 | −115.94 |
| 12 | 1st | 97 | #3 | NE | Lincoln | Jeans | Jordache | Stonewash | Small | 27 | 675 | 155.77 |
| 13 | 1st | 97 | #3 | NE | Omaha | Jeans | Wrangler | Stonewash | Large | 10 | 380 | −42.22 |
| 14 | 1st | 97 | #3 | NE | Omaha | Jeans | Wrangler | Black | Large | 22 | 836 | 278.67 |
| 15 | 1st | 97 | #1 | MO | St. Louis | Jacket | Jordache | Blue | Large | 73 | 1897.27 | −813.12 |
| 16 | 1st | 97 | #1 | MO | St. Louis | Jacket | Wrangler | Black | Medium | 46 | 2805.54 | 935.18 |
| 17 | 1st | 97 | #1 | MO | St. Louis | Jeans | Jordache | Stonewash | Medium | 58 | 1450 | 334.62 |
| 18 | 1st | 97 | #2 | MO | Springfield | ActiveWear | Jerzees | Yellow | X-Large | 49 | 1124.06 | −749.37 |
| 19 | 1st | 97 | #3 | MO | Springfield | ActiveWear | Jerzees | Red | Medium | 47 | 703.12 | 117.19 |

The support counts of PROFIT are then calculated. Step 4 of the algorithm generates two sets of candidate rules, one at the granularity level and the other at the aggregation level. Step 5 of the algorithm selects two sets of rules from the candidate sets. The resulting rules coming out of the first five steps of this algorithm are shown in Tables 8.6 and 8.7, respectively.

Step 6 of the algorithm compares the contents of Tables 8.8 and 8.9, and reveals that rules 1–3 have the same assertions at both levels. Therefore, they are considered as valid influential association rules. These rules are then confirmed as part of the final rules to be presented. Table 8.5 shows these rules

**Table 8.6 Influential Rules at Granularity Level**

| No. | Granularity Level | Confidence |
|---|---|---|
| 1 | ⟨STATE: KS⟩ ⇒ ⟨PROFIT: High⟩ | 32% |
| 2 | ⟨STATE: IA⟩ ⇒ ⟨PROFIT: Very_High⟩ | 40% |
| 3 | ⟨STATE: NE⟩ ⇒ ⟨PROFIT: Non_Profitable⟩ | 36% |
| 4 | ⟨STATE: MO⟩ ⇒ ⟨PROFIT: Medium⟩ | 32% |

**Table 8.7 Rules Discovered at Aggregation Level**

| No. | Aggregation Level | Aggregate |
|---|---|---|
| 1 | ⟨STATE: KS⟩ ⇒ ⟨PROFIT: High⟩ | 1848.95 |
| 2 | ⟨STATE: IA⟩ ⇒ ⟨PROFIT: Very_High⟩ | 5614.30 |
| 3 | ⟨STATE: NE⟩ ⇒ ⟨PROFIT: Non_Profitable⟩ | −1966.96 |
| 4 | ⟨STATE: MO⟩ ⇒ ⟨PROFIT: Very_High⟩ | 2487.42 |

**Table 8.8 Discovered Influential Association Rules**

| No. | Influential Association Rules | Confidence | Aggregate |
|---|---|---|---|
| 1 | <STATE: KS⟩ ⇒ <PROFIT: High⟩ | 32% | 1848.95 |
| 2 | <STATE: IA⟩ ⇒ <PROFIT: Very_High⟩ | 40% | 5614.30 |
| 3 | <STATE: NE⟩ ⇒ <PROFIT: Non_Profitable⟩ | 36% | −1966.96 |

**Table 8.9 Refined Influential Association Rules**

| No. | Refined Rule | Summary |
|---|---|---|
| 4 | <STATE: MO⟩ ⇒ <PROFIT: Very_High⟩ | 2500.74 |

Much of the PROFITS come from:

| QUARTER | YEAR | STORE | CITY | PRODUCT | BRAND | COLOR | SIZE |
|---|---|---|---|---|---|---|---|
| 1st | 97 | #1 | St. Louis | Jacket | Wrangler | Black | Medium |

which indicate that the PROFIT made in Kansas, Iowa, and Nebraska are categorized as "high," "very high," and "nonprofitable," respectively.

Step 6 of the algorithm also discovers a noncompatible assertion at the granularity level (Table 8.6) and the aggregation level (Table 8.7). It is seen that while the measure attribute PROFIT has a value of "Medium" for STATE: MO at the granularity level, the value of the same measure attribute is "very high" at the aggregation level. Hence the refinement of this rule is needed. Steps 7–9 of the algorithm are then applied. The refined rule 4 resulting from these steps is shown in Table 8.9.

This rule particularly tells us that though the "PROFIT" is "very high" in "STATE: MO", much of the profit came from a specific store due to its sale of certain merchandise in the specific quarter of a year. Such kind of influential association cannot be discovered simply by a OLAP process or a traditional association method alone. Here, the integration of the OLAP and data mining processes we developed enables us to discover this particular influential association pattern.

This example demonstrates the discovery of four influential association rules by the prototype system in an automated manner. The results are obtained by first invoking an OLAP process, and then integrating it with a data mining process to extract the influential association rules with the data records retrieved from a transaction database. The business values of these rules lie in the fact that, according to these rules, decisionmakers will be able to decide what to do with respect to their sales and profit objectives.

As a new research frontline the influential analysis algorithm does not well address at least two important issues. The first issue is the multiple dimensions and measures. This algorithm did not well explain how to apply it for multiple dimensions and measures. The complexity of combination is exponential to both number of dimensions $K$ and number of measures $J$. To efficiently process large volume of data, a more efficient algorithm is needed. Another issue is the resolution of *incompatible candidate rules*. In mining conventional association rules, occurring frequency of an association pattern is the sole measurement to judge the importance of the pattern. In the context of a multidimensional data model, we also consider the influencing effect of conditional item sets on the overall value (aggregation value) of target numeric measures. Occurring frequency of an influential association pattern and its influenced aggregation value should be considered relatively equally important unless users have specified the primary concern for further refinement of candidate rules.

Therefore, more efficient algorithm and more reasonable pruning and refining scheme for mining influential association rules are needed. Recently a new strategy has been developed to take advantage of the efficiency of bitmap indexing. The basic idea of bitmap indexing was introduced in Section 3.2.3. Bitmap indexing techniques are gaining more popularity in indexing technology for large volume of high read update ratio data in the data warehousing environment. Due to the space limitation, only the outline of the algorithm for computation of candidate influential association rules using bitmaps is given below. For more details of this approach see Zhang (2001).

**Computation of Candidate Influential Association Rules**
```
/* Algorithm of computing candidate influential association
rules from bitmaps */
/* input:
        B_d, bitmap index for the set of dimensions
        B_m, bitmap index for the set of measures
        C_min, user-specified minimum confidence
        N, the size of each bit vector within B_d and B_m */
/*output: S, the set of candidate influential association rules
*/
S ← ∅
for j ← 1 up to N do
        f_j = f_j.Bd ∪ f_i.Bm
    if f_j ∈ S
        then f_j.count ← fj.count + 1
        else S ← S ∪ {f_j}
            f_j.count ← 1
/* computation the confidence and aggregation value */
for each mapping function f_j in set S
        if f_j.count / f_j.Bd.SUPPORT < C_min
            then S ← S - {f_j}
            else f_j.CONFIDENCE = f_j.count/f_j.Bd SUPPORT
                for each measure m_k in M
                    f_j.m_k.AGGREGATION = SUM (m_k|f_j)
```

### 8.3.4  Case Study 4: *k*-Means Algorithm with Initial Points Refining

We now present another case study to illustrate a particular data mining task, namely, clustering. This also illustrates the important concern of sampling techniques for data mining (as discussed in Chapter 3). We apply an algorithm (Sun et al. 2000) that modifies the $k$-means and $k$-modes algorithms in selecting and refining the initial settings of the clusters so as to cluster data set results with a better local maxima. The rationale for this algorithm is that both $k$-means and $k$-modes algorithms converge finitely to a point (set of parameter values) that is locally maximal for the likelihood of data with the given model. The deterministic mapping means that the locally optimal solution is sensitive to the initial point choice.

This initialization problem can be solved via parameterization of each cluster model. This parameterization can be performed by determining the *centroids* (maxima) of the joint probability density of the data and placing a cluster centroid on each model. A clustering approach is used to estimate the density and attempt to find the maxima of the estimated density function.

The basic heuristic is that severely subsampling the data will naturally bias the sample to representatives "near" the models. In general, one cannot guard against the possibility of points from the tails appearing in the subsamples. Figure 8.2 shows data drawn from a mixture of two Gaussians (clusters) in 2-D with means at [1.5, 1.5] and [4, 4]. A small subsample is shown in Figure 8.2, which provides information on the modes of the joint probability density function. Each point in Figure 8.3 may be considered as a "guest" at the possible location of a mode in the underlying distribution. The figure shows that there is good separation between the two clusters. This observation indicates that the solutions obtained by clustering over a small subsample may provide good refined initial estimates of the true means, or centroids, in the data. However, this method often produces noisy estimates due to single small subsamples, especially in skewed distributions and high dimensions. This behavior is fairly common when clustering over small subsamples.

As discussed above, the solutions obtained by clustering over a small subsample may provide good initial estimates of the true means, or centroids, in

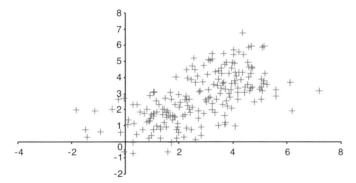

**Figure 8.2**   Samples of Gaussian distribution in two dimensions.

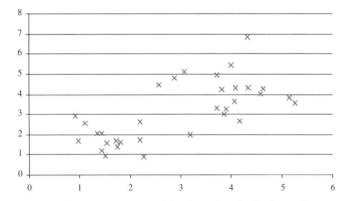

**Figure 8.3**   Small sample sets of the Gaussian distribution in Figure 8.2.

the data. Since one cannot prevent the possibility of the subsample resulting from the tail portion of a Gaussian distribution, the refinement algorithm will use multiple data subsamples to find the best solution as the initial points. The refinement algorithm initially chooses $J$ small random subsamples of data, $S_i, i = 1, \ldots, J$. The subsamples are clustered via the $k$-means (or $k$-modes) algorithm. The sets $CM_i, i = 1, \ldots, J$ are these clustering solutions (cluster means) over the subsample $S_i$. Let $CM$ be the union of $CM$, $CM = \bigcup\limits_{i=1}^{J} CM_i$.

Now $CM$ is treated as the data set and clustered via the $k$-means (or $k$-modes) algorithm. The $CM$ is clustered $J$ times using $CM_i, i = 1, \ldots, J$ as the initial point each time. All clustering solutions over $CM$ form the sets $FM_i, i = 1, \ldots, J$. Let $FMS$ be the union of sets $FM$, $FMS = \bigcup\limits_{i=1}^{J} FM_i$.

The distortion is used to evaluate the $FM_i, i = 1, \ldots, J$. Given the estimation by the $k$-means or $k$-modes algorithm, the distortion value that we consider is simply the sum of the distance between the data items and the means of their assigned cluster. A smaller value for the distortion measure indicates that the model parameters (i.e., means) are a better fit to the data provided the $k$-means (or $k$-modes) assumptions are true. The refined initial point is then chosen as the $FM_i$ having minimal distortion over the set $CM$.

Clustering $CM$ is a smoothing over the $CM_i$ to avoid solutions "corrupted" by outliers included in the subsample $S_i$. The refinement algorithm takes these parameters as input: $SP$ (initial starting point), $D$ (the data set), $K$ (number of desired clusters), and $J$ (number of small subsamples to be taken from data). The algorithm is described as follows (using $k$-means as an example):

**Algorithm Refinement of Initial Points ($SP, D, K, J$)**

```
CM = 0
For i = 1, . . . , J
      Let Sᵢ be a small random subsample of D
      Assign CMᵢ = Kmeans (SP, Sᵢ, K)
      CM = CM ∪ CMᵢ
      FMS = 0
For i = 1, . . . , J
      Assign FMᵢ = Kmeans (CMᵢ, CM, K)
      Assign FMS = FMS ∪ FMᵢ
      Assign FM = ArgMin{Distortion(FMᵢ, CM)}
               FMᵢ
Return (FM)
```

Several experiments have been carried out. Synthetic data were created for dimension $d = 10, 20, 40, 100$. The goal of this experimental is to evaluate how close the means estimated by the $k$-means algorithm are to the true Gaussian means used to generate the synthetic data. Two initializations are compared:

- *No Refinement*—random starting point chosen uniformly on the range of the data.
- *Refinement* ($J = 10$)—a starting point refined from refinement algorithm.

The random subsamples are 10% of full data set size and the number of sub-samples taken is 10.

Michalski's soybean disease data set (Michalski and Stepp 1983) can be used to test the $k$-modes algorithm with our initial point refinement algorithm. The problem is to reconstruct a classification of selected soybean diseases. Given are 47 cases of soybean diseases, each characterized by the 35 multi-valued variables. These cases are drawn from four populations representing the following soybean diseases:

$D1$—Diaporthe stem canker

$D2$—Charcoat rot

$D3$—Rhizoctonia root rot

$D4$—Phytophthorat rot

Ideally, a clustering method should partition these given cases into four groups corresponding to the diseases.

We used the $k$-modes algorithm to cluster each test data set of soybean disease data into four clusters with two initial starting point selections:

- *No Refinement*—random starting modes chosen uniformly on the range of the data
- *Refinement* ($J = 10$)—a starting point refined from the refinement algorithm

The program was executed 20 times, and 20 clustering results were produced. The results were then compared using clustering accuracy $r$ defined as $r = \Sigma_{i=1}^{k} a_i/n$, where $a_i$ is the number of instances occurring in both cluster $i$ and itscorresponding class, $k$ is the number of clusters (4 in this case), and $n$ is the number of instances in the data set (47 in this case). The clustering error is defined as $e = 1 - r$.

The 20 results are summarized in Table 8.10. The results show that 70% (14 cases) of the results had an accuracy of 0.98 (only one case missed) for refinement initializations, and 45% of the results had an accuracy of 0.89 or above for no refinement initialization. This demonstrates that the refinement

Table 8.10  Summary of 20 Clustering Results

| Accuracy | Cases with Refinement | Cases with No Refinement |
|---|---|---|
| 0.98 | 14 | 5 |
| 0.94 | — | 2 |
| 0.89 | — | 2 |
| 0.77 | — | 3 |
| 0.68 | — | 5 |
| 0.70 | 1 | — |
| 0.66 | 5 | 3 |
| Total | 20 | 20 |

initialization algorithm yields better clustering results than does the nonrefinement initialization method. These results are very similar to those reported by Huang (1998), but the refinement initialization algorithm is more practical than the initialization method used there for large databases with high dimensions.

In this case study, a fast and efficient algorithm for refining an initial starting point for a general class of clustering algorithms the *k-means* and *k-mode* has been presented. The refinement algorithm operates over small subsamples of a given database, hence requiring a small proportion of the total memory needed to store the full database and making this approach very appealing for large-scale clustering problems. The procedure is motivated by the observation that subsampling can provide guidance regarding the location of the modes of the joint probability density function assumed to have generated the data. By initializing a general clustering algorithm near the modes, not only are the true clusters found more often, but it follows that the clustering algorithm will iterate fewer times prior to convergence. Computational results on synthetic Ganssian data indicate that solutions computed by the *k*-means algorithm from the refined initial points are superior to the random initial starting points, especially over high-dimensional data sets. The clustering performance of the *k*-modes algorithm has been evaluated using a real-world data set (soybean diseases). The results have demonstrated the effectiveness of the *k*-modes algorithm in discovering relating structures in large data sets.

## 8.3.5  Case Study 5: A Reduction Approach to Data Mining

***8.3.5.1  Overview***  The purpose of this last case study is to illustrate how reductionism, such as the basic ideas used in the rough set theory, can be used for data mining. Explanation of a reimplementation of rough set rule reduction utilizing an algorithm proposed by Cercone et al. (1997) is given. Data structures used are detailed along with methodologies. A key feature of the system is the assignment of an integer identification value to each attribute and the utilization of those integer values in determining cardinality for rough set reduction. A unique decision tree structure is built using data analyzed by the program. This structure is used during activation of the system to dynamically build the queries and determine the path that the decision search takes. Examples are given so that the state of the data can be tracked as it passes through the various phases of the program. It is important to note that our reimplementation is not intended to simply redo what was already done. Instead, our purpose was to explore alternative ways to demonstrate the use of reductionism, the philosophical backdrop of rough set theory.

As discussed in Chapter 7, rough set theory has found its way into a number of theoretical and practical knowledge-based systems, particularly when inconsistent, imprecise, and ambiguous data are involved. Numerous approaches have been developed. One such system in the area of data mining is explained and analyzed by Cercone et al. (1997), who give details on the DBLEARN/ DB-Discover system. An algorithm applying rough set theory to attribute-oriented data was proposed and was used to demonstrate the concept and use of rough sets. This system consists of three phases:

- An analysis phase in which data for condition and decision attributes are collected and a reduct set of attributes produced
- A rule generation phase in which the reduct set of attributes is used to generate a rule set
- A third phase that allows the use of the rule set in the decision process

In particular, the following components are used in the system. Algorithm for computing a reduct (GENRED) assigns a significance value based on an evaluation function to each attribute and sorts the attributes according to their significance values. A *forward selection method* is then employed to create a smaller subset of attributes with the same discriminating power as the original attributes. At the end of this phase, an attribute set, denoted as SM, contains the good performing attribute subset found so far. Finally, to compute a reduct, a *backward elimination method* removes attributes, one by one, from the set SM. The lower the significance value is, the earlier the attribute is processed. The degree of dependency is calculated at each step according to the remaining attributes in SM. If the degree of dependency is changed, the attribute is restored to the set SM; otherwise it is permanently removed. Attributes remaining in the set SM for the reduct; other attributes may be removed. Algorithm GENRULE computes a set of maximally generalized rules in the following manner. It considers each rule in the set of specific decision rules for dropping conditions until a set of maximally general rules remains. The process of dropping conditions should first drop the conditions with values of lower significance.

***8.3.5.2 Methodology of Study*** We have used an object-oriented language C++ to implement all major steps of algorithms in Cercone et al. (1997) at the conceptual level for reduction, without necessarily using rough set concepts. To compare our result with the original algorithms used in Cercone et al. (1997), we used the same data for testing of our implementation. The attributes used in the test consist of the following attributes: make, fuel, displacement, weight, cylinders, power, turbocharged, compression, transmission, and mileage, the decision attribute. A sample tuple after attribute-oriented induction is

```
USA EFI medium medium 6 high yes high automatic medium
```

*Data Setup*   As user data are entered, a linked list of stAttribute structures is created along with an instance of the Attribute class for each attribute. These are attached to the structure via the "attrobject" element. As each Attribute class object is created, it is assigned a unique ID based on its order of input. A value of 100 was used as the index factor for this implementation; thus the first attribute input would have an ID of 100, the second 200, and so on. Note that this allows up to 99 unique values of the attribute, which can be handled by the program as each unique value is also assigned an ID on input.

   On completion of the user input process, the processing of the original data begins. As each line of the file is read, the individual values for the attributes are added to the appropriate object. As the values are on the line in the order in which the attributes were input, this is a matter of iterating through the linked list of stAttribute structures for each line and accessing the attached Attribute object. As this is done the attached "range" Value object linked list is searched to see if the input value is unique. If it is, a new Value object is created and added to the linked list, and the variable "rangect" incremented. The "rangect" value also becomes the ID of the range value. Thus the "rang'" values are numbered consecutively from 1 on. The instance is then automatically added to the "values" linked list of Value objects and the "valuect" incremented. Each value in the "values" linked list then represents the value for that attribute in the order in which it was input; thus, the first member of the linked list is the value for that attribute input from row 1 of the file.

*Data Analysis*   Chi-square analysis can be used to calculate the differences among the subjects in a research study to determine whether extraneous variables influenced the outcome. If the calculated chi-square value is high enough, we can conclude that the frequencies found would not be expected on the basis of chance alone and the null hypothesis would be rejected.

   The formula for chi-square analysis is

$$\chi^2 = \sum \frac{(|E - 0| - 0.5)^2}{E}$$

where $\chi^2$ is the chi squared, $E$ is an expected cell value, and $O$ is an observed cell value.

In our implementation using C++, the analysis of data begins with the creation of a Table class object for each attribute that is used in the chi-square analysis. The format of the table is unique instance values of the condition attribute (the range values) versus the unique instance values of the decision attribute. The condition attributes are the rows, while the decision attributes are the columns. The individual cells of the table then contain a count of the number condition attributes that participated in the indicated decision attribute. Table 8.11, which was built from the input data for the automobile domain, illustrates this concept. This would be the correct table for the first attribute the "make" consisting of the range values "USA" and "Japan" versus the "mileage" decision attribute with the range of "low," "medium" and "high."

Once created, these tables are input to a routine that determines the chi-square value for the particular attribute. The table is then attached via a pointer to the object to the stAttribute structure for that attribute. It is used later on in the program for rule creation.

The chi-square function is used to quantify the degree of interaction of an attribute with a decision attribute. Thus, the higher the significance value determined by the function, the greater the interaction. Using Table 8.11, the method used will be explained. First, as shown, the rows and columns are totaled. These values are used to calculate the expected value for each row/column combination; the formula used is

$$(\text{Row total}) \times \left( \frac{\text{column total}}{\text{table total}} \right) = \text{expected value}$$

For example, row 1/column 1 would yield

$$(0.6+3.0+2.4) \times \left( \frac{0.6+1.4}{0.6+3.0+2.4+1.4+7+5.6} \right) = 6 \times \frac{2}{20} = 0.6$$

Table 8.12 shows the expected values for each instance using the chi-square analysis. The difference between the observed values and the expected values is then calculated, the value squared, and the total divided by the expected value. This is done for each cell of the table; the total is the chi-square value for the table.

**Table 8.11   Mileage of Cars Manufactured in Different Countries**

| Make | Low | Medium | High | Row Total |
|------|-----|--------|------|-----------|
| Japan | 0 | 0 | 6 | 6 |
| USA | 2 | 10 | 2 | 14 |
| Column total | 2 | 10 | 8 | 20 |

**Table 8.12    Chi-Square Analysis of Mileage**

| Make | Low | Medium | High |
|------|-----|--------|------|
| Japan | 0.6 | 3.0 | 2.4 |
| USA | 1.4 | 7 | 5.6 |

**Table 8.13 Attributes Ordered with Decreasing Chi-Square Value**

| Attribute (Feature, Condition Variable) | $\chi^2$ Value |
|------------------------------------------|----------------|
| Weight | 17.5357 |
| Make | 12.8571 |
| Displacement | 7.08333 |
| Cylinders | 5.9375 |
| Power | 5.67955 |
| Transmission | 4.53333 |
| Compression | 3.83838 |
| Fuel | 0.625 |
| Turbocharged | 0.625 |

After the chi-square value is determined for each attribute, the contents of the linked list of stAttribute structures is used to create a one-dimensional array of the structures, so that they can be sorted. The array is then sorted in descending order on the chi-square values using an efficient sorting method. The resulting ordering produced by the program is shown in Table 8.13. This ranked list of attributes is used as the basis for the forward elimination process.

*Forward Elimination Process*    The basis for Cerone et al.'s entire reduct (GENRED) algorithm is the degree of dependency formula where $K(C, D) =$ card(LOW(C,D))/card(U) and the fact that if $K(C, D)$ is equal to 1, then all values of $D$ (the decision attribute) can be uniquely determined by the values of $C$ (the condition attributes), whereas, if $K(C, D)$ is equal to 0, then none of the $D$ attribute values can be so determined.

To start the forward elimination process, a Table class object is instantiated and built using the ordered list built as in Table 8.13. The first column would be composed of the weight attribute values; the second, the make values; and so on for each attribute. The rows would constitute each automobile instance entered from the file. The cell values are composed of the attribute ID added to the value ID assigned when the data were entered. Each attribute is represented by the order appearing in the table containing the original data. In addition, each possible value for an attribute is represented by integers assigned according to the order of their appearance in the data. Assuming that each attribute may have up to 99 values, two digits are sufficient to denote all possible values for an attribute. For example, the attribute weight appears in the original table in column 4, and the value for weight in the first row is 1, so 1 is assigned for medium. Since the second value of weight ever appearing in the table is heavy, a value 2 is assigned for "heavy." The only other value appeared in the table for weight is 3, so 3 is assigned for "light." Therefore, "weight is medium" is represented as 401. Each row in the original data table is represented as a sequence of such numbers, ordered by decreasing ranking produced from the chi-square value. The last column is the decision attribute. In our testing case, since there are nine condition attributes, the decision variable is labeled as 10. The first two rows generated for the automobile data are offered as an illustration:

```
ROW: 1
401 101 301 501 601 901 801 201 701 1001
ROW: 2
401 101 301 501 601 902 802 201 702 1001
```

Interpreting row 1, we have: weight—medium, make—USA, displacement—medium, cylinders—6, power—high, transmission—automatic, compression—high, fuel—electronic fuel injection, turbocharged—yes, and mileage —medium. Row 2 differs from row 1 only in columns 6: transmission—manual; column 7, compression—no; and column 9, turbocharged—no.

This table of integer values is utilized to determine cardinality by first performing addition on the values in each row. The values are then added to a linked list of stCardinalNo structures depending on whether they are in fact unique. This is determined by a search of the existing linked list for equal integers. If an equal integer is found in the list, a further check is performed. This consists of a comparison of values column by column (or, in essence, attribute by attribute) for equal values. If no unequal values are found, the instances are the same and the total is not added to the list. If the comparison yields a different value in any of the columns, then that total, along with the row number, is added via the stCardinalNo structure. At the end of the process, all members in the linked list are counted. This is the cardinality of the set of attributes analyzed.

In this manner the card(U) of the entire table is first determined. Next, beginning with the first column in the ordered table (the weight attribute), the cardinality of each attribute is determined. If the cardinality so determined is not equal to card(U), then $K(C, D)$ cannot be equal to 1, and the conditional attributes cannot uniquely determine the values of the attributes in $D$. If this is the case, the next column is considered by determining the cardinality of the first and second columns. Addition of attributes continues until the cardinality of all the attributes in the subset equals that of the entire universe. For the domain of automobiles used as a test in this implementation, the subset consisting of seven attributes was determined to be equal to card(U), as shown in Table 8.14.

**Table 8.14 Reduced Number of Attributes Ordered with Decreasing Chi-Square Value**

| Attributes | $\chi^2$ Value |
| --- | --- |
| Weight | 17.5357 |
| Make | 12.8571 |
| Displacement | 7.08333 |
| Cylinders | 5.9375 |
| Power | 5.67955 |
| Transmission | 4.53333 |
| Compression | 3.83838 |

Each row in the table is now represented by only these seven attributes. For example, incorporating the values of each attributes, the first two rows now become

```
ROW: 1
401 101 301 501 601 901 801 1001
ROW: 2
401 101 301 501 601 902 802 1001
```

*Backward Elimination Process* To set up the data for the backward elimination process, the preceding subset of attributes is used to build another array of pointers to Attribute class objects. This array is then sorted on the chi-square value ascending and a new table is generated from the results. After this process, the two first two rows would look like this:

```
ROW: 1
801 901 601 501 301 101 401 1001
ROW: 2
802 902 601 501 301 101 401 1001
```

Now, applying the Cercone et al. algorithm for backward elimination and the cardinality function, the set of attributes is checked attribute by attribute for degree of significance. This is done by totaling each row without the attribute value, and using these totals in the cardinality calculation. If the cardinality of this subset of attributes is not the same as the original cardinality, the attribute is essential to keeping $K(C, D) = 1$ and must be retained. If the cardinality is equal to the original, the attribute can be eliminated. The attribute is eliminated in the process by zeroing out the value in each row for the entire column before the next calculation is performed.

For backward elimination, the cardinality check is implemented in the following manner. If, after the columns are checked for similar values, the rows are found to be exactly the same (this again without the column being checked), the row and decision attribute values of the row are added to a second linked list of stCardinalNo structures. When the total number of unique row values is tallied at the end of the cardinality process, this list is also used by considering the decision values for each row. If all of these values are the same, their count is added to the count of the other cardinal list. This is done because, if all the decision values are the same, the value of the attribute left out has no effect on the decision, and is not essential in making the decision.

Applying this method to the automobile domain, it was found that the cylinder and displacement attributes could also be eliminated. So, at the end of this process the rows would look like this (note that the values to be eliminated are represented by zeros):

```
ROW: 1
801 901 601 0 0 101 401 1001
ROW: 2
802 902 601 0 0 101 401 1001
```

*Rule Generation*   The rule generation process utilizes the table of attributes that is the result of the cardinality analysis and the individual tables generated for each attribute (viz., those tables generated for the chi-square function), to build a decision tree structure. Objects of the RNode class are used as nodes of the tree.

To begin, the list of essential attributes is sorted (descending) on the chi-square value after the chi-square values are zeroed for the nonessential attributes. This new list is then used to create yet another table, which contains only those attribute values necessary to determine the decision attribute.

Again the sample rows are presented by way of illustration:

```
ROW: 1
401 101 601 901 801 1001
ROW: 2
401 101 601 902 802 1001
```

An analysis is now performed on the individual observed value tables generated for each attribute for the chi-square analysis. As an example, consider the one used above for the "make"–"mileage" comparison, as shown in Table 8.15. By looking at the table, it can be seen that if the make of vehicle is Japan, then the mileage can only be high. This observation can be incorporated into the decision process, so that if the make of vehicle is indicated as

**Table 8.15   Individual Observed Values for Mileage**

| Make | Low | Medium | High |
|------|-----|--------|------|
| Japan | 0 | 0 | 6 |
| USA | 2 | 10 | 2 |

Japan, then the decision of high can be made without considering the other attributes.

To incorporate this observational fact into the table, the columns (up to the decision attribute) of the rows with a make of Japanese were zeroed out. An example of a row is shown below.

```
ROW: 12
401 102 0 0 0 1001
```

The actual decision tree is built by going through the table one row at a time and instantiating RNode objects for each attribute value if it has not already been created. If it has, the children of the node are checked to see if the next attribute is present among its children. This continues until the decision attribute is reached, as this node having no children. Each node contains the attribute name (character string), attribute value (character string) and ID, the decision value (character string), a count of the children, and an array of pointers to its RNode object children.

***8.3.5.3 Queries*** Using the tree structure presented above, decisions based on user input to system-generated queries can be rendered. The system generates the queries using the attribute name and attribute value character strings of the nodes as it tracks through the system. The root node is of course displayed first, which in the case of the automobile domain would be the weight. The following is an example from the program echo:

```
Enter done to exit or categorize weight from the following:
medium
heavy
light
→
```

The value entered determines the next node to be visited in the process. If the node selected has only one child, then no prompt for a selection is made. This process continues until a node is encountered that has no children, and a decision can be displayed. In addition, as in many expert systems, at any time a "why"-type question can be entered by the user, and a trace of the decision process will be displayed. The trace is also displayed when the decision is rendered, again from the program echo:

```
Enter done to exit or categorize trans from the following:
  manual
  automatic
  → automatic
  weight = heavy
  by induction → make_model = USA
```

```
by induction → power = high
trans = automatic
by induction → comp = medium
Decision → mileage is low.
```

The attributes indicated by induction are nodes that are the only child from a parent.

#### 8.3.5.4  *Conclusion of the Data Reduction Case Study*   The implementation described above demonstrates basic idea of a reduction approach to data mining. The original algorithm was developed on the basis of rough set theory, and although our implementation follows the algorithm at the conceptual level, it does not follow all the details of the algorithm, particularly when the rough set aspects are concerned. Therefore, this case study indicates an alternative way of implementation of the reduction approach discussed by Cercone et al. (1997). There are some features used in our implementation. The first of these is the assignment of the integer ID value to both the attribute category and the values of the individual themselves. This allows the data to be analyzed and manipulated as arithmetic values instead of strings and results in a much faster and more straightforward process. Also, the algorithm for determining cardinality is structured, so that it can efficiently make a determination. The application also shows what can be done with such reduced sets of data. Using an effective analysis of the data at hand, it tailors an efficient tree structure of rule nodes that can be utilized to dynamically query a user while at the same time making a decision. Finally, although not exploited in this application, the use of integer ID values could lend itself to attribute and rule storage in object-oriented databases.

### 8.4   DATA MINING SOFTWARE TOOLS

The main purpose of this book is to discuss useful methodology for integrated data mining. Nevertheless, we offer some general remarks on existing data mining software tools. According to Han and Kamber (2000), there are several criteria for choosing a data mining system, such as data types that can be processed by the software, operating systems required by the software, data mining functions and methodologies, the method of coupling data mining with database and/or data warehouse systems, scalability (row scalable or column scalable), accommodation of visualization, data mining query language, and graphical user interface.

The data mining research community and commercial vendors have begun to elaborate an ideas to support the whole process instead of simply supporting single mining algorithms. Dedicated KDD support environments offer powerful preprocessing operators on the data.

There are several notable aspects related to data mining software tools in general. As indicated in earlier chapters, there are two general ways to carry out data mining: (1) taking a database-centric perspective and supporting algorithms to carry out one or more data mining tasks (association, classification, etc.) or (2) taking a more computation-oriented perspective and utilizing some uncertain reasoning techniques (e.g., neural networks or fuzzy set theory) to achieve the goal of one or more data mining tasks (e.g., classification or clustering). Another notable feature is that many products were either outgrown from, or attached to, some other existing software provided by the same vendor. For example, data mining products could be provided by database management system (DBMS) vendors, or by vendors who offer statistical analysis packages. Finally, although many data mining products are provided by software vendors, there are also products that originated as research projects from academic institutions. This is clear evidence that the data mining field has been nurtured by both academia and industry.

The following are some sample software products to illustrating the preceding remarks:

- Intelligent Miner from IBM provides a wide range of functionality for various data mining tasks, including association, classification, and clustering, as well as predictive modeling. It is tightly integrated with DB2 relational database system. Therefore, Intelligent Miner is an example of data mining products provided by a DBMS vendor.

- DBMiner, developed by DBMiner Technology Inc., supports various data mining tasks, with data cube–based online analytical mining and attribute-oriented induction techniques as its unique features. DBMiner is an example of a data mining tool developed from database-centric perspective, as well as an example of a product born in an academic environment.

- Clementine, now acquired by SPSS Inc., provides several data mining methods, including neural networks, rule induction, and visualization tools. Clementine is an example of data mining product initiated from uncertain reasoning perspective, as well as an example of a product provided by a vendor offering statistic packages.

Various data mining algorithms or techniques have been supported by different products. The following is a sample list of algorithms (or methods) along with products or vendors supporting them:

- *Logical Rules.* The key proponents of generalized rule systems are Information Discovery, Inc. and Ultragem Corporation, using rule induction (among other techniques) or genetic algorithms.

- *Decision Trees.* A really large number of vendors offer software packages based on decision tree methods such as CART. These include IBM, Pilot Software, Business Objects, Cognos, NeoVista, SAS, Angoss, and Integral Solutions (ISL). Most of these systems allow for the interactive exploration of the data with decision trees.

- *Artificial Neural Network.* A large number of other vendors have provided neural net systems. These include IBM, NeoVista, TMC, SAS, ISL, and Magnify.

- *k-Nearest Neighbor.* A well-known example of a product with a *k*-nearest-neighbor component was the Darwin (trademark) system from Thinking Machines Corporation (TMC).

Description of other software products can be found in Westphal and Blaxton (1998). Goebel and Gruenwald (1999) provided a survey of data mining and knowledge discovery software tools. It is interesting to note that although data mining is at the core of the overall knowledge discovery process, this step usually represents only a small part (estimated at 15–25%) of the overall effort.

Although there are many software products available for data mining, an appropriate application of the operators on the underlying data sources with respect to the great variety of mining algorithms and their features remains a very difficult and case-specific problem.

Goebel and Gruenwald (1999) identified some research issues related to software development for knowledge discovery and data mining. These issues echo many key points emphasized in this book (including future trends discussed in Chapter 2):

- Integration of different techniques, including interplay of different data mining algorithms, as well as integration of uncertain reasoning techniques into data mining algorithms developed from a database-centric perspective
- Extensibility so that a software product is ready to allow new methods to be incorporated
- Seamless integration with databases
- Support for both experts and novice users
- Managing changing data in a dynamic environment
- Ability to deal with complex data types

## 8.5 SUMMARY

In this chapter, we have described several case studies for integrated data mining and provided observations on several software products. The case studies were developed mainly to illustrate the diversity of data mining activities around the data mining cycle. Each case study focuses on either the whole mining process, or some specific stages in this process. The case studies have illustrated many aspects of integrated data mining, such as data preparation, data reduction, sampling, integration of uncertain reasoning with basic data mining tasks, and incorporation of OLAP operations. However, there are still many other aspects not covered, such as dealing with the scaleup problem when various algorithms or techniques are used.

As for the software tools sketched in this chapter, unlike case studies, rather than illustrating the diversity involved in data mining process, they clearly indicate the diversity of different orientations and different functionalities. The implication of this observation is at least twofold: First, users of existing software tools should carefully and skillfully map their specific data mining problems into available mining tools. The second indication is that, because of the limitation of existing software, it is likely that for some applications, there may be no appropriate software to use (or the software may be able to solve only a portion of the problem). Therefore, enterprises may have to develop their own data mining systems. In this case, a careful examination of existing software still makes good sense, because this examination may offer meaningful insight or important lessons for the development of the new data mining software (even if this software itself is not for sale, i.e., not available on the market).

The diversity involved in integrated data mining reminds us of the need for a systematic study of methodology in integrated data mining. Unlike a study of an individual algorithm or method, the study of *methodology* refers to an in-depth, holistic examination of the overall mining process and development of useful insights for better data mining. This examination requires good understanding of the mining process, as well as detailed implementation knowledge of each individual algorithm or technique that is useful in data mining. The study of methodology is a necessary extension, as well as a technical exploration of the philosophical and theoretical foundation of data mining (as discussed in Chapter 2). Sample issues that can be considered include top-down versus bottom-up approaches in data mining, technical invariants, and meta reasoning, as well as many others. [A general discussion on some methodological issues in the context of decision making as a whole, can be found in Chen (1999).]

# 9

# INTELLIGENT CONCEPTUAL QUERY ANSWERING WITH UNCERTAINTY: BASIC ASPECTS AND CASE STUDIES

## 9.1 OVERVIEW

Data mining is important to database management, not only because it is able to process ad hoc decision support queries but also because it broadens the scope of functionality of database management systems. In this last chapter we examine an interesting issue related to this feature, namely, intelligent conceptual query answering with uncertainty, and apply data mining techniques to it. This examination extends our discussion of integrated data mining to a wider perspective. We discuss three related aspects, each presented as a case study. These topics exemplify the rich contents of data mining. We also illustrate how uncertain reasoning issues are incorporated into the intelligent conceptual query answering process.

The first topic is concerned with the basics of conceptual queries and intensional answers. In Section 9.2 we show how attribute-oriented data mining can benefit intensional answering of conceptual queries. Related to this aspect, in the second case study as studied in Section 9.3, we further demonstrate how conceptual query answering can tolerate dirty data—another way of dealing with uncertainty. Finally, in Section 9.4, we investigate the issue of selecting conceptual query answers for OLAP using a concept called *query entropy* (or Q-entropy for short). Here we encounter a different kind of uncertainty, namely, which answer is the best. The theoretical basis of this new approach is first presented, followed by the presentation of the case study proper.

Section 9.5 concludes this chapter, as well as the whole book.

## 9.2  INTELLIGENT CONCEPTUAL QUERY ANSWERING

### 9.2.1  Conceptual Queries and Intensional Answers

A *query* is a user's statement for requesting the retrieval of needed information. Conventional queries conducted in database management systems, which are expressed with precise conditions directly based on data stored in databases, are not always the best means of efficient and effective communications between users and database system. A *conceptual query* involves a mechanism that is able to answer queries specified with general and abstract terms rather than primitive data stored in databases. Conceptual query answering is a process to provide answers to imprecisely specified queries with some general terms (Yoon 1997). Conceptual query answering may be carried out through two phases: preprocessing and execution. Conceptual queries provide users with the flexibility of expressing query conditions at a relatively high-level concept and allow them to pose more general questions to a database. It is important to be able to pose queries in terms of abstract terms, rather than expression based directly on primitive data.

The connections between conceptual queries and intensional answers in database management systems are discussed; both of these concepts are closely related to data mining, which are concerned with the overall process and specific techniques of the nontrivial extraction of implicit, previously unknown, and potentially useful information from data.

On one hand, an *intensional answer* to a query is a set of characterizations of the set of database values that satisfy the query (the actual data retrieved are referred to as the *extensional answer*). Intensional answers are derived from the extensional information in the database (Motro 1994; Han 1996; Han et al. 1996). For example, for the query of finding excellent students, an intensional answer could be some common features (such as a good GPA) shared by these students, rather than the names of these students. On the other hand, the task of *conceptual* (or *intelligent*, or *cooperative*) query answering is to map users' conceptual queries to actual database queries and to produce answers for the users' queries (Imilienski 1987).

Studies in intensional answers and conceptual query answering have been done largely by researchers in different camps. Traditionally, conceptual query answering handles conceptual queries by providing extensional data, while intensional answers handle conventional queries by providing abstract data. Although some authors started investigating their connections, a general methodology that deals with *how* to provide intensional answers for conceptual answers has yet to be developed. For example, on the basis of an attribute-oriented data mining technique, an outline of cooperative query answering using multilayer databases (MLDBs) was proposed in (Han et al. 1994).

Intensional answers for conceptual queries are particularly important for processing users' ad hoc decision support queries for online analytical processing (OLAP) in data warehousing environments. Relaxation can be used to automatically identify new queries that are related to the user's original query (Gaasterland 1997). A related but more radical concept is query-free information retrieval (Hart and Graham 1997).

### 9.2.2   Conceptual Query Answering

*9.2.2.1   Basics of Conceptual Query Answering*   Conceptual query answering in databases refers to mapping users' conceptual queries to actual database queries and producing answering for the users' queries. Conceptual query answering is a process to provide answers to imprecisely specified queries with some general terms (Yoon 1997). Examples of conceptual query answering are: "What are the common professions of people who have bought expensive houses in West Omaha in the last 2 years?" In this query terms such as "expensive" and "West Omaha" are not attributes or values in the actual database. A conceptual query can be expressed in terms of predefined abstract terms such as "expensive," and "West Omaha" that can be derived from primitive informal in a database.

Conceptual queries provide users with the flexibility of expressing query conditions at a relatively high-level concept, which relaxes the requirement of the preciseness of query conditions, and allowing them to ask more general questions to a database. It is important to be able to pose queries in terms of abstract terms, rather than expression based directly on primitive data. Since aggregation data can be viewed as a kind of conceptualization, conceptual query answering may be used as an effective tool for OLAP.

Combining the different criteria, query answering mechanisms can be grouped into four categories:

A. *Data Query and Direct Answering*. This is intended to provide direct answers to data queries. Traditional database queries fall into this category.

B. *Data Query and Conceptual (Intelligent) Answering*. This is intended to provide intelligent answer to data queries.

C. *Knowledge Query and Direct Answering*. This is intended to provide direct answering of knowledge queries.

D. *Knowledge Query and Conceptual Answering*. This is intended to provide conceptual answering of knowledge queries.

This case study is concerned with knowledge query and conceptual answering. Conceptual answering of knowledge queries means that a knowledge query is answered in an intelligent way by analyzing the intent of the query and providing generalized, neighborhood, or associated information.

### 9.2.2.2 Using Data Mining Techniques for Conceptual Query Answering

The concept of conceptual query answering for database queries has been studied by many authors. Yoon (1997) proposed an approach that uses concept hierarchy as background knowledge for formulating and answering conceptual queries. Han et al. (1998) uses data mining techniques to construct multiple layered database for conceptual query answering. We will use the idea proposed by Han et al. (1998) to construct a multiple layered database.

A great number of data are being and will continue to be collected in many databases by various kinds of data gathering tools, which creates a need for extracting knowledge from databases. Studies have shown that data mining greatly broadens the spectrum of conceptual query answering and has a lot of implications on query answering in data and knowledge base systems.

Since data mining techniques are developed at a rapid pace, the applications of the data mining technology in querying database knowledge and the impact of the technology on the development of conceptual query answering mechanisms in database systems are being widely studied. Techniques have been developed for conceptual query answering using discovered knowledge and/or knowledge discovery tools, which include generalization, data summarization, data characterization, concept clustering, rule discovery, query rewriting, deduction, lazy evaluation, and application of multiple layered databases. Although applying data mining techniques for data cleansing has been an experience of industry (Berson and Smith 1997), the opportunities of using data mining techniques for conceptual query answering through lazy data cleansing have never been explored.

### 9.2.2.3 Constructing Multilayer Abstract Database for Conceptual Query Answering

A multilayer database can be constructed to facilitate the analysis and understanding of database contents, and hence the information exchange among heterogeneous databases. Although conceptual query answering also requires integrated use of data from different sources, it does not need data to be cleaned as required by conventional queries. This is because frequently inconsistency among data from different sources may disappear during conceptual query processing. In fact, in many situations, data cleansing can be avoided entirely, and will be carried out only when necessary.

A multilayer database (MLDB) is a database composed of several layers of information, where the lowest layer corresponds to the primitive information stored in a conventional database, and with higher layers storing more general information extracted from lower layers. In the case of MLDB, high-level queries or conceptual queries answering can be obtained directly from a MLDB because a MLDB provides some generalized neighborhood or associated answers.

***Example 9.1***   Suppose that we have a company database and that the company office database contains employee, customer, and billing relations. Consider the following employee relation:

```
Employee (firstname, lastname, SSN, birth_date, address,
phone, extension, education, position, salary, supervisor,
children, . . . , spouse)
```

This relation is layer-0 relation in the MLDB. Since a database may contain different kinds of data, different methods will be used for generalization of each kind of data, including unstructured and structured values, and spatial and multimedia data. Generalization of numerical attributes can be performed similarly but in a more automatic way by the examination of data distribution characteristics. Suppose that the database contains the concept hierarchies for salary ranges, positions, education, and other information. An MLDB can be constructed as follows.

First, the Employee relation can be generalized to higher relation Employee1. The generalization can be performed as follows: (1) transform the birth_date to age, that is, from "4/23/60" to 39; (2) remove information associated with family members, and generalize salary to salary_range; and (3) generalize the education to education_range, position to department.

The generalized relation Employee1 can be considered as the lay-1 information of the Employee relation, and its schema is presented as follows.

```
Employee1 (firstname, lastname, SSN, age, address, phone,
education_range, department, salary_range)
```

Second, further generalization on Employee1 can be performed to produce an even higher-layer relation, Employee2. For example, generalization may be performed as follows: (1) generalize age to age_range using cluster method; (2) remove rarely used attribute, such as education_range; and (3) generalize address to area. The generalized relation Employee2 could be as follows.

```
Employee2 (firstname, lastname, SSN, age_range, area, phone,
salary_range)
```

Similarly, relation Customer can be generalized to Customer1, Customer2, and so forth, forming multiple layers of a customer relation. Multiple layers can also be formed in a similar way for the billing relation.

Queries can be answered efficiently and intelligently using the MLDB. For example, a user may ask for education of people who have an income of over 100K ($100,000/year). Since the attributes education range and income range are in relation Employee1, the query can be answered indirectly by using Employee1, which may return "80% has college education, and 20% has advanced education."

### 9.2.2.4 *Conceptual Query Answering in Multilayer Databases* A
MLDB may greatly facilitate cooperative query answering. Many conceptual query answering techniques need certain kinds of generalization; whereas different kinds of frequently used generalizations are performed and stored in the higher layers of an MLDB. Also, they often need to compare the "neighborhood" information. The generalized neighborhood tuples are usually stored in the same high-layer relations, ready for comparison and investigation. Moreover, they often need to summarize answer-related information, associated with data statistics or certain aggregations. Interestingly, a higher-layer relation not only presents the generalized tuples but also the counts of the identical tuples or other computed aggregation values (sum, average, etc.). Such high-level information with counts conveys important information for data summarization and statistical data investigation.

Furthermore, since the layer selection in the construction of a MLDB is based on the study of the frequently referenced attributes and frequently used query patterns, the MLDB itself embodies rich information about the history of the most regular query patterns and also implies the potential intent of the database users. It forms a rich source for query intent analysis and plays the role of confining the cooperative answers to frequently referenced patterns automatically.

Finally, a MLDB constructs a set of layers step by step, from most specific data to more general information. It facilitates progressive query refinement, from general information browsing to specific data retrieval.

### 9.2.3 An Approach to Intensional Conceptual Query Answering

### 9.2.3.1 *Overview* In the following paragraphs we focus on an approach where conceptual queries can be answered by intensional answers or can be answered through a query-invoked knowledge-reorganization process. The query-invoked process to produce necessary intensional answers for a conceptual query can be carried out in several different ways, including application of data mining techniques to obtain intensional answers so that they can be used later (an "eager" approach), or to have conceptual queries serve as a trigger to activate an intensional answer generation process (a "lazy" approach). We present an outline of a methodology that provides intensional answers for conceptual queries using attribute-oriented data mining techniques. In order to incorporate the eager approach, an abstract database should be constructed to handle frequently submitted queries. The process of generating intensional answers for conceptual queries is then outlined. The actual steps of generating intensional answers for conceptual queries are then discussed.

The construction of an abstract database can be summarized as follows.

*Step 1.* In frequently used relations, keep only those frequently referenced attributes.

*Step 2.* On the basis of the given concept hierarchies and statistical information, generalize the values of the retained attributes level by level, from the most specific layer to the most general layer.

*Step 3.* Merge identical tuples in each generalized relation and update the count or vote of the generalized tuples. (The purpose of using vote or count is to control the quality of generalization using a predefined threshold for frequency of tuples appeared.)

*Step 4.* On the basis of the given information of query access patterns, some relations may be joined together to form a new relation. The join operation should be performed on primitive relation to avoid key removing. After the join operation, perform steps 1–3.

*Step 5.* Keep the record for every new schema for generalized relations, and also keep the record of different concept levels for every attribute in each relation.

As an example, let us consider a database consisting of information of house buyers, along with the furniture purchased. Figure 9.1 depicts a concept hierarchy for family-income in relation to House-buyer. Figure 9.2 depicts a concept hierarchy for household-appliances in relation to Family-purchase. Table 9.1 shows a portion of the generalized relation of House-buyer after the conceptual hierarchies are applied. Table 9.2 shows a portion of the generalized relation after House-buyer and Family-purchase are joined (Lu 1999). Note that votes are used to provide an effective control to deal with uncertainty.

**9.2.3.2 *Generating Intensional Answers for Conceptual Queries***    The general process of generating intensional answers for conceptual queries is sketched below. We assume the existence of related conceptual hierarchies, as

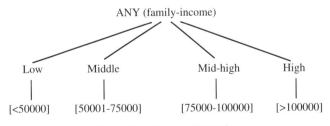

**Figure 9.1**   Income hierarchy.

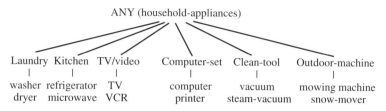

**Figure 9.2**  Appliances hierarchy.

**Table 9.1   House Relation (Part)**

| Age | Family-income | House-price | House-type | Vote |
|-----|---------------|-------------|------------|------|
| Young | High | Expensive | Two-story | 12 |
| Middle | Middle–high | Medium–expensive | Two-story | 54 |
| Young | Middle | Medium | Trilevel | 88 |
| Young | Low | Medium | Trilevel | 40 |
| Old | Low | Low | Ranch | |
| Young | Middle–high | Expensive | Two-story | 33 |

**Table 9.2   Family Appliances (Part)**

| Age | Family-income | House-price | Furniture | Furniture-Price | Household-Appliances (HA) | HA-price, $ |
|-----|---------------|-------------|-----------|-----------------|---------------------------|-------------|
| Young | High | Expensive | Bedroom Living room Dining room | 5400 | TV/video Kitchen Laundry Outdoor-machine | 3400 |
| Middle | Middle–high | Medium–expensive | Bedroom Living-room | 2200 | Laundry Outdoor-machine | 1700 |
| Young | Middle–high | Medium | Dining-room Living-room Study-room | 3750 | Computer-set TV/video | 3000 |

well as a related abstracted database. Conceptual query answering consists of three steps (Lu and Chen 1998).

*Step 1.  Analyzing Query Type.* On receiving a query, we analyze the conditions involved in the query and decide which type it belongs to. In general, we distinguish three types of query: (a) simple conceptual query (which can be answered directly using the abstract database), (b) complex conceptual query (which should be mapped to abstract database), and (c) mixed queries (which contain a part that can be directly answered by the abstract database and another part that needs to be mapped to the abstract database).

*Step 2. Acquiring the Extensional Answer.* For consideration related to efficiency, some attributes may be removed first. We then process the query and acquire the answer.

*Step 3. Producing Intensional Answers.*

The answers acquired in step 2 may be of a different format. Although the result of simple queries might already be in the form of an intensional answer with high-level concepts, the result of complex queries will still be in conventional form (viz., extensional answer). For extensional answers, further data mining is needed, which can be carried out using the steps such as removal of irrelevant attributes, with the user's help, if necessary; generalization of each specific value to a higher level (one level at a time); and generating an intensional answer from the generalized result.

### 9.2.4    Method for Intensional Conceptual Query Answering

We now provide more detail on generating intensional conceptual query answers. In general, we can distinguish three cases:

*Case 1.* Queries can be answered directly by search-only abstract database. This is an extreme case and demonstrates the typical eager approach.

*Case 2.* Queries cannot be answered by the abstract database. This is another extreme case and demonstrates the typical lazy approach.

*Case 3.* Combination of cases 1 and 2, which combines the eager and lazy approaches.

Since case 3 is the combination of cases 1 and 2, we use the following example to illustrate case 3. Consider a database containing information about the housing market in Omaha. The original relation schema is

```
House-sold (original-owner, address, location, house-price,
house-type, floor-area, construction-data, school-area,
distance-to-school, day-of-sale).
```

In addition, using conceptual hierarchies, a relation with the following schema is generated and is stored in an abstract database House-for-sale (in general, an abstract relation for relation $r$ is denoted as $r'$):

```
House-for-sale (address, location house-price, house-type,
floor-area, construction-date).
```

Note that although attributes in the abstract database may have the same name as those in the actual database, the domains of these attributes are usually different. For example, the values for the floor area in the actual database are numerical values in square feet, while the values in the abstract database are qualitative values such as large, medium, and small.

A user who just relocated in Omaha may want to submit the following query: "Find a house for sale in *West Omaha*, which should be located *near a school*, and the price of the house should be in the *middle range*, with *middle size* floor area, and the *average price* of the houses in this residential quarter should have increased *mostly* in the past 3 years."

Note that in this query, some needed information (e.g., distance to school) is in the actual database while some other information (e.g., middle-size floor area) will make use of the abstract database. Therefore, to answer this query, both the original and the abstract databases should be accessed. In addition, the conceptual hierarchies used for the construction of the abstract database may also be needed.

The following are the major steps involved in answering this query:

*Step 1.* Remove nonreferenced attributes from relation House-sold.

*Step 2.* Select the tuples with the values of attribute day-for-sale equal to 1995, 1996, and 1997.

*Step 3.* Map the abstract terms "West Omaha," "middle," and "near to school" to their corresponding primitive values and select these tuples satisfying the conditions in the query.

*Step 4.* Group the tuples by location.

*Step 5.* For tuples in each location, further group them by year.

*Step 6.* Calculate the average sales prices for different years for every location.

*Step 7.* Create a new attribute increase-rate for every location and calculate the increase-rate per the values of average sales price for different years.

*Step 8.* Select attributes location and increase-rate from the relation House-sold and join with the generalized relation House-for-sale in the abstract database using key location.

*Step 9.* Find the location(s) with middle house price, middle size floor area, near to school, and with the largest value of increase-rate.

The final answer to the query contains one or few locations. These steps illustrate a general methodology for intensional conceptual query answering.

## 9.2.5  Functionality of CQIA System

Figure 9.3 illustrates an implemented conceptual query—intensional answering (CQIA) system.

The implemented system has the following functionalities—it should

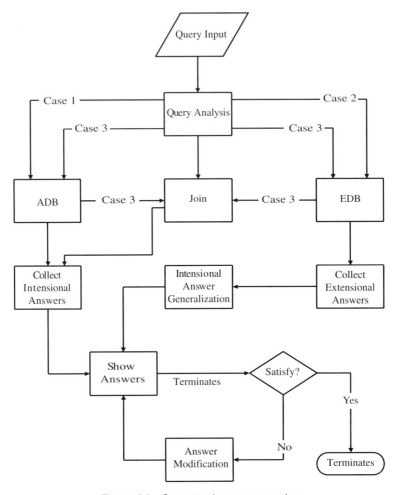

**Figure 9.3** Conceptual query processing.

- Be able to display the metadata (i.e., what data relations are stored in the database and what scheme it has for every data relation), which enhances the user's knowledge of the information in the database and provides scope for queries
- Be able to display all hierarchy information stored in the database, which allows the user to easily make the conceptual queries
- Be able to process several general cases of conceptual queries and generate intensional answers
- Allow the user to select the levels of concept in the hierarchies for the preferable intensional answers and generate the different levels of intensional answers based on user preference.

More details of the CQIA system can be found in Lu and Chen (1998) and Lu (1999).

## 9.3  LAZY DATA CLEANSING FOR CONCEPTUAL QUERY ANSWERING

### 9.3.1  Data Cleansing and Its Relevance to Conceptual Queries

As discussed in Section 9.2, conceptual query answering in databases refers to mapping users' conceptual queries to actual database queries and producing answering for the users' queries. Data warehousing provides excellent environments for conceptual query answering; however, building a data warehouse is expensive, and conceptual query answering may not require a full-fledged data warehouse environment. Data cleansing is the process of modifying existing data so that it meets a quality standard high enough to provide good data warehousing and data mining results. Because of the problems with existing data cleansing techniques and the fact that accurate data are not always required, conceptual queries can be answered without establishing data warehouse. In this study, we provide a simple and efficient approach to process conceptual queries using *lazy data cleansing* by constructing a MLDB (Jiang 1999). Lazy data cleansing is applied to large databases from multiple data sources that contain inconsistent data. We discuss various data mining techniques to produce conceptual queries and minimize the need for data cleansing. An approximate join algorithm is developed to process conceptual queries using lazy data cleansing. A trigger system is presented to alert the database users to the need for data cleansing (in case the data inconstency has exceeded a certain threshold). Lazy data cleansing is a very viable alternative to existing data cleansing techniques in answering conceptual queries. This research work contributed to the field of conceptual query answering and filled in the research gap of data cleansing in large databases through a "virtual" data warehousing approach.

In the following discussion we elaborate the proposed concept of lazy data cleansing in the context of conceptual query answering in multidatabase systems. The task is to use lazy data cleansing and apply this concept in conceptual query answering from a number of different databases, typically in an inconsistent and often incorrect fashion. Our focus is on conceptual query answering, but without the use of data cleansing in advance. Data cleansing is the process of modifying existing data so that it meets a quality standard high enough to provide good data warehousing and data mining results. Data cleansing is usually a prerequisite for building integrated data warehouses. However, an ideal, domain-independent method for data cleansing is not easy to find. The intuition behind our study is that since conceptual queries are not aimed at actual data retrieval, in many cases, an application program should be able to answer queries without cleaning the data in advance. Data cleansing will be carried out only when it is necessary. In case the need for cleansing is justified, a warning from the application program will be triggered to remind the user. This approach is referred to as "lazy data cleansing", and how to carry it out is the focus on this research. We first explain what lazy data cleansing is and why it is needed and then discuss how to apply this concept in conceptual query answering and develop a methodology of lazy data cleansing in the context of conceptual query answering. To facilitate database conceptual queries, we use data mining techniques to establish a multilayer database. We also develop an approximate join algorithm used in conceptual query answering. We discuss the different cases of using lazy data cleansing for conceptual query answering.

Recall that in Chapter 2, we discussed data cleansing (also called data cleaning) as the process of identifying and correcting incomplete and incorrect information in databases. It is an important component of data warehousing. Data cleansing has been used as a preparation step for OLAP processing because accuracy and consistency of data is important. The large volume of data involved in many databases frequently renders human verification of accuracy impractical. As a result, it becomes necessary to implement computerized methods to do the data cleansing work. In many application fields such as financial markets and mailing lists, accurate data are important and data cleansing is an important and required step before the data can be used in the data warehousing environment. The area of financial markets is, in particular, a data-intensive industry. To make sound investment decisions, financial analysts purchase large amounts of data from financial data providers. They use this historical data to develop financial models for making predictions and assessing risk about current data. Unfortunately, these databases often contain errors and omissions of important information. Analysts are dependent on the quality of these databases—missing data can prevent computation of key values. Incorrect data can cause their models to produce erroneous results without the analyst's knowledge. Because of the importance of accurate data and the large volume of data involved, data providers and consumers have a need to develop advanced methods for data cleaning. A number of companies, such as Standard and Poor, Dow Jones, Bloomberg, Moody's, and Data Transmission Networks, are in the business of collecting, packaging, and selling data related to stock, bond, commodity, and currency markets.

Clustering data raises the issue of how well partitioned the data are after clustering. If the data from which the $x$-attribute key is extracted is distributed uniformly over its domain, we can expect all clusters to have approximately the same number of records in them. But in reality, data are very unlikely to be uniformly distributed; instead, they are more randomly distributed, as skew elements and other hot spots will be prevalent, and thus, we must expect to compute very large clusters and some empty clusters.

### 9.3.2   Using Lazy Data Cleansing for Conceptual Query Answering

We now present our approach to process conceptual queries using lazy data cleansing. We first include the motivating example to help the reader understand how we process conceptual query answering. We describe the basic ideas of lazy data cleaning; that is, we conduct lazy data cleansing only when it is needed; specifically, databases will be cleansed when skeptical data in the databases exceed our tolerance level or threshold, which will trigger the need for data cleansing. This trigger is implemented by a counter that we set up. We also present a multiple database schema. We conduct a case study centered on conceptual query answering involving multiple databases in an Omaha community in which lazy data cleansing is involved. We analyze and generalize different cases to illustrate how conceptual answering can be carried out using lazy data cleansing. Some examples are included to illustrate different cases of lazy data cleansing.

***9.3.2.1 Multilayer Database*** As discussed in Section 9.2, conceptual queries can be answered efficiently and effectively using a multilayer database (MLDB). The following example shows how conceptual query answers are carried out in MLDB environments and helps lay a foundation for a better and fuller understanding of how we process conceptual query answering. For example, a query such as "What are the education levels of employees who have an annual salary of $50K?" can be answered using an MLDB efficiently and effectively, as shown bellow.

*Step 1.* We relax the query conditions using high layer relations. Instead of answering the query using "salary = $50K", the condition can be relaxed to about $50K. The top layer is examined first with general data presented. The salary range covering $50K in a high-layer relation, such as Employee1, can be used for query answering. Once the query is mapped to a level that fits a corresponding database layer, it can be processed within the layer.

*Step 2.* Instead of printing all the employees' education levels within this salary range, it searches through the high-layer Employee1, and prints the generalized answers, such as "60% of employees have bachelor's degrees, 30% of employees have advanced degree, 10% of employees have high school diploma." With the availability of MLDBs, such kind of generalized answered can be obtained from a high layer of database by summarization of the answers (presenting percentage, general view, etc.) at a high layer.

***9.3.2.2 Skeptical Data and the Basic Idea of Lazy Data Cleansing*** In some areas, consistent data in the database are not very critical, as data retrieval from the database can be executed while tolerating some kind of data inconsistency. It is possible to answer some conceptual queries without requiring consistent data. Moreover, although data cleansing is important for data warehousing, extensive data cleansing steps are not necessarily taken at all times. For conceptual queries, we may need to analyze only the trend of data, not the individual tuples of the data when data mining is involved. That is why lazy data cleansing is a very viable alternative, which is worth exploring.

Lazy data cleansing described here is applied to databases from multiple data sources that have inconsistent or incorrect data in them. We use the term *skeptical data* in this context to refer to data in the database that are typically in an inconsistent or incorrect fashion. They might include data that are duplicated, missing, or incomplete and incorrect information in the database. For example, names are routinely misspelled, and salutations are at times included as well as nicknames in the same field.

In conceptual query answering, a MLDB can be constructed to facilitate the analysis and understanding of database contents, and hence the information exchange among heterogeneous databases. The MLDB can greatly facilitate efficient and intelligent query answering. The examples in the next section show that the heterogeneous databases can be used to answer conceptual queries even before the data are cleansed.

To carry out effective lazy data cleansing, we need to know the rationale of this new cleansing approach and the circumstances under which it is effectively applied and the standards used to achieve our data cleansing goal. The basic idea of *lazy data cleansing* is that we can defer the data cleaning steps until a later time instead of cleaning the data before they are used, and then to alert the users to the need for data cleansing when the inconsistency among data exceeds some predefined limit (viz., the threshold). These skeptical data need to be cleansed when the degree of inconsistency or incorrectness is so great that they negatively affect the understanding of the database and merit data cleansing to serve the database readers.

In this sense, lazy data cleansing shares some common concern with active databases. Active databases not only store data, but also carry out actions to respond to events, such as data change (Silberschatz et al. 1996). Active databases support the specification and execution of rules in the database. Active rules used to alert users to unusual activities in the database system or enforce integrity constrains will specify when and what action is to be taken. We also need to set up a standard under which the need for cleansing is triggered. A "trigger" is a statement that is executed automatically by the system as a side effect of a modification to the database. Triggers are useful mechanisms for alerting humans, or for performing certain tasks automatically when certain conditions are met. A trigger definition, as used in active data mining and other applications, has three sections: events, conditions, and actions (Agrawal and Psaila 1995). This definition, which is to be used to conduct our lazy data cleansing analysis, specifies that rules are triggered by events; the database system checks the conditions of rules that have been triggered; and if the conditions are met, the database system executes the actions specified by the rules.

When we answer conceptual query using lazy data cleansing, we use triggers to alert users when data need to be cleaned. A counter will be employed to trace the inconsistency existing among the assessed data. When the maximum tolerance of inconsistency has been reached, say, 5%, a message will be triggered to inform the user the need for data cleansing.

The different cases of using lazy data cleansing for conceptual query answering are discussed as follows.

***9.3.2.3 Sample MLDB Schema***  Lazy data cleansing is used when multiple databases are employed for conceptual query answering. In general, each database may consist of multiple relations. In order to more clearly focus our discussion of conceptual query answering, in this case study we assume that each database has already been joined into one relation, and the task of conceptual query answering is performed on these relations representing the multiple databases. In general, these relations are in "second normal form," which is acceptable in many real-world applications. (A brief discussion on normalization theory in relational database design can be found in Chen (1999).) In the following we describe a case study that uses a sample multiple layered database schema from multiple databases. For each relation R, we include the original schema of R, then the schemas on the abstract database R1, then its own abstract database R2.

1. Resident (firstname, lastname, SSN, address, birth_date, home_phone, work_address, work_phone, education, income, status, spouse_name, hobby)

   Resident1 (firstname, lastname, SSN, address, age, home_phone, education_range, income_range, status, hobby_type)

   Resident2 (firstname, lastname, SSN, area, age_range, phone, income_range, status)

2. Car (firstname, lastname, address, licence, value, year, model, make, type, color, doors, style)

   Car1 (firstname, lastname, address, license, value_range, car_old, make, model, type, color_range)

   Car2 (firstname, lastname, address, license, value_range, old_range, make, model)

3. Accident (ID, license, driver_firstname, driver_lastname, SSN, date, damage_amount, location)

   Accident1 (ID, license, driver_firstname, driver_lastname, SSN, year, damage_range, area)

4. House (address, owner_firstname, owner_lastname, price, style)

   House1 (address, owner_firstname, owner_lastname, price_range, style)

***9.3.2.4  Conceptual Query Answering without Data Cleansing during Generalization***   A generalization technique transforming low-level data into relatively high-level data is a data mining technique used in constructing multiple-layer databases. It is also an important step for lazy data cleansing.

A database may contain different kinds of data. Simple numerical and non-numerical data are the most commonly used attribute values in databases. We will show how different kinds of data can be cleansed during the generalization process.

1. *Skeptical data can be removed when generalizing nonnumerical values.* Generalization of nonnumerical values may rely on the available concept hierarchies specified by domain experts or users or implicitly stored in the database. A conceptual hierarchy could be given by users or experts, stored, or partially stored as data in a database, specified by some generalization metarules, such as deleting a street number from a street address, being derived from the knowledge stored elsewhere, or being computed by applying some rules or algorithm, such as deriving `1236 N 42nd St` ⇒ `Northwest Omaha` from a geographic map stored in a spatial data table. Some skeptical nonnumerical data, during the process of generalization, can be cleansed. These erroneous data, if they are expressed in a range, can be neglected because they don't affect the integrity of the database in any significant way. For example, in a house relation, we assume that `3544 N 102 St` is a skeptical data for the address while `3504 N 102 St` is a correct address. When we generalize this address to residential area, it becomes `Northwest Omaha`. This is the right area for address `3504 N 102 St`, so the skeptical data disappears after it is generalized to a high layer.

2. *Skeptical data can be removed when generalizing numerical values.* Generalization of numerical attributes can be performed similarly but in a more automatic way by the examination of data distribution characteristics. In many cases, it may not require any predefined concept hierarchies. Skeptical data can be removed if incorrect numerical values in the database can still be grouped under one category as long as the incorrect values are under the same category as the correct values. For example, employee annual income can be clustered into several groups, such as "below 20K, 20–30K, 30–50K, 50–70K, over 70K," according to a relatively uniform data distribution criteria or using some statistical cluster analysis tools. Assuming one of the employees' income is mistyped as "34K" by the accounting manager in spite of the fact that this employee is earning 36K. No matter the employee earns 34K or 36K annually, when we generalize it, it will fall into the salary range of 30–50K. So skeptical data are removed after generalization. For example, a query such as "What is the common price of houses in this community?" can be answered by using house relation. Instead of printing prices for thousands of houses in this community, it searches through the top layer of house relation, such as `House1`, and prints the generalized answer by summarization of the answers. Here we have a skeptical data "130K" for house price instead of 120K. When we generalize the house relation, the value of the house is in the price range of 100–150K, the skeptical data disappears. The general answer can be compared with its neighborhood answers, "50% 100–150K, 25% less than 100K, 20% over 300K, 5% 200–300K," then we can come to a conclusion that the common price of houses in this community is 100–150K.

3. *Skeptical data can be removed when generalizing structured data.* Set-valued attributes are simple structure-valued attributes. Typically set-valued

data can be generalized by generalization of each value in a set into its corresponding higher-level concepts. For example, the hobby of a person is a set-valued attribute that contains a set of values, such as {football, hockey, chess, violin, novel}. Among these values, football is wrongly listed. What we want in the list is basketball. Football can be generalized into a set of high-level concepts, such as {sports, music, video_games}. Since football and basketball can both be generalized to sports, skeptical data are corrected after generalization.

The preceding example shows how skeptical data can be removed using generalization in the process of constructing a multiple-layer database since we are concerned only about the general data. It proves that constructing a multilayer database is not only an essential step for conceptual query answering but also an important part of lazy data cleansing.

### 9.3.3  Conceptual Query Answering without Data Cleansing Using Approximate Join

On the basis of our observation, most of the conceptual queries are involved with two or more relations. Next, we will develop an approximate-join algorithm to explain how we answer the conceptual queries using lazy data cleansing.

Let $r(R)$ and $s(S)$ be the relations whose natural join is to be computed, and let $R \cap S$ denote their common attributes. Suppose that both relations are sorted on the attributes $R \cap S$, and the final table is $RS$. Since, in some relations, we could have two or more records that have the same value on join attributes, it will be more to one join. This algorithm works for both one-to-one join and more-to-one join. If it's a one-to-one join, the relation that has bigger size will be fit in main memory. If it's a more-to-one join, the relation $(R)$ that has two or more records with the same value on join attributes will be fit in main memory.

When we join two relations, we will keep only the attributes we need, and discard other attributes. Thus, this will save some memory; moreover, when we process the conceptual answer, it becomes more efficient.

This algorithm associates one pointer with each relation. These pointers point initially to the first tuple of the respective relations. As the algorithm proceeds, the pointers move through the relation. The tuples in relation $R$ will try to find a match with the tuple in $S$. If found, the join attributes will be in the final table; if not, only the tuple in $R$ will be in the final table.

Since the relations are in sorted order, tuples with the same value on the join attributes are in consecutive order. After merging the first tuple in join relations, the pointer moves to the next tuple in $R$, and the current tuple must be checked to see if it has the same value of join attributes as the previous tuple. If it does, it will be merged with the tuple in $S$. Otherwise, the pointer moves to the next tuple in $S$. The feature of this algorithm is that when the tuple in $R$ tries to match with the tuple in $S$, if one of the join attributes has the same value, and the value of another join attribute is very close, we will consider the value of the join attributes to be identical. In real life, people often type a wrong character or number.

Next, we will use three cases to illustrate how approximate join plays its role in conceptual queries answering using lazy data cleansing.

### 9.3.3.1 Dropping Unrelated (Noninterested) Attribute

Skeptical data can be discarded if they are not related to the attributes that we are interested in. According to the join algorithm, we only keep the common attributes and the attributes that we want in the final table after the join of the two relations. We discard those attributes if they are not common attributes in two tables or if they are not what we are interested in extracting. So the skeptical data are also discarded.

*Query 9.1*   What is the popular type of car that 30-year old people like?
This query can be processed in the following steps.

*Step 1.* We can consider a 30-year-old to be in the age range 25–35. Starting from the top layer, Resident2, we have age_range, and the car type is in Car1. So we join Resident1 and Car1. In the Car1 relation, we have one of the values of attribute "car door," which is obviously skeptical, because there is only one door. Since "door" is not an attribute we are interested in, we discard this attribute. As a result, the skeptical data are also abandoned and the query can be answered without cleaning the data.

*Step 2.* Since 60% of cars are sports cars, 20% are pickups, and 10% are passenger cars, we can conclude that the answer is "30-year-old people like sports cars."

### 9.3.3.2 Cleansing Data by Considering Approximate Data as Identical

In databases, some records may have some minor mistakes such as mistyped, or incomplete data, or last name or first name misplaced, reversed, or misspelled. Often, people receive mail even if their information on the envelope is wrong, such as last name Liu written as Lu or Lui, or 125th St. is written as 125th Ave. We develop this algorithm to tackle these errors if they refer to two records in which the values of one or more attributes are identical while the values of the other attribute have some discrepancy, and we consider that these records represent the same information.

*Query 9.2*   What kind of hobby do sports car owners have?
This query can be processed in the following steps.

*Step 1.* Starting from the top-layer Resident2, we can't find the attribute hobby type, and we go down to layer Resident1. Attribute car type is in relation `Car1`. We join relation `Resident1` and relation `Car1`. Now suppose we have one record in relation `Resident1`:

```
Steve   Carlson   5416 N 152 Ave
```

Suppose we also have record in relation `Car1`:

```
Steve   Carlson   5416 N 152 St
```

We use approximate algorithm to join these two relations. Their common attributes are last name and address. For these two records, the owners' last names are the same even though their addresses are slightly different, and we will consider that both addresses are identical and we join these two records. Under these circumstances, we think that the two records refer to the same person and we have obtained the information we need. No data are lost in the process of approximate join because one of the addresses is a bit incorrect.

*Step 2.* The general answer is compared with its neighborhood answers. We will get 67% sports cars, so we conclude that the answer is people with sports hobbies own sports cars.

#### 9.3.3.3  *Cleaning Data by Dropping Duplicate Records*   In a relation, we have duplicate records because one of the records' primary key is incorrect. The duplicate record will be dropped when we join two relations. When two relations are joined together, two records in a relation have the same value of the join attributes. Under this circumstance, one of the records is a duplicate. So we drop the duplicate one and join only one record with other relations.

Suppose in the Resident relation, we have two duplicate tuples:

```
Steve   Carlson 743236555   5416 N 151Th St
Steve   Carlson 743236558   5416 N 151Th Ave
```

When we join a resident relation with another relation, the second record will be dropped, so the query can be answered without cleaning the data.

### 9.3.4   Warning the Users about the Need for Cleansing

A key idea in lazy data cleansing is to alert the user to the need for data cleansing when the inconsistency among data exceeds some predefined tolerance limit (viz., the threshold). When we answer conceptual query using lazy data cleansing, we use triggers to alert users as to when data need to be cleaned. A counter will be employed to trace the inconsistency existing among the accessed data. When the maximum tolerance of inconsistency has been reached, say, 5%, a message will be triggered to inform the user of the need for data cleansing.

**Query 9.3** What kind of house style do people over 65 years old like?
  This query can be processed in the following manner:

*Step 1.* We can relax the query conditions using high-layer relations. Instead of answering the query using age = 65-years, we can relax the condition to over 60-year, which is in the age range over 60-years covering 65-year-olds in a high-layer relation Resident2. Attribute house type is in relation House1.

*Step 2.* Join relations Resident2 and House1 using the approximate-join algorithm. In this process, we use a counter as a tool to monitor the number of inconsistent data that have occurred. When the inconsistency has exceeded the maximum limit (5%), a data cleansing warning will be given to the user. The user will decide if whether to begin data cleansing.

### 9.3.5 Obtaining Conceptual Query Answers

Obtaining the answers is the final step of conceptual answering. After we establish a multilayer database (MLDB) and perform join using the approximate-join algorithm, we may still be faced with skeptical data in the joint table.

#### 9.3.5.1 *Query Answers Including Skeptical Data*  In some cases, the skeptical data still exist in the database after we have constructed a MLDB and joint tables. However, the skeptical data are in the range of our acceptance or tolerance level. We can tolerate the bad data and still obtain a good answer for queries. Our conceptual query answer is a general query answer, not one that is specific or precise. The purpose of conceptual query answering is to provide answers to imprecisely specified queries in general terms. Conceptual queries offer us the flexibility of expressing query conditions at a relatively high-level concept, which relaxes the requirement of the preciseness of query conditions, and allow us to ask more general questions to a database.
  We consider the following cases.

**Case 1**  For two relations, one of the common attributes has skeptical data. When we join two relations, part of the information will be lost for that tuple. If the tuple is one of the tuples we selected to obtain the answer, the skeptical data will slightly affect the answer if we use percentage to present answers. But we are dealing with the generalized answers, and one or two tuples contain skeptical data will not affect the answer. We still obtain the same answer.

**Query 9.4** What is the income range for people who have cars valued over $30K?
  This query can be processed in the following manner:

*Step 1.* The car valued over $30K is in the top layer `Car2` relation; income range is also in the top-layer `Resident2` relation.

*Step 2.* Suppose that we have a record in which the last name Miranda is misspelled as Miran in the `Car2` relation. When we join relations `Car2` and `Resident2`, we can't find a match for last name Miran. So, we lose resident information on Miranda for this record.

*Step 3.* With the skeptical data, we get 80% of people with income over $100K who have cars valued over $30K. If we clean the skeptical data, we will get 85% instead of 80%. The threshold we have used for answering conceptual queries is 50%, so the answer would be the same for both cases.

**Case 2**  Skeptical data in a tuple exist in the final table after join, and the tuple is selected for the answer. But the skeptical data do not belong to the range for the answer, so we still obtain the right answer.

**Query 9.5**  What is the price range of houses for people who own cars valued over $30K?

This query is processed in the following manner. The price range is in high-layer relation `House1`, car value range is in high-layer relation `Car2`, join relation `House1`, and relation `Car2`. Suppose that we have a skeptical data "100–150K" for the house price in relation `House1`, and we have the tuples as shown in Table 9.3.

The record containing skeptical data "100–150K" will not be selected as the final answer. So we obtain the same answer for our query, which is 83% of houses valued over $300K are owned by people whose cars are valued over $30K.

### 9.3.5.2  Query Answers without Using Skeptical Data  Consider the following scenario. For two relations, the value of the common attributes has skeptical data. However, it is not the attribute that we are interested in, so it will not affect the answer.

**Query 9.6**  What is the most popular color of cars do 50-year-old people like?

This query can be processed in the following manner. Relaxation of query

Table 9.3  Tuples in Generalized Relation House1

| Name | Car Value Range | Price Range |
|---|---|---|
| Miran | >30 K[a] | >300 K |
| Miranda | >30 K | >300 K |
| Pave | >30 K | 100–150 K |
| Matt | >30 K | >300 K |
| Taylor | >30 K | >300 K |

[a] K = thousand U.S. dollars ($1000).

**Table 9.4    Tuples in Relation Car2**

| Name | Age | Color |
|------|-----|-------|
| Latzal | 45–55 | Dark |
| Latzal | 45–55 | Dark |
| Johnson | 45–55 | Dark |
| Johnson | 45–55 | Bright |
| Sweet | 45–55 | Dark |

conditions is achieved by using high-layer relations. Instead of answering the query using `age = 50-year`, we relax the condition to about 50-year-olds or age range "45–55 years," which is a high-layer relation covering 50-year-olds. `Resident2` can be used for query answering, and `color_range` is a high-layer relation in relation `Car2`.

Join `Resident2` and `Car2` relation; `Car2` is the main one in the final table, and this is a more-to-one join. Although the last name Anang in the `Car2` table is misspelled as Anan, the record about Anang is not in the records that we are interested in. Suppose that we have five records after join, as shown in Table 9.4.

We have 80% dark-colored cars. The answer is that 50-year-old people like dark-colored cars. The skeptical data are the value of the attribute that we are interested in. But they are not in the final records we have selected, so it will not affect the answer.

**Query 9.7**    What is the education level of people who own houses valued less than $100K?

This query can be processed in the following manner. Join `Resident2` and `House1`. Suppose that we have skeptical data in the house value. It should be "200–300K," not "150–200K", but it's not in the range that we are interested in and won't be selected when we obtain the answer from the final table after join, so the query can be answered without cleansing the data.

**9.3.5.3  Limitation of Lazy Data Cleansing**    Lazy data cleansing is an effective tool in cleansing data in large databases where accurate data are not the foremost concern for database users. The proposed method may not work, for example, in many application fields where accurate data are critical, and we will not get good answer for conceptual query. Banking is a case in point. A mistyped or misplaced number in the database can create chaos for banks and consumers alike. So we must use lazy data cleansing appropriately and under the right circumstances to achieve the intended goals and maximize its effectiveness. Also, if the databases have been cleansed using some existing data cleansing techniques, the lazy data cleansing technique for conceptual query answering will be less effective.

### 9.3.6  A Prototype System

As a case study, a portion of the implemented prototype system is depicted in Figure 9.4, which illustrates how to deal with a typical query:

```
Select a1 and a2
From R and S
where q1 = c1 and q2 = c2
```

### 9.3.7  Summary of Lazy Data Cleansing

Lazy data cleansing is a viable alternative to many existing data cleansing techniques that are applied to the academic study and commercial applications of conceptual query answering. Lazy data cleansing has filled the blank in the research in the arena of data cleansing in large databases without building expensive data warehouses.

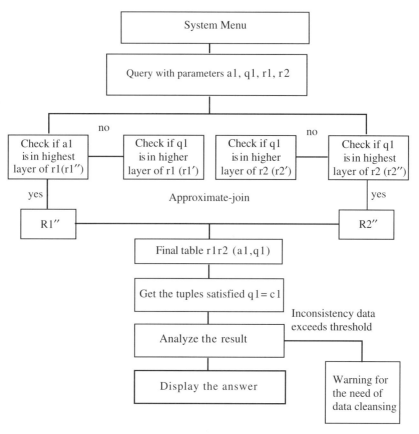

**Figure 9.4**  Part of a prototype system.

## 9.4 SELECTING CONCEPTUAL QUERY ANSWERS USING QUERY ENTROPY

### 9.4.1 Overview

The concept of entropy has shown its importance in variance branches of sciences, for example, as indicated in Chapter 5, Kawano and Hasegawa (1996) used entropy for attribute-oriented induction. In this chapter, we examine the use of entropy in a broader perspective, namely, using entropy to select appropriate answers for database queries. Query answering with aggregate data plays an important role of online analytical processing (OLAP) in data management systems. In this section we describe an exploration aspect related to intelligent query answering concerning aggregate answers: namely, in case multiple answers exist, how to evaluate them and select the best answer. This study illustrates an approach to dealing with uncertainty using extended entropy theory, and can be combined with intelligent query answering using data mining techniques. Entropy theory provides a powerful tool in the field of intelligent database query answering. Traditionally, Shannon entropy and conditional entropy are used to measure the amount of information stored in a message. However, mathematically they may not be the best method for our task. In this work, a new entropy function, *query entropy* (or *Q-entropy* for short), is proposed to replace the computing-intensive Shannon and conditional entropy. A new algorithm based on this Q-entropy was developed to solve the one-level optimal database query answering problems. In addition, this Q-entropy algorithm was implemented and evaluated with a sample database involving a survey of the 50 states of the United States. In most cases the algorithm answer agrees well with the optimal query answer based on the Shannon and conditional entropy. Sometimes there is some discrepancy between the algorithm answer and the optimal answer. Such discrepancy was found to be due to the tradeoff of accuracy for time efficacy of the new algorithm since in all cases the optimal answer identified from the Q-entropy was the same as that from the traditional Shannon/conditional entropy. Nevertheless, the new algorithm usually gives good, if not optimal, answers to a given query with regard to the information behind a real-world database. The following symbols are used in this section:

$|C_i|$ Cardinality of the $i$th concept

$E$ Expression

$G$ Quadratic approximation of Shannon entropy

$H$ Shannon entropy

$H_R$ Conditional entropy

$k$ Threshold of expression length

$p$ Probability

$Q$ Query entropy

*r*    Probability of the event that a randomly selected individual in a concept (node) is a qualified individual

### 9.4.2  Importance of Selecting a Probabilistic Answer

As the online availability of data is exploding, business firms have begun to use such data to help to *make better decisions* for their business. For example, an auto manufacturer may want to know which type of vehicles made the highest profit in the previous year, or which generation of people could be the ideal target population for auto purchase and what are their "tastes." For such inquiries, a conventional answer—usually a list of all individual objects—is not always the best means of information exchange between the user and the database. Frequently people feel the need for better decision support based on data analysis and knowledge discovery from the primitive data.

Intelligent query answering is based on the amount of information contributed from each property of an instance. The optimal answer to a given query is the one that contains more information than other competing answers. In the entropy theory, the information stored in an expression is measured by the empirical Shannon entropy and conditional entropy. However, both Shannon entropy and conditional entropy are computationally intensive. The algorithm for the selection of the optimal expression is of iterative nature and thus very time-consuming. This perhaps is one of the reasons why the entropy theory has not been applied to solve real-world data mining problems yet. In the following text, we show how to use a new entropy function, Q-entropy, to replace the computing-intensive Shannon entropy and conditional entropy. A simpler algorithm based on Q-entropy was also developed and implemented. The performance of the Q-entropy function and the new algorithm were evaluated using a sample database.

### 9.4.3  Advantages of Intelligent Database Query Answering

The following examples illustrate the advantages of intelligent database query answering.

***Example 9.2***    Suppose that the Board of Directors of a company wants to know something about the salary levels of its employees. A question could be a query like: "In our company, who is making more than $100,000 a year?" We may expect to receive several types of answer to this query. The traditional answer, although not an efficient method for information exchange, is just to list all qualified individuals. A better answer from data mining could be "All directors and most managers." It gives some qualitative description about the common characteristics of those qualified individuals. Another type of query answer is the aggregate expression. An *aggregate expression* is a sequence of terms that are in the format of "*r/t C*," where *C* represents a concept with a total number of *t* individuals, while *r* is the number of these individuals who belong to the answer (Motro 1994). As to the query above, an aggregate answer could be "8/8 directors + 27/32 managers." From this example it can be seen that an aggregate answer is superior to the qualitative answer "all directors and most managers," in that the aggregate answer not only covers all the information released in the latter but also provides more quantitative information towards the overall picture of the database.

***Example 9.3***   Imagine the CEO of a retail chain (such as Wal-mart Corporation) would like to know what are the most important factors determining the overall performance of its stores. Such factors could be region (West Coast, Midwest, etc.), distance to downtown, manager's age and the size of that store. Given the fact that the Wal-Mart database contains a huge amount of information about those thousands of chain stores nationwide, practically it is impossible for one to go through all the data to draw a conclusion. In this case, the setup of an appropriate decision tree is extremely useful for the organization of available information. To give the best aggregate answer, terms containing the maximum amount of information are identified to form the answer. However, how to quantitatively measure the information and how to extract terms with the largest amount of information within a reasonable period of time remains a challenge in the application of data mining theories to real-world problems.

### 9.4.4   Relationship to Previous Work

#### 9.4.4.1   *Entropy Theory*   Usually, there are more than one answer to a query. The question is how to obtain the best (optimal) one from those candidate answers. Compared with the route map and positive/negative theory (Shum and Muntz 1989), the entropy theory is the most promising approach for intelligent database query answering.

The term *entropy* was derived from chemistry, where it means *randomness*. In the information theory, it refers to the amount of uncertainty associated with an expression. In Section 5.3.1, the notion of information gain (as used in ID3 algorithm), actually employs the concept of entropy. Given a query, the more information contained in an answer, the lower its entropy will be. This is the logical basis for applying the entropy theory in database query-answering problems.

An *expression* is constructed from a collection of terms. A term is represented by the ratio of qualified individuals and total individuals in that concept. The length of an expression measures conciseness, while the entropy of the expression measures preciseness. An expression is said to be the optimal answer to a given query if it has the lowest entropy value.

***9.4.4.2  Shannon Entropy and Conditional Entropy***  Shannon proposed an empirical function to quantitatively measure the information content of a message in 1948. The concepts of Shannon entropy and conditional entropy are briefly described here. For details, see Shum and Muntz (1988).

***Definition 9.1***  Let $S$ be a finite probability space composed of two mutually disjoint events $E_1$ and $E_2$ with probability $p$ and $1 - p$, respectively. Then the *Shannon entropy* of the space $S$ is given by

$$H(S) = H(p_1, p_2) = -p \log p - (1 - p) \log (1 - p) \tag{9.1}$$

(special restriction: $p \log p = 0$ if $p = 0$). Shannon entropy is used to quantify information stored in a single term.

Most expressions contain more than just one term. To measure the amount of information stored in a long expression, the concept of conditional entropy was introduced. Simply speaking, conditional entropy can be regarded as the weighted average of Shannon entropy of each term across the whole expression.

***Definition 9.2***  Let $S$ and $R$ be two finite probability spaces with events $\{S_i\}$ $(i = 1,2\}$ and $\{R_k\}$ $(k = 1,2,\ldots,m)$, respectively. Then the *conditional entropy* of the space $S$ averaged over the space $R$ is

$$H_R(S) = \sum_{k=1}^{m} p(R_k) H_{Rk}(S) \tag{9.2}$$

***Example 9.4***  Consider a bilevel taxonomy $T$ of five concepts, as depicted in Figure 9.5. The number on the right side of each node shows the fraction of individual items in that concept belong to the extensional answer $A$.

The fraction on the right side of each concept is the probability of the event that a randomly selected individual in that concept belongs to the extensional answer. The *Shannon entropy* values of terms $C_2, C_3, C_4$ are:

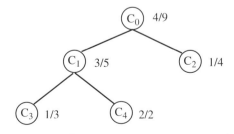

**Figure 9.5**  A bilevel taxonomy $T$ of five concepts.

$$H_{C_2}(S) = -(\tfrac{1}{4}\ln\tfrac{3}{4} + \tfrac{3}{4}\ln\tfrac{3}{4}) \tag{9.3}$$

$$H_{C_3}(S) = -(\tfrac{1}{3}\ln\tfrac{1}{3} + \ln\tfrac{2}{3}) \tag{9.4}$$

and

$$H_{C_4}(S) = -(\tfrac{2}{2}\ln\tfrac{2}{2} + \tfrac{0}{2}\ln\tfrac{0}{2}) \tag{9.5}$$

respectively. The *conditional entropy* for the expression "$\tfrac{1}{4}C_2 + \tfrac{1}{3}C_3 + \tfrac{2}{2}C_4$" is:

$$
\begin{aligned}
H_R(S) = {} & \tfrac{4}{9}H_{C_2}(S) + \tfrac{5}{9}[\tfrac{3}{5}H_{C_3}(S) + \tfrac{2}{5}H_{C_4}(S)] \\
= {} & \tfrac{4}{9}[-(\tfrac{1}{4}\ln\tfrac{1}{4} + \tfrac{3}{4}\ln\tfrac{3}{4})] + \tfrac{5}{9}\{\tfrac{3}{5}*[-(\tfrac{1}{3}\ln\tfrac{1}{3} + \tfrac{2}{3}\ln\tfrac{2}{3})] \\
& + \tfrac{2}{5}*[-(\tfrac{2}{2}\ln\tfrac{2}{2} + \tfrac{0}{2}\ln\tfrac{0}{2})]\}
\end{aligned}
\tag{9.6}
$$

### 9.4.4.3 Algorithm for Optimal Expression

The intuition to apply the entropy concept in the information theory to intelligent database query answering was formalized by Shum and Muntz (1988). Since entropy represents the uncertainty associated with an expression, the problem becomes how to locate the expression with the lowest entropy value in a time-efficient way, assuming that the threshold of the expression length is set.

The naive approach in which all possible expressions are formed and ranked by their entropy values quickly becomes impractical as the taxonomy (decision tree) and allowable length of expressions grow. Following is the greedy approach proposed by Shum and Muntz (1988).

It was suggested that the root concept be included in the final answer, for the purpose of "completeness." This means that one can deduce some other useful information from the given expression when the root concept is included.

In addition to the greedy approach for one-level taxonomy problem, Shum and Muntz (1988) proposed a heuristic approach. It involves the ranking and rearranging of leaf concepts according to the probability of qualified individuals in each concept. For details, see Shum and Muntz (1988).

**Algorithm for One-Level Taxonomy Problem**

> *Input*:  A one-level taxonomy with root concept R and leaves {C_1, . . . C_N}
>
> An extensional answer A classifiable by T
> Length threshold of expressions k (k < N)

*Output*: Expression E for A over T with length k

```
begin
```

$$E := \frac{|A \cap R|}{|R|} R;$$

```
        while the length of E is less than k
        do
                begin
```

add a term $\frac{|A \cap C_i|}{|C_i|} C_i$ to E to form E'

such that H(E) − H(E') is maximum
                        (comment: break ties arbitrarily)
                    E := E'
                end

```
end
```

#### 9.4.4.4 *Problems with Existing Approaches* The entropy theory has been in existence since 1950. Most studies conducted so far have focused on the theoretical part of the potential application of the entropy theory in optimal expression problems. Although the entropy theory itself seems to be well developed, there has been little (if any) evidence that it has been successfully applied to solve practical problems.

Shannon entropy and associated conditional entropy are widely used today in information theory applications. However, practical application of the entropy theory is hindered by the inherent computing burden of Shannon entropy and conditional entropy. One has to be very clear with the taxonomy in order to obtain the probability of the event that an individual in a concept belongs to the extensional answer and the probability of the event that a randomly chosen individual belongs to a concept. Another barrier is that the algorithm is iterative and time-consuming. Computing time explodes with more complex taxonomy. For a real-world problem, to obtain the optimal answer to a query, a decision tree has to be built first from the primitive information stored in a given database. Since the taxonomy structure is query-dependent, a dynamic linking between the database and a computer program is also essential to the successful implementation of the intelligent query-answering algorithm. This project attempts to ameliorate the computing burden by introducing a new entropy function, and to implement the optimal query-answering algorithm to solve some real-world problems.

### 9.4.5 Using Query Entropy (Q-Entropy)

#### 9.4.5.1 *Simplification of Shannon Entropy*  The function of Shannon entropy can be expanded at the point $p = \frac{1}{2}$ using the simplest quadratic Taylor expansion:

$$H \cong H_{1/2} + \frac{H_{1/2}}{2}(p - \frac{1}{2})^2$$

When a natural logarithm is used, this gives

$$H \approx -2(p - \frac{1}{2})^2 + \ln 2 \qquad (9.7)$$

The amount of information in an expression is meaningless unless it is compared with that stored in another expression. It is the RELATIVE magnitude of entropy that is useful for the selection of the optimal expression. Therefore, the constant 2 and $\ln 2$ in Equation (9.7) can be omitted. This gives us a new function $G$, which is the simplest quadratic function approximating the shape of a Shannon entropy curve:

$$G = -(p - \frac{1}{2})^2 \qquad (9.8)$$

Compared with Equation (9.1), Equation (9.8) is a much simpler mathematical expression.

#### 9.4.5.2 *Simplification of Conditional Entropy*  In addition to Shannon entropy, the calculation of conditional entropy provides another barrier for a time efficient algorithm. As shown in Equation (9.2), the calculation of conditional entropy involves not only the Shannon entropy of each leaf concept but also the probability of the event that a randomly selected individual is in that concept.

It has been proposed that $|R_k|$, the cardinality (number of elements) of $R_k$, can be used to replace $p(R_k)$ in the calculation of conditional entropy [equation (9.2)]. An underlying assumption is that as far as the finite domain $D$ with classifiable taxonomy $T$ is determined, the total number of individuals in $D$ (i.e., the cardinality of root concept $C_0$) is fixed. Usually this assumption is satisfied without confusion.

***Example 9.5***  Consider (again) the bi-level taxonomy in Figure 9.5. The conditional entropy for answer " $\frac{1}{4}C_2 + \frac{1}{3}C_3 + \frac{2}{2}C_4$ " is

$$H_R(S) = \tfrac{4}{9} H_{C_2}(S) + \tfrac{5}{9}\left[\tfrac{3}{5} H_{C_3}(S) + \tfrac{2}{5} H_{C_4}(S)\right]$$

$$= \tfrac{4}{9} H_{C_2}(S) + \tfrac{3}{9} H_{C_3}(S) + \tfrac{2}{9} H_{C_4}(S)$$

Since this taxonomy has nine individuals, constant 9 can be omitted. Thus, we can calculate $H_R'(S)$ instead of $H_R(S)$:

$$H_R'(S) = 9 H_R(S) = 4 H_{C_2}(S) + 3 H_{C_3}(S) + 2 H_{C_4}(S)$$

Note that 3,2,4 are just the cardinalities of node $C_3, C_4, C_2$, respectively. Theorem 9.1 follows.

**Theorem 9.1**   No matter how many layers a taxonomy may have, multiplications of probabilities during the calculation of conditional entropy will eventually give a simple ratio of the cardinality of a concept with that of the root concept.

Since the cardinality of the root concept is a constant, we can ignore it. Therefore, the modified conditional entropy of an expression is simply the weighted sum of the entropy value of each concept appearing in that expression (weight is simply the cardinality of that concept):

$$H_R'(S) = \sum_{k=1}^{m} |C_{R_K}| \cdot H_{R_k}(S) \tag{9.9}$$

In this way, the computing burden of conditional entropy is largely removed.

**9.4.5.3   Query-Entropy**   To take advantage of the approximation of Shannon entropy and the simplification of conditional entropy, we introduced a new mathematical expression *query entropy* (or Q-entropy for short).

**Definition 9.3**   Let R be a finite space consisting of mutually disjointed subsets $R_1, R_2, \ldots, R_k$ with cardinalities $|C_1|, |C_2|, \ldots, |C_k|$, respectively. The probability of the event that an individual in set $R_i$ is a qualified individual is denoted as $r_i$. Then the Q-entropy is defined as

$$Q = \sum_{i=1}^{k} |C_i| * G_i = \sum_{i=1}^{k} -|C_i| * \left(r_i - \tfrac{1}{2}\right)^2 \tag{9.10}$$

Figure 9.6 depicts a three-dimensional plot of Q-entropy versus plot of the Q entropy of a term versus $|C|$ and $r$ of that term (i.e., $k = 1$).

It should be noted that as the case of Shannon and conditional entropies, the requirement of completeness should be persisted when the Q-entropy of an expression is being calculated. "Completeness" means that the summa-

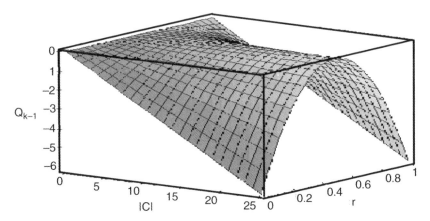

**Figure 9.6** A three-dimensional plot of Q (query) entropy.

tion of all terms in an expression should reflect the overall picture of the root taxonomy. If an expression is incomplete, a *virtual term* should be generated to "complete" the answer. The *virtual term* is simply a "hidden" (or "ghost") term that represents the complement of the expression with regard to the root concept. Although it does not appear in the expression, the virtual node has to be included in the calculation of the entropy value for that expression.

***Example 9.6*** For the bilevel taxonomy in Figure 9.5, the Q-entropy for the expression "$\frac{1}{4}C_2 + \frac{1}{3}C_3 + \frac{2}{2}C_\ell$" is

$$Q = Q_{C_2} + Q_{C_3} + Q_{C_4} = -4*\left(\frac{1}{4}-\frac{1}{2}\right)^2 - 3*\left(\frac{1}{3}-\frac{1}{2}\right)^2 - 2*\left(\frac{2}{2}-\frac{1}{2}\right)^2 \qquad (9.11)$$

which is much simpler than the corresponding conditional entropy [Equation (9.6)].

As can be seen from Example 9.6, when the new function is used, calculations become much easier because of the quadratic approximation of Shannon entropy but also because the burden of conditional entropy calculation has been eliminated. The entropy of an expression is simply the sum of the entropy of every term in that expression, which is conceptually straightforward.

Now there is a question: "Will the result from this Q-entropy be comparable to that from the conventional Shannon/conditional entropy?"

***Example 9.7*** Consider a taxonomy $T$ of four concepts with $C_0 = \{d_1, d_2, d_3, d_4, d_5\}$ as the root concept, and let $C_1 = \{C_3, d_3\}$, $C_2 = \{d_4, d_5\}$ and $C_3$

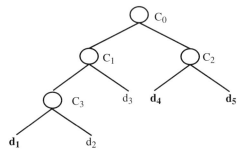

**Figure 9.7**   A bilevel taxonomy $T$ of four concepts.

$= \{d_1, d_2\}$, as depicted in Figure 9.7. Further, let $A = \{d_1, d_4, d_5\}$ be the extensional answer to a query.

There are three candidate expressions:

(I)    $\frac{1}{2}C_3 + \frac{2}{2}C_2$

(II)   $\frac{1}{3}C_1 + \frac{2}{2}C_2$

(III)  $\frac{3}{5}C_0$

If the natural logarithm is used, the calculated Shannon/conditional entropy values are

$$H_R(\text{I}) = \frac{3}{5}\left\{\frac{2}{3}H(\tfrac{1}{2}, \tfrac{1}{2})\right\} + \frac{1}{5}H(0,1) + \frac{2}{5}H(\tfrac{2}{2}, \tfrac{0}{2})$$

$$= 0.28$$

$$H_R(\text{II}) = \frac{3}{5}H(\tfrac{1}{3}, \tfrac{2}{3}) + \frac{2}{5}H(\tfrac{2}{2}, \tfrac{0}{2}) = 0.38$$

$$H(\text{III}) = -\left(\tfrac{3}{5}\ln\tfrac{3}{5} + \tfrac{2}{5}\ln\tfrac{2}{5}\right) = 0.67$$

Since $H(\text{I}) < H(\text{II}) < H(\text{III})$, the first expression is the best answer of the three. Note that a "virtual" node, $\frac{0}{1}C_{\text{virtual}}$, is generated for the first expression since it is an incomplete answer.

Now let's use the new Q-entropy function to select the best answer.

(I)    $\frac{1}{2}C_3 + \frac{2}{2}C_2$:

$$Q(\text{I}) = -2*(\tfrac{1}{2} - \tfrac{1}{2})^2 - 2*(\tfrac{2}{2} - \tfrac{1}{2})^2 - 1*(\tfrac{0}{1} - \tfrac{1}{2})^2 = -0.75$$

(II) $\frac{1}{3}C_1 + \frac{2}{2}C_2$ :

$$Q(II) = -3 * \left(\frac{1}{3} - \frac{1}{2}\right)^2 - 2 * \left(\frac{2}{2} - \frac{1}{2}\right)^2 = -0.58$$

(III) $\frac{5}{3}C_0$ :

$$Q(III) = -5 * \left(\frac{2}{5} - \frac{1}{2}\right)^2 = -0.05$$

Similar to Shannon/conditional entropy, $Q(I) < Q(II) < Q(III)$. Therefore, the best answer, (I), will be selected regardless of which entropy function is being used.

Shum and Muntz (1988) proposed the heuristic for one-level taxonomy problems. It can be proved that our Q-entropy function is compatible with all related lemmas and theorems of the heuristic associated with Shannon/conditional entropy (Luo 1999). Therefore, it is anticipated that the adoption of Q-entropy in solving optimal expression problems will give the same results as those from Shannon and conditional entropy.

**9.4.5.4  *An Algorithm for Selecting Probabilistic Query Answer with Single-Level Taxonomy***   The Q-entropy of a give expression is simply the sum of the Q-entropy of each term in that expression. Therefore, identifying the optimal expression boils down to selecting those terms with the lowest Q-entropy values. There is no need to perform further calculations of those probabilities associated with the conditional entropy and even the Q-entropy of an expression itself. This idea is formalized in the following algorithm for one-level taxonomy problem.

**Algorithm for Selecting Probabilistic Query Answer with One-Level Taxonomy**

```
Input:  Database and Query
Preset: k, expression length threshold

        (For concise answer, set k = 1 or 2;
        Increase k for more detailed answer)

Output: An expression E with length k.

        begin:
            Generate a decision tree based on the query
            (one-level taxonomy);
```

```
      Find all qualified individuals, i.e.,
   extensional answer A;
Locate root concept C₀ and r₀ = |A|/|T|;
   For every leaf concept (node) of the tree do
```

$$r_i = |A \cap C_i|/|C_i|$$

$$Q_i = -|C_i| * \left(r_i - \frac{1}{2}\right)^2;$$

```
      Find n-k + 1 nodes with the highest Qᵢ
   values:
               node.status = "discard"
            (Comment: break ties arbitrarily)
   Print out remaining (k - 1) concepts with rational
      number rᵢ as well as C₀ and r₀
end
```

The performance of this Q-entropy algorithm that we proposed is expected to be comparable with the greedy approach for Shannon/conditional entropy (Shum and Muntz 1988). However, since this algorithm itself does not involve iterative calculation, evaluation, and comparison of the conditional entropy for each intermediate expression, it theoretically should be much more efficient. To apply this algorithm to solve a real-world problem, a decision tree needs to be built first according to the chosen database and the query provided by the user.

The multilevel taxonomy problem is inherently much more complicated than the one-level taxonomy presented above. The naïve idea of simply picking concepts with the lowest entropy values (as formalized in one-level taxonomy) cannot be extended readily to multilevel taxonomy problems. Another problem with multilevel taxonomy is that usually it is less practical to fulfill the "completeness" in the answer; that is, the inclusion of the root concept may provide little help in effective conveyance of information. We also proposed a new Q-entropy algorithm for multilevel taxonomy problems. However, this algorithm has not been tested and implemented yet. Interested readers are referred to Luo (1999).

### 9.4.5.5 Implementation and Evaluation

*Experimentation 1: Population and Region*   Suppose that we are interested in the distribution of population across the United States. Consider the query "among nine geographic regions in the United States, which tend to have a large population (>3 million/state)?"

Figure 9.8 depicts the actual input/output window of the implemented program. Note that the population data in the database has a unit of kilo. So

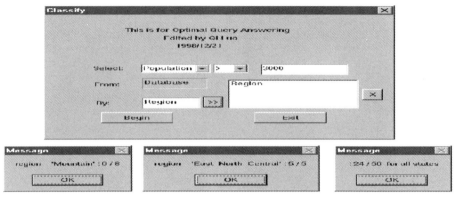

**Figure 9.8** The input/output windows for the first test, population, and region.

3 million represents an input of 3000 (kilo). The Q-entropy value itself is meaningless and is thus omitted from the output. When the user chooses the option "Begin," a decision tree based on the query is built. Then, the Q-entropy of each concept (node) is calculated. According to the new algorithm, two leaf nodes with the lowest entropy values are selected and combined with the root node to form the "optimal" answer to that query (the threshold for the expression length is set at 3).

For this query, it can be verified that the optimal answer based on Shannon/conditional entropy is 24/50 All States + 0/8 Mountain + 5/5 East_north_central, which is exactly the same as the program output.

*Experimentation 2: Income and High School Graduate Percentage*   In most cases the algorithm answer agrees very well with the optimal answer given by Shannon/conditional entropy. Here a special case is presented in which the answer from the implemented algorithm is not the optimal answer.

In this database, Hs_grad represents the percentage of population in a state who had successfully finished their high school education. Arbitrarily, we denote the graduate percentage "very high" if it is greater than 60%; "high" if 55% < Hs_grad ≤60%; "average" if 50% < Hs_grad ≤55%; "poor" if 40% < Hs_grad ≤50%, and "very poor" if the high school graduate percentage is less than 40%. Note that the program can classify the data and create a decision tree automatically according to the classification criterion specified by the user. The generation of a secondary database in which each numerical datum is converted to a categorical symbol is unnecessary (Luo 1999).

We would like to know something about high school graduate percentage and the average capitation income in a state. A sample query one may ask is

"Among states with different levels of high school graduate percentage, which is (are) likely to have a high capitation income (>\$4500)?"

The answer from the program is `26/50 All States + 0/4 Very Poor + 7/8 Very High`. This indicates that the average income is closely related to the educational level in a state. In plain English, none of the four states with very poor high school graduation percentages has an average income higher than \$4500, while among those eight states with the highest graduation percentage, seven have an average income exceeding \$4500 per year. The national median is approximately \$4500 as twenty-six states earn higher than this figure while 24 states fall below it.

However, for this query, the optimal answer from Shannon/conditional entropy is `26/50 All States + 0/4 Very Poor + 2/10 Poor`. It can be verified that this answer is also the optimal expression identified using Q entropy. Therefore, the discrepancy between the program output and the true optimal answer comes from the developed algorithm, but not from the adoption of Q entropy.

The reason for such a discrepancy is that in this new algorithm there is a tradeoff for time-efficiency. The price we paid is the ignorance of the "virtual" node formed by subtracting chosen leaf nodes from the root node.

When searching for the optimal answer, for each candidate expression it is very tedious to disjoint the root node every time to give the "virtual" node and then calculate the entropy value of this node. Therefore, this "virtual" node is neglected in the new algorithm, and instead the root node (rather than the "virtual" node) is included for completeness. Usually for a given query, entropy contributions from different "virtual" nodes are less variable than those from nodes being selected. In such cases, the relative magnitude of entropy values of different expressions is determined mainly by those selected leaf nodes rather than their "virtual" nodes. The algorithm is expected to work well in identifying the optimal answer. However, in some cases, there is a larger degree of variation in entropy contributions from those "virtual" nodes. If this is the case, ignoring the "virtual" node may cause a subtle entropy difference between the algorithm answer and the true optimal answer. Nevertheless, the algorithm answer is still considered a good answer to that query. For example, the answer `26/50 All States + 0/4 Very Poor + 7/8 Very High` given by the algorithm is not that bad. It reveals the trend behind these two properties; specifically, a state having greater high school graduate percentage tends to have higher capitation income.

### 9.4.5.6 *Summary of Q-Entropy Case Study*

In this work, a new mathematical function, Q entropy, is proposed to replace the computationally intensive Shannon/conditional entropy. Theoretical proofs (Luo 1999) as well as practical applications using a real-world database demonstrated that the Q-entropy function is favorably compatible with the traditional Shannon/conditional entropy. The entropy value of an expression is simply the sum of Q-entropy values of all terms in that expression. Therefore, the adoption of the Q-entropy in database query answering will greatly alleviate the computational burden of the Shannon entropy, and it renders the calculation of conditional entropy unnecessary.

Algorithms based on Shannon/conditional entropy are inherently tedious and of iterative nature because of the extra complexity associated with the calculation of conditional entropy for every intermediate expression. A new algorithm based on Q-entropy has been proposed (Luo 1999) to solve the one-level taxonomy problems. Leaf nodes with the lowest Q-entropy values are selected along with the root concept to form the algorithm answer to a given query.

The algorithm implemented the Microsoft Visual C++ to solve some optimal expression problems. In all tests the performance of the Q-entropy was in good agreement with that of the Shannon/conditional entropy. In most cases, the answer given by the new algorithm was the same as the optimal answer identified from both Shannon/conditional entropy and the Q-entropy. In some cases, although the algorithm answer was not the optimal answer, it was still a good answer revealing the main features of the taxonomy.

As to the future studies, although the new algorithm has been successfully implemented to solve one-level taxonomy problems, it may not work well with multilevel taxonomy problems, which are inherently much more complicated. The next step is to refine and validate the Q-entropy algorithm for multilevel taxonomy. If this can be done and the algorithm is successfully implemented to solve some real-world problems, it would be a big leap forward for the application of the entropy theory in database knowledge discovery.

## 9.5  CONCLUDING REMARKS

In this chapter we presented several additional case studies that are concerned mainly with applying data mining techniques to extended database functionalities. The particular aspects we have focused on are how to perform intelligent conceptual query answering, and how to incorporate uncertain reasoning issues into this process.

Intelligent conceptual query answering extends conventional database queries in two ways: (1) queries have been extended to conceptual forms, and (2) answers have been extended to intensional answers. As we have seen from case studies, data mining methods can play important roles in both aspects, thus effectively facilitating intelligent conceptual query answering. For example, both of the first two case studies (in Sections 9.2 and 9.3) extensively use attribute-oriented induction and related conceptual hierarchies to reduce conceptual queries to conventional queries, or to derive intensional answers from extensional data. In the third case study (in Section 9.4), we evaluate answers that take the form of aggregate expressions. Since aggregate expressions can be obtained by using some data mining techniques (including attribute-oriented induction), the third case study can be viewed as a post-processing step of data mining.

The central theme of this book is integrated treatment of data mining and uncertain reasoning. Discussions and examples in the previous chapters have explained this in detail. The case studies presented in this chapter have strengthened this perspective in various ways. For example, the first case study describes the overall process of achieving intelligent conceptual query answering. Although our focus was not on uncertainty itself, we had to deal with uncertainty issues along the way, including the use of votes to decide the strength of each derived tuple. The second case study deals with uncertainty in a more direct manner. We introduced a new concept, lazy data cleansing, to answer conceptual queries in the presence of uncleaned data. The data used for this study were acquired from different data sources and may be inconsistent to each other in some ways. The objective of this case study is how to produce satisfactory answers even when such inconsistency exists. The merit of the approach taken is that in certain cases, intelligent answers can be produced with existing dirty data, and data cleansing can be deferred at a later stage (or avoided altogether). Since data cleansing is considered a necessary step for data preparation in most applications, this case study demonstrates the iteration involved in the basic data mining cycle (as discussed in Chapter 4). Finally, in the third case study, we discussed the issue of selecting the "best" answer (in the form of aggregate expression) from several contenders. A new concept of entropy has been proposed to measure the quality of the answers, and, following comparison of the quality, the "best" answer is selected. The use of entropy demonstrates one way of dealing with uncertainty involved in competitive answers. Apparently, other uncertain reasoning techniques (e.g., fuzzy logic) can be considered to develop alternative approaches for solving the same problem (or similar problems).

In summary, the case studies discussed in this chapter have broadened our vision of integrated data mining. The additional insight gained from this chapter allows us to wrap up the whole book with the following final remarks:

- Data mining is an integrated process requiring various kinds of methods of its own, and can be aided by various techniques developed for uncertain reasoning (as discussed in Chapters 4–7).
- Data mining is an interplay between various techniques (as indicated in case studies in Chapter 8), and is usually only a part of a larger intelligent problem solving (as indicated in the case studies of Chapter 9).
- Data mining is not an isolated phenomenon, and for organizations who are interested in applying data mining, it is important to consider various issues related to infrastructures of data mining (as discussed in Chapter 2) and enabling techniques (as discussed in Chapter 3).

- The future development of data mining is closely tied to the development of several related areas, particularly with the development of database management systems (Silberschaz et al. 1999). Data mining stimulates new research directions in DBMS.

- As indicated in Chapter 1, we have tried to make our discussion concise so that a reader who is not familiar with data mining will not get lost in the forest of the data mining wonderland. At the end of this book, it is time to think about moving ahead. In order to apply appropriate techniques for data mining, a deeper understanding of various methods sketched in Chapters 5–7, as well as related background (e.g., knowledge of machine learning, artificial intelligence and database management systems) is needed (which can be gleaned from references provided at the end of this book).

- Because of the vast amount of data encountered in various real-world applications, in order to make data mining successful, it is important to focus on issues related to implementation, with particular emphasis on scaleup, as discussed in various places in this book (Chapter 2, 3, and 5).

- Various issues warrant further investigation, including research issues discussed in Chapter 2 and practical issues discussed in Chapter 8.

- There is a need for better understanding of the theoretical foundations as discussed in Chapter 2, and an in-depth study of data mining process and various data mining techniques are prerequisites for this kind of study.

- Data mining is also an interesting playground of many "meta-issues". In Chapter 3, we discussed relationships between metadata and data mining. In fact, knowledge patterns mined from data mining can be considered as metadata, as well. In addition, metaknowledge (such as templates) can be used to guide data mining.

- Although data mining is a new phenomenon, many ideas used in data mining are not new at all. For example, throughout this book, we have seen how statistics and probability theory have contributed to data mining. Readers who are familiar with various branches of mathematics (such as mathematical analysis) may have noticed many striking similarities between mathematics and data mining. For example, discovery of a small number of knowledge patterns from a large volume of data resembles selecting a small number of representative data elements (points or intervals) from an infinitive data set. Such comparative study may shed some interesting insight on the abstract process of human problem solving process in general.

Finally, we should keep in mind that data mining is still a rapidly developing field; new results and new challenges arrive every day. Although we have tried to present a comprehensive and up-to-date picture of integrated data mining, still many issues are not discussed or not emphasized in this book. (For example, although we discussed various numerical approaches in dealing with uncertainty, we did not pay much attention to logic-based approaches.) Therefore, we hope that you have enjoyed your journey through this book, and we wish you good luck in making even more interesting journeys on your own!

# REFERENCES

*AAAI Workshop on Semantic Approximation, Granularity, and Vagueness*, available at http://www.citizen.infi.net/~ledragon/KR2000sem_approx_workshop.html, 2000.

R. Agrawal and G. Psaila, Active data mining. *Proc. KDD 95*, 1995.

R. Agrawal and R. Srikant, Fast algorithms for mining association rules, *Proc. Very Large Data Bases (VLDB'94)*, 1994.

R. Agrawal and J. C. Shafer, Parallel mining of association rules, *IEEE Trans. Knowl. Data Eng.* **8**(6), 962–969 (1996).

R. Agrawal and R. Srikant, Privacy-preserving data mining, *Proc. ACM SIGMOD Conf. Management of Data*, 2000.

A. Al-Attar, A hybrid GA-heuristic search strategy, *AI Expert*, September 1994. See also http://www.attar.com/pages/attar_md.htm.

A. Al-Attar, *Data Mining—Beyond Algorithms*, http://www.attar.com/pages/attar_md.htm., 1999.

E. Baralis and G. Psaila, Designing templates for mining association rules, *J. Intelligent Inform. (JIIS)* **9**(1), 7–32 (1997).

R. J. Bayardo Jr., R. Agrawal, and D. Gunopulos, Constraint-based rule mining in large, dense databases, *Proc. ICDE'99*, 1999.

A. Berson and S. J. Smith, *Data Warehousing, Data Mining, & OLAP*, McGraw-Hill, New York, 1997.

E. A. Bender, *Mathematical Methods in Artificial Intelligence*, IEEE Computer Society, Los Alamitos, CA, 1996.

M. J. A. Berry and G. Linoff, *Data Mining Techniques for Marketing, Sales, and Customer Support*, Wiley, New York, 1997.

G. Bojadziev and M. Bojadziev, *Fuzzy Logic for Business, Finance, and Management*, World Scientific, Singapore, 1997.

R. J. Brachman and T. Anand, The process of knowledge discovery in databases, in U. M. Fayyad, G. Piatetsky-Shapiro, and P. Smyth (eds.), *Advances in*

*Knowledge Discovery and Data Mining*, AAAI Press, Menlo Park, CA, 1996, pp. 37–57.

S. Brin, R. Motwani, J. D. Ullman, and S. Tsur, Dynamic itemset counting and implication rules for market basket data, *Proc. SIGMOD '97*, 1997.

B. Brumen, T. Welzer, and H. Jaakkola, Predicting data mining costs: Additive approach, in Paper presented at 12th International Conference on Systems Research, Informatics and Cybernetics, 2000.

C. J. C. Burges, A tutorial on support vector machines for pattern recognition, *Data Mining Knowl. Discovery* **2**(2), 121–167 (June 1998).

C. L. Carter and H. J. Hamilton, Efficient attribute-oriented generalization for knowledge discovery from large databases, *IEEE Trans. Knowl. Data Eng.* **10**(2) (March/April 1998).

C. Carter, H. J. Hamilton, and N. Cercone, Shared based measures for itemsets, *Proceedings PKDD'97*, pp. 14–24, 1997.

N. J. Cercone, H. J. Hamilton, X. Hu, and N. Shan, Data mining using attribute-oriented generalization and information reduction, in T. Y. Lin and N. Cercone (eds.), *Rough Sets and Data Mining: Analysis of Imprecise Data*, 1997, pp. 199–227.

S. Chaudhuri, Data mining and database systems: Where is the intersection? *Data Eng. Bull.* **21**(1), 4–8 (1998).

S. Chaudhuri and U. Dayal, An overview of data warehousing and OLAP technology, *SIGMOD Record* **26**(1), 65–74 (1997).

S. Chaudhuri, D. Madigan, and U. Fayyad, KDD-99: The fifth ACM SIGKDD International Conference on Knowledge Discovery and Data Mining, *SIGKDD Explor.* **1**(2), 39–41 (2000).

M.-S. Chen, J. Han, and P. S. Yu, Data mining: An overview from a database perspective, *IEEE Trans. Knowledge Data Eng.* **8**(6), 866–897 (1996).

X. Chen, Z. Chen, and Q. Zhu, From OLAP to data mining: An analytical influential association approach, *J. Comput. Sci. Inform. Manage.* (Special Issue) (June 1999).

Z. Chen, Qualitative reasoning for system reconstruction using Lebesgue discretization, *Int. J. Syst. Sci.* **25**(12), 2329–2337 (1994).

Z. Chen, *Computational Intelligence for Decision Support*, CRC Press, Boca Raton, FL, 1999.

Z. Chen, Intelligent agents, *The IEBM Handbook of Information Technology in Business*, Thompson Learning, London, 1999A, pp. 561–569.

Z. Chen and Q. Zhu, Query construction for user-guided knowledge discovery in databases, *Inform. Sci.* **109**, 49–64 (1998).

Z. Chen, A. M. Fanelli, G. Castellano, and L. C. Jain, An Introduction to computational intelligence paradigms, in N. Baba and L. C. Jain (eds.), *Computational Intelligence in Games*, Physica-Verlag, Heidelberg, 2000, pp. 1–38.

K. J. Cios, W. Pedrycz, and R. Swiniarski, *Data Mining Methods for Knowledge Discovery*, Kluwer, Boston, 1998.

R. Cooley, B. Mobasher, and J. Srivastava, *Web Mining: Information and Pattern Discovery on the World Wide Web*, 1997, available at
http://www-users.cs.umn.edu/~mobasher/webminer/survey/survey.html.

G. F. Cooper, An overview of the representation and discovery of causal relationships using Bayesian networks, in C. Glymour and G. F. Cooper (eds.), *Computation, Causation, and Discovery*, AAAI Press, Menlo Park, CA, 1999.

O. Cordon, F. Herrera, and M. Lozano, A classified review on the combination fuzzy logic-genetic algorithms bibliography: 1989–1995, in E. Sanchez, T. Shibata, and L. A. Zadeh (eds.), *Genetic Algorithms and Fuzzy Logic Systems*, World Scientific, Singapore, 1997, pp. 209–240.

T. Dean, J. Allen, and Y. Aloimonos, *Artificial Intelligence: Theory and Practice*, Benjamin/Cummings, Redwood City, CA, 1995.

C. Domingo, R. Gavaldà, and O. Watanabe, Adaptive sampling methods for scaling up knowledge discovery algorithms, *Proc. 2nd Int. Conf. Discovery Science (DS'99)*, 1999.

D. Dubois and H. Prade, Putting rough sets and fuzzy sets together, in R. Slowinski (ed.), *Intelligent Decision Support*, Kluwer, Dordrecht, 1992.

Fanelli, A. M., G. Castellano, and L. C. Jain, *An Introduction to Neural Networks*, KBS Research Lab, Australia, 1999.

U. M. Fayyad, G. Piatetsky-Shapiro, P. Smyth, and in R. Uturusamy (eds.), *Advances in Knowledge Discovery and Data Mining*, AAAI/MIT Press, Cambridge, MA, 1996.

A. Feekin and Z. Chen, Duplicate detection using *K*-way sorting method, *Proc. ACM Applied Computing*, 2000, pp. 323–327.

A. A. Freitas, Understanding the crucial differences between classification and discovery of association rules—a position paper, *SIGKDD Explor.* **2**(1), 65–69 (2000).

A. A. Freitas and S. H. Lavington, *Mining Very Large Databases with Parallel Processing*, Kluwer, Boston, 1998.

Y. Fu and J. Han, Meta-rule-guided mining of association rules in relational Databases, *Proc. KDOOD/TDOOD*, 1995, pp. 39–46.

T. Gaasterland, Cooperative answering through controlled query relaxation, *IEEE Expert* **12**(5), 48–59 (1997).

S. I. Gallent, *Neural Network Learning and Expert Systems*, MIT Press, Cambridge, MA, 1993.

H. Garcia-Molina, J. D. Ullman, and J. Widom, *Database System Implementation*, Prentice-Hall, Upper Saddle River, NJ, 2000.

C. Glymour and G. F. Cooper (eds.), *Computation, Causation, and Discovery*, MIT Press, Cambridge, MA, 1999.

M. Goebel and L. Gruenwald, A survey of data mining and knowledge discovery software tools, *SIGKDD Explor.* **1**(1), 20–33 (1999).

J. Gray, A. Bosworth, A. Layman, and H. Pirahesh, Data cube: A relational aggregation operator generalizing group-by, cross-tab, and sub-totals, *Proc. Int. Conf. Data Engineering (ICDE 96)*, 1996.

R. Groner, M. Groner, and W. F. Bischof (eds.), *Methods of Heuristics*, L. Erlbaum Assoc., Hillsdale, NJ, 1983.

R. Groth, *Data Mining: Building Competitive Advantage*, Prentice-Hall, Upper Saddle River, NJ, 2000.

J. W. Gryzmala-Busse, *Managing Uncertainty in Expert Systems*, Kluwer, Boston, 1991.

D. Gunopulos and R. Rastogi, Workshop report: 2000 ACM SIGMOD Workshop on research issues in data mining and knowledge discovery, *SIGKDD Explor.* **2**(1), 83–84 (2000).

J. Han, Intelligent query answering by knowledge discovery techniques, *IEEE Trans. Knowl. Data Eng.* **8**, 373–389 (1996).

J. Han and M. Kamber, *Data Mining: Concepts and Techniques*, Morgan Kaufmann, San Francisco, 2000.

J. Han, Y. Fu, and R. Ng, Cooperative query answering using multiple layered databases, *Proce 2nd Int. Conf. Cooperative Information Systems*, 47–58 (1994).

J. Han, Y. Fu, R. Ng, and S. Dao, Dealing with semantic heterogeneity by generalization-based data mining techniques, in M. P. Papazoglou and G. Schlageter (eds.), *Cooperative Information Systems: Current Trends & Directions*, Academic Press, 1998, pp. 207–231.

J. Han, Y. Huang, N. Cercone, and Y. Fu, Intelligent query answering by knowledge discovery techniques. *IEEE Trans. Knowl. Data Eng.* **8**(3), 1996.

J. Han, L. V. S. Lakshmanan, and R. T. Ng, Constraint-based, multidimensional data mining, *Computer* **32**(8), 46–50 (1999).

J. Han, J. Pei, and Y. Yin, Mining frequent patterns without candidate generation, *Proc. 2000 ACM SIGMOD Int. Conf. Management of Data (SIGMOD'00)*, Dallas, 2000, pp. 1–12.

D. J. Hand, Statistics and data mining: Intersecting disciplines, *KDD Explor.* **1**(1), 16–19 (1999).

E. N. Hanson, Rule condition testing and action execution in Ariel, *Proc. SIGMOD 92*, 49–59 (1992).

P. Hart and J. Graham, Query-free information retrieval, *IEEE Expert* **12**(5), 32–37 (1997).

M. A. Hernandez and S. J. Stolfo, The merge/purge problem for large databases, *Proc. ACM SIGMOD Conf.*, 1995, pp. 127–138.

C. Hidber, Online association rule mining, *Proc. SGIMOD'99*, 1999.

J. Hipp, U. Guntzer, and G. Nakhaeizadeh, Algorithms for association rule mining—a general survey and comparison, *SIGKDD Explor.* **2**(1), 58–64 (2000).

M. Holsheimer, M. Kersten, H. Mannila, and H. Toivonen, A perspective on databases and data mining, *Proc. Knowledge Discovery Databases (KDD'95)*, 1995.

X. Hu, *Knowledge Discovery in Databases: An Attribute-Oriented Rough Set Approach*, Ph.D. Dissertation, Dept. Computer Science, University of Regina, Canada, available at xiaohua@cs.uregina.ca (univ), tonyhu@bnr.ca (company), June 1995.

Z. Huang, Extensions to the $k$-means algorithm for clustering large data sets with categorical values, *Data Mining Knowl. Discovery* **2**, 283–304 (1998).

T. Imielinski and H. Mannila, A database perspective on knowledge discovery, *Commun. ACM* **39**(11), 58–64 (1996).

W. H. Inmon, *Building the Data Warehouse*, Wiley, New York, 1996.

A. K Jain, M. N. Murty, and P. J. Flynn, Data clustering: A review, *ACM Comput. Surv.* **31**(3), 264–323 (1999).

N. Japkowitz, The class imbalance problem: Significance and strategies, *Proc. Int. Conf. Artificial Intelligence (IC-AI' 2000)*, 2000, Vol. I, pp. 111–117.

Q. Jiang, *Lazy Data Cleansing for Conceptual Query Answering*, M.S. Thesis, Dept. Computer Science, University of Nebraska at Omaha, 1999.

B. Kappen and C. Gielen, Neural networks: Artificial intelligence and industrial applications, *Proc. 3rd Annual SNN Symp. Neural Networks*, Springer, London, 1995.

N. K. Kasabov, *Foundations of Neural Networks, Fuzzy Systems, and Knowledge Engineering*, MIT Press, Cambridge, MA, 1996.

R. Katayama, K. Kuwata, and L. C. Jain, Fusion technology of neuro, fuzzy, genetic and chaos theory and its applications, in *Hybrid Intelligent Engineering Systems*, World Scientific Publishing Company, Singapore, 1996, pp. 167–186.

H. Kawano and T. Hasegawa, Data mining algorithms with entropy-based cost functions, *Proc. 11th Int. Conf. Systems Eng.*, Las Vegas, 1996, pp. 957–962.

H. Kawano, S. Nishio, J. Han, and T. Hasegawa, How does knowledge discovery cooperate with active database techniques in controlling dynamic environment? *Proc. 5th Int. Conf. Database Expert Systems Appl. (DEXA'94)*, Athens, Greece, September 1994, pp. 370–379.

R. L. Kennedy, Y. Lee, B. van Roy, C. D. Reed, and R. P. Lippman, *Solving Data Mining Problems through Pattern Recognition*, Prentice-Hall, Upper Saddle River, NJ, 1997.

R. Kimball, L. Reeves, M. Ross, and W. Thornthwaite, *The Data Warehouse Lifecycle Toolkit*, Wiley, New York, 1998.

G. Klir, *Architecture of Systems Problem Solving*, Plenum, New York, 1985.

R. Kosala and H. Blockeel, Web mining research: A survey, *SIGKDD Explor.* **2**(1), 1–15 (2000).

M. Kryszkiewicz, Representative association rules, *Proc. PAKDD'98*, 1998.

M. Kubat, I. Bratko, and R. S. Michalski, A review of machine learning methods, in R. S. Michalski, I. Bratko, and M. Kubat (eds.), *Machine Learning and Data Mining: Methods and Applications*, Wiley, Chichester, UK, 1998 (Chapter 1).

P. Langley, H. A. Simon, G. L. Bradshaw, and H. M. Zytkow, *Scientific Discovery: Computational Explorations of the Creative Processes*, MIT Press, Cambridge, MA, 1987.

W. Lee, S. J. Stolfo, and K. W. Mok, A data mining framework for building intrusion detection models, *Proc. IEEE*, 1999, pp. 120–132.

B. Lent, A. Swami, and J. Widom, Clustering association rules, *Proc. ICDE'97*, 1997.

D.-I. Lin and Z. M. Kedem, Pincer-search: A new algorithm for discovering the maximum frequent set, *Proc. 6th EDBT*, 1998, pp. 105–119.

B. Liu, W. Hsu, and Y. Ma, Integrating classification and association rule mining, *Proc. 4th Int. Conf. Knowledge Discovery and Data Mining (KDD 1998)*, 1998, pp. 80–86.

H. Lu, R. Setiono, and H. Liu, Effective data mining using neural networks, *IEEE Trans. Knowl. Data Eng.* **8**(6) (December 1996).

P. Lu, *Intensional Answering for Conceptual Queries: An Experimental Study of a Methodology*, M.S. Thesis, Dept. Computer Science, University of Nebraska at Omaha, 1999.

P. Lu and Z. Chen, Intensional conceptual answering through data mining, *Proc. Joint Conf. Info. Sci.* (Vol. III), 1998, pp. 479–482.

G. Luger and W. Stubblefield, *Artificial Intelligence: Structures and Strategies for Complex Problem Solving* (3rd ed.), Addison-Wesley Longman, Harlow, England, 1998.

Q. Luo, *Database Query Answering Using Q-entropy*, M.S. Thesis, Dept. Computer Science, University of Nebraska at Omaha, 1999.

H. Mannila, Theoretical frameworks for data mining, *SIGKDD Explor.* **1**(2), 30–32 (2000).

B. Masand and M. Spiliopoulou, WEBKDD'99: Workshop on Web usage analysis and user profiling, *SIGKDD Explor.* **1**(2), 108–111 (2000).

J. McCarthy, *Phenomenal Data Mining: From Observations to Phenomena*, 1996, available http://www-formal.stanford.edu/jmc/data-mining/data-mining.html.

M. Mehta, R. Agrawal, and J. Rissanen, SLIQ: A fast scalable classifier for data mining, *Proc. of the 5th Int. Conf. Extending Database Technulogy*, Avignon, France, 1996.

J. Mena, *Data Mining Your Website*, Digital Press, Boston, 1999.

R. Meo, G. Psaila, and S. Ceri, An extension to SQL for mining association rules, *Data Mining Knowl. Discovery* **2**(2), 195–224 (1998a).

R. Meo, G. Psaila, and S. Ceri, A tightly-coupled architecture for data mining, *Proc. ICDE 1998*, 1998b, pp. 316–323.

R. S. Michalski, I. Bratko, and M. Kubat (eds.), *Machine Learning and Data Mining: Methods and Applications*, Wiley, Chichester, UK, 1998.

R. S. Michalski and R. E. Stepp, Automated construction of classifications: Conceptual clustering versus numerical taxonomy, *IEEE Trans. Pattern Anal. Machine Intelligence* **5**(4), 396–410 (1983).

A. Monge and C. Elkan, An efficient domain-independent algorithm for detecting approximately duplicate database records. *Proc. 1997 SIGMOD Workshop on Research Issues on Data Mining and Knowledge Discovery*, May 1997, pp. 23–29.

A. Motro, Intensional answers to database queries, *IEEE Trans. Knowl. Data Eng.* **6**(3), 444–454 (1994).

R. Musick, *Belief Network Inductor*, Ph.D. Dissertation, University of California, Berkeley, 1999.

R. E. Neapolitan, *Probability Reasoning in Expert Systems: Theory and Algorithms*, Wiley, New York, 1990.

M. G. Negoita, Book review, *Data Mining Methods for Knowledge Discovery*, *SIGKDD Explor.* **1**(2), 118–119 (2000).

R. Ng and J. Han, Efficient and effective clustering method for spatial data mining, *Proc. 1994 Int. Conf. Very Large Data Bases*, 1994, pp. 144–155.

T. Palpanas, Knowledge discovery in data warehouses, *SIGMOD Record* **29**(3) (2000).

S. Parsons, Current approaches to handling imperfect information in data and knowledge bases, *IEEE Trans. Knowl. Data Eng.* **8**(3), 353–372 (1996).

K. Parsaye, OLAP & data mining: Bridging the gap, *Database Progr. Design* **10**(2), 30–37 (1997).

K. Parsaye, *A Characterization of Data Mining Technologies and Processes*, Information Discovery, Inc. (White Paper), 1999.

K. Parsaye, *DataMines for DataWarehouses—Data Mining Above, Beside and Within the Warehouse to Avoid the Paradox of Warehouse Patterns*, Information Discovery, Inc. (White Paper), 1999A.

Z. Pawlak, *Rough Sets: Theoretical Aspects of Reasoning About Data*, Kluwer, Dodrecht, 1991.

Z. Pawlak, Rough sets present state and further prospects, in P. P. Wang (ed.), *Advances in Machine Intelligence and Soft-Computing*, 1997, Vol. IV, pp. 4–16.

J. Pearl, *Probabilistic Reasoning in Intelligent Systems: Networks of Plausible Inference*, Morgan Kaufmann, San Mateo, CA, 1988.

J. Pearl, *Causality: Models, Reasoning, and Inference*, Cambridge University Press, Cambridge, UK, 2000.

W. Pedrycz, *Computational Intelligence: An Introduction*, CRC Press, Boca Raton, FL, 1998.

G. Piatetsky-Shapiro and W. Frawley (eds.), *Knowledge Discovery in Databases*, AAAI/MIT Press, Menlo Park, CA, 1991.

D. Pyle, *Data Preparation for Data Mining*, Morgan Kaufmann, San Francisco, CA, 1999.

R. Ramakrishnan and J. Gehrke, *Database Management Systems*, 2nd ed., McGraw-Hill, New York, 1999.

N. Ramakrishnan and A. Y. Grama (eds.), Data mining: From serendipity to science, *IEEE Computer* **32**(8), (Special issue) 34–75 (1999).

J. F. Roddick and M. Spiliopoulou, A bibliography of temporal, spatial, and spatio-temporal data mining research, *KDD Explor.* **1**(1), 34–38 (1999).

A. Roy, Artificial neural networks—a science in trouble, *SIGKDD Explor.* **1**, 22–28 (2000).

S. Russell and P. Norvig, *Artificial Intelligence: A Modern Approach*, Prentice-Hall, Englewood Cliffs, NJ, 1995.

S. Sarawagi, S. Thomas, and R. Agrawal, Integrating association rule mining with relational database systems: Alternatives and implications, *Proc. SIGMOD'98*, 1998. (Chap. 5).

S. Sarawagi, R. Agrawal, and N. Megiddo, Discovery-driven exploration of OLAP data cubes. *Proc. Int. Conf. Extending Database Technology*, 1998, 168–182.

T. Schreck and Z. Chen, Branch grafting method for R-tree implementation, *J. Syst. Software* **53**(1), 83–93 (2000).

G. Shafer and J. Pearl (eds.), *Readings in Uncertain Reasoning*, Morgan Kaufmann, San Mateo, CA, 1990.

L. Shastri (guest ed.), A fuzzy logic symposium, *IEEE Expert* **9**(4), 2–49 (1994).

C. D. Shum and R. Muntz, An information-theoretic study on aggregate responses. *Proc. of the 14th VLDB Conf.* Los Angeles, CA, 1988, pp. 479–490.

C. D. Shum and R. Muntz, Implicit representation for extensional Answers, in L. Kerschberg (ed.), *Proc. 2nd Intl. Conf. Expert Database Systems*, Benjamin/Cummings, Redwood City, CA, 1989, pp. 497–522.

L. Siklossy and M. Ayel, Data discovery, in X. Liu, P. Cohen, and M. Berthold (eds.), *Advances in Intelligent Data Analysis* (*IDA'97*), LNCS 1280, 1997, pp. 459–463.

A. Silberschatz and A. Tuzhilin, What makes patterns interesting in knowledge discovery systems, *IEEE Trans. Knowl. Data Eng.* **8**(3), 970–974 (1996).

A. Silberschatz, H. Korth, and S. Sudarshan, *Database System Concepts*, 3rd ed., McGraw-Hill, New York, 1997.

A. Silberschatz, M. Stonebraker, and J. D. Ullman, Database system: Achievements and opportunities, *Commun. ACM* **34**, 94–109 (1991).

C. Silverstein, S. Brin, and R. Motwani, Beyond market baskets: Generalizing association rules to dependence rules, *Knowl. Discovery Data Mining* **2**(1), 39–68 (1998).

C. Silverstein, S. Brin, R. Motwani, and J. Ullman, Scalable techniques for mining causal structures, *Data Mining Knowl. Discovery* **4**(2/3), 163–192 (2000).

H. Singh, *Interactive Data Warehousing*, Prentice-Hall, Upper Saddle River, NJ, 1999.

D. Skillicorn, Strategies for parallel data mining, *IEEE Concurrency*, 29–35 (Oct.–Dec. 1999).

R. Srikant and R. Agrawal, Mining generalized association rules, *Proc. VLDB'95*, 1995.

R. Srikant and R. Agrawal, Mining quantitative association rules in large relational tables, *Proc. SIGMOD'96*, 1996.

R. Srikant, Q. Vu, and R. Agrawal, Mining association rules with item constraints, *Proc. KDD'97*, 1997.

J. Srivastava and P.-Y. Chen, Warehouse creation—a potential roadblock to data warehousing, *IEEE Trans. Knowl. Data Eng.* **11**(1), 118–126 (1999).

J. Srivastava, R. Cooley, M. Deshpande, and P.-N. Tan, Web usage mining: Discovery and applications of usage patterns from Web data, *SIGKDD Explor.* **1**(2), 12–23 (2000).

T. Stohr, R. Muller, and E. Rahm, An integrative and uniform model for metadata management in data warehousing environments, *Proc. Int. Worskhop on Design and Management of Data Warehouses (DMDW'99)*, 1999.

Y. Sun, Q. Zhu, and Z. Chen, A modified $k$-means algorithm for categorical data clustering, *Proc. Int. Conf. Artificial Intelligence*, Vol. I, 2000, pp. 31–38.

B. Thuraisingham, *Data Mining: Technologies, Techniques, Tools, and Trends*, CRC Press, Boca Raton, FL, 1999.

H. Toivonen, Sampling large databases for association rules, *Proc. VLDB'96*, 1996.

P. D. Turney, Cost-sensitive classification: Empirical evaluation of a hybrid genetic decision tree induction algorithm, *J. AI Research* **2**, 369–409 (1995).

J. Vesanto, *Data Mining Techniques Based on the Self-Organizing Map*, Helsinki University of Technology, 1997.

C. Warrender, S. Forrest, and B. Pearlmutter, Detecting intrusions using system calls: Alternative data models, *Proc. IEEE*, 1999, pp. 133–145.

M. Weiss, *Data Structures and Algorithm Analysis in C++*, 2nd ed., Addison-Wesley, Reading, MA, 1998.

S. M. Weiss and N. Indurkhya, *Predictive Data Mining: A Practical Guide*, Morgan Kaufmann, San Francisco, CA, 1998.

C. Westphal and T. Blaxton, *Data Mining Solutions: Methods and Tools for Solving Real-World Problems*, Wiley, New York, 1998.

J. Widom and S. Ceri, *Active Database Systems: Triggers and Rules for Advanced Database Processing*, Morgan Kaufmann, San Francisco, CA, 1996.

L. Xiao, Z. Chen, and Q. Zhu, Mining causal patterns from frequent itemsets, *J. Intelligent Information Sys.*, 2001 (to appear).

R. R. Yager (ed.), *Fuzzy Sets and Applications: Selected Papers by Lotfi Zadeh*, Wiley, New York, 1987.

S. C. Yoon, Towards conceptual query answering, in S. W. Ras and A. Skowron (eds.), *Foundations of Intelligent Systems* Lecture Notes in Artificial Intelligence 1325, 1997, pp. 187–196.

C. Yu and W. Meng, *Principles of Database Query Processing for Advanced Applications*, Morgan Kaufmann, San Francisco, CA, 1998.

M. J. Zaki, Parallel and distributed association mining: A survey, *IEEE Concurrency* 14–25 (Oct–Dec. 1999).

M. J. Zaki, Scalable algorithms for association rules, *IEEE Trans. Knowl. Data Eng.* (2000a).

M. J. Zaki, Generating non-redundant association rules, *Proc. KDD'2000*, 2000b.

X. Zhang, Discovery of Influential Association Rules Using Bitmap Indexing, Department of Computer Science, University of Nebraskra at Omaha, 2001.

# INDEX